PIONEERS IN ENTREPRENEURSHIP AND SMALL BUSINESS RESEARCH

INTERNATIONAL STUDIES IN ENTREPRENEURSHIP

Series Editors:
Zoltan J. Acs
University of Baltimore
Baltimore, Maryland USA

David B. Audretsch
Indiana University
Bloomington, Indiana USA

Other books in the series:

PIONEERS IN ENTREPRENEURSHIP AND SMALL BUSINESS RESEARCH

Hans Landström
Institute of Economic Research, Lund University School of Economics, Lund, Sweden

 Springer

HB
615
.L267
2005

Library of Congress Cataloging-in-Publication Data

Pioneers in Entrepreneurship and Small Business Research
  By Hans Landström

ISBN 0-387-23601-5   eISBN 0-387-23633-3

Printed on acid-free paper

Printed in the United States of America.

9 8 7 6 5 4 3 2   SPIN 11499640

springeronline.com

Contents

Foreword

It is almost ten years now since the FSF-NUTEK International Award was introduced, the first award winner being appointed 1996. The objective of introducing an award of the sum 50 000 USD is to promote outstanding research in the area of small business and entrepreneurship.

The award is bestowed upon an individual researcher or group of researchers who have made significant contribution to increasing understanding of entrepreneurship, small business development, the role and significance of new business start-ups, and the impact of small business on economic development.

The award has since it started 1996 been giving to a number of very distinguished researchers from US and Europe. From David Birch and his ideas about the importance of small business as job creators to Paul Reynolds and his ideas of how to measure and compare the entrepreneurial spirit of nations.

In this book *Pioneers in Entrepreneurship and Small Business Research* you can read of most of these excellent researchers. For Paul Reynolds and William J Baumol special papers have been produced about their research. You can also read more about the different award winners on the websites www.fsf.se and www.nutek.se.

Around the world an increasing interest can be seen concerning issues of small business and entrepreneurship, and it is of vital importance to learn about the existing research knowledge about the individuals which start business, the characteristics of spin-offs from universities, the importance of clusters and industrial districts, the domain of the policy areas for small business. Reasons why there are so few really innovative entrepreneurs to give some examples. Therefore it is a book of great importance not only for researchers but also for service providers and policy-makers.

In a time with a lot of myths and opinions of the role of entrepreneurs and small business it is vital to like in this book summarize the knowledge that can be learned from really outstanding research. Such knowledge is often build upon empirical oriented methods giving a lot of policy relevant results of what to do or not to do in creating a society for small business owners and entrepreneurs.

The Swedish Foundation for Small Business Research (FSF) and The Swedish Business Development Agency (NUTEK) will continue to support the creation and dissemination of knowledge from excellent research to make better use of such knowledge among both the research society and politicians or service providers. This book is therefore an important piece in this work. Read it, discuss it and find interesting ideas for your future work.

Stockholm in September 2004

Anders Lundström   *Sune Halvarsson*
President, FSF   Deputy Director General, NUTEK

Acknowledgements

In this book I will provide a historical-doctrinal review of the development of entrepreneurship and small business research as well as presenting some of the researchers who created and shaped the field – the pioneers of entrepreneurship and small business research. Such an undertaking is always associated with risk. Many people have their own "images" of history, and history can be depicted from many different perspectives as well as focusing on various aspects. I therefore wish to stress that this is my own subjective description of history, where I have chosen to focus on the individuals and events that, in my view, have been important in the shaping of the research field. There is also a risk that some readers will use a book such as this as an easy route to the core works of the research field. This book is not intended as a substitute for in-depth study of the original works, but instead I hope that it will stimulate such reading – a challenge that is both fascinating and highly recommended. My motivation for writing this book, despite the risks involved, is that entrepreneurship is a young and quickly growing research field and I believe it is beneficial to stop now and again to reflect on the knowledge acquired through research in order to establish a basis for further development.

Even if this book is to a great extent a personal reflection, I have received considerable help and valuable comments and views from many of my colleagues. First, I would like to mention some good friends and colleagues who have assisted me in the writing of this book. Many of the initial ideas for the book were developed in collaboration with Morten Huse, and our close collaboration over many years has been both fruitful and stimulating. I would also like to mention my long and exciting collaboration with Bengt Johannisson. Bengt has not been directly involved in the writing of this book, but my discussions with him over many years of friendship have influenced my views on entrepreneurship and small business as a research field and given me a great deal of ideas on the history of the field and where it is heading.

Second, the book focuses on the first recipients of the FSF-NUTEK International Award for Small Business Research, and I am very grateful to the award winners David Birch, Arnold Cooper, David Storey, Ian MacMillan, Howard Aldrich, Zoltan Acs, David Audretsch, and Giacomo Becattini for making time for the interviews and for many intellectually stimulating discussions. In this connection I also wish to extend my heartfelt thanks to Thomas Mattsson of the entrepreneurship library at Jönköping International Business School, who always located the literature necessary for this project with great enthusiasm and efficiency.

Third, in the course of this project, a number of researchers have been interviewed, who have contributed their knowledge and views on the development of the research field. I would like to thank Jon Aarum Andersen, Per Davidsson, Frederick Delmar, Gunnar Eliasson, Marlene Fiol, Richard Harrison, Magnus Henrekson, Colin Mason, Rita McGrath, Dale Meyer, Charlene Nicholls-Nixon, and Roy Thurik for giving me access to their knowledge and reflections on the development of the field.

Fourth, the book also contains a review of entrepreneurship and small business research in different countries. I have visited a number of countries and interviewed researchers with a good overview of the research field in the respective country. In this respect I wish to thank: Josef Mugler, Hermann Frank, Hanns Pichler, Nikolaus Franke, David Smallbone, David Kirby, Robert Blackburn, Gabi Dei Ottati, Isabelle Marchini, Guido Corbetta, Massimo Columbo, Antoinio Ramos Rodrigues, Lars Kolvereid, Mette Mönsted, Poul Dreisler, and Annaleena Parhankangas. A special thank to Damian Hine for his efforts regarding the analysis of the development of entrepreneurship and small business research in Australia.

Fifth, several people have read at least part of the book and given me feedback on the manuscript, and I am therefore very grateful to Poul Dreisler, Damian Hine, David Kirby, Josef Mugler, David Smallbone, and Joakim Winborg for their efforts and challenging comments, which have helped me improve upon the quality of the manuscript.

Sixth, parts of the book have been presented at a number of seminars, conferences and especially at a large number of doctoral courses around Europe. It would be impossible to individually mention the large number of people who have discussed the subject with me, but our discussions have always been fruitful and on many occasions have caused me to reflect on my own views.

Finally, the book has taken a longer time to complete than I had anticipated. The Swedish Foundation for Small Business Research (FSF) has funded the project, and Anders Lundström, President of FSF, has shown admirable patience with regard to the completion of the book.

The same is true of Kluwer Academic Publishers, who with an equal measure of patience and good will have waited for a manuscript that never seemed to assume its final form. I also wish to thank Gullvi Nilsson and Monique Federsel, who have helped me handle the English language in a most exemplary way.

Hans Landström
Institute of Economic Research
Lund University School of Economics and Management
Lund, Sweden

A HISTORY OF ENTREPRENEURSHIP AND SMALL BUSINESS RESEARCH

Chapter 1

INTRODUCTION

The aim of *Pioneers in Entrepreneurship and Small Business Research* is first to provide a historical-doctrinal review of the development of entrepreneurship and small business research and, second, to present some of the pioneers that have shaped the research field during the past three decades. In this introductory chapter I wish to lay the foundation of the book by presenting some of the main themes and discussions (section 1.1.). A problem in entrepreneurship research is the difficulty of defining the concept of "entrepreneurship" and, in section 1.2., some of the definitions employed in the research over the years are presented. The chapter concludes with section 1.3., which presents an outline of the structure and content of the book.

1.   THE DEVELOPMENT OF ENTREPRENEURSHIP AND SMALL BUSINESS RESEARCH

1.1   Entrepreneurship in Society and Academia – a Long Standing Interest

Historically, entrepreneurship is one of the oldest activities. To discover or identify new business possibilities and to exploit these possibilities in new ventures for economic gain has always been important in human life. Entrepreneurial activities in society are mentioned by the ancient Greeks, and it was the philosopher Xenophon (approx. 430-354 B.C) who recognized the adventurous and opportunity seeking activities of oversea merchants (Karayiannis, 2003).

"So deep is their love of corn that on receiving reports that it is abundant anywhere, merchants will voyage in quest of it: they will cross the Aegean, the Euxine, the Sicilian sea; and when they have got as much as possible, they carry it over the sea, and they actually stow it in the very ship in which they sail themselves. And when they want money, they don't throw the corn away anywhere at haphazard, but they carry it to the place where they hear that corn is most valued and the people prize it the most highly, and deliver it to them there." (Oeconomicus, quoted in Karayiannis, 2003, p. 558)

Throughout history we have seen many important examples of entrepreneurial activities. One wave of entrepreneurial activities took place during the last few decades. In the 1970s and 1980s we experienced huge structural changes in society worldwide – oil crises, economic recessions, technological progress, increasing globalization, etc., as well as far reaching political changes in favor of a stronger market-oriented ideology. This created the uncertainty and disequilibrium that constitute breeding grounds for new business opportunities and new ventures (Bettis & Hitt, 1995; Meyer & Heppard, 2000). As a consequence, new and small firms have been seen by politicians and decision-makers as the main contributors to the development of the economy and wealth-creation in society.

This interest in entrepreneurship and small firms on the part of society has also had an impact on the academic world. The study of entrepreneurship and small business has become one of the most popular fields of research in management studies. The research has grown exponentially, the number of positions and chairs in entrepreneurship and small business has increased dramatically, and PhD programs specializing in entrepreneurship have been introduced at various universities (Finkle & Deeds, 2001). In the US, entrepreneurship is taught at over 1,600 schools in more than 2,200 courses. At the same time 277 endowed positions have been established, and there are 44 English-language refereed academic journals within the area (Katz, 2003). It is no exaggeration to say that entrepreneurship and small firms have been a "hot topic" in society as well as in education and academic research in recent decades.

The rapid development of the research within the field has, however, had some adverse effects – observers from (more) mature fields of study, looking at this growing body of entrepreneurship and small business research, have questioned whether the research really has created a coherent research stream that advances the field. For example, concerns have been raised in respect of (i) the problem of defining entrepreneurship and the uncertainty in the domain of entrepreneurship and small business research, and (ii) the fact that the field still suffers from a "liability of newness" (Stinchcombe, 1965), which among other things is evidenced by fragmented research and a transient research community, and consequently a lack of a theoretical foundation. Seen in this light, the research still has a long way to go before it can be regarded as an established scientific discipline, including (Molander, 1988): a *social structure* expressed in terms of organized forums for communication between researchers within the field, an established organization that ensures its survival, and role models and ideals as well as educational programs that provide and define the minimum competence required of researchers within the field, in addition to a *cognitive structure* including a general delimitation of and wide ranging background knowledge about the study object as well as accepted methods and ways of reasoning.

In the book I will show how scholars from different disciplines have taken an interest in entrepreneurship and small firms since the 18th century, represented by precursors such as Richard Cantillon and Jean Baptiste Say, and Austrian economists like Carl Menger and Joseph Schumpeter. The interest was intensified during the 20th century, when it spread to many different academic disciplines. Entrepreneurship and small business research gradually changed from being a topic within economic science, becoming a part of behavioral science, before finally moving into the area of management science. There is, thus, a long research tradition to build on, and the purpose of this book is to shed light on it with reference to the development of entrepreneurship and small business research throughout history. In the book I will also argue that the interest in entrepreneurship and small business research seems to appear at different eras and peaks during periods characterized by powerful dynamics and societal development. Thus, there seems to be a strong link between societal development and the interest in entrepreneurship and small business research.

1.2 The Emergence of Entrepreneurship and Small Business as a Field of Research

Even if scholars within different scientific disciplines have long taken an interest in entrepreneurship and small business, it is only in the past two decades, or not more than half an academic career, that the study of entrepreneurship and small business has been conducted more systematically and that a research field has started to emerge. This development has been characterized by exponential growth, which is obvious almost irrespective of the measures employed. The field seems to have been especially successful when it comes to building a strong social structure with an advanced infrastructure in terms of number of journals, conferences, educational programs, etc., but this advanced infrastructure has not been fully paralleled by a corresponding cognitive development. However, the field is still young, and today we know a great deal more about the entrepreneur, entrepreneurship and small firms than we did twenty years ago.

In the book I will try to describe the emergence of entrepreneurship and small business research during the 1980s and 1990s and the development of the field from a discovery-oriented research approach toward strong empirically-based research and the increasingly theoretical interest that we can find today. Entrepreneurship and small business research generally seems to follow the existing pattern for the development of new fields of research. I will argue that today there seem to be two different, and partly contradictory, tendencies: one converging more and more toward a "normal science approach" – mainly based on a US research tradition – and another in the form of increased heterogeneity within the research, which is based on differing contextual preconditions and research traditions in various countries. Against this background, the efforts to attain coherence by unified entrepreneurship and small business research are open to question.

1.3   The Contributions of the Pioneers

In emerging phases of new research fields, such as entrepreneurship and small business research, some individuals seem to be more important than others – a few researchers who ask the interesting and important questions and who make new phenomena visible, who attract other researchers (pioneers who open up new territories of research) but also researchers who start to organize colleagues with similar interests, maintain informal contacts with other researchers, recruit and train new doctoral students for the field, etc. – pioneers who create a research community. In this way these pioneers have a substantial impact upon the emerging research field in terms of setting the norms and maintaining the cohesion of the area. Put in another way, these pioneer researchers seem to play a major role in giving direction to the emerging field of research as well as influencing the selection of research problems (Crane, 1972). In a similar way, Aldrich and Baker (1997) argued that "Influences come from exemplary research, not from the propagation of rules or admonitions. The field will be shaped by those who produce research that interests and attracts others to build on their work" (p. 398).

In this book I wish to highlight the contributions of these pioneers – researchers that have been highly influential in the development of the research field. It is my wish that the reader will not only gain an insight into the key contributions of these pioneers but also get to know them as individuals and researchers. However, the field of entrepreneurship and small business includes many individual researchers that can be regarded as pioneers, and I do not claim to provide a complete picture of the contributions of all pioneers in the field. The pioneers selected for inclusion in this book have all received the International Award for Small Business Research – an award established in 1996 by the Swedish Foundation for Small Business Research (FSF) and the Swedish National Board for Industrial and Technical Development (NUTEK). The Award is presented annually to a researcher who has produced scholarly work of outstanding quality and importance within the field of entrepreneurship and small business research.

I will demonstrate that the contributions of these pioneers are not based on chance or flashes of genius but that their ground-breaking works are the result of solid empirical research based on new measuring instruments resulting from the development of information technology and new databases as well as their openness to ongoing societal changes. As in most radical ventures, courage is required in order to free oneself from the rules and knowledge of established disciplines, in combination with the motivation necessary to question conventional wisdom within the discipline and society at large, in addition to "timing" – their findings were presented at exactly the right time when new and small firms were in vogue. As a consequence, the pioneers focused their attention on important questions relevant for wealth creation in society and presented interesting theories about the phenomenon – theories that involved a certain movement of the minds of the audience.

2. THE MYSTERY OF ENTREPRENEURSHIP

A long-standing difficulty is how to define the central concepts within entrepreneurship and small business research and to demarcate the entrepreneurial domain. As far back as 1971, Peter Kilby observed that the entrepreneur has a lot in common with the "Heffalump", a large animal that competed for honey in A.A. Milne's *Winnie-the-Pooh*. The "Heffalump" is described as:

> "... a rather large and important animal. He has been hunted by many individuals using various trapping devices, but no one so far has succeeded in capturing him. All who claim to have caught sight of him report that he is enormous, but disagree on his particulars."

The "Heffalump" still seems to exist in entrepreneurship research, and in this section I will present some definitions of the entrepreneur and entrepreneurship that have been used in research over the years.

2.1 Early Definitions of Entrepreneurship

The phenomenon of entrepreneurship is far from novel, and the use of the concept of "entrepreneurship" goes back a long time both in the

French and in the English language (see Redlich, 1949; Hoselitz, 1951; Gopakumar, 1995).

2.1.1   Entrepreneurship in the French Vocabulary

"Entrepreneur" was originally a French word. The word appeared for the first time in the 1437 *Dictionnaire de la langue francaise*. Three definitions of the "entrepreneur" are listed in this dictionary. The most common meaning was "celui qui entreprend quelque chose", referring to a person who is active and achieves something. The corresponding verb is "entreprendre", which means to undertake something. The word has been a part of the French language since the 12th century, and many French authors referred to the term "entrepreneur" during the medieval period, often in connection with brutal war-like activities. An example of this was Lemaire de Belges, who described Hector and other Trojan warriors as "entrepreneurs". Other French authors referred to the entrepreneur as someone who is tough and prepared to risk his own life and fortune.

At the beginning of the 17th century the risk taking component became more apparent, and an entrepreneur was understood as a person who took risks. However, not all individuals taking risks were considered as entrepreneurs. Only those individuals involved in really big undertakings could be called entrepreneurs. Most often it was a question of large contracts between the state and some competent, wealthy person, with the objective of undertaking a major building scheme or supplying the army with equipment, etc. The typical entrepreneur was thus a person that was contracted by the state to perform specific services or to supply the state with certain goods. The price was fixed in the contract, and the entrepreneur assumed the risk of making a profit or loss. This meaning of the word "entrepreneur" was reflected in the French dictionaries of that time, in which the concept was defined as "entrepreneur, qui entreprend un bastiment pour un certain prix", which means that the entrepreneur has been contracted to perform a certain task at a fixed price. This definition of the "entrepreneur" concept was very common in the French legal and economic literature of the 17th and 18th centuries.

2.1.2   The Entrepreneur as a Building Contractor – Construction Entrepreneurs

In light of the increased use of the concept of entrepreneurship to denote a person having the technical and managerial responsibility for major public undertakings, most often the construction of public buildings, it may be of value to reflect on the role of the entrepreneur as a building contractor.

The typical entrepreneur in medieval times was thus a person with responsibility for major constructions such as castles, public buildings and churches. Up until the end of the 12th century it was most often the clergy who were responsible for such constructions of churches. However, the clergy did not assume any private financial risk. At the beginning of the 13th century the clergy were replaced by persons who specialized in construction work. They may be considered the first construction entrepreneurs. Their roles were, however, not clearly defined. In some cases they were responsible for the whole undertaking, whereas in other cases they appear to have had an exclusively advisory function.

As secular power increased, the influence of the clergy as builders decreased and finally disappeared completely. The major constructions were no longer churches or cathedrals. As a result of evolving capitalism, the planning and construction of buildings, etc. continually became more rationalized and the role of the builder more specialized. There was a successive increase in the division of work between architects and engineers specialized in the technical aspects of the construction and entrepreneurs who were responsible for commercial issues. With the growing importance of secular public buildings and intensification in the division of work, the entrepreneur increasingly developed dual roles. The first role was that of organizer and administrator, while the second was the role of capitalist. The organizing role involved integrating various production factors such as labor, material and machines. The role of capitalist implied taking the risk that costs would not exceed the contracted price.

2.1.3   The Entrepreneur Concept in the English Language

For a long time no similarity to the French "entrepreneur" concept existed in the English language. The most closely related term was "undertaker" and even "adventurer". The latter concept was used since the 15th century to refer to real estate speculators in Ireland. However, during the 18th century this definition became obsolete, and in *A Dictionary of the English Language* from 1755 the following definition was used: "Adventurer, he that seeks occasion of hazard; he that puts himself in the hand of chance".

The word "undertaker" was probably a more commonly used concept even though the meaning was not quite clear. Historically the word had certain parallels to the French "entrepreneur" concept. During the 14th and 15th centuries it simply denoted a person who undertook a certain task. Later on the concept developed into that of a person who undertook a task for the state at his own risk. As time went by the concept became more broadly defined and came to represent situations where one person engaged in projects involving risk where the profit was uncertain. The term "undertaker" thereby came closer to the concept of "projector", although there are indications that a "projector" was often considered to be a swindler or speculator, while an "undertaker" was an honest man involved in business with uncertain results. The definitions, however, are not quite clear, and some evidence also suggests that during the 17th and 18th centuries the term "undertaker" also referred to the owner-managers of big businesses. At this time the original meaning of an "undertaker" as someone involved in state undertakings had disappeared, and by the middle of the 18th century an "undertaker" was simply defined as a businessman, which meaning is exemplified by Adam Smith in *Inquiry into the Nature and Causes of the Wealth of Nations* (1776), in which he writes about "the undertaker of a great manufacture". By the end of the 18th century the concept had become obsolete in this connection and was gradually replaced by the "capitalist" concept. "Undertaker" later came to mean someone who organises funerals.

2.2   What do We Mean by Entrepreneurship?

Recent entrepreneurship research is characterized by ambiguity about the content of the concepts "entrepreneur" and "entrepreneurship". Different studies have used many various definitions, the number of which more or less equals the number of authors. For example, Morris (1998) found 77 different definitions in a review of journal articles and textbooks over a five-year period, while Gartner (1990) reviewed the concept as it was understood by academics, business leaders and politicians and listed 90 different attributes associated with the entrepreneur. Some common definitions are given in Figure 1-1.

The lack of a single clear definition has been considered as a barrier to the development of a research field (see e.g. Low & MacMillan, 1988; Bygrave & Hofer, 1991). It could be argued that without clear definitions of central concepts, each researcher would make his/her own interpretation of the concepts, which may limit the knowledge accumulation within the field.

Author	Definition
Drucker (1985)	Entrepreneurship is an act of innovation that involves endowing existing resources with new wealth-producing capacity.
Stevenson (1985)	Entrepreneurship is a process by which individuals pursue and exploit opportunities irrespective of the resources they currently control.
Gartner (1988)	Entrepreneurship is the creation of organizations, the process by which new organizations come into existence.
Timmons (1997)	Entrepreneurship is a way of thinking, reasoning, and acting that is opportunity driven, holistic in approach, and leadership balanced.
Venkataraman (1997)	Entrepreneurship is about how, by whom, and with what consequences opportunities to bring future goods and services into existence are discovered, created, and exploited.

Figure 1-1. Definitions of entrepreneurship (see also Meyer et al., 2002).

On the other hand it can also be argued that a research field may have different definitions of the main concepts (Landström, 2000). Firstly, entrepreneurship has been studied from various disciplines, and researchers try to focus on various aspects of entrepreneurship, which makes it only natural that different researchers use different definitions for central concepts. Secondly, entrepreneurship is in itself a complicated, ambiguous and changeable phenomenon, and it is reasonable to believe that this will also characterize the definitions used in the research. And finally, we should acknowledge that disagreements and shifts in opinion regarding how to define a phenomenon have characterized almost all fields of research in their early years of development (Hagstrom, 1965) and that even well established fields of research struggle with difficulties in defining core concepts, with which the researchers in these fields have learnt to live (Gartner & Bird & Starr, 1992). The conclusion could be that the problem is not that the definitions lack clarity, but rather the uniqueness of entrepreneurship research: What is the core of entrepreneurship research? Why is entrepreneurship research so unique that it cannot be properly understood in established research fields? What makes entrepreneurship research unique? What are the contributions of entrepreneurship research?

Although it may be difficult to define entrepreneurship as a field of research, many have attempted to do so. Some definitions are related to entrepreneurship as a societal phenomenon, while others are related to the need to define entrepreneurship as a scholarly domain.

2.2.1   Entrepreneurship as a Societal Phenomenon

Davidsson (2001; 2003) argues that we need to distinguish between "entrepreneurship as a societal phenomenon" and "entrepreneurship as a scholarly domain". In society at large, entrepreneurship is often related to a successful outcome. Thus, seen as a societal phenomenon, entrepreneurship as a function of society will only take place if the activities are successful enough to affect the market in a positive way, i.e. only successful entrepreneurship will be recognised. In this respect entrepreneurship can be defined as "the introduction of new economic activities that lead to changes in the marketplace".

The question is: What is new economic activity? Following the reasoning of Davidsson, "new activities" are something that gives buyers new choices and reasons and that forces competitors to consider altering their own products – thus driving the market process. To elaborate on different kinds of entrepreneurship in relation to the creation of new activities, a distinction can be made between "new" to the market and to the firm (see Figure 1-2).

		To Market	
		New	Old
		I	**II**
	New	New offer and new competitor (incl. imitative entry)	Organizational change (acquisition, internal re-organization, buy-outs, etc.)
To Firm			
	Old	**IV** Geographic market expansion (internationalization)	**III** Business as usual

Figure 1-2. Entrepreneurship as related to firm and market newness (source: Davidsson, 2001; 2003).

Few would argue for the exclusion of entrepreneurship in quadrant I (as long as entrepreneurship influences the market, which indicates that both imitative and innovative entrepreneurship could be included), and few would hesitate to exclude quadrant III from the definition of entrepreneurship. Quadrants II and IV are more problematic. It can be argued that the firm's geographic expansion (quadrant IV) could drive the market process on these new markets and therefore could qualify as entrepreneurship, whereas internal changes within an organization (quadrant II), radical as they may be to the firm, do not per se constitute entrepreneurship.

As indicated above, in society entrepreneurship is often linked to a successful outcome, and in this respect it is important to define what is meant by a successful outcome. The entrepreneurial outcome can be considered on two levels: the venture and society. Ventures that are successful in themselves and that produce net utility to society are unproblematic, similar to failed ventures on the micro level, which have no net effects at societal level. More interesting are unsuccessful ventures on the micro level, which nevertheless drive the market process because they inspire other actors on the market, therefore contributing to entrepreneurship as a societal phenomenon, i.e. micro level failures may be positive when viewed on a societal level and can be considered as entrepreneurship. It is even more difficult to classify ventures that yield a surplus on the micro level while the societal outcome is negative, for example, trafficking in illegal drugs. If we use the argument that entrepreneurship should drive the market process, such activities cannot be regarded as entrepreneurship. (Davidsson, 2003)

However, this definition of entrepreneurship as a societal phenomenon is inadequate for entrepreneurship as a scholarly domain, i.e. what entrepreneurship research should study – as it would exclude real time studies of entrepreneurship and studies of failures, etc. Thus, the successful outcome criterion would be a burden for entrepreneurship as a scholarly domain, and therefore other definitions are required.

2.2.2 Entrepreneurship as a Scholarly Domain

Identifying entrepreneurship as a scholarly domain is no simple matter. As indicated above, the research in entrepreneurship has shown a great variety and ambiguity in the use of different definitions. However, it is possible to identify a number of fundamental approaches to defining entrepreneurship: (i) entrepreneurship as a function of the market, (ii) the entrepreneur as an individual, and (iii) entrepreneurship as a process. These different approaches are grounded in different disciplines and their divergent focuses on different aspects of the concept.

Entrepreneurship as a function of the market. Entrepreneurship has a long tradition within economics, but it is difficult to identify any uniformity among researchers with regard to their use of definitions. However, the differences seem rather obvious considering that the definitions have been developed during different time eras and social structures – what they have in common is the researchers' interest in the function of entrepreneurship in the market place, in an attempt to answer the question: "What happens on the market when the entrepreneur acts?" (Stevenson & Jarillo, 1990), and five entrepreneurial functions can be identified (see also Hébert & Link, 1989):
- The entrepreneur as risk-taker/risk-manager (see e.g. Cantillon, 1755; Say, 1803; Knight, 1916).
- The entrepreneur as opportunity creator/innovator (see e.g. Schumpeter, 1912; Dahmén, 1950; Baumol, 1993).
- The entrepreneur as coordinator of limited resources (see e.g. Say, 1803; Casson, 1982).

- The entrepreneur as alert seeker of opportunities (see e.g. Mises, 1951; Kirzner, 1973).
- The entrepreneur as capitalist (see e.g. Smith, 1776; Ricardo, 1817; Marshall, 1890).

Thus, we can establish that economists have defined the function of entrepreneurs in the market in slightly different ways. These differences are reflected in Schumpeter (1934) and Kirzner's (1973) views on entrepreneurship. According to Schumpeter, the entrepreneur creates imperfections in the market by introducing new innovations. Kirzner, on the other hand, saw the entrepreneur as a seeker of imbalances, which she/he aims to remove by means of her/his entrepreneurial activity. The entrepreneurial function includes the co-ordination of information obtained for the purpose of identifying gaps between supply and demand, and acting as a broker, in order to make money on the difference.

With regard to the so-called production possibility curve (see Figure 1-3), Schumpeter's view is that society is on the edge of the curve and that the entrepreneur pushes the curve outwards by the introduction of innovations. This differs from the view taken by Kirzner, who argues that society is within the curve and reaches the edge with the aid of the entrepreneur, i.e. the entrepreneur is the person who pushes the economy toward the edge of the production possibility curve. Kirzner's entrepreneur does not create anything new, whereas Schumpeter's does. According to Kirzner, the entrepreneur is a sort of intermediary who recognises and exploits what is already there, which others are not aware of. By this means, we can make better use of existing resources, thus reaching the edge of the production possibility curve.

In his 1973 book, Kirzner puts forward several simplified lines of reasoning, and he also highlights the differences between his and Schumpeter's view on entrepreneurship. However, in later work, Kirzner moderated his reasoning somewhat in terms of, among other things, his view on entrepreneurs' creative ability (Kirzner, 1985). Hereby, the differences between Schumpeter's and Kirzner's views on entrepreneurship appear less obvious – instead they tend to complement each other in that Schumpeter's entrepreneur creates disequilibrium in the market while Kirzner's entrepreneur identifies and acts on it.

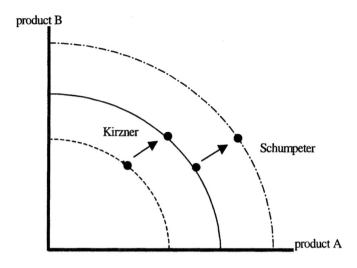

Figure 1-3. The production possibility curve in relation to Schumpeter's and Kirzner's view on entrepreneurship.

Critics have even argued that the two lines of reasoning are more or less identical – the differences are rather to be found in the points of departure underlying the reasoning – it is a question of viewing the "glass as half full or half empty".

The entrepreneur as an individual. Naturally, behavioral-science research focuses more strongly on the entrepreneur as an individual, which is also mirrored in the definitions used, and for a behavioral-science researcher, the following questions are relevant: "Who is the entrepreneur?" and "Why do they act?" (Stevenson & Jarillo, 1990). The definitions used are in most cases related to the personality traits of the entrepreneur.

Such definitions are by no means new. For example, as long ago as the 18th century, Cantillon defined the entrepreneur as a rational decision maker who assumed risk and provided management for the firm. Since then, many authors have defined the entrepreneur by means of various sets of personality traits. Some early definitions of the entrepreneur as an individual are:

Schumpeter (1934)   The entrepreneur is an innovator introducing new combinations of resources.

Cole (1959)   … an individual or group of individuals who initiate, maintain or expand a profit-oriented business unit for production or distribution of economic goods and services.

Shapero (1975)   The entrepreneur takes initiatives, organizes social and economic mechanisms and accepts the risk of failure.

Brockhaus (1980)   … a major owner and manager of a business venture.

For a long time, there has been a tendency to equate entrepreneurs with small business owners. However, as far back as the 1980s, Carland et al. (1984) argued that it is important to differentiate between these two functions (p. 358):

"An entrepreneur is an individual who establishes and manages a business for the principal purposes of profit and growth. The entrepreneur is characterized principally by innovative behavior and will employ strategic management practices in the business.

A small business owner is an individual who establishes and manages a business for the principal purpose of furthering personal goals. The business must be the primary sources of income and will consume the majority of one's time and resources. The owner perceives the business as an extension of his or her personality, intricately bound with family needs and desires."

Thus, the entrepreneur is not the same as a small business owner and, in entrepreneurship research, the entrepreneur has been given a range of different meanings, depending on the perspective of the researcher. Cunningham and Lischeron (1991) have summarized some main approaches to describing the entrepreneur as an individual (Figure 1-4).

Based on the view of the entrepreneur as an individual, Johannisson (1992) developed a line of reasoning about the logics of entrepreneurship that goes beyond the traditional "trait" orientated definitions. Johannisson considers that the entrepreneur is existentially motivated – it is a way of life – and that entrepreneurship involves a total commitment on the part of the individual. At the same time, the integration of entrepreneurship and personal life/family life implies responsibility – for the family, colleagues, employees, etc.

Entrepreneurial approach	Characteristics
"Great person" school	The entrepreneur has an intuitive ability – a sixth sense – and inborn traits and instincts.
Psychological characteristics school	Entrepreneurs are driven by unique values, attitudes, and needs.
Classical school	The central characteristic of entrepreneurial behavior is innovation, and the entrepreneur is therefore creative and discovers new opportunities.
Management school	Entrepreneurs are organizers of an economic venture; entrepreneurs are people who organize, own, manage and assume the risk.
Leadership school	Entrepreneurs are leaders of people; entrepreneurs have the ability to adapt their style to the needs of the people.
Intrapreneurship school	Entrepreneurship skills can be useful in complex organizations; intrapreneurs who develop independent units to create markets and expand services.

Figure 1-4. Different approaches to describing the entrepreneur as an individual (source: Cunningham & Lischeron, 1991, p. 47).

Entrepreneurship also demands creativity – the creation of something new that builds on the entrepreneur's readiness to learn and self-reliance, which makes the entrepreneur dare to challenge established practice. Herein lies a paradox – on the one hand, self-reliance leads to the belief of "owning the truth" while, on the other hand, the entrepreneur has to be responsive to alternative images of reality (readiness to learn).

The entrepreneur must also possess a competency – a competency that includes the ability to handle another paradox, namely that of employing empirical knowledge as a key source of information (i.e. a knowledge beyond formal education) as well as reflecting over and questioning practical experience. The entrepreneur's commitment and responsibility, creativity, and competence form the basis of their entrepreneurial mission to create visions for new activities and transforming these visions into actions. An illustration of Johannisson's reasoning is presented in Figure 1-5.

Entrepreneurship as a process. Entrepreneurship research has, in recent decades, gained an increasingly stronger foothold in the area of management studies, resulting in a partial shift in the research questions. The question "How is entrepreneurship developed?" (Stevenson & Jarillo, 1990) has gained topical interest – a question that in turn calls for a more process-oriented definition.

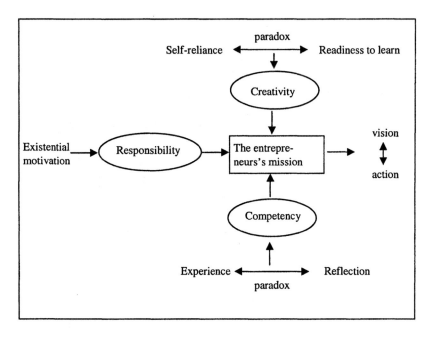

Figure 1-5. The entrepreneurial logic (source: developed from Johannisson, 1992, p. 120).

One of the early exponents of this shift in view – from a focus on the individual to a process based orientation – was William Gartner, who in the late 1980s wrote the article "Who is an entrepreneur? is the wrong question" (1988), where he argued that entrepreneurship concerns a process – the emergence of new organizations. William Bygrave and Charles Hofer (1991) pursued a similar line of reasoning, stating that "the entrepreneurial process involves all the functions, activities, and actions associated with the perceiving of opportunities and the creation of organizations to pursue them" (p. 14), and they argued that this entrepreneurial process could be characterized as: An act of human volition that involves a change of state, and it is a unique and dynamic process which involves numerous antecedent variables, and its outcomes are extremely sensitive to the initial conditions of these variables.

However, there has been a lack of consensus among entrepreneurship researchers regarding what should form the focus of studies on the entrepreneurial process. Two different streams of interest can be discerned: the emergence of new organizations and the emergence of opportunities.

- The emergence of new organizations

The chief exponent of a definition that focuses on the emergence of new organizations is perhaps William Gartner (1988; 1990; 1993), who talks about a process of organizational emergence. In Gartner's life cycle model, the process of entrepreneurship starts with "initiating", i.e. when the entrepreneur makes the decision to start a company, and ends with "the establishment", when the entrepreneur has to obtain external resources and create a market niche. Gartner uses the "organizational emergence" concept to depict how an organisation manifests itself. Thus, this is a process that predates the existence of the organisation. Consequently, it is not possible to talk about new or young companies. Gartner focuses on those activities that enable a person to create an organization, which can take place in many different contexts. Therefore, "the emergence of new organizations" in Gartner's sense should not be read as the creation of formal and legally defined organizations – Gartner is explicitly also interested in internal venturing in existing organizations.

The view of entrepreneurship as the emergence of new organizations has found expression in two international research projects: The Entrepreneurship Research Consortium (ERC) and the Global Entrepreneurship Monitor (GEM). Both studies have their basis in Paul Reynolds' reasoning on "nascent entrepreneurs" (Reynolds, 2000), where entrepreneurship is defined as individuals that are in the process of establishing a company or that have recently started a company (within the last 42 months).

- The emergence of opportunities

The main exponents of a definition that focuses on the emergence of opportunities, rather than new organizations, are Sankaran Venkataraman and Scott Shane. The difficulty in defining entrepreneurship as a scholarly domain led Venkataraman (1997) to argue that in most research fields it is not appropriate to define the topic in terms of the object of study. Likewise in entrepreneurship research, a definition of the "entrepreneur" is not relevant to entrepreneurial issues. Venkataraman argues that entrepreneurship as an area of research may be defined through the research questions that are central and unique to the field. Inspired by Austrian economics, he argued that entrepreneurship as a scholarly field "seeks to understand how opportunities to bring into existence 'future' goods and services are discovered, created, and exploited, by whom, and with what consequences" (1997, p. 120). Accordingly, the core of entrepreneurship should be concerned with (Venkataraman, 1997; Shane & Venkataraman, 2000):

1. why, when and how opportunities for the creation of goods and services come into existence,
2. why, when, and how some people are able to discover and exploit these opportunities while others cannot or do not, and
3. why, when, and how different modes of action are used to exploit entrepreneurial opportunities.

The article by Shane and Venkataraman (2000) has been the reference point for many discussions about entrepreneurship as a distinct domain in relation to other areas of research. In this debate the question about the "outcomes" of exploiting entrepreneurial opportunities has been in focus (see e.g. Zahra & Dess, 2001), especially in relation to the field of strategic management (Alvares & Busenitz, 2001). Many entrepreneurial efforts succeed and lead to wealth creation for both the entrepreneur and society but, more typically, new ventures fail. Thus, even if performance and wealth creation are not unique to entrepreneurship as a research area – for example, it is also a central paradigm in strategic management – it appears to be central to entrepreneurship research, and the outcomes of entrepreneurial activities therefore need to be included in entrepreneurship research, as they represent the fourth core of entrepreneurship:

4. what are the economic, psychological, and social consequences of this pursuit of a future market, not only for the entrepreneur but also for the other stakeholders and for society as a whole?

In this respect, entrepreneurship is not a fixed characteristic that differentiates some people from others, but rather a tendency of certain people to respond to situational cues of opportunities. Neither does entrepreneurship require, although it can include, the creation of new organizations, and entrepreneurship can occur in different contexts, such as existing organizations. Thus, Shane and Venkataraman's framework is much broader than the emergence of new organizations.

2.3 Accepting Entrepreneurship as a "Multiplying" Phenomenon

Many researchers hold that the problem of achieving a widely recognized definition of entrepreneurship research has a major bearing on the possibilities of the research field to develop and mature – and perhaps also for survival. Without unambiguous definitions of central concepts, there is a risk that entrepreneurship research will be fragmented – a potpourri of research – without the necessary knowledge accumulation. Against this background, voices have been raised in favor of a unification of entrepreneurship research – not only in the area of central concepts, but also in frameworks and methodological approaches, thus developing the field in line with a normal-science approach (Aldrich & Baker, 1997).

However, I will argue that such a development can be questioned. Entrepreneurship is an inherently complicated and ambiguous phenomenon, and the content of the concept changes over time. Because the phenomenon in itself is complicated, ambiguous and tends to vary, it is reasonable to expect that our definitions of the concept will also be ambiguous and changeable (Landström, 2000). We have also to remember the history of entrepreneurship research – a diverse group of scholars from various disciplines rushed into this promising field of research, and the researchers brought with them a range of different definitions, theoretical frameworks, levels of analysis and methodological approaches – which can be regarded as one of the strengths of the field in order to study and understand a multifaceted and complex phenomenon. In this situation, it can be questioned whether or not it is reasonable to sustain the dream of a unified science. Steyaert and Hjorth (2003) talk about "multiplying entrepreneurship", indicating that there are "many entrepreneurships" in terms of focus, definitions, scope, and paradigms. They argue that we not only accept and recognize different positions, but also systematically develop them, for example, by intensifying our efforts to connect scholars working with similar themes, frameworks or approaches (see also Gartner, 2001).

For this reason I will not attempt to define entrepreneurship, and the book includes various definitions of the concept by different researchers. It should also be noted that several of the pioneers presented have not focussed on the entrepreneur or entrepreneurship but on existing small businesses – businesses with certain characteristics, for example, small market share, personalized management, and independence of owner decision-making (Bolton, 1971), and with certain size (even if the criteria for measuring small firms may vary depending on context). On the other hand, entrepreneurship does not imply small scale nor does it have the status of a special legal entity – entrepreneurial processes exist independently of organizational boundaries. Dealing with entrepreneurship and small business at the same time naturally involves difficulties, and there is a risk that rigor will suffer in some descriptions. However, in the light of the close link that has traditionally existed been entrepreneurship and small business in research, I believe that it is necessary to treat the two areas as a whole.

3.   THE CONTENT OF THE BOOK

The book consists of four parts. Part I contains a historical-doctrinal review of the development of entrepreneurship and small business research. This part comprises five chapters. Chapter 1 includes, in addition to a presentation of the aims of the book, an attempt to summarize the existing definitions of entrepreneurship as a societal phenomenon and as a research field. In chapter 2, early entrepreneurship and small business research is described, from the early thinking of the 18th century to the contributions of Schumpeter and McClelland in the 20th century, and the development of entrepreneurship and small business research is placed in a larger societal context. In chapter 3 the emergence of a field of research during the 1980s and 1990s is discussed in terms of the social and cognitive development of the field. Chapter 3 mainly covers the development of entrepreneurship research from a US perspective. Therefore, chapter 4 provides an international picture of the development of entrepreneurship and small business thinking in different parts of the world – with a focus on Europe and Australia. Finally, in chapter 5 the pioneers in entrepreneurship and small business research will be identified together with a brief presentation of those who have received the FSF-NUTEK International Award for Small Business Research.

Parts II and III are devoted to a couple of pioneers that have received the International Award for Small Business Research, and the contributions made by the award winners will be described in greater detail – a chapter is devoted to each of them. In Part II, chapters 6 to 9, the contributions to entrepreneurship and small business research made by the award winners with a focus on macro-level analysis will be presented, whereas in Part III, chapters 10 to 12, will be devoted to award winners with a focus on a micro-level analysis. The chapters not only set out to describe the contributions to research made by the individual pioneers but also to give a picture of them as a person and their view on the development and future of entrepreneurship and small business research.

In Part IV, chapter 13, the book ends with an epilogue in which I will summarize some of the main arguments in the book and address some ideas for the future development of the research field.

REFERENCES

Aldrich, H.E. & Baker, T.B., 1997, Blinded by the cites? Has there been progress in entrepreneurship research?, in Sexton, D.L. & Smilor, R.W. (eds.), *Entrepreneurship 2000*, Chicago: Uppstart, 377-400.

Alvarez, S.A. & Busenitz, L.W., 2001, The entrepreneurship of resource-based theory, *Journal of Management*, 27, 755-775.

Baumol, W.J.,1993, Formal Entrepreneurship Theory in Economics, Existence and Bounds, *Journal of Business Venturing*, 3, 197-210.

Bettis, R.A. & Hitt, M.A., 1995, The new competitive landscape, *Strategic Management Journal*, 16, 7-19.

Bolton, J.E., 1971, *Report on the Committee of Inquiry on Small Firms*, CMNO 4811, London: Her Majesty's Stationary Office.

Brockhaus, R.H., 1980, Risk taking propensity of entrepreneurs, *Academy of Management Journal*, 23, 509-520.

Bygrave, W.D. & Hofer, C.W., 1991, Theorizing about entrepreneurship, *Entrepreneurship Theory and Practice*, 16, 2, 13-23.

Carland, J.W. & Hoy, F. & Boulton, W.R. & Carland, J.C., 1984, Differentiating Entrepreneurs from Small Business Owners: A Conceptualization, *Academy of Management Review*, 9, 2, 354-359.

Casson, M., 1982, *The Entrepreneur. An Economic Theory*, Oxford: Martin Robertson.

Cole, A., 1959, *Business Enterprise in its Social Settings*, Cambridge, MA: Harvard University.

Crane, D., 1972, *Invisible collegues. Diffusion of knowledge in scientific communities*, Chicago: University of Chicago Press.

Cunningham, J.B. & Lischeron, J., 1991, Defining Entrepreneurship, *Journal of Small Business Management*, 29, 1, 45-61.

Dahmén, E., 1950, *Svensk industriell företagsverksamhet*, Stockholm: Industrins Utredningsinstitut.

Davidsson, P., 2001, Towards a Paradigm for Entrepreneurship Research, paper at the XV RENT Conference, Turku, Finland.

Davidsson, P., 2003, The Domain of Entrepreneurship Research: Some Suggestions, in Katz, J. & Shepherd, D. (eds.), *Advances in Entrepreneurship, Firm Emergence and Growth*, Vol 6, Greenwich, CT: JAI Press.

Drucker, P., 1985, *Innovation and entrepreneurship*, New York: Harper & Row.

Finkle, T.A. & Deeds, D., 2001, Trends in the market for entrepreneurship faculty 1989-1998, *Journal of Business Venturing*, 16, 613-630.

Gartner, W.B., 1988, "Who Is an Entrepreneur?" Is the Wrong Question, *American Journal of Small Business*, Spring, 11-32.

Gartner, W.B., 1990, What are we talking about when we talk about entrepreneurship, *Journal of Business Venturing*, 5, 1, 15-29.

Gartner, W.B., 1993, Words Lead to Deeds: Towards an Organizational Emergence Vocabulary, *Journal of Business Venturing*, 8, 231-239.

Gartner, W.B., 2001, Is there an elephant in entrepreneurship? Blind assumptions in theory development, *Entrepreneurship Theory and Practice*, 25, 4, 27-39.

Gartner, W.B. & Bird, B.J. & Starr, J.A., 1992, Acting As If: Differentiating Entrepreneurial From Organizational Behavior, *Entrepreneurship, Theory and Practice*, Spring, 13-21.

Gopakumar, K., 1995, Entrepreneur in Economic Thought: A Thematic Overview, *Journal of Entrepreneurship*, 4, 1, 1-17.

Hagstrom, W.O., 1965, *The scientific community*, Carbondale, IL: Southern Illinois University Press.

Hébert, R.F. & Link, A.N., 1989, In Search of the Meaning of Entrepreneurship, *Small Business Economics*, 1, 39-49.

Hoselitz, B.F., 1951, The Early History of Entrepreneurial Theory, *Exploration in Entrepreneurial History*, 3, 4, 193-220.

Johannisson, B., 1992, *Entreprenörskap på svenska*, Malmö: Almqvist & Wiksell.

Karayiannis, A.D., 2003, Entrepreneurial functions and characteristics in a proto-capitalist economy: The Xenophanian entrepreneur, *Wirtschaftspolitische Blätter*, 50, 553-563.

Katz, J.A., 2003, The chronology and intellectual trajectory of American entrepreneurship education 1876-1999, *Journal of Business Venturing*, 18, 283-300.

Kilby, P. (ed.), 1971, *Entrepreneurship and Economic Development*, New York: Free Press.

Kirzner, I.M., 1973, *Competition and Entrepreneurship*, Chicago: Chicago University Press.

Kirzner, I.M., 1985, *Discovery and the Capitalist Process*, Chicago: Chicago University Press.

Knight, F.H., 1916/1921, *Risk, Uncertainty and Profit*, New York: Houghton Mifflin.

Landström, H., 2000, *Entreprenörskapets rötter*, Lund: Studentlitteratur.

Low, M.B. & MacMillan, I.C., 1988, Entrepreneurship: Past Research and Future Challenges, *Journal of Management*, 14, 2, 139-161.

Meyer, G.D. & Heppard, K.A. (eds.), 2000, *Entrepreneurship as Strategy*, Thousand Oaks, CA: Sage.

Meyer, G.D. & Neck, H.M. & Meeks, M.D., 2002, The Entrepreneurship – Strategic Management Interface, in Hitt, M.A. & Ireland, R.D. & Camp, S.M. & Sexton, D.L. (eds.), 2002, *Strategic Entrepreneurship*, Oxford: Blackwell.

Mises, L. von, 1951, *Planning for Freedom*, South Hollan, Ill: Libertarian Press.

Molander, B., 1988, *Vetenskapsfilosofi*, Stockholm: Thales.

Morris, M.H., 1998, *Entrepreneurial intensity: sustainable advantages for individuals, organizations, and societies*, Westport, Conn: Quorum.

Redlich, F., 1949, On the Origin of the Concepts of 'Entrepreneur' and 'Creative Entrepreneur', *Explorations in Entrepreneurial History*, 1, 2, 1-7.

Reynolds, P.D., 2000, National panel study of US business start-ups: Background and methodology, in Katz, J.A. (ed.), *Advances in Entrepreneurship, Firm Emergence, and Growth*, Vol 4, Stanford, CT: JAI Press, 153-227.

Schumpeter, J.A., 1912, *Theorie der Wirtschaftlichen Entwicklung*, Leipzig: Dunker & Humblot.

Schumpeter, J.A., 1934, *The Theory of Economic Development*, Cambridge, MA: Harvard University Press.

Shane, S. & Venkataraman, S., 2000, The Promise of Entrepreneurship as a Field of Research, *Academy of Management Review*, 25, 1, 217-226.

Shapero, A., 1975, The Displaced Uncomfortable Entrepreneur, *Psychology Today*, 9, 83-88.

Smith, A., 1776/1976, *An Inquiry into the Nature and Causes of the Wealth of Nations*, Oxford: Clarendon Press.

Stevenson, H.H. & Gumpert, D., 1985, The Heart of Entrepreneurship, *Harvard Business Review*, March-April, 85, 2, 85-94.

Stevenson, H.H. & Jarillo, J.C., 1990, A Paradigm of Entrepreneurship: Entrepreneurial Management, *Strategic Management Journal*, 11, 17-27.

Steyaert, C. & Hjorth, D., 2003, *New Movements in Entrepreneurship*, Cheltenham, UK: Edward Elgar.

Stinchcombe, A.L., 1965, Social Structure and Organizations, in March, J.G. (ed.), *Handbook of Organizations*, Chicago: Rand McNally, 142-193.

Timmons, J.A., 1997, *New Venture Creation*, Homewood, Ill.: Irwin.

Venkataraman, S., 1997, The Distinctive Domain of Entrepreneurship Research, in Katz, J.A. (ed.), *Advances in Entrepreneurship, Firm Emergence, and Growth*, Volume 3, Greenwich, Connecticut: JAI Press.

Zahra, S. & Dess, G.G., 2001, Entrepreneurship As a Field of Research: Encouraging Dialogue and Debate, *Academy of Management Review*, 26, 1, 8-10.

Chapter 2

THE ROOTS OF ENTREPRENEURSHIP AND SMALL BUSINESS RESEARCH

In this chapter I will focus on the roots of entrepreneurship and small business research. I will start by discussing some of the early thoughts about entrepreneurship and the introduction of entrepreneurship into economic literature (section 1). Joseph Schumpeter is an important figure in economic research on entrepreneurship, and his work is presented in section 2, followed by a discussion on the post-Schumpeterian development in economic science in section 3. Entrepreneurship and small business research gradually changed from being an economic discipline to a research area within behavioral science. The contribution of David McClelland is presented in a section in which I discuss the stream of research that attempts to answer the "who is an entrepreneur" question (section 4). In recent years entrepreneurship and small business research has also moved into the area of management science, as described in section 5. The chapter concludes with a discussion in section 6 in which I relate entrepreneurship and small business research to the development of society.

1. EARLY THINKING ON ENTREPRENEURSHIP

Although the term "entrepreneur" has been a part of the French language since the 12th century, the European economy remained locked in the feudal system for a long time, which hampered entrepreneurship and innovation. However, during the middle ages, the situation gradually changed, especially in Italy, France and Southern Germany, which were the driving forces in the European economy at that time. The rise of the cities created a breeding ground for entrepreneurship, and it was especially among the merchant class, who supplied raw materials and marketed the finished goods, that entrepreneurship thrived. By the 18th century feudalism had disappeared, and legal and institutional conditions had greatly changed in favor of entrepreneurship and innovation, as evidenced by the burgeoning of the joint stock company and development of a banking system. (Wennekers & Thurik, 1999)

Economists were the first to attempt to endow the concept of entrepreneurship with greater scientific meaning. The development of entrepreneurship within the area of economic science has been described in depth by Hébert and Link (1982; 1989). Part of the following section is drawn from their review

1.1   Entrepreneurship in an Economic Context

Entrepreneurship appeared in the economic science literature primarily through the writings of Richard Cantillon (approx. 1680-1734), an Irish-born banker who lived in Paris and whose work *Essai Sur la Nature du Commerce en Général*, published posthumously in 1755, endowed the concept with economic meaning and the entrepreneur with a role in economic development. Cantillon's work received considerable attention in France, and it circulated as a manuscript before it was finally published. Cantillon recognized that discrepancies between demand and supply in a market create opportunities for buying cheaply and selling at a higher price and that this sort of arbitrage would bring equilibrium to the competitive market. The assumption was that the entrepreneur would buy products at a fixed price, have them packaged and transported to market and sell them at an unpredictable, uncertain price. People who took advantage of these unrealised profit opportunities were called "entrepreneurs". A basic characteristic of Cantillon's analysis was the emphasis on risk – entrepreneurship is a matter of foresight and willingness to assume risk, but this is not necessarily connected with the manufacturing of goods and employment of labor in a productive sense. Cantillon thus focused on the function of the entrepreneur – he made a clear distinction between the function of the entrepreneur and the capitalist (who provided the capital) – and not on the personal attributes of the former. He was, however, of the opinion that the entrepreneur makes conscious choices about resource allocation in order to exploit resources so as to achieve as high a financial return as possible.

By the mid 18th century, changing production conditions, social relations, and a new way of thinking began to emerge. These changes also affected the intellectual and academic environment. In the realm of economic science, "classical" economic theory developed and is generally regarded to have its origin in Adam Smith's (1723-1790) *Inquiry into the Nature and Causes of the Wealth of Nations* (1776/1976) – a work which in many ways set the trend for economic theory and in which Smith laid the foundation for the analysis of the way the market economy functions. Smith's work influenced the view taken of the entrepreneur in economic science: he did not distinguish between the capitalist as the provider of the "stock" of the enterprise and the entrepreneur as the ultimate decision-maker, neither did he deal with the entrepreneurial function in the economy – instead, it was the capitalist who became the central actor in Smith's analysis. This failure to isolate the entrepreneurship function from pure ownership of capital became standard practice among classical economists.

There were, however, a number of economists who maintained a certain amount of interest in entrepreneurship, at least to a limited extent, among them the philosopher Jeremy Bentham (1748-1832). He criticized Smith for not considering the role of the entrepreneur in society. Although Bentham emphasized the role of the entrepreneur in economic development in various ways, in his reasoning the entrepreneur was no more than an individual who undertook certain tasks on contractual terms. Another of the economic classics that should be mentioned is John Stuart Mill (1806-1873). He has been recognized as the person who established the word "entrepreneur" for a more general use than that attributed to it by economists.

However, it was the French economist Jean Baptiste Say (1767-1832), a great admirer of Adam Smith, who really changed the contemporary trend. In his works, *Traité d'économie politique* (1803/1964) and *Cours complet d'économie politique practique* (1828), Say defined entrepreneurship as the combining of factors of production into an organism, and he provided an empirical description of what the entrepreneur does as well as an analysis of the entrepreneurial function in the economy. Say's entrepreneurship theory starts by dividing industrial development into three distinct activities: research that is conducted by researchers for the purpose of generating knowledge, adjustment of this knowledge to usable products via entrepreneurs, who organize production factors, and finally the production that is performed by the workers. He saw the entrepreneur as a "broker", who organizes and combines means of production with the aim of producing goods. But this adjustment is not just something that occurs by chance, and it must lead to the development of a good or a service that provides some form of value or utility. In addition, Say did not take the view that the entrepreneur was only a coordinator of the means of production – he was also the one who carried out these activities at his own risk.

1.2   From Macro to Micro Economics

The end of the 19th century heralded a transition in economic science from macroeconomic considerations to a greater focus on microeconomic ones. This new focus was dominated by a theory of equilibrium where individuals were either producers or consumers and where the search for equilibrium became the most important aspect of economic analysis. In this situation, the entrepreneur was overlooked. One of the few classical economists who retained an interest in entrepreneurship was Alfred Marshall (1842-1924). Even though Marshall was aware of Say's and Cantillon's emphasis on coordination and risk taking as the basic characteristics of an entrepreneur, in his earlier work *Principles of Economics* (1890) Marshall followed the English tradition and considered the entrepreneur as a multifaceted capitalist, and in the equilibrium of a perfectly competitive market, there was no place for "entrepreneurs" as generators of economic activity. However, in his more institutional work (Marshall, 1919), he placed greater emphasis on entrepreneurship and referred to it as "the best educators of initiative and versatility, which are the chief sources of industrial progress." (p. 249)

It is interesting to observe that at the same time there were also contributions to entrepreneurship theory from researchers in Germany and Austria. The analyses from these countries belonged to a tradition that emphasised administration and politics. One economist that deserves to be mentioned is von Thünen (1783-1850), who argued that there is a theoretical difference between entrepreneurship and management, and he regarded the entrepreneur as both an innovator and a risk bearer. Another is Mangoldt (1824-1868), who regarded entrepreneurial profits as the rent of ability, indicating that the entrepreneur should be regarded as a separate factor of production. But there were also other Austrian economists, for example Menger (1840-1921), who saw the entrepreneur as someone who transformed goods from one stage to another in the production chain, involving time, risk and uncertainty, and his disciples Böhm-Bawerk (1852-1914) who regarded the entrepreneur as a capitalist, and Wieser (1851-1926), who considered the entrepreneur as "a jack-of-all-trades" (Ahl, 2002).

Carl Menger is, above all, considered to be the ideological founder of the so-called Austrian tradition of economic thoughts (see subsection 3.2.). His contribution to classical economics is mainly at the methodological level. In his seminal work *Grundsätze der Volkswirtschaftlehre* (1871/1981) he introduced a subjectivistic view on the economy. He was the proponent of methodological *subjectivism,* where economic phenomena are not perceived as relations between objects but between people. In order to understand such relations, economic theory must proceed from the social, cultural and economic conceptions that govern human actions. Unlike the natural sciences, economics cannot ignore the perceptions, wishes and views of the people studied. This view is also reflected in Menger's methodological *individualism*. Within society and economics, the actors are individuals – not a group or social class – which means that explanations of economic phenomena have to proceed from or at least be possible to refer back to individuals' actions (Pålsson-Syll, 1998). Thus, economic changes do not take place in a vacuum but are created by individuals' awareness and understanding of a given situation. This means that the entrepreneur can be considered as an "agent of change", who transforms resources into useful products and services.

1.3   From Europe to the US

In the late 19th century, the European discussion on entrepreneurship found an audience in the United States, which in that period was well on the way to becoming a major industrial power. Some of the American economists who continued to develop the discussion about entrepreneurship were Francis Walker, Fredrick Hawley, and John Bates Clark. Perhaps the best-known economist in this context was Frank Knight (1885-1972). In his thesis *Risk, Uncertainty and Profit* (1916, revised 1921), Knight made a distinction between three types of future uncertainties – risk exists when outcomes are uncertain, but the outcomes can be predicted with some degree of probability, uncertainty arises when the probability of outcomes cannot be calculated, and "true uncertainty" occurs when the future is not only unknown, but also unknowable with unclassifiable instances and a non-existent distribution of outcomes (Sarasvathy et al., 2003). Knight argued that entrepreneurship is mainly characterized by true uncertainty. Opportunities arise out of the uncertainty surrounding change – if change is predictable there is no opportunity for profit. Thus, the entrepreneur receives a return for making decisions under conditions of true uncertainty. Entrepreneurial return, therefore, results from the fact that individual activity cannot be predicted, and entrepreneurial competence is the individual's ability to deal with uncertainty. Incidentally, it should be mentioned that Knight was later considered a central figure within economics, among other things due to being the founder of the so-called Chicago-school of economics. He also published several seminal contributions, for example, *Economic Organization* (1933), which is considered a classic of micro economic theory.

At the beginning of the 20th century, there was already an extensive theoretical base around the concept of the entrepreneur and entrepreneurship. However, even if certain common ground existed when it came to the way entrepreneurship was viewed by the early authors, it is difficult to identify a consensus that would enable us to speak of a "theory". Furthermore, the entrepreneur was still regarded as being on the periphery of economic analysis.

2.   JOSEPH ALOIS SCHUMPETER

It was Joseph A. Schumpeter (1883-1950) who tried once again to make the entrepreneur a central figure in economic theory. The turn of the 19th century was characterized by the development of new industries

and the building of modern enterprises, and many authors claimed to see
the death struggle of small firms in the economy (Bögenhold, 2000).
However, in this respect, Schumpeter was inspired by Gustav Schmoller
(1838-1917), who, in his analysis of the historical-economic
development, was convinced that there exists a unique and central factor
in all economic activity – the entrepreneur – who is a key figure due to
his/her ability as a creative organizer and whose role is to develop
innovations and initiate new activities.

Schumpeter is regarded as a social scientist, and his extensive
scientific production encompasses a wide field within economic theory.
In his scientific production Schumpeter tries to build a new economic
theory as a reaction to the equilibrium ideal that was developed and
promoted by Leon Walras (1834-1910). Although Schumpeter himself
was a great admirer of Walras, he considered that the equilibrium theory
was incomplete. There was some "energy" within the economic system
that created disequilibrium in the market, and Schumpeter tried for the
first time to communicate these thoughts in his book: *Theorie der
Wirtschaftlichen Entwicklung* (1912, second edition 1926) or *Theory of
Economic Development* (1934), which is the English translation of the
second edition. The first and second editions are rather different. Of the
two, the first edition is more original and bears all the signs of youthful
enthusiasm. Nevertheless, it is the second edition – especially the
English version – that is most often cited. This edition is more
streamlined and, in it, Schumpeter attempted to relate his work to the
mainstream of economic thinking at that time.

2.1   The Life of Joseph Schumpeter

Joseph Schumpeter was born on 8th February 1883 in the small town
of Triesch (presently Trest in the Republic of Slovakia). The family was
Catholic and for several generations belonged to the elite of the town,
but his father who was a textile manufacturer died when Joseph was only
four years old. At the beginning of the 1890s the family moved to
Vienna. The ten-year-old Schumpeter was sent to a very exclusive
private school. In 1901 he graduated with top grades and immediately
enrolled at the law department of the University of Vienna (economics
was taught at the law department). Several of the world's most famous
economists, such as Carl Menger, Eugen von Böhm-Bawerk and
Friedrich von Wieser were working there at that time. In 1906 at the age
of 23, Schumpeter took his doctoral degree in economics (formally law).
He made rapid progress and in 1908 he completed his "habilitation"
thesis. The thesis was about Walras' equilibrium theory. In 1911 he
became professor of economics at the University of Graz. (Swedberg,
1994; 2000)

Schumpeter also took an interest in politics, and in 1919 he was
asked by the Social Democratic Party to become Minister of Finance in a

coalition government. He accepted the offer even though he was not a supporter of the Social Democrats. However, he was abruptly replaced after six months, which marked the end of his short-lived political career. Business also attracted Schumpeter, and at the beginning of the 1920s he began a career as an investor and venture capitalist. For a couple of years he was a very successful financier. However, the economic crisis that rocked Austria during the mid 1920s resulted in him losing everything, including his position, and he amassed large debts. (ibid.)

In 1925 Schumpeter was offered a new professorship, on this occasion at the University of Bonn. His mother and wife both died at around this time, which left him free to travel abroad more often. He visited the US and lectured at Harvard University. At Harvard his talents were clearly seen, and he was offered a professorship that he accepted in 1932 after long consideration. During the Harvard period he wrote several large volumes such as *Business Cycles* (1939) and *Capitalism, Socialism and Democracy* (1942). These contributions met with a very mixed reception.

Schumpeter had a very conservative political attitude. As the Second World War broke out, the FBI initiated investigations and surveillance of Schumpeter that lasted for several years, and friends and colleagues started to avoid him. Rumors that Schumpeter supported Hitler started to flourish. In retrospect, it was evident that Schumpeter had no sympathies for Nazism. The result was, however, that he started to withdraw from the public eye. He started to work intensively on his next and final volume, *History of Economic Analysis* published in 1954. The work was almost completed when he died of a cerebral haemorrhage on the night of 7th to 8th January 1950, at the age of 66.

2.2   The Theory of Economic Development (1934)

In *The Theory of Economic Development* (1934) Schumpeter tries to build a new economic theory, and the book thus contains lines of reasoning about the importance of capital, the creation of wealth, and economic cycles. It is only the second chapter that is devoted to the entrepreneur, and it is primarily this chapter that has had a major impact, while his other thoughts have not been easily accepted in economic theory.

Schumpeter's basic realization was that economic growth resulted not from capital accumulation, but from innovations or "new combinations". His point of departure was that equilibrium is predominant in the economic system. He regards the economic system as a closed circular flow (*der Kreislauf*) due to the fact that a seller of a certain commodity will subsequently be the buyer of other commodities. The system is in a state of equilibrium, resulting in a continuous reiteration of the flows. However, this does not mean that changes do not occur but rather that all actors involved adapt to the new situation as soon as the changes are detected. Sometimes, however, radical changes occur in the system, due to a tendency of the entrepreneur to break the equilibrium by introducing innovations in the form of new products, methods of production, markets, investment goods, or organization of industrial units and branches.

Once Schumpeter had recognized the crucial role of innovation in economic growth, he understood that innovation had to be implemented by someone, and this ability to break with established practice was primarily related to individual entrepreneurs. He argued that entrepreneurship demands a specific type of personality, which differs from that of the simple, rational conduct of the economic man – a personality made up of a mix of rational-utilitarian elements (a large measure of prediction and planning) in addition to emotional elements (Martinelli, 2004). According to Schumpeter, entrepreneurs are characterized by the desire to found private kingdoms, the will to conquer, and the joy of creating, or in more modern parlance (Swedberg, 2000, p. 16): (i) the desire for power and independence, (ii) the will to succeed, and (iii) the satisfaction of getting things done – money per se is not the driving force behind the entrepreneur. Thus, entrepreneurship is a creative act and deviates from the bourgeois culture, which defines rationality from a narrower viewpoint of short-term advantages. In this respect Schumpeter diverges from the assumptions of both classical and neo-classical economists who, in different ways, tended to equate utilitarian rationality with capitalism (Martinelli, 2004).

However, these innovations, which change the established pattern, tend not to occur evenly over time but in "swarms". The fact that entrepreneurs break down barriers stimulates other individuals to follow their lead. The upturn in the economy brought about by these innovations has, however, qualitative effects on the economic system in the form of what Schumpeter calls "creative destruction", where the positive economic development leads to a crisis. When an entrepreneur enters an existing market dominated by a few large suppliers, the innovative new firms will increase the overall demand for the product or service offered, but will also capture market shares from existing suppliers, i.e. the new firm will expand the overall economic activity as well as redistributing wealth by destroying the market structure and shifting market shares from existing firms to the new one.

2.3   Schumpeter's View on Entrepreneurship

It should be noted that Schumpeter's work and view on entrepreneurship underwent a change over time. Up to about 1940, he was mainly interested in developing his mode of reasoning about entrepreneurship and in integrating these trains of thought in his new economic theory. However, during the interwar period in the US, he had encountered a different corporate world to that found in the Austria of his youth. In the

US, the corporate scene was dominated not by small firms with clearly distinguishable entrepreneurs but by large companies with advanced research departments engaged in planned research. This spurred Schumpeter's interest in innovative activities in existing organizations, while at the same time he developed a growing interest in economic history. This change in focus finds expression in, among other things, his book *Capitalism, Socialism and Democracy* (1942), where he focused on the institutional structure of society. In this book, he raised the question as to whether capitalism as an economic system would be able to survive and predicted that socialism would eventually displace capitalism in Western democracies.

	Mark I regime	Mark II regime
Book	– *The Theory of Economic Development* (1934) – based on Schumpeter's 1912 book	– *Capitalism, Socialism and Democracy* (1942)
Industry characteristics	– Less concentrated market structures (competitive markets). – Low entry barriers. – A large number of small companies with a base of applied knowledge (few science based firms).	– More concentrated market structures (oligopolistic and monopolistic markets). – High entry barriers. – The firms grew larger by exploiting economies of scale, with a declining number of small firms in most industries.
Similarities	– Innovations (or new combinations) are central to economic development. – Entrepreneurship is a function that is delimited in time. – The capitalist assumes the risk.	
Differences	– Focus on the individual – the entrepreneur is an individual.	– The function is in focus – entrepreneurship need not be carried by a single individual but can be the responsibility of a group, a network or an organization. Above all, Schumpeter highlights innovative activities by large and established organizations.
	– Only "first degree" innovations are counted – i.e. only the important and truly pattern breaking innovations create economic development.	– A lower requirement on innovative aspects – "followers" can also be regarded as entrepreneurs.

Figure 2-1. Schumpeterian Mark I and Mark II regimes.

Schumpeter predicted a decline in the economic importance of the entrepreneur; a fact that he considered would be one of the major forces in the transformation from capitalism to socialism. In his book he argues that increased rationality and routine in society weakens entrepreneurship, thus leading to the stagnation of capitalism. Innovations would no longer be related to the expertise of a single individual but become the fruits of the organized efforts of large teams, most efficiently performed within the framework of large corporations – making the large corporations increasingly predominant in the economy. Thus, Schumpeter's prediction was that, due to economies of scale in the production of new economic knowledge, large corporations would have an innovative advantage over small firms, but also that the economic landscape would be dominated by giant corporations. Schumpeter's views on the mechanisms behind economic development and the shifts in these views are generally referred to as the Schumpeterian Mark I and Mark II regimes. Figure 2-1 presents a summary of Schumpeter's views on economic development during these two regimes.

It is interesting to note that John Maynard Keynes (1883-1846) published his work *General Theory of Employment, Interest and Money* (1936/1973) several years after Schumpeter's English version had appeared. Keynes, however, did not go into detail regarding entrepreneurship and did not give the entrepreneur a central role in economic development. In comparison with Schumpeter, Keynes' reasoning had a much more profound effect on the economic debate, which may be due to the fact that he was more normative and emphasized, to a greater degree, the state's opportunities to influence economic development. In addition, the Great Depression in the 1930s made Schumpeter's theories seem irrelevant and even wrong. It must also be admitted that his own turgid prose may be another reason for the modest inroad of Schumpeter's thoughts within as well as beyond economics – Schumpeter was not always easy to read or understand (Sandberg, 2001). Thus, Schumpeter was totally swamped by the Keynesian Revolution, and for most economists the question of entrepreneurship was not problematic. Entrepreneurship was just a variable dependent upon economic factors, such as availability of capital, labor, material, etc., and entrepreneurial activities would emerge more or less spontaneously when economic conditions were favorable (Martinelli, 2004). The result was that, once more, the entrepreneur had to take a backseat in economic theory.

3.   THE POST-SCHUMPETERIAN DEVELOPMENT OF ECONOMIC SCIENCE

Schumpeter's reasoning has remained a basic point of reference for many of his successors. Later developments can be roughly divided into two categories: the Schumpeterian tradition and the Austrian tradition.

3.1   Schumpeterian Tradition

Schumpeter's ideas were developed at the Research Center in Entrepreneurial History at Harvard University. The Center was founded by Arthur H. Cole in 1948, and it was here that Schumpeter worked until his death in 1950 although he only devoted part of his time to it. Other members of the Center were among others Hugh Aitken, Fritz Redlich, Alexander Gerschenkron, Talcott Parsons, and Thomas Cochran. These members were not Schumpeterian in the true sense of the word. The researchers at Harvard had slightly different perceptions of the nature of entrepreneurship, but they did agree that entrepreneurship consisted of three different dimensions: (i) changes in the economic system, (ii) creation of organizations as a prerequisite for the commercialization of innovations, and (iii) the fact that the task of the entrepreneur was to create profits and that this occurs through the production and distribution of goods and services, i.e. entrepreneurship was related to a certain sector in society. Research Center in Entrepreneurial History ceased to exist in 1958 but Schumpeter's lines of reasoning still exert an influence. Some of the economists that have continued the tradition and developed Schumpeter's ideas are:

Erik Dahmén (1950; 1970) formulated the concept of "development blocks" to describe an integrated industrial system within a nation. In a development block, different kinds of complementarities are developed, i.e. different institutions and companies support each other because they work with the same basic material or have other production-related points of contact. New innovations such as railway construction, electrification and motorization give rise to new complementarities in society. These development blocks have a fundamental impact on society, contributing to the establishment of old companies in new locations as well as radically new companies that have been able to utilise these changes. Thus, development blocks lead to the creation of the swarms of innovations described by Schumpeter.

William Baumol's (1968; 1990; 1993) basic thesis is that the supply of entrepreneurs in a society is constant but that the societal value of their self interest driven ingenuity varies according to the rewards available. This indicates that, in order to encourage entrepreneurship, it is necessary to create conditions that allow the entrepreneurial pursuit of self-interest to accord with social wealth creation. In this respect,

Baumol argues that entrepreneurship can be found in many societies throughout history, but while it is productive in some, it is unproductive and even destructive in others. In other words, entrepreneurial activities may have negative consequences in terms of decreased social income and welfare – the entrepreneur earns money at the expense of other citizens in society. For example, different types of company acquisitions can sometimes turn into unproductive entrepreneurship and, quite often, legislation and the legal system prevent or delay the exploitation of new ideas.

3.2   Austrian Tradition

This tradition originated at the end of the 19th century and is based on the thoughts of the Austrian economist Carl Menger (see subsection 1.2.) but also Friederich von Wieser and Eugen von Böhm-Bawerk, whose ideas were further developed by two other Austrian economists: Frederick von Hayek (1899-1992) and Ludwig von Mises (1881-1973). The thinking within this tradition is based on the view that the individual is an independent economic entity and that his or her actions to a great extent influence the economic conditions in society. Thus, the focus is on the individual's actions on the market. According to Mises (1951) entrepreneurship is a question of correctly anticipating the market. If the entrepreneur is successful in anticipating the market, he or she will be able to produce more cheaply than their competitors and earn profit by being useful to the customer – the more useful, the more profit will be made – and therefore it is destructive to tax or confiscate the profit of the entrepreneur in other ways. Furthermore, Mises (1949/1963) observed that people are not only calculating creatures but also alert to making use of opportunities, which caused him to introduce the concept of "human action" to describe this behavior. Hayek (1945) pointed out that in a market economy, knowledge is often divided among different individuals, so that no one individual possesses the same knowledge or information as another. This means that there are only a few people who know about special shortages or resources that are not used to maximum effect. This knowledge is unique since it is obtained through each individual's special situation, occupation, social network, etc. This division of knowledge explains the presence of uncertainty, which gives rise to market opportunities.

During recent decades, one of Mises' students at New York University, Israel Kirzner, has stood out as the leading exponent of the Austrian tradition. In his book *Competition and Entrepreneurship* (1973), Kirzner develops arguments raised by Mises and Hayek. According to Kirzner, it is fundamental for an entrepreneur to be alert in identifying   and   dealing   with   profit-making   opportunities ("entrepreneurial alertness"), i.e. the entrepreneur tries to discover profit opportunities and helps to restore equilibrium to the market by acting on these opportunities. In this respect Kirzner gives a precise meaning to the word "entrepreneurship": entrepreneurship is "alertness" to new opportunities, and entrepreneurs act on these opportunities. The entrepreneurial function involves the coordination of information, which is based on identifying the gap between supply and demand, as well as acting as the brokers between supply and demand, making it possible to earn money from the difference. Thus, the entrepreneur searches for imbalances in the system. In such situations, there is an asymmetry of information in the market, which means that resources are not coordinated in an effective way. By seeking out these imbalances and by constantly trying to coordinate the resources in a more effective way, the entrepreneur leads the process toward equilibrium. Thus, Kirzner regards the entrepreneur as a person, who is alert to imperfections in the market thanks to information about the needs and resources of the different actors and, with the help of this information, is able to coordinate resources in a more effective way, thereby creating equilibrium.

4. FROM ECONOMIC TO BEHAVIORAL SCIENCE

In the course of the last half century, it seems that entrepreneurship has more or less been overlooked in economic models, with a few exceptions. An intra-scientific explanation is that economic science has focused more and more strongly on equilibrium models – which constitute the dominant paradigm in the field, and in which there does not seem to be any room for the entrepreneur (Barreto, 1989; Kirchhoff, 1994). Another, more extra-scientific explanation may be that, since Schumpeter, attention in society has moved away from trying to explain entrepreneurship toward developing it. For example, in the 1950s the availability of entrepreneurial ability was considered a vital factor in economic development. After World War II it was important to stimulate individuals to start businesses and get development in society under way. It was tempting to find an individual profile leading to entrepreneurial success (or failure). If this were possible it would also be possible to identify and encourage those with appropriate personalities to engage in an entrepreneurial career. However, economists could not play a useful role in identifying and developing this ability. Instead, behavioral science researchers, and especially psychologists, saw an open field and increasingly assumed responsibility for continuing the theoretical development. Thus, after World War II behavioral scientists came to dominate the research field. The point of departure was: Why do some individuals tend to start their own business whereas others do not? The answer was: It depends on the fact that some individuals have certain qualities that others lack. In order to understand the entrepreneur as an individual, behavioral science researchers have mainly asked the questions: "Who is an entrepreneur?" and "Why does the entrepreneur act?" (Stevenson & Jarillo, 1990).

4.1   Who is an Entrepreneur?

When it comes to what motivates entrepreneurs to strive for success in the economic sphere, behaviorists tend to emphasize the psychological factors involved. One of the pioneers that should be mentioned in this respect is Everett Hagen who, in a massive work *On the Theory of Social Change: How Economic Growth Begins* (1962), studied how a more traditional society is transformed into an economic growth society. Hagen uses two personality types: the authoritarian and the innovative, and the conclusion is that the number of innovative personalities in a society is decisive for its economic growth. Hagen also explores how social exclusion and degradation produce individuals determined to accumulate wealth. He argues that people who have grown up in certain minorities develop a much stronger psychological propensity for entrepreneurship than those who have not.

However, the most well-known pioneer among behavioral scientists with an interest in entrepreneurship is David McClelland who was one of the first to present empirical studies in the field of entrepreneurship that were based on behavioral science theory.

4.1.1   David McClelland

David McClelland was born on 20th May 1917 in Mt.Vernon, New York – one of five children of a Methodist college president (McClelland himself later became a committed and active Quaker) – and he died on 27th March, 1998. His religious background may explain his desire and energy in applying psychology to solve "real-world problems", for example, to develop training courses in India in order to increase the achievement motive among local business people, his interest in re-socializing alcoholics in the US, etc. After McClelland received his PhD in 1941 from Yale University, he joined the faculty of Wesleyan University in Connecticut in 1942, where he remained until 1956. From 1956 to 1987 he was professor at Harvard University. During his long career he wrote or edited 16 books and published over 185 papers and book chapters (Winter, 2000). His most well known books are *Personality* (1951), his classical textbook on personality psychology, and *Human Motivation* (1987), which summarizes and synthesizes most of McClelland's work on motivation in over forty years of research.

David McClelland was a personality and motivation psychologist and is most widely known for his research on the achievement motive. His interest in the need for achievement motive (nACH) developed from his wartime experience when he served as assistant personnel officer of the

American Friends Service Committee, and later on, with his background in experimental psychology, he developed a method for scoring the Thematic Apperception Test (TAT) – a test that was developed by Henry Murray in the 1930s. Over the next several decades his research interest became broader, and he became interested in many interdisciplinary topics – linking personality to fields like economics, history, political science, and biology. After 1970, McClelland shifted away from the study of achievement to a stronger focus on the power motive, but he continued his interdisciplinary journey, exploring the links between power, affiliation, and achievement motives, and different aspects of psychological functioning (Winter, 2000).

Throughout McClelland's career he was guided by his motto "if something exists, it exists in some amount and can be measured" and that a theory cannot be accepted until tested by rigorous quantitative measurements. McAdams (1987) identified a couple of salient themes in McClelland's production that characterize his research on human motivation:

– A fascination with Freud and the unconscious – McClelland believed that the important motives in human life reside beneath the surface of everyday awareness.
– A commitment to measurement – everything could be measured and transformed into numbers.
– An implied dimensional view of people – McClelland studied underlying dimensions of the personality that motivate (direct or select) behaviour. Thus, he believed that the motives should crystallize into concrete behavior.
– A belief that motives can be changed – during his career he developed different education programs for altering people's motivational profiles.
– A preoccupation with major questions of human adaptation and a concern about the welfare of society – McClelland was interested in the big issues in society, for example, Why do nations make war? Why are some people more successful than others?, etc.

To entrepreneurship researchers, McClelland's reasoning about the achievement motive, developed in his book *The Achieving Society* (1961), is what has primarily made an imprint on the doctrinal history of entrepreneurship. McClelland had the ability to obtain large research grants, and his studies were often based on gigantic empirical data material and included a large number of researchers around the world. This was also the case with the studies focusing on nACH, the results of which showed, among other things, that people who have a strong need for achievement are not artistically sensitive. They are entrepreneurs with a drive to constantly improve themselves – to find a shorter route to the office or a faster way of reading their mail – they are not gamblers, they want to win by personal effort – as opposed to luck (Harris, 1971). The achievement motive is often described as the entrepreneurial motive, and it has been shown that entrepreneurs in small firms score higher on nACH than their associates, whereas in larger companies it is more complex, as it seems that power motives become more important for managers in large companies.

4.1.2   The Achieving Society (1961)

In his pioneering work *The Achieving Society* (1961), McClelland discussed the question: Why do certain societies develop more dynamically than others? For example, "Why did medieval Florence become the hub of the Renaissance?" and "Why did the same development not appear in other places with seemingly similar preconditions?" Here McClelland builds further on Max Weber's reasoning in *The Protestant Ethic and the Spirit of Capitalism* (1904/1970), in which Weber made an analysis covering the interplay between culture and the economic development in a society. Weber's argument is that certain puritan traits in the Protestant moral code resulted in a combination of thrift, a sense of duty, industriousness and self-denial and that these characteristic traits made the development of capitalism possible. For McClelland, the point of departure was that the norms and values that prevail in a given society, particularly with regard to the need for achievement (nACH), are of vital importance for the development of that society.

By means of a large number of experimentally constructed studies, McClelland demonstrated the link between a nation's need for achievement and its economic development. For example, as an indicator of the degree of need for achievement in a society, he studied popular legends and fairy tales, both modern and historical, from different parts of the world in order to relate them to the nation's economic development. The results show that there appears to be a relation between a nation's degree of need for achievement and its economic development. He points out, however, that economic development is a complex phenomenon, which cannot be explained merely in terms of need for achievement. Consequently, other variables need to be considered, such as the individual's relationship motive and need for control. He concluded that economically better developed countries are characterized by a lower focus on institutional norms and a greater emphasis on openness toward other people and their values, as well as communication between people. It is in this context that entrepreneurs become the important driving force in the development of a country. In other words, a country's achievement level is transformed into economic growth through the medium of the entrepreneur. If the level of need for achievement in a country is high, there will probably be individuals who behave as entrepreneurs. Entrepreneurs are, in this respect, people who have a high need for achievement, great self-confidence, independent problem-solving skills, and who prefer situations that are characterized by moderate risk, follow-ups of results and feedback, and the acceptance of individual responsibility.

McClelland's contribution meant that the personal qualities of the entrepreneur occupied a prominent position in entrepreneurship research within the field of behavioral science during the 1960s and 1970s. There are a large number of studies that try to identify the particular qualities of the entrepreneur, and some of the individual characteristics assumed to be related to entrepreneurs are (Delmar, 2000):

- Need for achievement; which is one of the most popular characteristics associated with entrepreneurs and which is based on McClelland's 1961 study.
- Risk-taking propensity; the role of the entrepreneur as economic risk-taker or risk-bearer in the economic system can be traced back to early writers in economic sciences, not least Knight (1921).
- Locus of control; the concept, developed by Rotter (1966), concerns whether a potential goal can be attained through one's own action or follows from uncontrolled external factors.
- Over-optimism; entrepreneurs often show a high degree of over-optimism, as reported by Cooper, Woo and Dunkelberg (1988).
- Desire for autonomy; entrepreneurs seem to have a high need for autonomy (Sexton & Bowman, 1985) and a fear of external control (Smith, 1967).

A review of psychological approaches to entrepreneurs would be incomplete without mentioning the contributions made within the psychoanalytical oriented tradition, which assumes that the behavior of the individual is best understood by a number of intrinsic qualities. The foundation of these qualities is laid early in life. The main exponent of this research tradition is perhaps Ketz de Vries, who in his work "The Entrepreneurial Personality" (1977) takes the view that entrepreneurial behavior is the result of experiences in early youth, characterized by an unhappy family background with various kinds of psycho-social problems. Because of this, the individual acquires a deviant personality, does not function in a structured social environment, and has difficulty accepting authority and working together with others.

The number of traits identified in research has gradually increased and, with a few exceptions (e.g. "need for achievement"), it has proven difficult to link any specific traits to entrepreneurial behavior (Delmar, 2000). For this reason, research into individual traits has been extensively criticized, both on conceptual and methodological grounds, but also due to the fact that an increasing number of companies are founded by teams and not by a single individual. Despite this, the notion of trying to identify entrepreneurial traits in various individuals still persists, but current research is more rigorous in terms of concept development as well as more sophisticated in the use of methods. The models have also become more complex, taking into account the situation and the individual's perception of the situation.

4.2   Different Categories of Entrepreneurs

For behavioral science researchers, it was not only of interest to define who the entrepreneur is but also to show how he/she differs from other groups of leaders. As entrepreneurs constitute a fairly heterogeneous group of people, it was essential to classify them in comparison with other groups of leaders as well as within the group of entrepreneurs. Several researchers have discussed these differences. Among the pioneers in this field are Orvis Collins, David Moore and Darab Unwalla, who examined the differences between managers in large businesses and entrepreneurs, and Norman Smith, who identified different types of entrepreneurs.

Collins, Moore and Unwalla (1964) build on an earlier study by Warner and Martin *The Industrial Man* (1959), in which the authors attempted to characterise the successful business leader. Collins et al. found differences between managers and entrepreneurs in terms of their views on authority and their insight into the need for social skills. The manager fits into the system and considers it natural to make a career in the hierarchy, whereas the entrepreneur feels that he or she is a prisoner of the system and wants to break free. They also found that entrepreneurs constitute a heterogeneous group of individuals and that there is a need to classify different types of entrepreneurs. The best known classification is perhaps that of Smith, who in his work *The Entrepreneur and his Firm* (1967) distinguished between the "craftsman entrepreneur" and the "opportunistic entrepreneur". Both of these types are a reflection of each other. The craftsman is described as a person who is qualified in a limited field, not very flexible, and who focuses on the past and present. Smith was also interested in the connection between the type of entrepreneur and the type of company he created. He found that the company run by a craftsman is rigid in that the changes in customer groups and products are small, the production equipment is located in the same place and the market is local or regional, in contrast to the opportunistic entrepreneur, who often tends to start more adaptive companies. The heterogeneity of entrepreneurs and the need to focus on the differences between the two types of entrepreneurs have resulted in Smith's typology being used and developed in a large number of studies over the years.

4.3   Entrepreneurship in a Broader Behavioral Sense

The interest in entrepreneurship is not only evident within psychology but also within other behavioral sciences such as sociology and social anthropology, even if the interest is relatively marginal.

Sociology has mainly contributed to entrepreneurship knowledge in its attempt to increase understanding of how society or context can influence the propensity to undertake entrepreneurial activities and of the role of entrepreneurship in society. Within sociological theory, the reasoning in the area of entrepreneurship can be traced back to works by Max Weber (1864-1920). Weber was originally a historian but is best known for his sociological contributions. His ideas on entrepreneurship cannot be found in any specific piece of work but exist in several different works. Weber's main aim was to explain how social systems change from one stable position to another. Mostly, a "charismatic leadership", i.e. a special type of individual with the ability to make other people follow him or her, plays an important role in these changes. This "charismatic leadership" could have some resemblance with the type of person that we call "entrepreneur". However, although often misinterpreted, Weber's concept of charisma is not identical to entrepreneurship. Weber argues that the charismatic leader has only functioned as an important motor of change during the early stages of mankind and is less important in a capitalistic society. For Weber, entrepreneurship had more to do with the skilful direction of enterprises that respond to opportunities in the market economy, than with the economic operations of a single individual. The drivers of entrepreneurial force in society were also important for Weber, and in his well-known work *The Protestant Ethic and the Spirit of Capitalism* (1904/1970) he placed a strong emphasis on religious connections, primarily the Protestant ethic. He was of the opinion that this ethic created a positive attitude to work and to earning money, which facilitated the development of capitalism and entrepreneurship. Finally, Weber made some contributions to entrepreneurship in his later, more political writings during the 1910s, when he contrasted the entrepreneur with the bureaucrat. As society becomes more rationalized, bureaucracy tends to increase in importance and may be allowed to dominate in individual enterprises. However, the entrepreneur is the only person who can keep the bureaucracy at bay – only the entrepreneur has better knowledge of a firm than the bureaucrats (Swedberg, 1998; 2000).

The content of sociology is very extensive and entrepreneurship has never constituted a dominant theme within the subject. Entrepreneurship research conducted within the field of sociology can be related to the following areas (see e.g. Martinelli, 1994; 2004):

- Entrepreneurship as deviant behavior – entrepreneurs are deviant because of their marginal status (Hoselitz, 1963). Acting in a hostile social milieu and being outside the dominant value system leads individuals in marginal groups to concentrate on business, thereby being subject to lesser sanctions for their deviant behavior. In this respect Young (1971) stresses the importance of "organic solidarity" within the group. It is not important to be deviant with regard to society at large but to have access to resources within the group, which can overcome the lack of social recognition and denial of access to important social networks (see also Aldrich & Waldinger,

1990, for research on ethnic marginalism and entrepreneurship related to ethnicity).

- Entrepreneurship and culture, represented by for example historians such as Landes (1951) and sociologists such as Lipset (1967). Landes explained the differences between the development of industrialization in France and the US in the light of their different historical heritages. France with its feudal heritage had residual social attitudes that were hostile to entrepreneurship, whereas in the US the absence of a feudal past allowed the growth of a social culture that was receptive to entrepreneurship. Lipset compared the US and Latin America and explained differences in economic development in terms of the degree of legitimation of entrepreneurship.

- The influence of the structural context on entrepreneurship, for example, research on class affiliation and entrepreneurship (e.g. Dobb, 1946; Moore, 1966; Wallerstein, 1979). Historically it can be shown that in modern capitalist societies it is likely that entrepreneurs will be recruited from main or even dominant groups in society, and entrepreneurship is also a major avenue for upward social mobility, for example, among marginal groups like immigrants.

- Entrepreneurship and networks. In his seminal article in 1985, Granovetter (1985) presented major arguments concerning the social embeddedness of economic activity and the particular relevance of social networking when applied to entrepreneurship (see e.g. early research by sociologists such as Aldrich & Zimmer, 1986, but also researchers in the area of management such as Birley, 1985). In particular, the network approach has been considered as a function of bridging activities that have been separated, or to use Burt's expression (1992) "structural holes" in networks. Entrepreneurial networks have also been associated with the entrepreneurs' ties in the overall personal network (Granovetter, 1973; Aldrich et al., 1987).

In contrast to sociology, few studies of entrepreneurship can be found in social anthropology, but some of the most interesting pioneering work produced in entrepreneurship is by anthropologists such as Fredrik Barth (1963; 1967) and Clifford Geertz (1963). The early studies concentrated primarily on social change and economic development but social anthropologists subsequently took an interest in the interaction between local entrepreneurship and the social pattern of the individual.

One of the pioneers within the area was Fredrik Barth, who in his book *The Role of the Entrepreneur in Social Change in Northern Norway* (1963) presented an analysis of entrepreneurship based on studies of a small community in the northern part of Norway. A few years later he made a study of a Central African village (Barth, 1967). Barth argues that entrepreneurship has to do with connecting two spheres in society in which different norms and values exist – something that is cheap in one sphere may be expensive in another. For example, in the Norwegian study, the economic sphere and politics constitute two different spheres, and even if it may be difficult, it is lucrative to transfer value from one sphere to the other. Thus, the entrepreneur has the ability to transcend the boundaries between these different spheres and create something new.

Barth focused on what the entrepreneur actually does and analysed why individuals make different choices within the framework of a given context. The entrepreneur is not a person but rather a role played by an individual. This role means breaking with traditional patterns and differs from more conventional roles particularly within three areas: (a) the entrepreneur concentrates more single-mindedly on maximizing his or her own advantages (financial profit), (b) the entrepreneur's activities are more experimental and less institutionalized, and (c) the entrepreneur is more prepared to take risks. However, the entrepreneur cannot act in a rational fashion on the basis of his or her own goals but must, according to Barth, take account of the norms and restrictions of the local community or social structure. The entrepreneur is, however, not "locked" into the local norms although they may restrict or hinder his or her options.

Much of the subsequent social anthropological research has investigated small firms rather than entrepreneurship, especially really small firms, and has focused on entrepreneurship in relation to ethnic groups and family businesses. Some examples of themes examined within social anthropology are the entrepreneur's personal networks, the level of entrepreneurship among different societal groups and the importance of entrepreneurship in regional economic development.

5.   ENTREPRENEURSHIP AND SMALL BUSINESS IN MANAGEMENT SCIENCE

After the Second World War, Keynesian economic theory, suggesting increased government interventions to manage cyclical fluctuations, seemed to be working, and there was a positive economic development in society. The importance of entrepreneurship and small businesses seemed to fade away, and many scholars supported Schumpeter's declaration (1942) that "what we have got to accept is that the large-scale establishment has come to be the most powerful engine of progress" (p. 106). At the same time, during the 1950s and 1960s there was also a widespread fear of the Soviet Union, due to its ability to concentrate economic resources and utilize economies of scale (Acs, 1992). In order to compete, many western societies, not least the US, assumed industrialization and economic development to be based on mass production, and large companies were seen as superior in efficiency as well as the most important driving force behind technological development. It was argued that economies of scale were of paramount importance for industrial development, that only large firms could produce output in sufficient quantities to take advantage of these economies and that, as a consequence, government policies in many countries favored large businesses.

The notion that large-scale production and a social order with strong collectivistic elements were conducive to economic development was firmly established among social scientists at the time – and beliefs in the potential of economies of scale can be traced back to economists like Adam Smith and Karl Marx. One of the most influential thinkers was John Kenneth Galbraith who, in his books *American Capitalism* (1956) and especially in *The New Industrial State* (1967), provided an important rationale for an economic policy oriented toward the large corporations. Galbraith argued that innovative activities as well as improvements in products and processes were most efficiently carried out in the context of large corporations. Similarly, in *The Rise of the Western World* (North & Thomas, 1973) Nobel Laureate Douglass North gave the entrepreneur a very minor role in economic development – and hardly mentioned the topic at all, while Servan-Schreiber warned Europeans to be aware of *The American Challenge* (1968) in the form of the "dynamism, organization, innovation, and the boldness that characterize the giant American corporation" (p. 153).

However, during the 1970s visible changes began to appear and with them the first signs that large systems are not always preferable. The "twin oil" crises triggered an appraisal of the role of small and medium-sized firms. Many large companies were hit by severe economic difficulties, and unemployment became a major problem in many western societies. Large companies were increasingly seen as inflexible and slow to adjust to new market conditions. Based on the concerns about unemployment and the criticism levelled at large companies, economic activity moved away from the large companies to smaller firms. There may be several explanations for this shift in focus from large companies to small firms. Carlsson (1992), for example, found two explanations: (i) a fundamental change in the world economy, related to the intensification of global competition, the increase in the degree of uncertainty, and the growth of market fragmentation, and (ii) changes in the characteristics of technological progress, i.e. the recession of the 1970s and 1980s initiated a series of technological waves – first the development of information technology followed by the biotechnological wave. According to Audretsch and Thurik (2000), globalization and technological advances were the necessary preconditions for the knowledge-based economy becoming the driving force behind the move from large to smaller businesses. Furthermore, Brock and Evans (1986; 1989) add four more reasons for the shift from large firms: the increase in the availability of labor, which resulted in lower real wages, changes in consumer tastes, relaxation of (entry) regulations, a privatization movement that swept over the world, and the fact that it was a period of "creative destruction" (or what Piore & Sabel, 1984 labelled the "industrial divide").

These changes were also reflected in the industrial structure. By the early 1970s a change in the industrial structure in the US had begun to emerge. During the period from 1958 to 1980 the importance of small businesses decreased, for example, the share of value added contributed from firms with 500 or less employees decreased from 57% to 52% (Brock & Evans, 1986). But during the 1970s the structure began to change, primarily in the manufacturing sector, where there was evidence that small firms were outperforming their larger counterparts, for example, in the US steel industry and in industries characterized by rapid innovative changes (e.g. electronics and software). In the period from 1982 to 1992 the small firms' share of added value in the US economy stabilized at about 51%. At the same time, in many sectors of the economy, the small firms' share of employment increased (Acs et al., 1999). Thus, there seems to be a major shift in the industrial structure in favor of small companies, a phenomenon that appears not be specific to the US – it was a trend in most developed Western countries.

As a consequence of this shift, new areas of interest emerged, and topics such as entrepreneurship, innovation, industrial dynamics, and job creation (Acs, 1992) increasingly came to dominate the political debate. This development received additional support from politicians such as Ronald Reagan in the US and Margaret Thatcher in the UK, who pursued a policy strongly in favour of promoting small business and entrepreneurship. For example, President Reagan referred to the decade as the "Age of the Entrepreneur" in his 1985 address to the nation.

It was in this context that David Birch presented his seminal work *The Job Generation Process* (1979). Birch was interested in understanding how jobs were created. The main problem was to obtain adequate data – existing databases were not equipped to cope with large longitudinal data. Birch used Dun & Bradstreet data in the US, and considerable efforts were made to facilitate the analysis of the data over time – Birch and his research group had data from 1969 to 1976. The study focused on job creation, and some interesting findings emerged. For example, migration of firms from one region to another played a negligible role, and job losses seemed to be about the same everywhere. Thus, it was not the rate of closures that varied from one region to another – it was the rate of job replacements that was crucial for the growth or decline of a region. But what kinds of firms played a critical role in job creation? Birch found that the majority of new jobs were created by firms – often independent and young firms – with 20 or less employees. The conclusion was that it was not the large firms that created new jobs, but the small and young firms in the economy.

The report was only sold in twelve copies, but its influence was enormous, not least on policy-makers. The report also had an enormous impact on the research community – even if it has been a source of considerable controversy and criticism (see e.g. Storey and Johnson, 1987; Storey, 1994; Kirchhoff, 1994). It provided the intellectual foundation for researchers throughout the world to incorporate smaller firms into their analyses of economic development, and many of the findings have proved very robust and have been verified in a host of later studies (see for example studies by David Storey, Bruce Kirchhoff, Paul Reynolds, and Per Davidsson).

However, David Birch was not the only one to observe the prevailing trend in society. For example, at the same time Alvin Toffler wrote his book *The Third Wave* (1980) in which he forecast that both offices and factories would be revolutionized in a way that would affect the structure of industry and the size of work units. But there were also other authors, such as Handy (1984), and Brock and Evans (1986), who challenged the previously held belief that jobs and dynamics in society always come from the large corporations. For example, Handy argued that the changes during the 1970s could be considered as a fundamental restructuring of work – large organizations began to decline and long-term unemployment became familiar.

Thus, it was possible to observe an increase in the dynamics of society, changes in the industrial structure and increased unemployment. This development was accelerated by a change in political ideology represented by Margaret Thatcher in the UK and Ronald Reagan in the US. Some authors could see what was happening and could challenge the assumptions of the past. Among them, David Birch is one of the major exponents in showing that the future differs from the past, not least in terms of the importance of entrepreneurship, innovation and industrial dynamics. At the same time, an academic community with scholars interested in entrepreneurship and small business began to emerge. The demand from students for entrepreneurship courses increased, and business schools in the US were quick to introduce entrepreneurship courses into their curricula. These courses mainly dealt with issues related to the development of new business opportunities and the establishment of firms and can be linked to normative-oriented issues, which were primarily the domain of scholars involved in management studies. Moreover, an infrastructure was taking shape in the form of professional organisations, academic conferences, etc. In entrepreneurship, the academic community consisted for the most part of researchers and academic teachers who focused on micro-level analysis. A new research field was starting to emerge.

6.   **ENTREPRENEURSHIP AND SMALL BUSINESS RESEARCH IN RELATION TO SOCIETAL DEVELOPMENTS**

Looking back at the history of entrepreneurship and small business research, it is interesting to observe that our knowledge about entrepreneurship and small firms seems to have been developed with a certain chronological regularity – "swarms" of entrepreneurship and small business research seem to have appeared at different times in history. For example, we can identify such "swarms" at the following points in time:

1860-1880   Austrian and German economists Johann von Thünen, Hans Emil von Mangolt, Carl Menger, Friedrich von Wieser, and Eugen von Böhm-Bawerk – research based on a tradition rooted in political science and administration.

1890-1920   Many of Joseph Schumpeter's thoughts on entrepreneurship were developed during this period. US economists such as Fredrick Hawley and John Bates Clark and, at a slightly later stage, Frank Knight had a major influence.

1950-1970   Based on a strong behavioral science tradition, this period includes pioneers such as David McClelland, Everett Hagen, Seymour Martin Lipset, and Fredrik Barth.

1985-   An increased interest from researchers within the field of industrial organization focusing on macro-level analysis, such as David Birch (the role of small firms in employment creation), Zoltan Acs and David Audretsch (small firms in innovation), Giacomo Becattini and Sebastiano Brusco (small firms and regional development), but also an increased interest among researchers within management studies – micro-level analysis – for example, Arnold Cooper (technology-based firms), Howard Aldrich (ethnicity and networks), Jeffry Timmons and William Wetzel (the role of venture capital), and Ian MacMillan, Peter Drucker, and Rosabeth Moss Kanter (entrepreneurship as a strategy).

Why, then, do these "swarms" of entrepreneurship and small business researchers appear at certain periods in time? A likely explanation is that there is a strong link between societal development and the interest in entrepreneurship and small business research – periods of economic difficulties and crises give rise to demands for change and the creation of new ways of thinking. Entrepreneurship and small business research thrives and peaks during periods characterized by powerful dynamics and development in society.

The Swedish economic historian Lennart Schön (2001) argues that the development of western economies follows long-term structural cycles of about 40 to 50 years and that each structural cycle is initiated and shaped by some form of international economic crisis. Each cycle can be divided into two periods, characterized by different behaviors:

- Transformation period – i.e. a period dominated by the transformation of industrial structures, in which resources are reallocated between industries, and by the diffusion of basic innovations within industry, thus providing new bases for such reallocation. During these periods, investment is generally long term and directed toward increasing capacity in new areas of production.
- Rationalization period – i.e. a period dominated by the concentration of resources in the most productive units within the industry and by measures to increase efficiency in the different lines of production, i.e. aimed at increased efficiency of existing structures and operations and decreased resource utilization. Investments, which are short-term in character, are directed toward reducing costs in existing structures and operations.

Although transformation and rationalization are processes that to a large extent take place simultaneously in an economy, historically there have been shifts in emphasis between periods of transformation and rationalization. These shifts occur with considerable regularity within a long structural cycle, for example 25 years of emphasis on transformation, followed by some 15 years of emphasis on rationalization. Thus, we can find a pattern of long cycles characterized by crisis – transformation – rationalization. Starting from the mid 19th century, the following long cycles can be identified in the world economy (Figure 2-2).

It appears obvious that the "swarms" of entrepreneurship and small business research are related to periods of transformation characterized by far-reaching societal renewal, the emergence of new structures giving rise to a new direction for economic growth, and the rapid spread of new technical solutions. At the risk of over-interpreting the material (societal changes vary in different countries and the duration of the phases is often poorly recorded), entrepreneurship research peaks seem to occur at the end of these periods of transformation – which mirrors the fact that research takes time due to the "natural conservatism" characterizing most research.

Crises → Transformation → Rationalization		Basis for the structural cycle
1845/50	1875	Breakthrough of mechanized factories and development of railways.
1890/95	1920	Breakthrough of the modern industrial society.
1930/35	1960	Breakthrough of electrification and the spread of automobiles.
1975/80	2000/05	Breakthrough of electronics, especially the microprocessor and information technology.

Figure 2-2. Long-term structural cycles.

On the other hand, interest in entrepreneurship and small firms appear to be less marked during periods of rationalization and more associated with stable societal relationships, increased production efficiency and short-term perspectives. Thus, one conclusion is that, throughout history, there has been a link between societal development and entrepreneurship and small business research (Figure 2-3).

	Transformation	*Research*	*Focus*
1845-1875	Mechanized factories and railways	Economics	Entrepreneurship as a function of the market
1890-1920	Modern industrial society	Economics	Entrepreneurship as a function of the market
1930-1960	Electrification and automobiles	Behavioral sciences	The entrepreneur as an individual (traits)
1975-2000	Electronics	Industrial Organization and Management studies	Entrepreneurship and small business as a process

Figure 2-3. Linkage between societal development and entrepreneurship and small business research.

What then, will the future be like? If we accept Schön's reasoning, society is currently on the brink of a shift from a "transformation period" dominated by changes in the industrial structure and reallocation of resources, to a "rationalization period", which will be characterized by a concentration of resources and an increased focus on efficiency in existing structures. It seems reasonable to assume that the character of entrepreneurship and small business in society will change while societal interest in it may decrease or at least assume a different shape from that of today. In view of the strong linkage between industrial development and the character of entrepreneurship and small business research, it can be expected that the research will develop a new form – whereby new research issues related to the future industrial structure will come to the fore. Thus, the future research agenda will be quite different.

REFERENCES

Acs, Z.J., 1992, Small Business Economics: A Global Perspective, *Challenge*, 35, 38-44.

Acs, Z.J. & Carlsson, B. & Karlsson, C., 1999, The Linkage Among Entrepreneurship, SMEs and the Macroeconomy, in Acs, Z.J. & Carlsson, B. & Karlsson, C. (eds.), *Entrepreneurship, Small & Medium-Sized Enterprises and the Macroeconomy*, Cambridge: Cambridge University Press.

Ahl, H.J., 2002, *The Making of the Female Entrepreneur*, JIBS Dissertation Series No 015, Jönköping International Business School, Sweden.

Aldrich, H.A. & Rosen, B. & Woodward, W., 1987, The Impact of Social Networks on Business Foundation and Profit, paper at the Babson Entrepreneurship Conference, Pepperdine University, Malibu, CA, 29 April – 2 May.

Aldrich, H.A. & Zimmer, C., 1986, Entrepreneurship Through Social Networks, in Sexton, D. & Smilor, R. (eds.), *The Art and Science of Entrepreneurship*, New York: Ballinger, 3-23.

Aldrich, H.A. & Waldinger, R., 1990, Ethnicity and Entrepreneurship, *Annual Review of Sociology*, 16, 111-135.

Audretsch, D.B. & Thurik, A.R., 2000, Capitalism and democracy in the 21st century: From the managed to the entrepreneurial economy, *Journal of Evolutionary Economics*, 10, 17-34.

Barreto, H., 1989, *The Entrepreneur in Economic Theory – Disappearance and Explanation*, London: Routledge.

Barth, F., 1963, *The Role of the Entrepreneur of Social Change in Northern Norway*, Oslo: Universitetsforlaget.

Barth, F., 1967, Economic Spheres in Darfur, in Firth, R. (ed.), *Themes in Economic Anthropology*, London: Tavistock.

Baumol, W.J., 1968, Entrepreneurship in Economic Theory, *American Economic Review*, 58, 2, 64-71.

Baumol, W.J., 1990, Entrepreneurship: Productive, Unproductive and Destructive, *Journal of Political Economy*, 98, 5, 893-921.

Baumol, W.J., 1993, Formal Entrepreneurship Theory in Economics: Existence and Bounds, *Journal of Business Venturing*, 3, 197-210.

Birch, D.L., 1979, *The Job Generation Process*, MIT Program on Neighborhood and Regional Change, Cambridge, MA.

Birley, S. 1985, The Role of Networks in the Entrepreneurial Process, *Journal of Business Venturing*, 1, 1, 107-117.

Brock, W.A. & Evans, D.S., 1986, *The Economics of Small Business: Their Role and Regulation in the US Economy*, New York: Holmes and Meier.

Brock, W.A. & Evans, D.S., 1989, Small Business Economics, *Small Business Economics*, 1, 7-20.

Burt, R.S., 1992, *Structural Holes: The Social Structure of Competition*, Cambridge: Harvard University Press.

Bögenhold, D., 2000, Limits to Mass Production: Entrepreneurship and Industrial Organization in View of the Historical School of Schmoller and Sombart, *International Review of Sociology*, 10, 1, 57-71.

Cantillon, R., 1755/1931, *Essai sur la nature du commerce en général*, London: MacMillan.

Carlsson, B., 1992, The rise of small business: causes and consequences, in Adams, W.J. (ed.), *Singular Europe, economy and policy of the European community after 1992*, Ann Arbor, MI: University of Michigan Press.

Collins, O. & Moore, D. & Unwalla, D.B., 1964, *The Enterprising Man*, East Lansing: Michigan State University.

Cooper, A.C. & Woo, C.Y. & Dunkelberg, W.C., 1988, Entrepreneurs' Perceived Chances of Success, *Journal of Business Venturing*, 3, 97-108.

Dahmén, E., 1950, *Svensk industriell företagsverksamhet*, Stockholm: Industrins Utredningsinstitutet.

Dahmén, E., 1970, *Entrepreneurial Activity and the Development of Swedish Industry*, Homewood, Ill: Irwin.

Delmar, F., 2000, The psychology of the entrepreneur, in Carter, S. & Jones-Evans, D. (eds.), *Enterprise and Small Business*, Harlow: Pearson Education.

Dobb, M., 1946, *Studies in the Development of Capitalism*, London: Routledge.

Galbraith, K.H., 1956, *American Capitalism*, Boston, Houghton Mufflin.

Galbraith, K.H., 1967, *The New Industrial State*, London: Hamish Hamilton.

Geertz, C., 1963, *Peddlers and Princes: Social Change and Economic Modernization in two Indonesian Towns*, Chicago: Chicago University Press.

Granovetter, M., 1973, The Strenght of Weak Ties, *American Journal of Sociology*, 78, 6, 1360-1380.

Granovetter, M., 1985, Economic Action and Social Structure: The Problem of Embeddedness, *Journal of Sociology*, 91, 3, 481-599.

Hagen, E., 1962, *On the Theory of Social Change: How Economic Growth Begins*, Homewood, Ill: Dorsey.

Handy, C., 1984, *The Future of Work*, Oxford: Basil Blackwell.

Harris, T.G., 1971, To Know Why Men Do What they Do – A Conversation with David C. McClelland, *Psychology Today*, January, 35-75.

Hayek, F., 1945, The use of knowledge in society, *American Economic Review*, 35, 519-530.

Hébert, R.F. & Link, A.N., 1982, *The Entrepreneur*, New York: Praeger.

Hébert, R.F. & Link, A.N., 1989, In search of the meaning of entrepreneurship, *Small Business Economics*, 1, 39-49.

Hoselitz, B.F., 1963, Entrepreneurship and Traditional Elites, *Explorations in Entrepreneurial History*, 2, 1, 36-49.

Kets de Vries, M.F.R., 1977, The Entrepreneurial Personality: A person at the Crossroad, *Journal of Management Studies*, 14, 34-57.

Keynes, J.M., 1936/1973, *General Theory of Employment, Interest and Money*, New York: Harcourt Brace.

Kirchhoff, B.A., 1994, *Entrepreneurship and Dynamic Capitalism*, Westport, CT: Praeger.

Kirzner, I.M., 1973, *Competition and Entrepreneurship*, Chicago: University of Chicago Press.

Knight, F.H., 1916/1921, *Risk, Uncertainty and Profit*, New York: Houghton Mifflin.

Knight, F.H., 1933, *Economic Organizations*, Chicago: University of Chicago Press.

Landes, D., 1951, French business and the businessman: a social and cultural analysis, in Earle, E.M. (ed.), *Modern France*, Princeton: Princeton University Press.

Lipset, S.M., 1967, Values, Education, and Entrepreneurship, in Lipset, S.M. & Solari, A. (eds.), *Elites in Latin America*, London: Oxford University Press.

McAdams, D.P., 1987, Foreword, in McClelland, D.C., *Human Motivation*, Cambridge: Cambridge University Press.

McClelland, D.C., 1951, *Personality*, New York: Holt, Rinehart & Winston.

McClelland, D.C., 1961, *The Achieving Society*, Princeton, NJ: van Nostrand.

McClelland, D.C., 1987, *Human Motivation*, Cambridge: Cambridge University Press.

Marshall, A., 1890, *Principles of Economics*, London: MacMillan.

Marshall, A., 1919, *Industry and Trade*, London: MacMillan.

Martinelli, A., 1994, Entrepreneurship and Management, in Smelser, N.J. & Swedberg, R. (eds.), *The Handbook of Economic Sociology*, Princeton, N.J.: Princeton University Press.

Martinelli, A., 2004, The Social and Institutional Context of Entrepreneurship, in Corbetta, G. & Huse, M. & Ravasi, D. (eds.), *Crossroad to Entrepreneurship*, Dordrecht: Kluwer.

Menger, C., 1871/1981, *Principles of Economics*, New York: New York University Press.

Mises, L. von, 1951, *Planning for Freedom*, South Hollan, Ill: Libertarian Press.

Mises, L. von, 1949/1963, *Human Action*, New Haven: Yale University Press.

Moore, B., 1966, *The Social Origins of Dictatorship and Democracy*, Boston: Beacon Press.

North, D. & Thomas, R.P., 1973, *The Rise of the Western World: A New Economic History*, Cambridge: Cambridge University Press.

Piore, M.J.. & Sabel, C.F., 1984, *The Second Industrial Divide. Possibilities for Prosperity*, New York: Basic Books.

Pålsson-Syll, L., 1998, *De ekonomiska teoriernas historia*, Lund: Studentlitteratur.

Rotter, J.B., 1966, *Generalised Expectations for Internal Versus External Control of Reinformcement*, American Psychological Association, Psychological Monographies, p 80, No 1.

Sandberg, L.G., 2001, The Entrepreneur: Innovator or Manager, Individualistic Hero or Factor of Production, in Henrekson, M. & Larsson, M. & Sjögren, H. (eds.), *Entrepreneurship in Business and Research*, Stockholm School of Economics: Institute for Research in Economic History.

Sarasvathy, S. & Dew, N. & Velamur, S.R & Venkataraman, S., 2003, Three Views of Entrepreneurial Opportunities, in Acs, Z.J. & Audretsch, D.B. (eds.), *Handbook of Entrepreneurship Research*, Dordrecht: Kluwer.

Say, J-B., 1803/1964, *Traité d'économie politique*, New York: Kelley.

Schumpeter, J.A., 1912, *Theorie der Wirtschaftlichen Entwicklung*, Leipzig: Dunker & Humblot.

Schumpeter, J.A., 1934, *The Theory of Economic Development*, Cambridge, MA: Harvard University Press.

Schumpeter, J.A., 1939, *Business Cycles*, New York: McGraw-Hill.

Schumpeter, J.A., 1942, *Capitalism, Socialism and Democracy*, New York: Harper & Row.

Schumpeter, J.A., 1954, *History of Economic Analysis*, London: Allen & Unwin.

Schön, L., 2001, Swedish Industrial Growth and Crises in the 20th Century, paper at the workshop Growth, crises and regulation in the European economies, University of Helsinki, 1-4 March 2001.

Servan-Schreiber, J.J., 1968, *The American Challenge*, London: Hamish Hamilton.

Sexton, D.L. & Bowman, N., 1985, The Entrepreneur: A Capable Executive and More, *Journal of Business Venturing*, 1, 129-140.

Smith, A., 1776/1976, *An Inquiry into the Nature and Causes of the Wealth of Nations*, Oxford: Clarendon Press.

Smith, N.R., 1967, *The Entrepreneur and His Firm*, Bureau of Business Research, East Lansing, Michigan: Michigan State University Press.

Stevenson, H.H. & Jarillo, J.C., 1990, A Paradigm of Entrepreneurship: Entrepreneurial Management, *Strategic Management Journal*, 11, 17-27.

Storey, D.J., 1994, *Understanding the Small Business Sector*, London: Routledge.

Storey, D.J. & Johnson, S., 1987, Are small firms the answer to unemployment?, London: Employment Institute.

Swedberg, R., 1994, *Schumpeter. Om skapande förstörelse och entreprenörskap*, Stockholm: Ratio.

Swedberg, R., 1998, *Max Weber and the Idea of Economic Sociology*, Princeton, NJ: Princeton University Press.

Swedberg, R. (ed.), 2000, *Entrepreneurship, The Social Science View*, Oxford: Oxford University Press.

Toffler, A., 1980, *The Third Wave*, London: William Collins.

Wallerstein, I., 1979, *The Capitalist World Economy*, Cambridge: Cambridge University Press.

Warner, W.L. & Martin, N.H., 1959, *The Industrial Man*, New York: Harper & Brothers.

Weber, M., 1904/1978, *The Protestant Ethic and the Spirit of Capitalism*, London: Urwin.

Wennekers, S. & Thurik, R., 1999, Linking Entrepreneurship and Economic Growth, *Small Business Economics*, 13, 1, 27-55.

Winter, D.G., 2000, David McClelland (1917-1998), *American Psychologist*, 55, 5, 540-541.

Young, F.V., 1971, A macrosociological interpretation of entrepreneurship, in Kilby, P. (ed.), *Entrepreneurship and Economic Development*, New York: Free Press.

Chapter 3

THE EMERGENCE OF AN ACADEMIC FIELD

In chapter 2 I presented some pioneers of entrepreneurship and small business research who have been of significant importance for the development of knowledge about entrepreneurship and small business. We have also seen the strong historical relationship between the economic development of society and the scientific interest in entrepreneurship and small firms. In this chapter, I will present and discuss some ideas about the development of entrepreneurship and small business research since the beginning of the 1980s – the time when the field started to emerge. The chapter will mainly describe the development in a US context, with a strong focus on entrepreneurship as opposed to small business research. The development of the field can be divided into cognitive aspects of research, which involve the substance of research, the content of the theories, the logic of the methods employed, and social aspects of research, which deal with the academic community and the organization of research (Crane, 1972; Becher, 1989). Section 1 describes the "social turmoil" that characterized the 1970s and that triggered an increasing interest in the economy in general as well as among researchers. Section 2 treats the social development that has taken place within entrepreneurship and small business research especially in the 1990s, which witnessed a large increase in the number of researchers and the creation of an infrastructure within the field. Section 3 focuses on the cognitive development within entrepreneurship and small business research, including the advances in knowledge and methodology in the field during the last decades. During the emergence of entrepreneurship and small business as an academic field, several "struggles" took place that have had a major influence – and in some instances have impeded this development. These controversies will be discussed in section 4.

1.   **THE DECADE OF THE PIONEERS AND THE
        ENTHUSIASTIC EMERGENCE OF THE FIELD**

Societal development has had a clear impact on the academic interest in entrepreneurship and small firms since the 1970s. In this section I will discuss different aspects of societal development that have influenced the emergence of an academic field of entrepreneurship and small business research.

1.1   Social Turmoil

In the preceding chapter (Chapter 2) it was established that major societal transformations took place during the 1960s and 1970s resulting in questions being raised about the efficiency of large systems, which coincided with a political will to create change – changes that were driven by entrepreneurship, industrial dynamics and job creation. Of course the causes underlying the increasing interest in entrepreneurship may be difficult to identify but some interaction factors seem to have been involved (see also a discussion in Swedberg, 2000; Bjerke & Hultman, 2002) – it is in this context possible to talk about a *social turmoil*:

–   Oil crises that triggered or coincided with fundamental changes in the world economy including intensified global competition, not least from countries in South East Asia, in addition to strong technological progress – the growth in importance of computers and microprocessors – which led to an increased uncertainty in the economy.
–   A recession in the economy of many countries and a deep concern about unemployment, as well as a general belief that new and small businesses were the solution to unemployment problems. It was realized that constant change and innovation were necessary for any business to survive in a changing global and technological world.
–   A change in "fashion" among young people – large firms were regarded as too large and bureaucratic and less interesting as work places, whereas small firms were increasingly regarded as dynamic and creative organizations to work in – "small is beautiful" became the catchword.
–   A revival of small business in Europe and in the US supported by a change in political ideology. The Keynesian model for dealing with cyclical fluctuations and the public economy was questioned to an increasing extent in favor of a more market oriented view – from Keynesianism to a radically pro-market ideology – represented by Margaret Thatcher in the UK (came to power in 1979) and Ronald Reagan in the US (came to power in 1980).

This "social turmoil" triggered a renewed interest in entrepreneurship and small firms not only among politicians and policy-makers but also within the economy in general, and a community of researchers with an interest in entrepreneurship and small business started to emerge.

1.2 Cognitive Development of Entrepreneurship and Small Business Research

Research about entrepreneurship and small business was limited but the late 1970s and early 1980s witnessed the publication of a number of pioneering scientific studies, mainly in the area of what can be termed "small business economics", which had a very strong influence on future development. The studies highlighted the phenomenon and demonstrated the importance of entrepreneurship and small business for societal dynamics and development. These studies thereby promoted interest in entrepreneurship and small business both in the research community and among politicians and decision makers. Thus, the research followed the prevailing societal trend within the political system as well as within academia.

One major theme in this pioneering research was focused on the dynamics of the economy and job creation in society. In Chapter 2 David Birch's path-breaking report *The Job Generation Process* (1979) was mentioned. The study had an enormous impact not only among researchers but also among politicians and policy-makers. A number of researchers interested in small firms and job creation, for example, David Storey in the UK, and Catherine Armington and Marjone Odle in the US, to mention a few, followed in David Birch's footsteps. But there were also researchers who showed a more general interest in new and small businesses. In this context, William Brock and David Evans' book *Economics of Small Business* (1986), in which the authors take a holistic view of small business economics as a distinct research area, deserves to be mentioned, as does Robert Hébert and Albert Link's book *The Entrepreneur* (1982) – describing the history of economic thought and the role of entrepreneurship.

Another theme of interest was small business and regional development. A loose configuration of researchers emerged, who studied the regional development in Italy, for example researchers like Giacomo Becattini and Sebastiano Brusco – two Italian economists, who resurrected the concept of industrial districts, originally formulated by Alfred Marshall at the turn of the 19th century. The empirical work of Becattini was mainly based on the development of the Tuscan economy, whereas Brusco studied the industrial district of Emilia Romagna. However, their results about the importance of small firms for regional development were not internationally recognized until Michael Piore and Charles Sabel published their book *The Second Industrial Divide* in

1984, in which they performed a macro-historical analysis of the transformation from Fordist mass production to flexible specialization using the Italian industrial districts as the main example.

David Audretsch and Zoltan Acs can be regarded as pioneers in their studies of the connection between smallness and innovation. Zoltan Acs' book *The Changing Structure of the US Economy: Lessons from the US Steel Industry*, 1984, argued that small firms should not be viewed as less efficient copies of large enterprises, since small firms have an innovative role in the economy. Acs' empirical data were collected from the US steel industry, and to elaborate on the findings from this industry, Zoltan Acs together with David Audretsch began to systematically investigate the determinants of innovative activities in different industries. David Audretsch and Zoltan Acs also played a crucial role in bringing together researchers with an interest in small business economics and organizing a number of seminars at the Wissenschaftszentrum Berlin für Sozialforschung in Berlin, where David Audretsch was active at that time. Later (1989) they also established *Small Business Economics* as an outlet for researchers interested in the economics of new and small firms.

As we have seen, a number of pioneering studies were published in the late 1970s and early 1980s, primarily within "small business economics". A factor contributing to the cognitive development of the field was the building of different databases of information about young and small companies, making it possible for researchers to identify new patterns that could not previously be discerned. The development of databases on young and small companies must also be linked to the increase in data capacity – it was not until the 1970s that it became possible to process large amounts of data. This aspect also contributed to making the research field attractive to researchers outside the management area. Researchers within the fields of economics, industrial organization, and economic geography became aware of the advantages of studying large amounts of data on small companies, which was not possible when studying large companies. Therefore, several of the researchers who opened up the research field and contributed to highlighting the importance of new and small companies for societal development – both to policy-makers and members of the research community, thereby having a considerable impact on the development of the research field – had a background in what we can call "small business economics", with an academic grounding in disciplines such as economics, industrial organization, and economic geography.

1.3 Social Development of Entrepreneurship and Small Business Research

At the same time as we can identify a cognitive development founded on "small business economics", a community of academic scholars emerged within the field of entrepreneurship and small business. This social development of the field had its academic origins in the area of "management studies". Entrepreneurship gained a foothold in the curriculum at US business schools and among scholars within management studies. Management studies are in themselves an eclectic research field, or what Whitley (1984) calls a "fragmented adhocracy" as well as a research field that lacks a strong paradigm. These facts naturally contributed to entrepreneurship gaining acceptance and legitimacy among scholars in management studies. We can also identify an increasing interest in entrepreneurship and small business management courses in the late 1960s and early 1970s in the US. However, this was many years before most business schools in the US and Europe began to offer such courses (Cooper et al., 1997). It could be argued that the development of entrepreneurship education was to a high degree demand driven, and Vesper (1982; see also Cooper, 2003) identified a couple of reasons behind the increase in the number of entrepreneurship courses in the US. First, a greater interest in entrepreneurship courses on the part of students during the 1960s. Leading schools like Harvard and Stanford, where the students are extremely demanding customers, introduced entrepreneurship courses at an early stage, whereas other universities gradually capitulated to student demand, leading to the introduction of a large number of entrepreneurship courses in the early 1970s. It was primarily the US business schools that were sensitive and responsive to this demand. After this wave of course introductions, the development continued – every school had at least a few faculty members who were in favor of the subject of entrepreneurship – and many schools, including some of the most respected institutions, launched entrepreneurship courses – which gave the courses a kind of legitimacy. Second, this was also a time when large resources were directed toward US entrepreneurship education programs – mainly from external donors. An inflow of money from wealthy alumni and foundations (e.g. the Coleman Foundation and the Kauffman Foundation) – whose wealth was often founded on successful entrepreneurship – therefore channeled their interest to fund entrepreneurship chairs, centers and awards. Finally, the increasing interest in entrepreneurship on the part of politicians and policy-makers also led to the initiation of several government support programs across the US and Europe aimed at stimulating entrepreneurship educations.

Thus, we can identify a whole line of scholars – especially in management studies – who were deeply involved in the education of students of entrepreneurship as well as pioneers who tried to encourage scholars interested in entrepreneurship to attend seminars, conferences, etc. – leading to the start of a community of entrepreneurship scholars. This early social development of the field was characterized by enthusiasm, individualism and the importation of knowledge from other research fields. Thus, it was a group of enthusiastic scholars in management studies that started to take an interest in a new topic. At the same time, the research community was small and could be characterized as fragmented and individualistic, i.e. entrepreneurship research was to a great extent dependent on individual initiatives and projects. There was however a successive increase in the number of scholars with an interest in entrepreneurship and small business. Due to the fact that the research field had not developed an identity of its own in terms of concepts, models and methods, it was easy for researchers from different disciplines to carry out entrepreneurship and small business research without experiencing obvious deficits in competence and "tacit knowledge" – it was a "low entry" field. As a consequence, the influence of researchers from mainstream disciplines was substantial, leading to a risk of the research being controlled by theories and models that were ill suited to reflecting the character of entrepreneurship (Brockhaus, 1988; Bygrave, 1989).

1.4   Social Turmoil and the Emergence of Entrepreneurship and Small Business Research

The major shifts identifiable during the 1970s that have had consequences for the cognitive and the social development of entrepreneurship and small business research are illustrated in Figure 3-1.

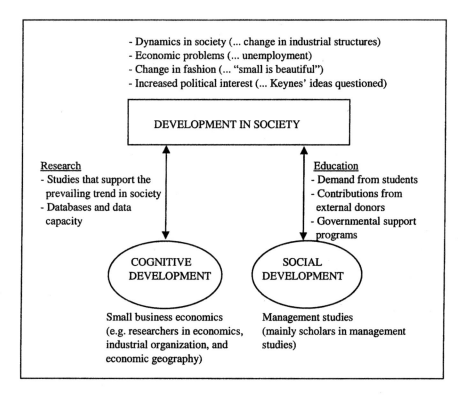

- Dynamics in society (... change in industrial structures)
- Economic problems (... unemployment)
- Change in fashion (... "small is beautiful")
- Increased political interest (... Keynes' ideas questioned)

DEVELOPMENT IN SOCIETY

Research
- Studies that support the prevailing trend in society
- Databases and data capacity

Education
- Demand from students
- Contributions from external donors
- Governmental support programs

COGNITIVE DEVELOPMENT

SOCIAL DEVELOPMENT

Small business economics (e.g. researchers in economics, industrial organization, and economic geography)

Management studies (mainly scholars in management studies)

Figure 3-1. Social turmoil and the emergence of entrepreneurship and small business research.

2. THE GROWTH OF ENTREPRENEURSHIP RESEARCH

Entrepreneurship and small firms have continued to be a "hot topic" in society as well as in academia, and the growth of the research community and the building of an infrastructure for research as seen during the 1990s will be discussed in this section.

2.1 The New Competitive Landscape

The interest in entrepreneurship and small business remained high within industry and society at large – an interest that was clearly visible in the 1990s. This interest seems to be related to the turbulence of the "new competitive landscape", resulting from rapid technological advances and the globalization of world trade, which created an uncertainty that is conducive to entrepreneurship (Bettis & Hitt, 1995;

Hitt & Reed, 2000). As a result, several new phenomena appear to have emerged that triggered new opportunities for entrepreneurship and new firms (Meyer & Heppard, 2000; Bjerke & Hultman, 2002):

- Many changes took place, resulting in, for example, changing consumer tastes, technological development, transformed industry structures – industry borders became blurred and knowledge was the dominant competitive factor.
- Everything seemed to move faster; information became more accessible, product cycles became increasingly shorter, etc. – it was more a question of the survival of the fastest than the survival of the fittest.
- An increased complexity in society and an increased uncertainty – genuine uncertainty – were part of the picture.

It is the quick changes, the complexity and uncertainty in society that constitute a hotbed for entrepreneurship, the dynamics of which facilitate the emergence and utilization of new business opportunities. These circumstances have meant that societal interest in entrepreneurship and small firms have remained high and that the subject has featured prominently on the political agenda in many countries. At the same time, the changes taking place within entrepreneurship and small business have constantly given rise to new research questions – old questions quickly disappear while new ones attract attention. As a consequence the field of entrepreneurship and small business research developed in many different directions, and it has been difficult to achieve a convergent theory development within the field.

2.2 Exponential Growth of the Research Community

Since the beginning of the 1990s we can find a growing research community in the field. This expansion can be measured in various ways – with respect to the number of researchers, the number of published articles, number of conferences and journals focusing on or opening up to entrepreneurship contributions – and this expansion is obvious, irrespective of the measurements employed. However, the research community has to a very great extent been fragmented. As mentioned in the discussion in Chapter 1, for a long time there has been ongoing uncertainty and debate on what entrepreneurship research is about. Therefore, entrepreneurship researchers have different views on the phenomenon we call entrepreneurship and form different pictures of it (Brazeal & Herbert, 1999). This uncertainty is also reflected in the article by Shane and Venkataraman (2000), in which they argue that entrepreneurship research "has become a broad label under which a hodgepodge of research is housed" (p. 217). In addition, entrepreneurship seems to be extremely difficult to study. It is a complex phenomenon, which includes many different approaches, levels of analysis, etc., and it is a dynamic phenomenon – entrepreneurship is constantly changing. This uncertainty in the domain of entrepreneurship research and the complex and dynamic nature of the phenomenon have contributed to a high degree of fragmentation in the field.

The field is not only fragmented but entrepreneurship and small business research can still be seen as a "low entry" field resulting in a "transient" research community. Based on a citation analysis, Landström (2001) showed that most of the researchers within the field rarely publish and if they publish, they are seldom cited. The researchers that have published in entrepreneurship constitute a rather heterogeneous group of researchers. Based on the number of articles published in the field and the number of citations, the research community can be divided into four categories (see Figure 3-2):

- Ad-hoc transients, i.e. researchers who appear only once and whose publication within the field of entrepreneurship is a one-off event.
- Influential transients, i.e. transient researchers who appear only once, but whose work is influential for entrepreneurship research.
- Craftsmen, i.e. researchers whose names tend to appear more frequently in entrepreneurship articles, which means that they have stayed within the field for a longer period of time.
- Core group, i.e. highly productive researchers in the entrepreneurship field, whose work Has a substantial impact upon the research field.

Among the researchers published in entrepreneurship, the vast majority could be regarded as transient researchers, i.e. researchers who belong to some form of mainstream research community and who only temporarily enter the field of entrepreneurship research, whereas the number of researchers who work with entrepreneurship research on a continual basis is rather small. In addition, the "core group" of influential researchers, i.e. researchers that have had an impact on the research community by providing comprehensive knowledge about the phenomenon or robust findings (methodological development) within the field, seems to be very small – most entrepreneurship researchers can be regarded as craftsmen who publish more or less frequently in entrepreneurship but have only marginal influence.

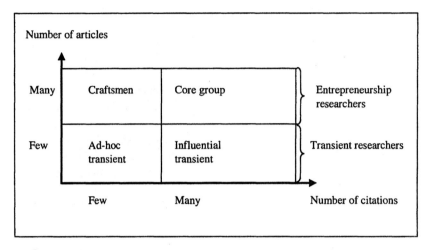

Figure 3-2. Categorization of the research community in entrepreneurship research.

It is also interesting to note that in many cases the work by the "core group" of researchers tends to be forgotten rather quickly, indicating that the field is rather ahistorical. Landström (2001) identified a small group of "core" researchers within entrepreneurship research, and a number of "core articles" written by them. The citation pattern shows that the core articles seem to be forgotten rather quickly. A general impression is that many researchers within the core group tend to focus on different research questions and publish articles on many different areas of entrepreneurship, which indicates that entrepreneurship research is unstable and that there is a lack of continuity – old topics fade out and new ones take their place on a continual basis – which may also be the reason why the works of the core group appear to fade away rather quickly.

In a similar way, Busenitz et al. (2003) argue that the boundaries of the entrepreneurship field remain highly permeable, which allows scholars from various disciplines to conduct research within the field of entrepreneurship, which also has its advantages. One example is an inflow of skilled researchers from other research fields. Moreover, researchers outside the entrepreneurship research community started to conduct studies of entrepreneurship, and they published their works in mainstream journals. Altogether, this has not only contributed to rendering the character of entrepreneurship research fragmented, transient and ahistorical but has also put pressure on those researchers calling themselves entrepreneurship researchers, thus enhancing the quality of the research.

2.3   Building of a Social Structure

By the late 1990s there was evidence of a growing internal culture and knowledge base as well as an increased social structure within the field, expressed in terms of (i) organized forums for communication between researchers (e.g. conferences and scientific journals), (ii) role models and ideals (e.g. chairs and awards for important scientific contributions), and (iii) education programs in entrepreneurship (Landström et al., 1997). To give some examples of this improved social structure in entrepreneurship and small business research:

−   At the start of the new millennium there were more than 2,200 courses in entrepreneurship and small business, 277 endowed positions in the US, and 44 English-language refereed academic journals (Katz, 2003).

−   The number of trade- and textbooks in entrepreneurship and small business has increased dramatically, and in 1998 numbering 3,555 titles in small business and 1,132 in entrepreneurship (Katz, 2003).

−   We can find an increased number of PhD entrepreneurship programs at various universities but also jointly organized doctoral programs, such as the European Doctoral Program in Entrepreneurship and Small Business Development.

From this development it is also possible to discern an increased "liberation" from mainstream disciplines, where the researchers increasingly start to view themselves as entrepreneurship and small business researchers. However, entrepreneurship is a complex phenomenon that can be studied from many different angles. It is therefore hard to include all research issues and questions under the "umbrella" of entrepreneurship. In this respect, we can see a trend toward an increased segmentation of the field (Reader & Watkins, 2001), i.e. the development of loosely related research subgroups – a phase of "emerging tribes". For example, Reader and Watkins identified nine, more or less homogeneous groups, and the analysis indicated that many of the researchers clustered together have social as well as intellectual connections.

Even if we can establish that the field of entrepreneurship and small business has made great advances in terms of the building of a strong social structure, it is still too early to assess if it can be said to be irreversibly anchored within academia. Finkle and Deeds (2001), among others, emphasize that many universities are still only willing to accept an entrepreneurship faculty to a limited extent and that entrepreneurship remains an electic subject in most universities in the US.

3.   THE COGNITIVE DEVELOPMENT OF
        ENTREPRENEURSHIP AND SMALL BUSINESS
        RESEARCH

In the last couple of decades entrepreneurship and small business research has shown a tremendous growth in the number of researchers within the field. At the same time, a research infrastructure has been built in the form of conferences, scientific journals, chairs, education programs, etc. This raises a fundamental question. Has this expansion been followed by a corresponding cognitive development of the field? This question will be discussed in this section. As an introduction, the changing character of the research, from discovery-oriented to empirical-oriented research, will be described. I will then review the content of the state-of-the-art books by Donald Sexton and various co-authors, in order to give an impression of the development of the field over the years. Finally, I will discuss whether or not there has been a convergence in entrepreneurship research, based on the Grégoire et al. (2001) analysis of the contributions to the Babson Kauffman Conference.

3.1   From Discovery-Oriented to Empirically-Oriented Research

In this subsection I will attempt to describe the cognitive development of entrepreneurship and small business research since the early 1980s, from a discovery-oriented research, which characterized much of the 1980s, to the mainly empirically based research of the 1990s.

3.1.1   From a Discovery-Oriented Research Approach ...

What characterized the field of entrepreneurship and small business research during the 1980s? The most prominent advances can be said to have taken place within what we today can call "small business economics", where researchers, mainly with a background in industrial organization but also in economics and economic geography, started to take an interest in the importance of small companies for example in the area of job creation, small firm innovation, as well as the role of small firms in regional development. Although management schools were mainly concerned with entrepreneurship education programs that were in most cases run by a part-time faculty with strong links to industry, it was possible to discern a growing interest in the development of research in the area. The researchers' interest initially concentrated on issues such as the entrepreneur as an individual, new technology based companies and venture capital. They also realized that entrepreneurship was a social phenomenon, which spurred their interest in social networks.

In the late 1980s, a number of reviews were conducted in order to summarize the achievements made in entrepreneurship and small business research during the decade (see e.g. Carsrud et al., 1986; Churchill & Lewis, 1986; Wortman, 1987; Low & MacMillan, 1988; Bygrave, 1989: VanderWerf & Brush, 1989; Bygrave & Hofer, 1991; Aldrich, 1992; Amit et al., 1993; Bull & Willard, 1993; Johannisson, 1994). Reviews of the early development of the field were often critical of the scientific progression of entrepreneurship and small business research. This criticism primarily concerned:
- the lack of consensus regarding the definition of entrepreneurship,
- the fragmentation of the research – in its topics and purpose as well as methodologies employed,
- the lack of a theoretical foundation,
- methodological inconsistencies in empirical research, and
- the lack of legitimacy within the wider research community.

Based on these reviews, it can be argued that the field was young and the phenomenon complex – the research could to a high degree be regarded as discovery-oriented – it focused on providing descriptions and insights about a phenomenon that was previously unfamiliar (Churchill & Lewis, 1986) while Carsrud et al. (1986) and Wortman (1987) emphasized that the level of methodological and statistical sophistication in most of the studies was quite low. The discovery-oriented character of the field made rigorous research methodologies for rigor's sake inappropriate (Churchill & Lewis, 1986).

3.1.2 .... to an Empirically-Oriented Research Approach

What changes can we observe in terms of the issues that have constituted the core of the research during the 1990s? One of the more fundamental changes that have taken place – which can more or less be regarded as a systematic shift – is that the research interest in the entrepreneur as an individual, i.e. entrepreneurial traits, has declined in favor of a focus on contextual and processual aspects. Here, the pioneering works of William Gartner deserve to be mentioned. As early as 1988, Gartner claimed "Who is the entrepreneur? is the wrong question", arguing that more relevant questions were: "How are new organizations created?" (Gartner, 1988). In a number of articles, Gartner (1990; 1993) has stressed that entrepreneurship is about "the creation of new organizations" (see similar reasoning in Bygrave & Hofer (1991) and more recently in the GEM project). Even if this development toward a process oriented approach has taken time, Gartner's ideas are now firmly anchored within entrepreneurship research.

Davidsson, Low and Wright (2001) argued that the focus of research seems to have shifted from a couple of "dead-ends" such as the psychological characteristics of the entrepreneur, toward topics that open up new possibilities such as behavioral and cognitive aspects of the entrepreneur, an increased emphasis on context and the entrepreneurial process (especially concerning the emergence of new entrepreneurial activities), and an introduction of theoretical perspectives into the research (e.g. the evolutionary approach and the resource-based view to mention a few). Davidsson and Wiklund (2001) modified this line of reasoning somewhat and provided a whole range of examples of progress in entrepreneurship and small business research, such as:

- The psychological traits approach has changed to an application of more modern psychological theory in entrepreneurship research (see e.g. Sarasvathy, 1999).
- There has been an influx of more theory-driven approaches within the field, for example, the increased popularity of the resource-based view, but also the evolutionary perspective developed by Howard Aldrich.
- A broader acceptance of entrepreneurship, which is not only restricted to independent small firms, indicating an increased interest in corporate entrepreneurship and in entrepreneurial strategies.
- Considerable progress has also been made regarding the influence of regional environments on entrepreneurship and small firms (see e.g. special issue of *Regional Studies*, 1994).
- An increased interest in cross-national studies. This research is still in its infancy, but initial attempts to compare institutional and cultural differences have been made in the Entrepreneurship Research Consortium (ERC) and Global Entrepreneurship Monitoring (GEM).

In a similar way Aldrich and Martinez (2001) argue that we have seen important advances in the area of theory – a shift in emphasis from the personal characteristics and intentions of entrepreneurs themselves to a stronger concentration on their actions and the outcomes. Empirically, the 1990s have led to an increase in our knowledge, not least regarding how entrepreneurs use knowledge, networks, and resources to launch new ventures, but also a more sophisticated taxonomy of environmental forces at different levels of analysis (population, community, and society).

Finally, an enhanced quality of entrepreneurship and small business research can also be observed when analyzing entrepreneurship articles in scientific journals, at least at the "top end" of research within the field – and we can observe that the structure of the field is becoming increasingly hierarchical. In their analysis of entrepreneurship articles published in seven leading management journals during the period 1985 to 1999, Busenitz et al. (2003) found that only 97 articles out of a total of 5,291 addressed entrepreneurship issues (1.8%). However, an increasing number of entrepreneurship articles tend to appear in major empirical management journals – whereas the share of theoretical articles has remained low – which indicates the dominance of empirical work within the field, but also that the quality of empirical research is high enough to warrant publication in high-quality journals (see also Low, 2001).

We can establish that, in the 1990s, entrepreneurship and small business research exhibited a progressively higher quality of empirical research. An indication of increased methodological awareness is found in Chandler and Lyon (2001), who analyzed 416 empirical articles in entrepreneurship and small business journals during the past decade. Their analyses show a trend toward the use of more sophisticated analytical and statistical methods in the research as well as greater awareness of reliability and validity problems. Thus, there seems to be increased sophistication in the statistical methods employed in entrepreneurship and small business research, which may be a sign of the progress of the field. However, Grégoire, Meyer and DeCastro (2002) question this progress. In their analysis of 104 empirical articles published in six mainstream management journals between 1985 and 2001, they found, on the one hand, that the field is converging in the use of some identifiable practices – an increased reliance on archival data and regression-based analysis techniques, in addition to the integration of econometric techniques – but, on the other and, it can be questioned whether this "crystallization" is a sign of progress – archival data may prevent the observation of many relevant dimensions of entrepreneurship.

The increased statistical sophistication has taken place in parallel with improved opportunities for constructing databases specifically designed to meet the aims of the entrepreneurship and small business researcher. This development has contributed to the acquisition of more robust knowledge. At the same time as the development toward increased statistical sophistication became evident – and the field began to attain the characteristics of a more "normal science approach" (Aldrich & Baker, 1997) – a longstanding feature of entrepreneurship researchers, namely their methodological openness and interest in experimentation, resulting from different approaches and data collection techniques, was put at risk. The new developments counteracted the original openness, threatening its existence.

3.2   State-of-the-art in Entrepreneurship and Small Business Research

Since the early 1980s, Donald Sexton and various colleagues have presented a number of state-of-the-art books, in which several core researchers within the field have described the current knowledge concerning certain central research topics. Thus, the books provide not only a picture of which researchers are regarded as important but also which research issues have been topical at different points in time. Figure 3-3 presents topics and authors described in the various books.

In *Encyclopedia of Entrepreneurship* (1982) Sexton and his colleagues highlight the links between the research field, behavioral science and economic research as well as representing the first attempt to summarize early entrepreneurship and small business research which emanated from management studies. The points of departure are the trends that were visible in society of the 1970s – entrepreneurship and small businesses received greater coverage from the media and popular literature, there were a growing number of academic courses in entrepreneurship, in addition to increasing governmental interest in entrepreneurship and small firms. The book included nearly 40 researchers – most of whom had their roots in management, although researchers within engineering, economics, behavioral sciences, and business history were also included. The book is characterized by curiosity and the search for available knowledge about this "new" phenomenon. Accordingly, its content is highly varied; part 1 summarizes existing knowledge about the entrepreneur as an individual, part 2 addresses the creation of new ventures (e.g. the process of starting a business, risk capital, and the performance of new firms), and part 3 discusses the contribution of entrepreneurship to economic progress. The chapters also differ in character, from reviews of early entrepreneurship and small business research within economics (Livesay and Kent), more traditional state-of-the-art articles, primarily within the behavioral science area (Brockhaus, and Shapero & Sokol), to chapters that mirror the way in which entrepreneurship is depicted in the non-academic literature (Hornaday, and McClung & Constantin) but also compilations of empirical research in the area (Timmons, Bruno & Tyebjee, Vesper, and Paulin & Coffey & Spaulding) and a presentation of the authors' own empirical studies within the field (Wetzel, Brophy, and Cooper). In 1992, ten years later, Churchill (1992) reflected on Sexton's state-of-the-art books, and he made an analogy to the story of the blind men and the elephant, where six men touch different parts of the elephant and give quite different descriptions of its characteristics. Churchill was of the opinion that the 1982 book shows a relatively unstructured exploration of the elephant. The researchers discovered that this animal was different, that it was composed of a number of rather unusual parts, and that it was quite large.

Kent, C.A. & Sexton, D.L. & Vesper, K.H., 1982, *Encyclopedia of Entrepreneurship*, Englewood Cliffs, NJ: Prentice-Hall
1. The Entrepreneur (Harold Livesay, John Hornaday, Robert Brockhaus, Albert Shapero & Lisa Sokol, Edwin Harwood)
2. Entrepreneurial Technology (Jacquetta McClung & James Constantin, Jeffry Timmons, William Wetzel Jr, David Brophy, Arnold Cooper, Hans Schollhammer)
3. Entrepreneurship and Progress (Calvin Kent, Wayne Broehl Jr, Israel Kirzner, O.J. Krasner, Albert Bruno & Tyzoon Tyebjee)
4. Entrepreneurship and Academia (Karl Vesper, William Paulin & Robert Coffey & Mark Spaulding)
Sexton, D.L. & Smilor, R. 1986, *The Art and Science of Entrepreneurship*, Cambridge, MA: Ballinger
1. Entrepreneurship Characteristics (Howard Aldrich & Catherine Zimmer, Robert Brockhaus & Pamela Horwitz, Robert Hisrich)
2. Risk and Venture Capital Financing (William Wetzel, David Brophy)
3. High-Tech Entrepreneurship (Arnold Cooper, Pier Abetti & Robert Stuart)
4. Growth and Entrepreneurship (Jeffrey Timmons, Ian MacMillan)
5. Research and Education (Max Wortman, Neil Churchill & Virginia Lewis, Karl Vesper
Sexton, D.L. & Kasarda, J.D., 1992, *The State of the Art of Entrepreneurship*, Boston, MA: PWS-Kent Publishers
1. Entrepreneurship Education (Zenas Block & Stephen Stumpf)
2. Entrepreneurship and Economic Development (Zoltan Acs & David Audretsch, Jon Goodman & James Meany & Larry Pate)
3. Entrepreneurship Research: Linkages and Methodology (Gregory Dees & Jennifer Starr, Diana Day, Gerald Hills & Raymond LaForge, Howard Aldrich, Andrew Van de Ven, Bruce Kirchhoff & Bruce Phillips, Paul Reynolds)
4. Entrepreneurial Firm Growth and Financing (Arnold Cooper & Javier Gimeno Gascon, Frank Hoy & Patricia McDougall & Derrick Dsouza, Dennis Slevin & Jeffrey Covin, David Brophy, Jeffrey Timmons & Harry Sapienza, William Bygrave, John Freear & William Wetzel Jr, Sankaran Venkataraman & Ian MacMillan & Rita Gunther McGrath)
5. International Entrepreneurship and Research Needs for the 1990s (Robert Hisrich, Robert Brockhaus, Neil Churchill)
Sexton, D.L. & Smilor, R.W., 1997, *Entrepreneurship 2000*, Chicago, IL: Upstart
1. Financing Growth (David Brophy, Jeffrey Timmons & William Bygrave, John Freear & Jeffrey Sohl & William Wetzel Jr, William Petty)
2. Growth Strategies (Jeffrey Covin & Dennis Slevin, Arnold Cooper & Catherine Daily, Sankaran Venkataraman & Ian MacMillan, Bruce Kirchhoff & Zoltan Acs)
3. Entrepreneurship Education (Marilyn Kourilsky & Sheila Carlson, John Young)
4. Broader Dimensions of Entrepreneurship (Nancy Upton & Ramona Heck, John Butler & Patricia Greene, Patricia McDougall & Benjamin Oviatt, John Yankey & Dennis Young)
5. Research Applications, Issues, and Needs (Bruce Phillips & William Dennis, Frank Hoy, Howard Aldrich & Ted Baker)

Sexton, D.L. & Landström, H., 2000, *The Blackwell Handbook of Entrepreneurship*, Oxford: Blackwell
1. Setting the Stage for International Research in Entrepreneurship (Howard Aldrich, Per Davidsson & Johan Wiklund, Michael Hitt & Duane Ireland, William Dennis)
2. Government Impact on Entrepreneurship (Dennis Dee, David Audretsch, Robert van der Horst & Andre Nijsen & Selcuk Gulhan, Josef Mugler, David Storey)
3. Financing Growth (Rik Donckels, Colin Mason & Richard Harrison, Sophie Manigart & Harry Sapienza, Raphael Amit & James Brander & Christoph Zott)
4. Achieving Growth: Internal and External Approaches (Sue Birley & Simon Stockley, Ben Arbaugh & Michael Camp, Erkko Autio, Arnold Cooper & Timothy Folta, Bengt Johannisson, Mark Weaver, Frank Hoy & John Stanworth & David Purdy)

Figure 3-3. State-of-the-art books on entrepreneurship research (Donald Sexton).

In the second book, *The Art and Science of Entrepreneurship* (1986), the growing field of entrepreneurship and small business research with its roots in management studies is summarized. Several of the names subsequently regarded as pioneers within entrepreneurship and small business research (e.g. Aldrich, Hisrich, Wetzel, Cooper, Timmons and MacMillan) are found in the book. It treats a number of topics within the emerging field, such as social networks (Aldrich & Zimmer), female entrepreneurs (Hisrich), venture capital (Wetzel and Brophy), high-tech entrepreneurship (Cooper), growth and entrepreneurship (Timmons) and corporate entrepreneurship (MacMillan). Several chapters are an attempt to summarize the mainly empirical research conducted in the early 1980s. It is noteworthy that almost a quarter of the book is devoted to examining the research within the field and assessing trends in entrepreneurship education programs. Thus, the book gives an overall picture of the character of the research and education within this growing area. One interesting observation in the book is that entrepreneurship is clearly something distinct from small business, even if the definition of the concepts was less clear. Using the analogy of the blind men and the elephant, Churchill (1992) argues that this second book reflects the fact that the general shape of the elephant had already been described. Some investigations had been carried out as to the nature of the different parts, and there was great excitement about the existence of the elephants – they were viewed as being a major stimulus to the economy. However, there was still a great deal to learn about them.

The third book, *The State-of-the-Art of Entrepreneurship* (1992), is the most comprehensive, consisting of 22 chapters and 600 pages. The greater part of the book reflects the expansion of entrepreneurship and small business research and the fragmentation of the field that took place in the late 1980s. A prominent feature is a certain trend toward liberation from behavioral science research, while on the other hand strengthening the link with management research. For example, several chapters are devoted to how entrepreneurship can be related to strategic management

(Day) and to marketing (Hills & LaForge). The book reflects the growth of entrepreneurship and small business research at both macro- and micro levels. The macro level focus was related to the economic impact of entrepreneurship (Acs & Audretsch), government intervention to stimulate entrepreneurship (Goodman & Meany & Pate), the prediction of new-firm birth (Reynolds), and the development of venture capital markets (Timmons & Sapienza, and Bygrave). At micro level, interest was focused on the process of founding and new-firm performance (Cooper & Gimeno-Gascón), high-growth firms (Hoy & McDougall & Dsouza), entrepreneurial teams (Slevin & Covin), venture capital (Timmons & Sapienza), informal risk capital (Freear & Wetzel), corporate entrepreneurship (Venkataraman & MacMillan & Gunther McGrath), and internationalization (Hisrich). It is interesting to note that research outside the US is also focused upon, with one chapter devoted to entrepreneurship education and research in Europe. In this book the intensity of the interest in entrepreneurship and small firms has increased significantly, better instruments, not least databases, have been developed and applied, and the scope of the research has been broadened significantly. In Churchill's (1992) elephant analogy, this was described as looking at different aspects of the "elephant", but also as an awareness of the complexity of the phenomenon. Thus, the picture presented is rather fragmented. The overall challenge for entrepreneurship research during the 1990s was "understanding" – a lot of work had been done to describe the phenomenon – now was the time to understand it.

The early years of the 1990s saw a huge expansion in entrepreneurship and small business research. This development is reflected by the fourth book *Entrepreneurship 2000*, which was published in 1997. It was no longer possible to cover the entire research field, and the book therefore focused on firm growth, especially on the problems of financing faced by growing firms – financing of entrepreneurial firms (Brophy), venture capital (Timmons & Bygrave), informal venture capital (Freear & Sohl & Wetzel) and harvesting firm value (Petty) – as well as growth strategies, such as high growth transitions (Covin & Slevin), entrepreneurial teams (Cooper & Daily) and organizational modes in new business development (Venkataraman & MacMillan). It is difficult to identify any distinct pattern in the different contributions but a certain theoretical focus can be discerned, not least related to strategic management research. The expansion and fragmentation of the research field that have taken place can be partly seen in the broader view of entrepreneurship and small business, including chapters on family business (Upton & Heck), ethnic entrepreneurship (Butler & Greene) and entrepreneurship in the non-for-profit sector (Hisrich & Freeman & Standley & Yankey & Young). The lasting impression of the book is, however, its questioning and criticism of recent entrepreneurship and small business research. For example, Aldrich and Baker argue that not much had changed in terms of methodology over the years. The research field was still to a large extent a monomethod field, depending on questionnaire-based techniques, with fairly unsophisticated data analyses. In addition, Hoy questions the relevance of the research and asks: Is entrepreneurship research being applied (in the sense of addressing the needs and concerns of practitioners)? His conclusion is ambiguous. Even though there seems to be an increase of practical and applicable findings from entrepreneurship and small business research, there is less evidence that applied findings are being effectively communicated to policy-makers and practitioners.

Nor does the fifth book, *The Blackwell Handbook of Entrepreneurship* (2000), lay claim to mirroring the entire research field – the field has expanded and diversified, thus making an overview and review of the field within the space of one book extremely difficult. Hence, the book concentrates on a number of themes: methodological aspects, government impact on entrepreneurship, and growth. It is also interesting to note that this was the first time that European researchers were deeply involved as editors and authors (about half of the authors are from Europe). The first part treats methodological considerations in entrepreneurship and small business research, for example learning from each other, not only within the international research community (Aldrich) but also across different research disciplines, particularly strategic management (Hitt & Ireland). An obvious difference in relation to previous state-of-the-art books, which were more critical of the methodology used within entrepreneurship and small business research, is the constructiveness of the methodological discussions. The second part of the book consists of a discussion about the opportunities for governments in various countries to stimulate entrepreneurship and small businesses. This is a traditional European theme and, consequently, the European researchers dominate this section of the book. The theme most extensively covered in the book is, however, growth. As in previous state-of-the-art books, the financial aspects of growth receive relatively large coverage, including both the informal capital market (Mason & Harrison) and the formal market (Manigart & Sapienza, Amit & Brander & Zott). However, other aspects of growth are also discussed, for example, entrepreneurial teams (Birley & Stockley), growth of technology-based firms (Autio), clusters (Cooper & Folta), and networks (Johannisson). Many of the contributions within the "growth" theme are reviews where the authors try to gather existing knowledge within the respective topic as well as suggesting directions for future research. Similar to earlier state-of-the-art books (especially in Sexton & Smilor, 1997), the influence of strategic management research is apparent. To continue the "elephant analogy", the book demonstrates awareness that there may be other elephants on other continents, that we need different stimuli to induce the elephants to contribute to societal development and that the researchers need to develop scientific methods that can be used to improve our understanding of the elephants.

3.3 Convergence in Entrepreneurship and Small Business Research

The above analysis has provided a picture of the core researchers within the field as well as a picture of the topics focused upon at different points in time. But this analysis does not tell us whether these scholars and their contributions have led to converging streams of research, and thus the potential to accumulate knowledge within the field. In this respect the study by Grégoire, Déry and Béchard (2001) is of great interest. They studied co-citation relationships between the most cited references used in 752 full-length papers published in the Babson Kauffman Conference's Frontiers of Entrepreneurship Research Proceedings between 1981 and 1999. The Babson Conference is an important forum for entrepreneurship and small business scholars – at least for entrepreneurship research based on the "US-tradition" – and may therefore be of interest in order to show the development of the field.

The results indicate that over the period 1981 to 1999 there were several emerging "conversations" in entrepreneurship and small business research. Firstly, there were two clusters focusing on *new venture performance*, both of which were based on Porter's seminal work *Competitive Strategy* (1980). One of the clusters tried to answer the question "How can we measure new venture performance?" (e.g. Sandberg & Hofer, 1986; Brush & Vanderwerf, 1992), whereas the other cluster focused on "How will various factors affect new venture performance?" (e.g. Sandberg & Hofer, 1987). Secondly, a relatively tight cluster can be found around *resources and capabilities* as the determining factor of competitive advantage, i.e. the resource-based view, represented by articles by, for example, Barney (1991), Wernerfelt (1984), Penrose (1959), and Miles and Snow (1978). Thirdly, the result shows two clusters anchored in McClelland (1961), which concern the *person of the entrepreneur*. One cluster comprises books and chapters that review past research on social or psychological dimensions of entrepreneurship (e.g. Brockhaus, 1982; Shapero & Sokol, 1982). Another cluster focuses on specific factors affecting a person's decision to launch a new venture, for example, risk-taking propensity (Brockhaus, 1982) or the subjective perception of risk and ability (Liles, 1974) but also on more immediate situational factors (Shapero, 1975). Fourthly, there is a cluster of works converging on *venture capitalists' role and practices*. This cluster is based on the study by MacMillan et al. (1985) of venture capitalists' decision criteria but is also closely linked to Tyebjee and Bruno (1984), Gorman and Sahlman (1989), and Sapienza (1992). Finally, two smaller clusters emerged in the analysis, one concerning *structural and economic dependence relationships* anchored in Pfeffer and Salancik's (1978) and Williamson's (1975) influential books, and the other around *the role of social networks in the entrepreneurial process*, based on the articles by Aldrich and Zimmer (1986) and Birley (1985). The main "conversations" in entrepreneurship research during the last two decades are summarized in Figure 3-4.

Cooper (2003) identified some similar paths in the development of entrepreneurship research. For example, there has been a long tradition of work, especially in the early days of entrepreneurship research, which seeks to determine whether entrepreneurs are different to other individuals and managers in general – what is often described as "trait" research. This path of research is based on seminal works of McClelland (1961), Collins, Moore and Unwalla (1964), and Brockhaus (1980). Trait research has been the subject of sharp criticism. Gartner (1988) was one of the first to argue that the focus in entrepreneurship research should be upon behaviors, not traits, and consequently a number of research streams have developed that examine the process of venture formation. Three areas have received particular attention: (i) venture finance (Bygrave & Timmons, 1992; MacMillan et al., 1985; Sahlman, 1992), (ii) the role of networks in entrepreneurship (Larson, 1992; Aldrich & Zimmer, 1986), and (iii) the role of new and small firms in innovation (Acs & Audretsch, 1990). From the earliest days of entrepreneurship and small business research we can identify a third stream of research that has been focused on predictors of performance, i.e. the extent to which the characteristics of the entrepreneur, the formation process, the nature of the firm, and environmental characteristics influence the survival and/or success of the new venture (Mayer & Goldstein, 1961; Brüderl et al., 1992; Gimeno et al., 1997). Finally, corporate entrepreneurship, i.e. how new ventures can be developed within existing firms, has been of interest in entrepreneurship research for many years (Fast, 1978; Kanter, 1983; Burgelman, 1983).

While the above gives a general picture of the research field over the entire period, the question is whether or not it is possible to identify any changes in the key research issues over time. In other words, are different issues more interesting than others at different periods? Grégoire et al. divided their analysis into four periods. They found that the period 1981 - 1985 was to a great extent characterized by concerns about the personal traits of entrepreneurs, with three underlying networks of researchers focusing on female entrepreneurs, technical entrepreneurs, and managerial concerns. On the other hand, during the period 1986 to 1990, a strong fragmentation emerged, with many parallel "conversations" but little convergence. A change occurred in the period 1991 to 1995 – the field was to some extent structured around a strategic perspective – and Porter (1980) became a principal anchor. In addition to the strategic impetus, a couple of parallel networks emerged, to some extent anchored in Vesper (1980) and Gartner (1985), which included conceptual works within the field, population ecology, personal antecedents and experiences, and psychological and social characteristics of the entrepreneurs. Finally, in the period 1996 to 1999 the strategic impetus was consolidated, especially around the resource-based view, and in recent years scholars from the field of strategic management as well as entrepreneurship have called for an integration of entrepreneurial and strategic thinking (see e.g. McGrath & MacMillan, 2000; Meyer & Heppard, 2000; Hitt et al., 2002). However, the focus was not only on strategic aspects; the latter half of the 1990s was mainly characterized by increased theoretical grounding of the research. Growth became a key concept in many studies, and an increasing number of cross-national studies were carried out. The large ERC-project and the GEM-project, in which Paul Reynolds was the driving force, constituted important sources of inspiration both among researchers and among policy-makers. An increasing number of researchers focused their interest on Reynolds' "nascent entrepreneurs" concept (even if a major part of the research results from these two international studies was not published until the early 2000s).

The conclusions drawn by Grégoire et al. (2001) were that there has been a convergence in entrepreneurship research over the years, even if the level of convergence is still relatively low and unstable (older topics decline in importance and are replaced by new ones). But some topics seem to have consistently interested entrepreneurship researchers – for example variables affecting new venture performance and a person's decision to launch a new venture as well as venture capitalists' practices and influence, the influence of social networks, and strategic considerations. The main conclusion of Grégoire et al. is that "entrepreneurship appears less characterized by a dominant paradigm as by successive pockets of convergence" – it is a situation characterized neither by the conformism of single paradigms nor by the anarchy of total fragmentation.

1980	1985	1990	1995

The entrepreneur as an individual
New venture performance/predictors of performance
Resources and capabilities
Venture capital (markets and behavior)
Social networks
The role of new and small firms in innovation
Corporate entrepreneurship

A "trait" approach		A "process" approach	

Personal characteristics
- female
  entrepreneurs
- technical
  entrepreneurs
- managerial concerns
	Strong fragmentation (many parallel conversations)	Increased strategic focus
		
		Parallel conversations:
		- conceptual works
		- population ecology
		- individual and
		  social characteristics
			Consolidation of strategic impetus (RBV)
			More theory-driven approaches
			
			- Growth
			- Cross-national
			  studies
			- Nascent
			  entrepreneurs

Figure 3-4. "Conversations" in entrepreneurship and small business research.

3.4   Progress in Entrepreneurship and Small Business Research

Has there been any progress in entrepreneurship and small business research during the last decades? Even though the field is still young and of an eclectic nature, much has been achieved, and we know a great deal more about, for example, the characteristics of the entrepreneur, the entrepreneurial process, the context of entrepreneurship, and the role of small businesses in the economy, than we did a couple of decades ago. It can nevertheless be concluded that the cognitive development of entrepreneurship research has been rather slow.

Returning to the original question posed in this chapter, namely whether the development of a greater emphasis on social aspects was accompanied by a corresponding cognitive development, the answer is clearly "no"; the advanced social structure that we find in entrepreneurship and small business research is not paralleled by a corresponding cognitive development of the field.

Why, then, has the cognitive development of the field progressed so slowly? There are of course many reasons, several of which have been discussed in this chapter. First, societal dynamics have remained on a high level, which has led to continuously changing forms of entrepreneurship and related problems – new questions are constantly arising before the old ones have been answered. Second, entrepreneurship has for a long time been an optional component primarily within management education programs, and the faculty has frequently consisted of external lecturers with a strong practical orientation, part-time teachers, adjunct professors from industry, in many cases without academic degrees, which has made it difficult to obtain permanent teaching posts. This has meant a lack of strong focus on research among scholars in the field. Third, the research community has lacked stability – it has primarily been transient – for which there are several reasons, for example that (a) the researchers represent many different disciplines, which creates a dichotomy between the focus on mainstream research and entrepreneurship, (b) in many cases the researchers have identified themselves with the specific problem rather than with entrepreneurship and small business as a research field, and (c) there is no connection between the enthusiastic community of researchers who routinely work on entrepreneurship and the transient researchers within the field. Finally, it has been difficult to obtain legitimacy for entrepreneurship and small business in the academic world – in contrast to its position in society, entrepreneurship is still on the margin of the academic world and has to struggle for legitimacy.

4. THE STRUGGLES

This chapter has treated the development of entrepreneurship and small business as an academic research field since the early 1980s. This development has not been without problems, and it is possible to discern a number of "struggles" that have impacted on the field in different ways and in some cases also impeded its development. These "struggles" concern, for example, the relation between disciplinary research and a separate domain of entrepreneurship and small business research, the view of entrepreneurship as a phenomenon, and the balance between exploitation and exploration of knowledge.

4.1 Disciplinary Research vs a Separate Domain of Entrepreneurship and Small Business Research

During the last couple of decades we can discern the development of entrepreneurship and small business research within existing disciplines toward the establishment of a distinct domain of research. What rationale can we find for this development? It could, for example, be argued that entrepreneurship and small business research is best pursued within established disciplines like economics, psychology and sociology. The reasoning behind this argument is that (i) there are few contingencies of interest to entrepreneurship scholars that are not contained in existing disciplines and therefore there is no need to reinvent the wheel, and (ii) within existing disciplines entrepreneurship and small business research is required to meet the quality criteria of the respective discipline, which is a way for the research to attain academic legitimacy (Davidsson, 2003). As a consequence it would be possible for entrepreneurship and small business researchers to use existing theories from psychology, sociology, etc. and test their explanatory value in the entrepreneurial context (Landström, 2000).

On the other hand, entrepreneurship (and small business) may be regarded as a complex phenomenon. Existing theories may not always be optimal for addressing these characteristics, which indicates a need to pose new questions and build concepts and models to explain the phenomenon (Landström, 2000; Davidsson, 2003). Leaving entrepreneurship and small business research to other disciplines also means the lack of a research community – a community with deep knowledge of and familiarity with entrepreneurship and small business as phenomena that transient visitors to the field do not possess. Without this kind of knowledge, an understanding of the entrepreneurial phenomenon will be difficult to achieve (Low, 2001). Finally, and most importantly, if entrepreneurship and small firms are left to other disciplines, there is no guarantee that research will focus on the most central questions of entrepreneurship and small business (Acs & Audretsch, 2003). These arguments are summarized in Figure 3-5.

Davidsson (2003) argues that in the future we need to combine topical and disciplinary knowledge. This can be achieved by (i) entrepreneurship and small business researchers who learn more about theory and method from the disciplines, (ii) disciplinary researchers who read a great deal of entrepreneurship and small business research, and (iii) collaboration between topical and disciplinary researchers – and, according to Davidsson, all three directions are likely to be explored in the presence of a distinct domain of research.

Disciplinary research ⟶	Domain of entrepreneurship and small business research
Integrated within main stream disciplines - no need to reinvent the wheel - entrepreneurship and small business research is required to meet the quality criteria of the discipline (academic legitimacy)	Liberation from main stream disciplines - complex phenomena (existing theories not always optimal) - research community in entrepreneurship and small business (tacit knowledge) - focus on the most central questions of entrepreneurship and small business

Figure 3-5. Disciplinary research vs a domain of entrepreneurship and small business research.

4.2 Entrepreneurship in an Innovative vs Firm-Organizing Sense

The lack of clear definitions of the central concepts in entrepreneurship has been the target of extensive criticism and discussion for a long period of time within the entrepreneurship and small business research community. The multidisciplinary character of the field adds to the problems – different disciplines focusing on different aspects of entrepreneurship, and each discipline has its own unique way of defining and viewing entrepreneurship (Herron et al., 1991).

However, looking at the definitions used in entrepreneurship research (see Chapter 1), two main perspectives can be discerned. One is Schumpeter's view, in which the entrepreneur is seen as an innovator, the creator of transformations in the market, or, in the words of Baumol (1993), "innovative entrepreneurship". It is the innovativeness or path-breaking aspect that is the motivating force behind the entrepreneur's actions. On the other hand, the entrepreneur can be regarded as an individual who creates and organizes a new business venture, irrespective of whether or not it comprises an innovative element, or to use Baumol's term "firm-organizing entrepreneurship". This type of entrepreneur tends to tap existing imperfections in the market, thereby guiding the market toward equilibrium. Both types of entrepreneurs are important for societal development but there is a clear difference between them in terms of their roles in the economy.

Without doubt, the difficulty of reaching consensus on the central concepts of entrepreneurship has been considered as constraining the development of the field, not least due to the fact that considerable energy and mental effort have been expended on the discussion about how to define the concept of entrepreneurship.

4.3   Exploration vs Exploitation of Knowledge

March (1991) made a distinction between "exploration" and "exploitation", where exploration includes such things as search, discovery, novelty and innovation and involves creating variation in experience, risk-taking, and experimentation. Exploitation, on the other hand, means refinement of existing knowledge, routinization and implementation of knowledge, involves efficiency and creates reliability in experience, as well as learning and tending to repeat successful past behavior.

Within the research community we often search for a strong "paradigm", and Kuhn argued that only a research field with a strong focus on exploitation can really lead to an accumulation of knowledge (see Landström & Johannisson, 2001). However, it could be argued that a focus on a strong paradigm and exploitation behavior could easily lead to what March (1999) calls a "success trap" – the research becomes blind to its own success and tends to only repeat past behavior. During the 1980s and 1990s entrepreneurship and small business research was characterized by the opposite situation. The research involves a high degree of variation and experimentation – having been built on exploration behavior. The risk inherent in extensive exploration is, according to March, a "failure trap" (March, 1999), where the research is trapped in an ongoing process of endless experimentation and introduction of new ideas that lead nowhere.

However, elaborating on March (1991), it could be argued that too rapid a development toward a strong paradigm could be potentially self-destructive for the research field. Within a research community there is mutual learning. The community socializes new researchers within the field, while, simultaneously, the community adapts to individual beliefs, i.e. mutual learning leads to convergence between the research community and individual beliefs. This convergence is generally useful, both for the individual and the community, especially in the short term. Furthermore, there will be a trade-off between exploration and exploitation, which involves a conflict between the short term and future development as well as between the gains made by individual knowledge and the benefits to collective knowledge. The major threat to mutual learning is the possibility that the individual will adjust to the paradigm within the community before the community can learn from the individual – fast learning is not always positive and may hurt the socializers in the long run, even if it may help those socialized. Therefore, a relatively slow socialization of new researchers within the field is preferable, and moderate turnover sustains variability in individual beliefs, which may in the long run improve the knowledge within the research community as well as the average individual knowledge.

Based on this reasoning, I will argue that it is not a question of either exploiting or exploring. A dynamic and innovative research field is characterized by a balance between exploration and exploitation. The picture I have painted of the progression of the research field during the past three decades shows that entrepreneurship and small business research is in a phase of maturity – *scientific maturation*. Such scientific maturation calls for a balance between exploration – the pursuit of new knowledge, for example, by introducing new concepts and theoretical frameworks to the field – and exploitation – the development of existing knowledge, by integrating and validating the knowledge base within the field. As indicated in this chapter, exploration has dominated entrepreneurship and small business research for a long time, and this can be regarded as beneficial for the development of the field. Based on the reasoning of Welsch and Liao (2003), one can argue that in this way the field has been enriched by innovative perspectives and methodological approaches – most of them imported from other fields – fields that harbour different philosophies, foci, concepts and theories, and methodological approaches. But entrepreneurship and small business researchers have also been highly innovative in finding ways to understand the complexity of entrepreneurship as a phenomenon – a complexity that presupposes a variety of perspectives and methodological approaches. However, this focus on explorative research has been made at the price of a lack of conceptual standardization and replication as well as fragmentation of the research. What is needed in the future is a stronger focus on exploitation – replication, integration and synthesis – in order to achieve a better balance between exploration and exploitation in entrepreneurship research.

In order to achieve scientific maturation, entrepreneurship and small business research needs to create a balance between explorative and exploitative research, and Welsch and Liao (2003; see also Landström, 2001) formulated it well in their strategies for future entrepreneurship and small business research.

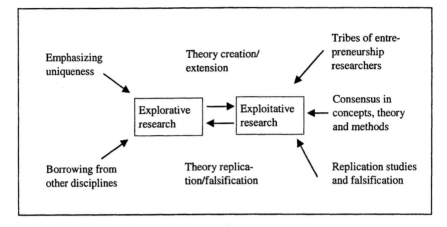

Figure 3-6. Creation of a balance between explorative and exploitative research (source: adapted from Welsch & Liao, 2003, pp. 29-33).

REFERENCES

Acs, Z.J., 1984, *The Changing Structure of the US Economy: Lessons from the Steel Industry,* New York: Praeger.

Acs, Z.J. & Audretsch, D.B., 1990, *Innovation and Small Firms,* Cambridge, MA: MIT Press.

Acs, Z.J. & Audretsch, D.B., 2003, Introduction to the Handbook of Entrepreneurship Research, in Acs, Z.J. & Audretsch, D.B. (eds.), *Handbook of Entrepreneurship Research,* Dordrecht: Kluwer, 3-20.

Aldrich, H.E., 1992, Methods in Our Madness? Trends in Entrepreneurship Research, in Sexton, D.L. & Kasarda, J.D. (eds.), *The State of the Art of Entrepreneurship,* Boston, MA: PWS-Kent Publishers, 191-213.

Aldrich, H.E., 2000, Learning Together: National Differences in Entrepreneruiship Research, in Sexton, D.L. & Landström, H. (eds.), *The Blackwell Handbook of Entrepreneurship,* Oxford: Blackwell, 5-25.

Aldrich, H.E. & Baker, T., 1997, Blinded by the cites. Has there been progress in entrepreneurship research? in Sexton, D.L. & Smilor, R.W. (eds.), 1997, *Entrepreneurship 2000,* Chicago, IL: Upstart., 377-400.

Aldrich, H.E. & Martinez, 2001, Many are Called, but few are Chosen: An Evolutionary Perspective for the Study of Entrepreneurship, *Entrepreneurship Theory and Practice,* 25, 4, 41-56.

Aldrich, H.E. & Zimmer, C., 1986, Entrepreneurship Through Social Networks, in Sexton, D.L. & Smilor, R. (eds.), *The Art and Science of Entrepreneurship,* Cambridge, MA: Ballinger, 3-23.

Amit, R. & Glosten, L. & Muller, E., 1993, Challenges to theory development in entrepreneurship research, *Journal of Management Studies,* 30, 5, 815-834.

Barney, J.B., 1991, Firm resources and sustained competive advantage, *Journal of Management,* 17, 99-120.

Baumol, W.J., 1993, *Entrepreneurship, Management and the Structure of Pay-offs,* Cambridge, MA: MIT Press.

Becher, T., 1989, *Academic tribes and territories. Intellectual enquiry and the cultures of disciplines,* Milton Keynes: Open University Press.

Bettis, R.A. & Hitt, M.A., 1995, The new competitive landscape, *Strategic Management Journal,* 16, 7-19.

Birch, D.L., 1979, *The Job Generation Process,* MIT Program on Neighborhood and Regional Change, Cambridge, MA.

Birley, S., 1985, The role of networks in the entrepreneurial process, *Journal of Business Venturing,* 1, 1, 107-118.

Bjerke, B. & Hultman, C.M., 2002, *Entrepreneurial Marketing,* Cheltenham: Edward Elgar.

Brazeal, D. & Herbert, T., 1989, The genesis of entrepreneurship, *Entrepreneurship Theory and Practice,* 23, 3, 29-45.

Brock, W.A. & Evans, D.S., 1986, *The Economics of Small Business: Their Role and Regulation in the US Economy,* New York: Holmes and Meier.

Brockhaus, R., 1980, Risk taking propensity of entrepreneurs, *Academy of Management Journal,* 23, 3, 509-520.

Brockhaus, R., 1982, The psychology of the entrepreneur, in Kent, C.A. & Sexton, D.L. & Vesper, K.H. (eds.), 1982, *Encyclopedia of Entrepreneurship,* Englewood Cliffs, NJ: Prentice-Hall, 39-57.

Brockhaus, R., 1988, Entrepreneurship research: Are we playing the correct game?, *American Journal of Small Business,* Winter, 55-61.

Brüderl, J. & Preisendorfer, P. & Ziegler, R., 1992, Survival chances of newly founded business organizations, *American Sociological Review,* 57, 2, 227-242.

Brush, C.G. & VanderWerf, P.A., 1992, A comparison of methods and sources for obtaining estimates of new venture performance, *Journal of Business Venturing*, 7, 2, 157-170.

Bull, I. & Willard, G.E., 1993, Towards a theory of entrepreneurship, *Journal of Business Venturing*, 8, 183-195.

Burgelman, R.A., 1983, A process model of internal corporate venturing in the diversified major firm, *Administrative Science Quarterly*, 28, 223-244.

Busenitz, L.W. & Page West, G. & Shepherd, D. & Nelson, T. & Chandler, G.N. & Zackarakis, A., 2003, Entrepreneurship in Emergence: Past Trends and Future Directions, *Journal of Management*, 29, 3, 285-308.

Bygrave, W.D., 1989, The entrepreneurship paradigm, *Entrepreneurship Theory and Practice*, 14, 8, 7-26.

Bygrave, W.D. & Hofer, C.W., 1991, Theorizing about Entrepreneurship, *Entrepreneurship Theory and Practice*, Winter, 13-22.

Bygrave, W.D. & Timmons, J.A., 1992, *Venture Capital at the Crossroad*, Boston, MA: Harvard Business School Press.

Carsrud, A.L. & Olm, K.W. & Eddy, G.G., 1986, Entrepreneurship: Research in Quest of a Paradigm, in Sexton, D.L. & Smilor, R. (eds.), 1986, *The Art and Science of Entrepreneurship*, Cambridge, MA: Ballinger, 367-378.

Chandler, G.N. & Lyon, D.W., 2001, Issues of Research Design and Construct Measurement in Entrepreneurship Research: Past Decade, *Entrepreneurship Theory and Practice*, 25, 4, 101- 113.

Churchill, N.C., 1992, Research Issues in Entrepreneurship, in Sexton, D.L. & Kasarda, J.D. (eds.), *The State of the Art of Entrepreneurship*, Boston, MA: PWS-Kent Publishers, 579-596

Churchill, N.C. & Lewis, V.L., 1986, Entrepreneurship Research: Directions and Methods, in Sexton, D.L. & Smilor, R. (eds.), *The Art and Science of Entrepreneurship*, Cambridge, MA: Ballinger, 333-365.

Collins, O. & Moore, D. & Unwalla, D.B., 1964, *The Enterprising Man*, East Lansing: Michigan State University.

Cooper, A.C., 2003, Entrepreneurship: The Past, the Present, the Future, in Acs, Z.J. & Audretsch, D.B. (eds.), *Handbook of Entrepreneurship Research*, Dordrecht: Klüwer, 21-34.

Cooper, A.C. & Hornaday, J.A. & Vesper, K.H., 1997, The field of entrepreneurship over time, Frontiers of Entrepreneurship Research, xi-xvii.

Crane, D., 1972, *Invisible colleges. Diffusion of knowledge in scientific communities*, Chicago: University of Chicago Press.

Davidsson, P., 2003, The Domain of Entrepreneurship Research: Some Suggestions, in Katz, J. & Shepherd, D. (eds.), *Advances in Entrepreneurship, Firm Emergence and Growth*, Vol 6, Greenwich, CT: JAI Press.

Davidsson, P. & Low, M.B. & Wright, M., 2001, Editor's Introduction: Low and MacMillan Ten Years On: Achievements and Future Directions for Entrepreneurship Research, *Entrepreneurship Theory and Practice*, 25, 4, 5-15.

Davidsson, P. & Wiklund, J., 2001, Levels of Analysis in Entrepreneurship Research: Current Research Practice and Suggestions for the Future, *Entrepreneurship Theory and Practice*, 25, 4, 81-99.

Fast, N., 1978, *The Rise and Fall of Corporate New Venture Decisions*, Ann Arbor, MI: UMI Research Press.

Finkle, T.A. & Deeds, D., 2001, Trends in the market for entrepreneurship faculty, 1989-1998, *Journal of Business Venturing*, 16, 613-630.

Gartner, W.B., 1985, A conceptual framework for describing the phenomenon of new venture creation, *Academy of Management Review*, 10, 696-706.

Gartner, W.B., 1988, "Who Is an Entrepreneur?" Is the Wrong Question, *American Journal of Small Business*, Spring, 11-32.

Gartner, W.B., 1990, What are we talking about when we talk about entrepreneurship, *Journal of Business Venturing*, 5, 1, 15-29.

Gartner, W.B., 1993, Words Lead to Deeds: Towards an Organizational Emergence Vocabulary, *Journal of Business Venturing*, 8, 231-239.

Gimeno, J. & Folta, T. & Cooper, A. & Woo, C., 1997, Survival of the fittest? Entrepreneurial human capital and the persistence of underperforming firms, *Administrative Science Quarterly*, 42, 4, 750-783.

Gorman, M. & Sahlman, W.A., 1989, What do venture capitalists do?, *Journal of Business Venturing*, 4, 231-248.

Grégoire, D. & Déry, R. & Béchard, J-P., 2001, Evolving Conversations: A look at the Convergence in Entrepreneurship Research, paper at the Babson Kauffman Entrepreneurship Research Conference, Jönköping, Sweden, June.

Grégoire, D. & Meyer, G.D. & DeCastro, J.O., 2002, The crystallization of entrepreneurship research dvs and methods in mainstream management journals, paper at the Babson Kauffman Entrepreneurship Research Conference, Boulder, Colorado, 6-8 June.

Hébert, R.F. & Link, A.N., 1982, *The Entrepreneur*, New York: Praeger.

Herron, L. & Sapienza, H.J. & Smith-Cook, D., 1992, Entrepreneurship Theory from an Interdisciplinary Perspectie, *Entrepreneurship Theory and Practice*, 16, 3, 5-11.

Hitt, M.A. & Ireland, R.D. & Camp, S.M. & Sexton, D.L., 2002, *Strategic Entrepreneurship*, Oxford, UK: Blackwell.

Hitt, M.A. & Reed, T.S., 2000, Entrepreneurship in the new competitive landscape, in Meyer, G.D. & Heppard, K.A. (eds.), *Entrepreneurship as Strategy*, Thousand Oaks, CA: Sage, 23-47.

Johannisson, B., 1994, On the status of entrepreneurship and small-business research. Strategies for enhanced legitimacy, paper at the 8th Nordic Conference on Small Business Research, Halmstad University, Sweden, June.

Kanter, R.M., 1983, *Change Masters*, New York: Simon and Schuster.

Katz, J.A., 2003, The chronology and intellectual trajectory of American entrepreneurship education, 1876-1999, *Journal of Business Venturing*, 18, 283-300.

Kent, C.A. & Sexton, D.L. & Vesper, K.H. (eds.), 1982, *Encyclopedia of Entrepreneurship*, Englewood Cliffs, NJ: Prentice-Hall

Kuhn, T.S., 1962/1996, *The Structure of Scientific Revolutions*, Chicago: Chicago University Press.

Landström, H., 2000, *Entreprenörskapets rötter*, Lund: Studentlitteratur.

Landström, H., 2001, Who Loves Entrepreneurship Research: Knowledge Accumulation Within a Transient Field of Research, paper at the XV RENT Conference, Turku, Finland, 22-23 November.

Landström, H. & Frank, H. & Veciana, J.M. (eds.), 1997, *Entrepreneurship and small business research in Europe*, Aldershot, UK: Avebury.

Landström, H. & Johannisson, B., 2001, Theoretical foundations of Swedish entrepreneurship and small-business research, *Scandinavian Journal of Management*, 17, 225-248.

Larson, A., 1992, Network Dyads in Entrepreneurial Settings: A Study of the Governance of Exchange Relationships, *Administrative Science Quarterly*, 37, 76-104.

Liles, P.R., 1974, Who Are the Entrepreneur?, *MSU Business Topics*, Winter, 5-14.

Low, M.B., 2001, The Adolescence of Entrepreneurship Research: Specification of Purpose, *Entrepreneurship Theory and Practice*, 25, 4, 17-25.

Low, M.B. & MacMillan, I.C., 1988, Entrepreneurship: Past Research and Future Challenges, *Journal of Management*, 14, 2, 139-161.

MacMillan, I.C. & Siegel, R. & SubbaNarishma, P.N., 1985, Criteria used by venture capitalists to evaluate new venture proposals, *Journal of Business Venturing*, 1, 1, 61-74.

March, J.G., 1991, Exploration and Exploitation in Organizational Learning, *Organization Science*, 2, 1, 71-87.

March, J.G., 1999, *The Pursuit of Organizational Intelligence*, Oxford: Blackwell.

Mayer, K.B. & Goldstein, S., 1961, *The First Two years: Problems of Small Firms Growth and Survival*, Washington DC: H.S. Government Printing Office.

McClelland, D.C., 1961, *The Achieving Society*, Princeton, NJ: van Nostrand.

McGrath, R.G. & MacMillan, I.C., 2000, *The Entrepreneurial Mindset*, Boston, MA: Harvard Business School Press.

Meyer, G.D. & Heppard, K.A., 2000, *Entrepreneurship as Strategy*, Thousand Oaks, CA: Sage.

Miles, R.E. & Snow, C.C., 1978, *Organizational Strategy, Structure and Process*, New York: MacGraw-Hill.

Penrose, E.T., 1959, *The theory of the growth of the firm*, Oxford: Blackwell.

Pfeffer, J. & Salancik, G.R., 1978, *The external control of organizations*, New York: Harper & Row.

Piore, M.J. & Sabel, C.F., 1984, *The Second Industrial Divide. Possibilities for Prosperity*, New York: Basic Books.

Porter, M.E., 1980, *Competitive Strategy*, New York: John Wiley.

Reader, D. & Watkins, D., 2001, The intellectual structure of entrepreneurship: an author co-citation analysis, paper at the XV RENT Conference, Turku, Finland, 22-23 November.

Regional Studies, 1994, Special issue: Regional Variations in New firm Formation, 28, 4.

Sahlman, W.A., 1992, Aspects of financial contracting in venture capital, in Sahlman, W.A. & Stevenson, H.H. (eds.), *The Entrepreneurial Venture*, Boston, MA: Harvard Business School Publications, 222-242.

Sandberg, W.R. & Hofer, C.W., 1986, The effects of strategy and industrial structure of new venture performance, Frontiers of Entrepreneurship Research, Wellesley, MA: Babson College.

Sandberg, W.R. & Hofer, C.W., 1987, Improving new venture performance: The role of strategy, industry, structure, and the entrepreneur, *Journal of Business Venturing*, 2, 5-28.

Sapienza, H.J., 1992, When do venture capitalists add value?, *Journal of Business Venturing*, 7, 9-27.

Sarasvathy, S., 1999, *How do firm come to be?: Towards a theory of the prefirm*, PhD Thesis, Pittsburgh, PA: Carnegie Mellon University.

Sexton, D.L. & Kasarda, J.D. (eds.), 1992, *The State of the Art of Entrepreneurship*, Boston, MA: PWS-Kent Publishers.

Sexton, D.L. & Landström, H. (eds.), 2000, *The Blackwell Handbook of Entrepreneurship*, Oxford: Blackwell.

Sexton, D.L. & Smilor, R. (eds.), 1986, *The Art and Science of Entrepreneurship*, Cambridge, MA: Ballinger.

Sexton, D.L. & Smilor, R.W. (eds.), 1997, *Entrepreneurship 2000*, Chicago, IL: Upstart.

Shane, S. & Venkataraman, S., 2000, The promise of entrepreneurship as a field of research, *Academy of Management Review*, 25, 217-221.

Shapero, A., 1975, The Displaced Unconfortable Entrepreneur, *Psychology Today*, 9, 83-88.

Shapero, A. & Sokol, L., 1982, The social dimensions of entrepreneurship, in Kent, C.A. & Sexton, D.L. & Vesper, K.H. (eds.), *Encyclopedia of Entrepreneurship*, Englewood Cliffs, NJ: Prentice-Hall, 72-90.

Swedberg, R. (ed.), 2000, *Entrepreneurship. The Social Science View*, Oxford: Oxford University Press.

Tyebjee, T.T. & Bruno, A.V., 1984, A Model of Venture Capitalist Investment Activity, *Management Science*, 30, 9, 1051-1066.

VanderWerf, P.A. & Brush, C.G., 1989, Achieving Progress in an Undefined Field, *Entrepreneurship Theory and Practice*, Winter, 45-58.

Vesper, K.H., 1982, Research on education for entrepreneurship, in Kent, C.A. & Sexton, D.L. & Vesper, K.H. (eds.), *Encyclopedia of Entrepreneurship*, Englewood Cliffs, NJ.: Prentice-Hall.

Vesper, K.H., 1980, *New Venture Strategies*, Englewood Cliffs, NJ: Prentice Hall.

Welsch, H.P. & Liao, J., 2003, Strategies for entrepreneurship development: striking a balance between explorative and exploitative research, in Steyaert, C. & Hjorth, D. (eds.), *New Movements in Entrepreneurship*, Cheltenham, UK: Edward Elgar, pp 20-34.

Wernerfelt, B., 1984, A Resource-Based View of the Firm, *Strategic Management Journal*, 5, 171-180.

Whitley, R., 1984, *The intellectual and social organization of the sciences*, Oxford: Oxford University Press.

Williamson, O.E., 1975, *Markets and hierarchies*, New York: Free Press.

Wortman, M.S., 1987, Entrepreneurship: an integrating typology and evaluation of the empirical research in the field, *Journal of Management*, 13, 2, 259-279.

Chapter 4

THE INTERNATIONAL PICTURE

Chapter three presented the development of entrepreneurship and small business research from a mainly US perspective. Compared to Europe, American society is more characterized by entrepreneurial ideology, and the international dissemination of entrepreneurship research has been dominated by US scholars, and therefore it is only natural that many of the works on the history of entrepreneurship and small business research reflect this bias. As a consequence, most of the history of entrepreneurship and small business research has been written by US researchers, for US researchers and about US research – it is an American story. Nevertheless, entrepreneurship and small business research in Europe has a long tradition, and Europe can in many ways be regarded as the birthplace of theoretical entrepreneurship studies (see Chapter 2), although for a long period entrepreneurship was ignored in policy and research. However, in the late 20th century, entrepreneurship and small business re-emerged on the political agenda across Europe, and during the 1980s and especially in the 1990s developed a foothold within European research. Entrepreneurship and small business research is to a great degree international, exhibiting the same positive development in Europe as in other parts of the world – not least in Australia. In this chapter I will therefore first present a description of European entrepreneurship and small business research. This is followed by a section about the development of entrepreneurship and small business research in Australia. Finally, some reflections and comparisons are made regarding the research in Europe, Australia and the US. Recent years have witnessed a trend toward a greater interest in the development of entrepreneurship and small business research in the US as well as in Europe and Australia, and the following review will describe this dynamic development.

The development of entrepreneurship and small business research in different countries can be described in several ways. Since the focus of this book is on research pioneers, the following chapters will consist of a review of the pioneers, their publications as well as events that have influenced the development of the field in the respective countries.

1.   ENTREPRENEURSHIP AND SMALL BUSINESS RESEARCH IN EUROPE

In this section entrepreneurship and small business research in Europe will be presented. This is, however, not entirely easy due to the great heterogeneity of the continent – which has resulted in divergent conditions for entrepreneurship and small businesses, but also very different research traditions between countries. I have therefore opted to describe entrepreneurship research in the various parts of Europe.

1.1   General Characteristics

Entrepreneurship and small business research in Europe has several characteristics (Huse & Landström, 1997; Landström et al., 1997). First, as already stated, Europe is a heterogeneous continent, and entrepreneurship and small business research is characterized by its diversity. There are major differences between countries and regions – there are various contextual settings that influence entrepreneurship and small businesses. Second, "small business" has received more attention than "entrepreneurship". In order to stimulate development in society, European research, and small business policies in Europe are both more controversial and more subject to intensive public attention than in the US. Taken together, this makes the research of contextual differences interesting. Contextual differences not only influence the research topics chosen but are also reflected in the level of analysis – European researchers focus more strongly than their US counterparts on small business and on an aggregate level of analysis, for example, comparing differences and similarities between industries, regions and countries (Landström & Huse, 1996). Third, there is an acceptance of a broader range of methodological approaches among European researchers, which means greater methodological openness, compared to US scholars. European researchers and doctoral students have consequently been trained in a greater range of methodologies than their US counterparts. This methodological openness is reflected in the methods used by European researchers. For example, Landström and Huse (1996) found a stronger tendency among US researchers to use surveys as the main methodological approach and questionnaires as the dominant data collection method, whereas European researchers showed a broader range of methodologies, including a greater number of qualitative approaches. Finally, the diversity of entrepreneurship research in Europe influences not only the methodological approaches used and the topics chosen but is also reflected in the research communities in the various countries. There is a very great variation in research traditions between countries (Hisrich & Drnovsek, 2002) – in terms of not only the size of the research community in each country but also the researchers' disciplinary backgrounds and epistemological concerns.

Due to the great heterogeneity and diversity of the continent, it seems difficult to give an adequate description of entrepreneurship research. However, in order to provide a more nuanced picture of European research, I will present the development of entrepreneurship and small business research in different parts of Europe.

1.2   United Kingdom

In Europe, Great Britain was one of the first countries to be hit by the economic structural changes at the end of the 1960s and early 1970s. The Northern part of England was a region especially affected by these structural changes, along with Wales, Scotland and other older industrial areas, resulting in business closures and a high rate of unemployment. It was this recession that prompted increased political interest in entrepreneurship and the small business sector. Due to their ability to create jobs, which large corporations were unable to provide, small firms were regarded as the answer to the employment problems resulting from structural changes. The growing political interest in small firms on the part of the UK government at this time led the British government to initiate a comprehensive inquiry into the role of small businesses in the economy. The final report, the Bolton report, was presented in 1971 and exerted significant influence on politicians, academics and the media. During the 1970s the political parties developed explicit small business policies and the media devoted more coverage to the small business sector, thus leading to an interest in small business research among academics in the UK.

The Bolton Committee commissioned 18 research reports covering different aspects of small business activities. In the report the conceptual problem of defining small businesses was highlighted, and the Committee established a qualitative conceptualisation of small business, stressing small market share, personalized management, and independence of owner decision-making (Bolton report, 1971, pp. 1-2). But it also emphasized the lack of adequate databases and the statistical problems of quantifying the small business sector. Based on their own calculations, the Committee concluded that the small business sector was in a state of long term decline and that this process seemed to have further advanced in the UK than elsewhere (ibid., p. 342). However, this pessimistic statement is open to question (Curran & Stanworth, 1982). It can be argued that the Bolton Committee was misled by the historical basis upon which the estimations of the decline were made, i.e. the selected period was historically atypical, and the conclusions made of the Bolton report were not actually verified in reality during the 1970s.

The Bolton report led to a great interest among individual UK researchers in the conditions and importance of small businesses. Two pioneers were James Curran and John Stanworth, whose book *Management Motivation in the Smaller Business* (1973) was perhaps the most interesting early contribution on the subject. Curran came from a sociological and Stanworth from an engineering research tradition, and their research was less policy-oriented than that of some more recent contributors. Another key figure was Allan Gibb of University of Durham. Due to his strong links with the north of England with its huge economic problems, company closures and high unemployment, he realized the need for small firms. He wanted to facilitate and stimulate entrepreneurship, and for this reason education and training were key activities in the Small Business Centre at the University of Durham, which Gibb established in the early 1970s. Together with Terry Webb of Ashridge Management College, he was also the instigator of an annual conference (the UK Small Business Policy and Research Conference), which originally attracted some 20 participants annually but which today is one of the largest conferences in Europe with several hundred participants. Among the researchers who presented their findings at the first conference in 1979 were: Michael Scott, Peter Johnson, David Kirby, Patrick Hutchinson, Douglas Donleavy, Tom Cannon and Joan Mitchell (Gibb & Webb, 1979). This annual conference is now in its 27th year with approximately 200 participants from the entrepreneurship and small business research and policy community.

The political agenda in terms of entrepreneurship and small business changed dramatically in the early 1980s when Margaret Thatcher came to power (1979). Thatcher had an ideological view of entrepreneurship and small businesses and initiated a large number of measures in order to change the mentality of the people in the UK – creating an entrepreneurial culture – including privatizations, deregulation, a new tax regime, and a large number of new instruments to stimulate new and small businesses. Entrepreneurship and competition were two central concepts in this policy, concepts which also influenced academia. The universities were expected to be increasingly self supporting, which led to increased competition between them. As a consequence, the research became more empirical and concentrated on areas that were likely to create revenue for the university in question – contract research offered one of few mechanisms for obtaining research funds in a situation where core research funding were extremely limited. At the same time, many education programs focussing on entrepreneurship and small business management were established at different universities, several of which emphasized training and education for small business managers (for example in Durham and Stirling). Thus, Thatcher had a very broad approach to entrepreneurship – it was a question of changing the minds of people – and she was very influential in this regard.

Small business research in the UK increased during the 1980s – the research field became established at various universities and new researchers became interested in the field. These researchers had a background in different social science disciplines – it was not only economists like David Storey but also researchers with a background in sociology (James Curran), psychologists such as Elisabeth Chell, management researchers (Sue Birley, David Kirby, and Allan Gibb) and economic geographers (Colin Mason) – a fact that has contributed to the multi character of UK research today.

At the end of the 1980s the UK Economics and Social Science Research Council (ESRC), in collaboration with private sector businesses and some government bodies, initiated a comprehensive small business research program (the ESRC Small Business Initiative) – an initiative which could be regarded as a real milestone and put small business research on the map. David Storey was appointed program coordinator. The ESRC Initiative focussed on four areas: (i) the economic role of small firms within a national and international context, (ii) local labor markets and small firms, (iii) structural and organizational issues, and (iv) determinants of the birth, survival and growth of small firms. A large number of projects were undertaken and three research centers were established (Kingston, Cambridge and Sussex universities). Storey decided to select several well known researchers who were not regarded as small business researchers, which afforded the program a diversity of interest, a multidisciplinary character, and ensured high quality research. The studies performed as part of the program were all very carefully designed with interesting analyses that have contributed a variety of new knowledge to the research in this field. Storey's book *Understanding the Small Business Sector* (1994) provides one of the most prominent summaries and syntheses of the knowledge generated by the program. The book can be regarded as a standard work in the field – but interesting summaries can also be found in the books co-edited by Storey *Finance and the Small Firm* (together with Allan Hughes), *Employment, the Small Firm and the Labour Market* (together with John Atkinson), and *Small Firms in Urban and Rural Locations* (together with James Curran) – books that constitute central sources of knowledge for small business researchers.

In the 1990s the interest changed toward growth oriented established businesses. Unlike Thatcher's extensive reforms at all levels, Tony Blair's approach was much more targeted, especially his strong focus on technology-based firms, but also more socially inclusive with entrepreneurship being seen as one way of revitalizing deprived areas. Government has also started to listen to the researchers to a greater extent – it finances the majority of externally funded small business research and thereby largely determines which research areas are to be covered. The significant amount of research funding from government departments also explains the strong empirical basis and policy orientation of small business research in the UK.

Research funding also influences small business research in the UK in another way. The universities are ranked on a five-year basis by a panel largely consisting of "mainstream researchers". This forces university based researchers to publish in highly rated, mostly main stream business and management journals. This has had two effects: a focus on quantitative methodological approaches that can generate many articles and lead to publication in mainstream journals – which, in most cases, are not read by other small business researchers. Furthermore, small business researchers have found it hard to gain recognition in these national evaluations, resulting in difficulties obtaining long-term "core money" and having to rely on "earned money" from government departments or private companies instead. Naturally, this makes long-term systematic research very difficult, contributing to the fragmentation of research and its agenda is only partly determined by the researchers themselves.

The 1990s witnessed the consolidation of small business research in the UK (the development of a community of researchers and the establishment of several institutions focusing on small business, etc. – the three leading centers during the 1990s were Warwick, Cambridge, and Kingston) while at the same time there is diversity and disparity. Today, small business research in the UK is characterized by:

– An increased interest in entrepreneurship.
– A large community of researchers – today we can find about 150 researchers and 70-80 PhD candidates with an interest in small business (or entrepreneurship), but at the same time the researcher community is rather fragmented – it is difficult to identify specific "schools of thought" within small business research in the UK.
– Extensive government research funding (commissioned research) and researchers that are successful in the search for external research funds.
– Empirical and policy-oriented research – with many researchers basing their work on a policy-agenda rather than on a scientific agenda (but an increased development toward more "theoretical" contributions).
– A clear division between research and education at universities.

1.3   Nordic Countries

The Nordic countries (Denmark, Finland, Norway and Sweden) have, despite their geographic proximity, quite different traditions of entrepreneurship and small business research and must therefore be treated separately (see e.g. Johannisson & Landström, 1997, Landström

& Johannisson, 2001; Spilling, 1997; Christensen & Axelsson, 1997, Malinen & Paasio, 1997).

In *Sweden* research in the area of entrepreneurship and small business is similar to international trends – indicating a steady increase in research since the early 1970s. Before the 1970s there were few studies conducted on entrepreneurship and small business, with the exception of a study by Axel Iveroth in 1943 *Småindustri och hantverk i Sverige* (The small business sector and craft industries in Sweden) and in particular Erik Dahmén's seminal work in 1950 *Svensk industriell företagsverksamhet* (Industrial activities in Sweden). However, it was not until the late 1960s that the interest in entrepreneurship and small business research re-emerged in Sweden – originating in the discipline of business administration. It was at the newly established Umeå University, in the Northern part of the country, that entrepreneurship and small business research was initiated, under Dick Ramström. The research was primarily directed toward describing the small firm structure in Sweden as well as their special needs, problems and advantages – it was a matter of trying to draw attention to and make small business visible – and it was small businesses, not entrepreneurship, that became the focus of the research.

During the recession in the Swedish economy in the 1970s, great hopes were pinned on small businesses, with the ensuing call for more knowledge about the sector. Research was, however, limited to a small number of researchers, in several cases with their roots at Umeå University. Bengt Johannisson became the leading exponent of entrepreneurship and small business research in Sweden. The research began to specialize in studies of networks and local entrepreneurial cultures. At the end of the decade there was a concentration of entrepreneurship research in two universities, Umeå and Växjö.

In the 1980s the state made considerable efforts to stimulate the small business sector, and throughout the decade there was a vigorous increase in entrepreneurship and small business research. Researchers attempted, in as far as possible, to link knowledge to concepts and models within the area of business adminstration, which resulted in the limited influence of other disciplines. The growth of research was characterized by (i) the spread of research to many universities throughout the country – a geographic diffusion of the research, (ii) a change as regards the object of study – from the traditional family business to new types of small firms, such as technology-based firms and fast-growing businesses, and (iii) although the research was rooted in the discipline of business administration, at this time it began to mould an identity of its own – the researchers began to regard themselves as specialists in entrepreneurship and small business. This process culminated in 1989 with the establishment of the first chair of "entrepreneurship and business development" at Lund University/Växjö University with Bengt Johannisson as the first incumbent.

During the 1990s entrepreneurship and small business research has been consolidated into an independent research field – a consolidation that includes at least two elements: the creation of more chairs at various universities in Sweden and the establishment of research centers both in collaboration between different universities (e.g. the Swedish Foundation for Small Business Research) and at individual universities such as Jönköping International Business School and the Stockholm School of Economics. This has resulted in several strong research environments and, by the late 1990s and early 2000s, Swedish entrepreneurship and small business research was internationally competitive (measured by the number of publications, awards at international conferences, etc.) – not least due to the research of Per Davidsson (Jönköping International Business School) and Johan Wiklund and Frederick Delmar at Stockholm School of Economics.

Among the Scandinavian countries only *Finland* shows a similar development to that of Sweden within the area of entrepreneurship and small business, and it is primarily since the mid 1980s that the research and education in this subject area have been greatly intensified. The first chair was established in 1984 at the Helsinki School of Economics and Business Administration with Veikko Leivo as the first incumbent, a position that was later taken over by Arto Lahti (1990). Early contributions to Finnish entrepreneurial and small business research were also made by Antti Paasio at the Turku School of Economics and Business Adminstration and Asko Miettinen at Tampere University of Technology. Today almost every university in Finland has a full or associate professorship in entrepreneurship – indicating that the number of chairs and researchers is relatively large in Finland, but also implies a fragmentation of the research despite the fact that a number of centers conducting more systematic research within the field have emerged.

The first thesis, *Företagsledning och motivation* (Management and motivation), was published as long ago as 1965 by Sven E. Kock and explored the relationship between the need for achievement and firm growth. However, it was not until the 1980s that entrepreneurship and small business research and teaching gained impetus with the creation of a number of chairs at various universities throughout Finland. Since the 1980s the number of theses increased dramatically, and by the end of the 1990s some 30 theses emerged within the area. At the same time Finnish entrepreneurship research has gained more international visibility and recognition, not least through the research of Erkko Autio and his colleagues at the Helsinki University of Technology.

In conclusion, Finland today has a large infrastructure in the area of entrepreneurship and small business research, as evident from the fairly large number of chairs and researchers within the field, and the soaring number of dissertations, but also a fragmentation and lack of long-term systematic research within the field.

Similar to the other Scandinavian countries, interest in the area of entrepreneurship and small business in *Norway* first appeared on the political agenda in the 1970s when the Norwegian government released a white paper on small business (Stortingsmelding nr 22, 1977-78, *Små og mellomstore industri bedrifter* [Norwegian Government White Paper on "Small and Medium-sized Manufacturing Firms"]). Looking at the history of entrepreneurship and small business research in Norway (the description is mainly based on Spilling, 1997) it can be concluded that, with a few exceptions, there was hardly any interest in the phenomenon of entrepreneurship and small business before the 1970s on the part of Norwegian researchers. One exception is the work of the economist F. Wedervang on *Development of a population of industrial firms* (1964), which covers the development of Norwegian manufacturing industries in the period from 1930 to 1948. The second exception is the work by the social anthropologist Fredrik Barth, who in his book *The Role of the Entrepreneur in Social Change in Northern Norway* (1963) analysed a small community in Northern Norway and discussed the "role" of the entrepreneur. However, it was not until the late 1970s that we could find an emerging interest in entrepreneurship and small business among researchers.

Since the 1980s entrepreneurship and small business have been on the agenda in several universities, but the efforts within the field have been uncoordinated and unsystematic. However, during the 1990s, Bodø Graduate School of Business in Bodø in the northern part of the country and Trondheim University of Technology have turned out to be the leading exponents of entrepreneurship and small business research, and we can find a more systematic form of entrepreneurship and small business research at these two universities. Under the direction of Lars Kolvereid, the business school in Bodø was the first to offer graduate courses in entrepreneurship in 1986, a master program was introduced in 1995, and a PhD program started in the early 2000s. The University of Technology in Trondheim has for many years offered the main engineering education in Norway, and students can specialize in innovation, entrepreneurship and small business management. Trondheim is also by far the most important university in terms of doctoral dissertations on entrepreneurship and small business in Norway. The first thesis, and the only one during the 1980s from a Norwegian university was Åge Garnes' thesis: *Etableringslyst? En undersøkning av ungdom i teknisk utdanningssituasjon om planer for og ønskje om oppstart av eiga bedrift* (Start-up interest among young people involved in technology studies) in 1982. It should however be born in mind that doctorates in management studies were introduced at a relatively late stage in Norway, which meant that many doctoral candidates had to sit their doctoral exam abroad.

During the 1990s entrepreneurship and small business research has grown significantly. Apart from the research groups in Bodø and

Trondheim, research on entrepreneurship and small business has been scarce and fragmented, although there is evidence of emerging interest in the field at, for example, the Norwegian School of Management in Oslo and also at other universities – although ususally the research only involved one or a few researchers. In addition, we can find few chairs in Norway dedicated specifically to entrepreneurship and/or small business research – the first chair was established at Bodø Graduate School of Business in 1986 with Sigmund Waagø as the first incumbent.

A key feature of the industrial structure in *Denmark* is the lack of large corporations. As a consequence, it has proved difficult to distinguish entrepreneurship and small business research from management studies in general. This has also resulted in the fact that there are few research centers dedicated to entrepreneurship and small business research, the research community is fragmented and dominated by researchers with many years experience of entrepreneurship and small business research, for example, Mette Mønsted and Poul Rind Christensen to name two of the best known within the field. Traditionally, governmental and regional institutions have also assumed responsibility for counselling and research, even if the importance of these institutions has gradually declined in line with the increasing importance of academic research. The first dedicated chair in entrepreneurship was not established until 1997 at Aalborg University with Urs Gattiger as the first incumbent.

Due to the fact that small businesses are extremely important for the Danish economy and that research is well-integrated within management studies, studies on small business emerged relatively early. In his book *Haandbog i Handelsvidenskap* (Handbook of Business Science) in 1894/1926, Christopher Hage discussed the role of small firms in Denmark, arguing that, due to economies of scale, small firms could only survive in sectors of the economy devoted to domestic consumption (e.g. construction, retailing, and crafts) and not in sectors exposed to international competition. The interest in the role of small firms in the economy remained low, and the first contribution after the Second World War was the work by Michael Bruun, Per Sørensen and Niels Ravn *Iværksætterundersøgelsen* (Investigation on start-ups) in 1978, which was a regional analys of Aarhus county in Denmark, in which they claimed that entrepreneurial activity and new business formation was to be found in the early and declining phases of a product life cycle. At the same time a couple of other studies emerged which indicated intensified activity in the area of small business research in Denmark. Several quantitative studies were presented, which focussed on the number of entrepreneurs and their socioeconomic importance. In the mid 1970s a regional theme was introduced, a theme that received more attention during the 1980s. Other themes of interest in entrepreneurship and small business research in Denmark during the 1980s were related to small businesses and their networks as well as the internationalization of small businesses, and a few significant contributions were made on the entrepreneur as an individual and his/her lifestyle.

Interest in entrepreneurship and the importance of the small business sector grew in the late 1980s and early 1990s, inspired by the high priority of entrepreneurship and business establishment on the political agenda. The mid 1990s witnessed a shift in Danish small business policy. Having formed an important part of job creation and social policy in terms of assisting unemployed people to start their own busineeses, interest in entrepreneurship changed due to the increasing political focus on renewal and dynamics in trade and industry, leading to increased interest in new innovative activities. The political shift was also related to the academic interest in entrepreneurship, and the Center for Innovation and Entrepreneurship (CIE) at Copenhagen Business School hereby acquired a prominent role. Active at the center were Mette Mønsted, Henrik Herlau and Helge Tetzchner (later professor in Esbjerg) – all with a genuine and long established interest in entrepreneurship and small business.

The linkage between knowledge development in entrepreneurship and the development of industry and trade has continued. For example, much of entrepreneurship research has been financed by government ministries and the academic interest in entrepreneurship and small business has continued. At the Copenhagen Business School, research has been channeled to the Department of Management, Philosophy and Politics, where the interest has been broadened and today involves several different research themes. Other strong research environments are University of Southern Denmark (Campus Kolding and Esbjerg) with the Center for småvirksomhedsforskning (CESFO), the exponents of which are Poul Rind Christensen and Torben Bager. Entrepreneurship and small business research has expanded in Denmark and today also encompasses for example the Aarhus School of Business and the University of Aalborg.

1.4 Central Europe

In the German speaking countries there is a long tradition of entrepreneurship research dating back to the early Schumpeterian theory of economic development. However, it is not pure entrepreneurship that has been the main characteristic of the German speaking countries but the dominance of small firms, especially in craft, retail and service businesses. Furthermore, the small business sector is based on strong members' associations, for example, in Austria the obligatory membership of every firm (even the smallest one) in regional and federal associations, which together form the Austrian Economic Chamber, and craftsmanship exams, which must be passed before one can start a business.

Naturally this structure has an impact on research, not only in terms of a strong focus on small businesses but also on the way of organizing research. After the First World War, initiatives were taken to improve the management of craft businesses, culminating in the founding of the Deutsches Handwerksinstitut in Karlsruhe in 1919 (an organization that still exists as an umbrella organization for seven autonomous institutes). Over the years, a number of research institutes have been established aimed at developing management practice and knowledge, mainly connected to different sectors of industry. Thus, there is extensive research on the small business sector conducted outside the academic setting, but in many cases with some form of link with the universities. The relationship between the Universities and the Institutes can be characterized by a division of labor, with the Institutes focussing on continuous observations of the sector and applied research, mainly on aggregate levels of analysis, whereas the Universities concentrate more on basic research.

This early interest in small business resulted in, among other things, the establishment of a chair of small business management at the Vienna Business School (Hochschule für Welthandel), today Vienna University of Economics and Business Administration, as early as 1936, with W. Bouffier as the first incumbent – probably the first small business chair in Europe or anywhere in the world. However, the activities were brought to a halt by the Nazi regime two years later, and even if there seems to have been an interim incumbent for some years during the War, the chair was not re-established until 1956 with E. Hruschka as professor from 1957 to 1980 and Josef Mugler since 1982.

There was also an early interest in small business research in Switzerland after the Second World War. This interest can mainly be linked to the personal initiatives of Alfred Gutersohn, who was an honorary professor at the University of St Gallen. With strong support from the Swiss small business community, he established the Swiss Research Institute for Small Business and Entrepreneurship at the University of St Gallen at the end of the 1940s. He also started to invite researchers from the field of small business to participate in an exchange of ideas, and together with W. Heinrich from Austria and K. Rössle from Germany he organized the first "Rencontres de St-Gall" in 1948 – probably the first conference on small business in the world. Even if the topical focus of the "Rencontres de St-Gall" conference has varied over the years as well as becoming more international in terms of its participants (Schmidt, 2002), it has retained its original structure of an intensive workshop with a selected and strictly limited number of delegates.

Since the start of "Rencontres de St-Gall", German speaking researchers have been very active over the years in the organization of small business and entrepreneurship research in Europe. The following are examples of researchers that deserve to be mentioned:

- Hans Jobst Pleitner, Switzerland, for many years director of the Swiss Research Institute at the University of St Gallen and former organizer of the Rencontres de St-Gall.
- Josef Mugler, Austria, initiator and first president of the European Council for Small Business (ECSB) in 1988, who has organized many international conferences, such as the Second RENT Conference in 1988, the ICSB World Conference in 1991, the IntEnt Conference in 1993, etc.
- Heinz Klandt, Germany, who has been responsible for the Internationalizing Entrepreneurship Education and Training (IntEnt) conference – since 1992 – which focusses on academic entrepreneurship education – as well as initiator of the so called G-Forum, specializing in entrepreneurship research in the German speaking area (since 1997).

In conclusion, the bulk of research within the German speaking countries has, due to the industrial structure and business culture, been focussed on small businesses and to a lesser extent on entrepreneurship. However, for a long time there have been individual initiatives aimed at highlighting entrepreneurship research. For example, in 1951, the new rector of the Vienna Business School, Karl Oberparleiter, held an inaugration address entitled "Das Unternehmer-Problem" (Problems of Entrepreneurship) and his message was that it was necessary to increase the level of entrepreneurship in society and deal with the specific problems encountered by the entrepreneur. Another individual contribution was the book by Michael Hofmann "*Das unternehmerische Element in der Betriebswirtschaft*" (The Entrepreneurial Element in Business Administration), 1968, in which he makes an analysis of the contributions of economics to the field of entrepreneurship. But these and other early initiatives did not lead to a stronger movement to establish entrepreneurship at German speaking universities.

However, a number of other initiatives proved to be of greater importance. For example the development which took place at the University of Cologne at the end of the 1970s, initiated by Norbert Szyperski and his assistants Klaus Nathusius, Detlef Müller-Böling, and Heinz Klandt, and at the Research Institute for Small and Medium-sized Businesses (Institut für Mittelstandsforschung) in Bonn, headed by Horst Albach from 1983 to 1987, inspired an increased interest in entrepreneurship research, an interest that found expression in, among other things, the seminal work by Szyperski and Nathusius *Probleme der Unternehmensgründung: Eine betriebswirtschaftliche Analyse Unternehmerischer Startbedingungen* (Problems of Start-ups: An Analysis of Start-up Conditions from the Perspective of Business Administration) (1977), in which the authors considered the problems of start ups as a complex phenomenon that cannot be ignored in view of the importance of entrepreneurship for structural change and job creation. Albach was a well recognized professor of business adminstration, who for a couple of years was chairman of the Research Institute for Small and Medium-sized Businesses, in which position he initiated a number of studies on small businesses as well as on entrepreneurship. Heinz Klandt later published his PhD thesis *Aktivität und Erfolg des Unternehmensgründers: Eine empirische Analyse unter Einbeziehung des mikrosozialen Umfeldes* (Start-up Ventures and the Success of the Entrepreneur: An Empirical Investigation Including the Micro-social Environment) (1984), in which he focussed on the founder and his/her environment. The thesis is one of the most cited publications in entrepreneurship within the German speaking research community. Klandt, Müller-Böling, Nathusius and Szyperski were also among the founders of the Förderkreis Gründungs-Forschung 1987, an organization whose mission is to stimulate and build an infrastructure for entrepreneurship research and education in the German speaking countires, by means of, among other things, lobbying, the building of a literature database (ELIDA), organizing conferences, etc.

Some years later a group of entrepreneurship researchers (Hermann Frank, Gerhard Plaschka and Dietmar Rössl) also emerged at the Vienna University of Economics and Business Adminstration, headed by Josef Mugler. In this connection Gerhard Plaschka's PhD thesis in 1986 *Unternehmenserfolg: Eine vergleichende empirische Untersuchung von erfolgreichen und nicht erfolgreichen Unternehmensgründern* (Business Success: A Comparison Based on Empirical Data between Successful and Unsuccessful Entrepreneurs), in which he compared successful and failed start ups in Austria, deserves to be mentioned. This thesis was one of the first to consider start up processes in a more comprehensive way.

A seminal work that ought to be mentioned in this context is the book by Joseph Brüderl, Peter Preisendörfer and Rolf Ziegler *Der Erfolg neugegründeter Betriebe. Eine Studie zu Chancen und Risken von Unternehmensgründungen* (The Success of Start-ups: An Investigation into the Opportunities and Risk of Start-ups) in 1996. The authors were sociologists from the University of Munich, and their contribution has been published in international journals including the *American Sociological Review* (the article: Survival chances of new founded business organizations, 1992). Their contribution may be one of the most internationally cited works by German speaking entrepreneurship researchers.

Hence, it can be seen that entrepreneurship elicited little response from German speaking researchers. The reasons for this are of course many and complex and we can only speculate as to some of them:
- The German speaking countries have to a great extent been characterized by a strong small business sector dominated by many craft businesses – a sector of industry that traditionally has not been seen as very innovative and dynamic.
- The consequences of two world wars, which necessitated huge efforts to reconstruct a destroyed economy. This task of reconstruction

called for planning and distribution of scarce resources in which the government and political institutions had to play an important role – there was no time for innovations and entrepreneurship.

- The German speaking countries have a long tradition of business administration (Betriebswirtschaftslehre) – before the Second World War, Germany was the leading country in Europe within the field, and the first Handelshochschulen were founded there (Leipzig in 1898, in the same year: Vienna (Austria) and St.Gall (Switzerland), and Cologne in 1901) – with a strong own identity. In addition, the academic organizations have, to a large extent, a very conservative structure (strong hierarchical structures, scientific journals in German, etc.), which means that changes within the discipline are very slow.

It was not until the latter half of the 1990s that interest in entrepreneurship research increased dramatically. At the end of the 1990s the time was ripe: a public awareness existed – politicians and policy-makers were aware of the importance of entrepreneurship (for example, the German economy began to slow down), there was an increased awareness of the development of entrepreneurship in other European countries, and the media started to discuss entrepreneurship. Even if some attempts were made to establish chairs in entrepreneurship in the early 1990s, for example at the University of Dortmund in Germany, it was not until 1997 that the first chair of entrepreneurship was established at the European Business School at the University of Schloss Reichartshausen in Germany (with Heinz Klandt as the first incumbent). Since then, around 50 additional endowed chairs have been established in the German speaking countries, most of them in Germany (Klandt, 2003).

In this regard Heinz Klandt deserves mention, in view of his valuable efforts to organize and manage the field of entrepreneurship in the German speaking countries, not least due to the fact that the so called G-Forum (G = Gründung [foundation]) seemed to be a focal point in the entrepreneurship research movement. The first conference took place in 1997 with 70 delegates from different universities and disciplines and since then has developed into one of the most important meeting places for entrepreneurship researchers in the German speaking countries.

These extensive research efforts in the German speaking countries indicate that the research is on the threshold of a breakthrough and is growing rapidly, although some decisive factors should be taken into account. For example, many of the chairs are endowed chairs sponsored by industry, banks and regional institutions, in many cases for practical purposes – to establish companies supported by universities – and the question is if the interest in entrepreneurship will be maintained in the long term even if the expectations are not fulfilled. Another central question is whether entrepreneurship research will succeed in breaking away from the much stronger business administration tradition that exists in these countries.

1.5   Mediterranean Countries

Both Italy and Spain are countries that have many small businesses, not least in the form of family-run firms in the tourism and service sectors. *Italy* has traditionally been dominated by a catholic, Marxist ideology and an idealistic intellectual climate, in which entrepreneurs have not enjoyed much popularity in society until the last twenty years (Amatori & Colli, 2004). The immediate post war period was characterized by a "massacre" of small industries, especially in the south of Italy, and a concentration of industrial activities in larger companies in the north-western part of the country. This period of Italian industrial development has often been called the "Italian miracle". It began with the reconstruction of the country after the war followed by the rapid growth of Italian industry – based on large scale industries such as automobile and steel production. However, in common with most industrialized countries, Italy experienced major changes in the industrial structure during the 1970s and at the start of the 1980s with the growing importance of small businesses for economic development and the high proportion of self-employment. The major fluctuations in the world economy in recent decades have had important consequences for Italian industry, as many sectors are strongly dependent on export. Despite this, Italy has been relatively successful, among other things due to the devaluation of the lira and the continuous undervaluing of the currency, which has made Italian products more competitive.

For many years small firms held no interest for economics and management scholars, but following the crisis during the 1970s and a seminal book by the sociologist Arnaldo Bagnasco entitled *Tre Italie* (Three Italies) in 1978, in which the old view of the industrial structure in Italy was questioned, the interest among scholars increased. Today, although small businesses constitute a natural empirical basis for economics and management research, there are nevertheless difficulties in establishing an autonomous research field focusing on small business – researchers prefer to see themselves as economists or management researchers rather than experts on small business research.

An Italian phenomenon that has attracted international attention is the industrial districts that emerged in the north-eastern regions of Italy in the 1950s and 1960s. The interest in this research has been huge and inspired many followers – one example is Michael Porter, who in his work on national competitive advantages was influenced by the work on industrial districts. The research focusing on the industrial districts has also influenced Italian small business research, as the researchers on industrial districts were very visible in the Italian scientific community and influenced many young researchers to enter the field. Consequently, small business research has been dominated by researchers with an academic background in disciplines such as economics, regional economics, and industrial economics. Examples of central research areas with a macro-level focus are (see also Cardini & Fumagalli, 1997):

– The Industrial District Focus

In the mid 1970s small businesses started to play a more important role. This gave rise to an extensive debate on the causes and origins of this development. One explanation for the growth in small businesses was a change in the production process, and the Italian industrial districts served as an example of these changes. The seminal works of Giacomo Becattini at University of Florence and Sebastiano Brusco at University of Modena represent contributions of great significance not only in Italy but also internationally, and the research on industrial districts is still a very important stream of research in Italy.

– The Small Business Focus

Research in this area focuses on the importance of small businesses for industrial development. Also here, the research was prompted by the social changes that could be identified during the 1970s as well as the Bolton report in Great Britain (1971) and David Birch's (1979) analysis of the importance of small companies for employment and industrial development in the US. The researchers have an economics background. Among the Italian pioneers that deserve to be mentioned are Gaetano Golinelli, who in the second half of the 1970s wrote one of the first books on small businesses in Italy based on reflections resulting from the Bolton report, and Giorgio Fuá who wrote a book to demonstrate the role of small businesses in the development of the Italian economy.

– The Industrial Enterprise Focus

Besides those researchers with their base in economics, there is another strong research theme in Italy focusing on the industrial enterprises and with a theoretical grounding in industrial economics. Among the most important Italian researchers are Ricardo Varaldo (export behavior of industrial enterprises in more mature industries), Mario Raffa (transfer of knowledge between large and small firms), Gianni Lorenzoni (networks), and Marko Vivarelli (growth of small firms).

Thus, economists and researchers within industrial economics have dominated Italian small business research for a long time. In recent years we can, however, discern an increasing interest in the situation of small companies among researchers with a focus on micro-level analysis – researchers in management studies, although it is difficult to identify something that is uniquely Italian in the research carried out – as it mainly follows the international research agenda.

One of the main characteristics of small business research in Italy is that the research is to a large extent individual and highly fragmented – it is hard to identify a homogeneous research community around small business research. In recent years, however, Italian small business research has increasingly acquired a stronger empirical foundation as well as a more international character (e.g. there are more articles published in English speaking journals).

In *Spain*, it is also only during the last decade that new and small firms have received attention, both from the scientific community and from politicians and policy-makers. According to Veciana and Genescà (1997), the first empirical research on entrepreneurs in Spain was carried out by two young sociologists in the early 1960s, Juan Linz and Amando de Miguel (1963-64), and published in the article "Fundadores, Herederos y Directores de las Empresas Españolas" (Founders, heirs and managers in Spanish firms). In the study they explored the individuals behind Spanish firms – their origin, education, experience – and also analyzed differences in the way they managed their firms. Although it was an interesting piece of work, its impact on the academic community was limited.

The first doctoral course on entrepreneurship, with the title "Historical Evolution of Entrepreneurship", was organized by José Veciana at Universitat Autònoma de Barcelona in 1976, followed by a second doctoral course at the same university in 1977 on "Entrepreneurship in Catalonia". In 1988 two chairs were created at Universidad de Navarro, one in Entrepreneurship and one in Family Business. It is also worth mentioning the creation of two governmental research institutes whose aim was to administer support programs for SMEs, but also to carry out research within the field: IMPI (Instituto de la Pegueña y Mediana Industria) in 1977, and IMPIVA (Instituto de la Pegueña y Mediana Industria Valencia) in 1984. Both institutes developed into important research centers for small business in Spain.

In order to give an overview of the entrepreneurship and small business research in Spain, José Veciana and Enric Genescà (1997) conducted a review of economics, business administration and management journals between 1980 and 1995 in order to analyze articles written by Spanish entrepreneurship and small business researchers. This analysis was later complemented by one conducted by Jimenez-Moreno and Garcia-Villaverde (2003), who reviewed articles published between 1996 and 2001. Based on these analyses, the Spanish entrepreneurship and small business research can be described as follows:

In Spain there was an early interest – and we are talking about the early 1970s – in the personal characteristics of the entrepreneur and the attitudes toward entrepreneurship among students and managers, an interest which grew strongly during the 1980s. The research on the characteristics of the entrepreneur as an individual has however stagnated, and research is instead directed toward topics such as the "economic and financial structure of SMEs" and "SME strategies", but also research on family businesses and public policies for SMEs has been fairly prominent.

During the initial period (1980 to 1995), a feature of the research was a lack of empirical studies – articles that informed about themes relating to small firms and entrepreneurship, but without a base in empirical studies. In the case of empirical studies, quantitative methodological approaches dominated. Today we can find an increased focus on qualititative approaches (e.g. case studies and action research), but quantitative studies are still the most popular (Jimenez-Moreno and Garcia-Villaverde, 2003).

Most articles on entrepreneurship and small business written by Spanish researchers are published in Spanish journals, not least in the journal *Economia Industrial* (Journal of Industrial Economics), which reflects the interest in "SME strategies" and "economic structure of SMEs" – both popular research themes – as well as the high scientific level of the journal. Publications in foreign journals are rather few.

To sum up, entrepreneurship research in Spain can be said to be emerging. As much of the research is performed by doctoral students, it is seldom presented in international scientific journals. Moreover, the publications are of a one-off character, i.e. there is a lack of continuity. The research is also strongly fragmented among different universities with an interest in entrepreneurship and small businesses.

1.6   Transition Countries

The characteristic of all European countries in transition is their move away from a centrally planned system to the adoption of some form of market economy – a process that started between 1988 and 1992 – and the development accelerated after the collapse of the "Berlin Wall" on 9 November 1989. One of the main issues facing the transition countries is the need to develop a private business sector. This development from public to private sector ownership has taken various forms including (i) a direct privatization of former state owned enterprises – in many cases managers of state-owned enterprises as well as former politicians (the nomenclatura) have used their influence to privatize "their enterprise", (ii) private firms tolerated during the socialist period, for example, craft enterprises in Poland, continued to exist during the transition period, and (iii) the creation of completely new businesses, including self-employment and part-time businesses (in many cases in order to provide "self help" for former employees of state-owned enterprises who were made redundant or have been forced to resign as well as many informal sector businesses). The transformation also includes a liberalization of markets where central control over prices is replaced by market mechanisms, but also the creation of market institutions such as banks, other financial intermediaries, training support services, etc. (Smallbone & Welter, 2001)

Many politicians and policy-makers saw the promotion and development of new and small firms as being the engine of economic reforms and the core of the transition process, but after more than ten years of transition it is still difficult to identify a successful outcome in the development of small firms in many of these countries. Entrepreneurial behavior in the transition countries often reflects the unstable and hostile nature of the external environment and scarcity of key resources, including (Welter & Smallbone, 2003; Catoiu & Veghes, 2003; Mateev, 2003):

– An unfavorable macroeconomic framework, characterized by a decrease in production, income and demand and high inflation, which impacts on the purchasing power of individuals as well as institutional consumers.
– A highly inadequate legal system involving the laws relating to property, bankruptcy, contracts, taxes, etc.
– Lack of a financial infrastructure where the risk capital market is virtually non-existent and the banking system typically follows a conservative strategy in relation to new private firms.

However, it should be emphasized that each transition was different and that the countries are now at different stages in their development toward a market economy – entrepreneurship seems to have developed more quickly in countries where reforms proceeded smoothly and quickly (Mugler, 2000) and where there has been a strong pre-socialist industrial tradition (Smallbone & Welter, 2001). The following groups of countries can be identified (Mugler, 2000):

Group 1 – the most advanced countries that started negotiations with the European Union in 1998 and that became EU members in May 2004, such as the Czech Republic, Estonia, Hungary, Poland and Slovenia.

Group 2 – countries at an intermediate stage, such as Bulgaria, Croatia, Romania and Slovakia, i.e. countries that have shown much slower and more hesitant progress in implementing market reforms.

Group 3 – the countries of the former Yugoslav Federation which have experienced long separatist wars and an extremely difficult political situation.

Group 4 – a heterogeneous group of countries that were once a part of the former Soviet Union, some of which are oriented toward Europe and EU, although most countries in this group are stuck somewhere in the middle between an Eastern and a Western orientation.

In transition economies, newly created businesses tend to break up the large industrial structures that dominated the centrally planned economies, and therefore small firms could be considered a synonym for economic transformation (Mugler, 2000). As a consequence, the interest in small business research increased dramatically. For example, considerable research has been conducted in the Czeck Republic,

Hungary, Poland and Slovakia due to the growth of entrepreneurship in these countries as well as to their membership of the OECD (the Organization for Economic Cooperation and Development) and various EU funding programs that have given domestic researchers the opportunity to collaborate with researchers in western countries.

One main problem is that the quality of aggregated economic data does not follow market principles or Eurostat (the Statistical Office of the European Union) standards, thus research based on official data should be treated with caution. In addition, the informal economy is widespread in the transition countries, which means that a large proportion of actual economic activity is not measured by formal indicators (Mugler, 2000).

The international research community has shown an interest in this transformation process and considerable research has been conducted both by native researchers and visiting researchers from Western countries, the results of which have been presented in many journals and at international conferences. In addition, a couple of specialized conferences have been established thus contributing to the diffusion of knowledge about the transition process, for example, the Management and Development Conferences (1994, 1996, 1998) in Portoroz, Slovenia, the conferences organized by the University of Split, Croatia, on Enterprise in Transition (1995, 1997, 1999, 2001, and 2003).

2. ENTREPRENEURSHIP AND SMALL BUSINESS RESEARCH IN AUSTRALIA

This section consists of a presentation of entrepreneurship and small business research in Australia including a description of the Australian small business landscape, the introduction and development of entrepreneurship and small business research during the 1980s and 1990s, and its linkages to policy, the development of academic teaching on entrepreneurship, and finally, an outlook to the future.

2.1 The Small Business Context

Historically, Australia is recognized as a country dominated by small business, in terms of the number of businesses, share of employment and GDP. In 1999 there were an estimated 1.3 million small businesses (Australian Bureau of Statistics) in a population of 18 million. With a relatively small, geographically dispersed liberal economy, small business formation and growth was not a serious political consideration until relatively recently. It was not until 1994 that responsibility for small business was incorporated into the portfolio of a cabinet ministry in the Federal Government. In fact policy focus has traditionally been directed toward large companies and large unions, being the two major players in Australian industry. This was exacerbated by the adversarial industrial relations system in Australia. It would be false to assume that the pivotal economic role of small and entrepreneurial businesses to national, state and local economies was recognized.

In the 1970s and 1980s, the emphasis of entrepreneurship and small business research was on the need for basic skills development, education and small business management training rather than on entrepreneurship. The demand for advanced, theoretical and conceptual research was not apparent to scholars until the early 1990s. Furthermore, there were simply not enough researchers to undertake the research that was needed. More recently, most research resources were devoted to mainstream issues as dictated by stakeholder needs, market failure and small business management deficiencies, such as the finance gap, failure rates and basic benchmarking.

In the 1990s, increasing recognition of the need for entrepreneurial activities as a means to global competitiveness for both individual firms and the economy as a whole, resulted in a more diverse demand for research. Studies into individual entrepreneurs, innovation, small business policy, internationalization, networking, regional and local economic development, life cycles and growth metrics began to appear as academics were enticed out of their original disciplines such as industrial economics, strategic management, organizational studies, psychology, sociology, international trade and finance, law and industrial relations. In this way the researchers differed little from the entrepreneurial businesses themselves, as they saw and seized opportunities in a young market. In terms of technology diffusion, however, all these adopters and adaptors needed an innovator in order to initially break into the market. These would be the people with the greatest influence on the progress and direction of research in the country. To grasp this developmental process, there is a need to know who the innovators were and what influence they had on the research field over more than thirty years.

2.2 The Introduction of Entrepreneurship and Small Business Research in Australia

At the start of entrepreneurship and small business research in Australia, which would be considered to be the late 1960s, there were a number of pioneering researchers, the most prominent being Geoffrey Meredith, Winston Dunlop, and Alan Williams. Recognition of these researchers, as with small business in general, was limited to the wider social science academic community. Their work was dominated by inquiry into small business start-ups and more particularly failure. The area was largely influenced by academics with a background in finance, management and accountancy. Thus, interest centred on benchmarking financial performance as a means of obtaining essential market information on small firms (Geoffrey Meredith in particular), failure rates (Alan Williams among others) and remedying the deficiencies in small business management skills (Winston Dunlop in particular). Sectoral emphasis was retail, trades, and those in traditional sectors of the economy, such as light manufacturing and engineering. The only service sectors to be seriously considered were retail, wholesale and financial areas. It would not be until the 1990s that the service sector was taken seriously as an economic contributor and a research target (LEK Partners, 1994). In those early days, entrepreneurship was deemed less important than small business ownership. All the major books of the 1960s and 1970s were based on small business owners, small business management and small business problems and issues.

Figure 4-1 provides an indication of the focus of research in three identifiable eras of entrepreneurship and small business research in Australia, including the researchers who gained recognition at a national and sometimes international level in each era.

Era	Focus	Recognized emerging researchers
Late 1960s	Small business recognition Small business failure rates	Geoffrey Meredith Winston Dunlop Alan Williams
1970s-1980s	Small business failure rates Accounting and financial issues facing small business Finance gaps Financial benchmarking	Rolffe Peacock Chad Perry Patrick Hutchinson Richard MacMahon John Bailey
1990s	Small business competitiveness Entrepreneurial businesses Profiling entrepreneurs Marketing issues	Scott Holmes John Breen Allan Brown Thierry Volery John Watson

Figure 4-1. Development of entrepreneurship and small business research in Australia.

2.3 Critical Junctures in the Development of Entrepreneurship and Small Business Research in Australia – the Overlap Between Policy and Research

There is general agreement that the event that started the Australian assistance program was a Committee established by the Federal Government in the 1960s – a Committee chaired by (the late) Sir Fred Wiltshire. Wiltshire was recognized as a member of a small business family with a national and international reputation. The Committee on Small Business (1971) was set up to "explore ways of providing guidance to small business management to help improve efficiency, with attention primarily on small manufacturing business" (p. iii). The Committee Report known as the Wiltshire Report was tabled in 1971. However, it was not to be acted upon by government until 1973. A federal election in 1972 saw a change of government, and the incoming Minister took up the recommendations of the Wiltshire Committee and established a National Small Business Bureau (NSBB) in Canberra in 1973. This was Australia's first government funded unit to "serve" small business owners and in retrospect can been seen as a significant outcome of the Wiltshire Report. In general, the report recommended assistance for small business owners, but considered that such assistance should be delivered via the private sector – industry associations as well as professional, consultancy and related organizations. Government did not implement this recommendation.

In 1969, Geoffrey Meredith, soon to be appointed Professor with major responsibility for small business management in Australia, was a major player in the Wiltshire report, having been invited onto the board where he provided substantial input into the recommendations on teaching and learning programs, on university funding for entrepreneurship and small business education and on the need for more research in the field with a clear Australian agenda and perspective. This was seen not only as recognition of the role of small business in the economy, but also of the need for education about small business and entrepreneurship, and hence the central role dedicated academics would play through both teaching and research.

From this point a circle could emerge in which industry and political recognition were supported by and supportive of applied research into the conditions under which small and entrepreneurial firms operated in the Australian environment. The political recognition of small business reached an all time high in 1994 when the portfolio of small business was first introduced into the Federal Cabinet with the appointment of a senior government minister.

Another critical event in the recognition of the importance of the small business sector occurred in the mid 1990s with a series of important reports, the most significant of which was the Karpin Report (1995) on business competitiveness, incorporating a major section on small businesses and the need to facilitate entrepreneurship. Other reports included: the Carmichael Report (1994) on training and skills development for Australia's small businesses; Australia's emerging exporters (Australian Manufacturing Council, 1993) and intelligent exports (LEK Partners, 1994). Each of these reports not only served to reinforce the importance of the small business sector in the economy, but also provided a national blueprint for research into the sector. These reports can be seen as recognition of the input of the pioneers of small business and entrepreneurship research in Australia, as well as a belated acknowledgement of the important role played by smaller firms in the economy at both national and local levels.

2.4 Milestones in Entrepreneurship and Small Business Research in Australia

The first major scientific work on small businesses in Australia is considered to be the book *The Australian Manual of Small Business Practice*, by Lisa Brodribb (1967) which resulted from her PhD study at the University of Melbourne and was followed some years later by the widely read and cited *Small Business in Australia: Problems and Prospects* written by Brian Johns, Winston Dunlop and Bill Sheehan in 1978. It is worth noting, however, that many researchers within the field regard the 1975 book by Geoffrey Meredith, *Small Business Management in Australia,* as the greatest achievement in the field in the last thirty years. It should also be noted that the contribution of this book was in its value to education rather than research. This is indicative of where progress has been made in the area. It is perceived that development of education and training resources for students and for existing and potential small business owners, entrepreneurs, policy makers, program directors and consultants has been the most important contribution of academics in Australia. In fact much of the research in the field has been applied, thus having the greatest possible influence on business and policy.

Furthermore, the first academic journal dedicated to entrepreneurship and small business was *Management Forum* published since 1975 by the University of New England (UNE), where Geoffrey Meredith had been appointed to the first Chair in 1970 with responsibilities for small business in Australia. In fact the UNE was seen to be the hotbed of entrepreneurship and small business research in the 1970s and 1980s. Other early dissemenation of research through journals was via *Accounting Forum*, launched by Rolffe Peacock and T.E. Bishop in 1978. Peacock remained editor for ten years, and the journal is still in existence today. These two early journals paved the way for entrepreneurship and small business research. However, they were artefacts of the "finance gap" era and did not have the scope to expand in line with the broadening research agenda that accompanied a growing field of research, policy and practice.

In fact the broadening research agenda and the greater recognition of small business as a salient sector of the economy inevitably led to the perceived need to establish a body which could provide a forum for researchers, educators, consultants, policy makers and practitioners in the field of small business and entrepreneurship. This culminated in 1985 with the establishment of the Small Enterprise Association of Australia and New Zealand – once again initiated by Geoffrey Meredith. SEAANZ has grown in membership and the number of participants at its conferences is in the hundreds. While international forums such as ICSB, WASME, ISBC, Academy of Management Entrepreneurship Division, and the Babson Conference provide ample opportunity for internationally focused work, SEAANZ remains an important outlet for doctoral scholars, early career researchers, practitioners and more senior researchers as mentors at a national level. An indication of the widening research agenda facilitated by SEAANZ was the establishment in 1987 of a new journal known today as *Small Enterprise Researcher: The Journal of SEAANZ*. It can be safely stated that every known researcher in Australia has published in this journal at some stage of his/her career, indicating the important developmental role this journal has played for entrepreneurship and small business research.

2.5   Education, Training and Small Business Skills Development

One of the areas of greatest concern and input of energy has been skills training and development for small business owners, entrepreneurs and those considering entering into small business. The report which first considered small business and entrepreneurship education and training as part of its brief was that commissioned in the 1960s and chaired by professor Cyert. It was established in order to consider a national postgraduate training facility. This led to the funding of the Australian Graduate School of Management in Sydney. A subsequent study recommended a similar arrangement for the Melbourne Business School. However, the Ralph Committee (1982) focussed on the training needs of small business, and the National Training Council commissioned a report into small business education and training needs, while Bailey and Royston (1980) also examined attitudes of small business owners to training. Following Ralph, the Commonwealth Tertiary Education Commission sought information on the available training programs and how they could be made more accessible to business owners. The report (Meredith, 1984a; b) was presented in 1983.

Since the 1980s the number of commissioned reports on aspects of small business education and training has been extensive. Bailey and Royston (1980) noted the resistance of owners to formal training programs, while Williams (1984) and Ralph (1982) concluded that small business management competencies were at a rudimentary stage and inadequate, thus contributing to business failure. The need for training in competencies was evident. Through the Australian National Training Authority, the federal government commenced an investigation in 1999 into small business competencies with the intention of incorporating such skills into small business training courses. By 2002, some 370 courses had been developed covering record keeping, administration, frontline management, legal services, marketing, sales, advertizing, governance, human resources, strategic management and e-business. Courses are available at varying levels – from Certificate to Advanced Diploma. These courses are delivered through Australia's technical education institutes or by approved private providers.

Most states offer courses in small business start up and management at high school level, with students encouraged to form companies and produce/sell/market products or services for profit with business owners acting as advisors. There is also an Australian Business Week (ABW) National Competition, in which senior high school students from most states and territories compete in establishing a small business concept over a one-week period.

Most universities offer a unit in Small Business Management and at least one course in Entrepreneurship at undergraduate level. Some universities such as Swinburne in Victoria and Newcastle in New South Wales offer majors in entrepreneurship and small business. At the post graduate level, Deakin University in Victoria was the first Australian University to include small business in an MBA program, although the University of New England (UNE) offered graduate courses in small business management, small business finance, small business policy and entrepreneurship at Graduate Certificate, Graduate diploma and Master of Economics degree levels. In 1993 UNE changed the approach to MBA courses at its Northern Rivers (NSW) Campus by offering an option of a major in small business and entrepreneurship as part of its MBA, so that with course work and a project, candidates could research a wide area of small business operations. The same campus introduced Australia's first research based Doctor of Business Administration (DBA) in 1995, which degree can be completed with modules in management, research methods plus a research proposal and a thesis of some 50,000 words.

2.6   Coming of Age

While entrepreneurial small businesses are undeniably important to the Australian economy, interest in and research on the sector in Australia has been slow and at best intermittent. Despite consistent Federal Government commitment to the sector, small business and entrepreneurship research has struggled for funding and legitimacy. The orientation of government policies from the post-war period until the 1970s was focussed on large firms, large unions and large government agencies, and small firms were generally regarded as irrelevant. In more recent times, and possibly as a direct result of the neglect of the small business sector by policy makers, the quality of data upon which policy decisions have been made has been poor.

The research that has emerged over the last three decades corresponds closely with the policies and economic climate of the country. At times the research has been conducted in response to small business problems or to the prevailing political climate. On some occasions the research has even dictated policy and proactively created solutions for small and entrepreneurial businesses. The theoretical and practical contribution of entrepreneurship and small business research to the Australian economy continues to increase. The large volume and variety of reports, studies, papers, books and educational material provide a solid foundation on which to build a promising research agenda. There are a number of indications that entrepreneurship and small business research in Australia has come of age:

1. It is obvious that there are many more researchers in the area than there were ten years ago. As a result, the research topics are also more diverse than before.
2. Those who could be considered to have been in the second phase of entrepreneurship and small business research have senior positions such as heads of schools and departments both in the smaller, regional universities and in the larger metropolitan universities.
3. Australian researchers not only attend SEAANZ conferences; they are a major grouping at ICSB and other international small business conferences as well as participants at the Entrepreneurship Division of the Academy of Management
4. The term "entrepreneurship" is appearing more frequently in the titles of schools and centers at universities across the country.
5. The title Professor of Entrepreneurship is becoming more common, again not only in regional and niche universities, but also in the larger universities.

Increasing numbers of universities have Professors of Small Business or Entrepreneurship, including Bond and Griffith in Queensland, Newcastle in NSW and Swinburne in Victoria. A greater number of universities have centers for small business often linked to regional development. These include the University of Queensland, Southern Cross, Swinburne, Central Queensland, Griffith, Bond, Newcastle, Ballarat, Latrobe, Monash at Gippsland, Western Australia and Deakin. As noted above, small business policy issues have tended to be determined by the federal government, and government has also generally attempted to implement policy but with activities that are focussed on the short rather than the long term.

3. COMPARISONS BETWEEN EUROPE, AUSTRALIA, AND THE US

As shown by this review of entrepreneurship and small business research in Europe and Australia, there seem to be similarities but mainly substantial differences between entrepreneurship and small business research in Europe and Australia compared to the US. Starting with the similarities, Aldrich (2000) discussed a couple of similarities that can be found across nations, for example:

- A strong normative and prescriptive orientation underlies entrepreneurship and small business research in many countries.
- Entrepreneurship and small business research has historically focussed more on descriptions than hypothesis testing although signs of change are apparent.
- Research has focussed mainly on established organizations, rather than the founding process.

However, the main impression is that there are great differences in entrepreneurship and small business research between different continents (but also between countries). Although Europe is heterogeneous, thus making it difficult to provide a general picture of entrepreneurship and small business research, a number of differences between Europe, Australia and the US can be discerned (Figure 4-2).

First of all, differences in the thematic and conceptual development, where US research has a strong focus on entrepreneurship, and the level of analysis is mainly the firm whereas the research in Europe and Australia is mainly focused on small businesses. Furthermore, we can find various levels of research analysis, where European researchers have tended to favor more aggregated levels and to take a greater interest in policy-oriented research. US researchers also have a tendency to assume that their findings are universal, whereas their colleagues in Europe and Australia usually discuss the context in which their findings originate and tend to regard their results as nation-specific.

From a methodological perspective it is interesting to note that US entrepreneurship and small business researchers tend to constitute a community built on a single methodology that mainly relies on surveys and questionnaires as data collection methods in addition to sophisticated statistical analysis and focusing on generalization, parsimony and statistical rigor. In contrast, European research exhibits a great deal of openness toward different methodological approaches, including qualitative methods, leading to greater focus on realism, accuracy and complexity. In Australia a combination of methods have traditionally been used. This also reflects the tendency of policy oriented research to employ a qualitative approach, as opposed to accounting and financial research, which tend to adopt a more quantitative approach. While attempts have been made to compile national studies on entrepreneurship and small business, neither government nor researchers have been successful in this regard, at least not on a large scale.

The research community in the US is large and homogeneous – and constitutes a base for a "market". The internal competition among researchers thereby becomes important, which manifests itself in the necessity of having one's works published (publish or perish syndrome). In Europe the research community is in many countries rather small and with a very heterogeneous character – researchers come from different disciplines and with different theoretical frameworks and methodological approaches – which makes the internal market less visible. Due to its policy-oriented character, small business researchers in Europe tend to have many different external stakeholders, which means strong external competition for research funds. Australia has not had a solid funding base for entrepreneurship and small business research, and as a consequence the research has been largely characterized by its small scale and low cost. The focus of small business is most apparent at the level of the States, rather than the Federal level, as the States have differing agendas and economies. In recent years a strong interest in high technology industries can be identified, which has led to some convergence in the research agenda built around the commercialization imperative.

Will these differences be maintained or is there a pressure toward convergence? Research is global while international diffusion mechanisms have spread information about differences and similarities throughout the international research community – which makes the research more homogeneous – and this process seems to be gaining momentum in today's international environment. Scientific activities are also becoming increasingly global, and Ziman (1994) talks about a shift from "cosmopolitan individualism" to "international collectivism".

Aldrich (2000) talks about "isomorphism" as a mechanism through which scholars learn about each other's work. For example, forces that promote such imitative behavior are international journals, conferences, cross-national working groups, visiting scholars, etc. There are many forces that have the potential to bring scholars from different continents closer together (Aldrich, 2000): (i) research is becoming more and more international (conferences, visiting scholars, joint projects, etc.) and international activities are increasing in importance, which promotes the dissemination of approaches, (ii) the growing importance of international English-language journals, which promote a common standard of evaluation and professional prestige and which institutionalize norms of professionalism within the field, and (iii) similar reward systems are

	US	Australia	Europe
Thematic and conceptual development	– Focus on entrepreneurship.	– Focus on small business.	– Focus on small business and policy implications.
	– Individual and firm level analysis.	– Firm level analysis.	– Varying levels of analysis but some focus on more aggregated levels of analysis.
	– Tendency to build research on the assumption that their findings are universal.	– Researchers regard their results as nation (or even State) specific.	– Researchers regard their results as nation specific.
Methodological development	– One methodological field. Relying on surveys and questionnaires.	– Mixture of qualitative and quantitative methods, based on disciplinary background.	– Methodological openness. Relying more on qualitative fieldwork methods.
	– Focus on generalization, parsimony and statistical rigor.	– Leaning toward generalizability and statistical rigour.	– Focus on realism, accuracy and complexity.
Research community	– Market driven – established market system:	– Stakeholder driven – limited stakeholder heterogeneity:	– Stakeholder driven – many different external stakeholders:
	Driving force	Driving force	Driving force
	– Internal competition (publish or perish).	– Political forces and market mechanism support.	– Political forces and external competition (resources from external stakeholders).
	Community	Community	Community
	– Large and homogeneous.	– Small core, with a larger group of transient researchers.	– Small and heterogeneous.
	– Visible.	– Visibility has increased due to seniority of university-based researchers.	– Less visible.

Figure 4-2. Entrepreneurship research in Europe, Australia, and the US.

evolving in Europe as in the US. Collaboration may be enhanced by the phenomenon of "publish or perish", and a way to increase one's publication count is by collaborating – adding together "fractional papers". Price (1986, p. 126) states that "The most prolific man is also by far the most collaborating". Of course, if multiple authorship becomes the rule, researchers will increase their number of collaborators with every paper they write.

Thus, many forces are working toward international convergence and uniformity in entrepreneurship research – in common with most scientific fields. But as has been shown in this chapter, there is great heterogeneity between the continents (and even between countries) regarding the contextual settings for entrepreneurship and small business, and the research agenda is quite different. There are also large differences in research traditions between countries. This indicates that the trend toward convergence and uniformity will slow down and that different research traditions may develop in parallel and in accordance with their own preconditions. The emergence of powerful and influential research centers with the potential to build strong research environments and to systematically develop specific research areas and paradigms provides further evidence of this development.

REFERENCES

Aldrich, H.E., 2000, Learning Together: National Differences in Entrepreneurship Research, in Sexton, D. & Landström, H. (eds.), *The Blackwell Handbook of Entrepreneurship*, Oxford: Blackwell.

Hisrich, R.D. & Drnovsek, M., 2002, Entrepreneurship and small business research – a European perspective, *Journal of Small Business and Enterprise Development*, 9, 2, 172-222.

Huse, M. & Landström, H., 1997, European Entrepreneurship and Small Business Research. Methodological Openness and Contextual Differences, *International Studies of Management and Organization*, 27, 3, 3-12.

Landström, H. & Frank, H. & Veciana, J. (eds.), 1997, *Entrepreneurship and Small Business Research in Europe*, Aldershot: Avebury.

Landström, H. & Huse, M., 1996, Trends in European Entrepreneurship and Small Business Research, SIRE Working Paper 1996:3, Universities of Halmstad and Växjö, Sweden.

Price, D.J. de S., 1986, *Little science, big science ... and beyond*, New York: Columbia University Press.

Ziman, J., 1994, *Prometheus Bound: Science in a Dynamic Steady State*, Cambridge: Cambridge University Press.

UK

Bolton, J.E., 1971, *Report of the Committee of Inquiry on Small Firms*, CMND 4811, London: Her Majesty's Stationery Office.

Curran, J. & Stanworth, J., 1982, The Small Firm in Britain – Past, Present and Future, *European Small Business Journal*, 1, 1, 16-25.

Gibb, A. & Webb, T. (eds.), 1979, *Policy Issues in Small Business Research*, Westmead, Hants: Teakfield.

Stanworth, M.J. & Curran, J., 1973, *Management Motivation in the Smaller Business*, Epping, Essex: Gower Press.

Storey, D.J., 1994, *Understanding the Small Business Sector*, London: Routledge.

Nordic countries

Barth, F. (ed.), 1963, *The Role of the Entrepreneur in Social Change in Northern Norway*, Oslo: Universitetsforlaget.

Bruun, M. & Sørensen, P. & Ravn, N., 1978, *Iværksætterundersøgelsen*, Aarhus: Jysk Teknologisk Institut.

Christensen, P.R. & Axelsson, L., 1997, How entrepreneurial is the research into sall business and entrepreneurship in Denmark?, in Landström, H. & Frank, H. & Veciana, J. (eds.), *Entrepreneurship and Small Business Research in Europe*, Aldershot: Avebury.

Dahmén, E., 1950, *Svensk industriell företagsverksamhet*, Stockholm: IUI.

Hage, C.F., 1894/1926, *Haandbog i Handelsvidenskab*, Copenhagen.

Iveroth, A., 1943, *Småindustri och hantverk i Sverige*, Stockholm: IUI.

Jensen, T.B., 1979, *Nogle udviklingstendenser for fremstillingsvirksomhet i Danmark*, Copenhagen.

Johannisson, B. & Landström, H., 1997, Research in entrepreneurship and small business – state of the art, in Landström, H. & Frank, H. & Veciana, J. (eds.), *Entrepreneurship and Small Business Research in Europe*, Aldershot: Avebury.

Landström, H. & Johannisson, B., 2001, Theoretical foundations of Swedish entrepreneurship and small business research, *Scandinavian Journal of Management*, 17, 225-248.

Malinen, P. & Paasio, A., 1997, Entrepreneurship and small business research in Finland, in Landström, H. & Frank, H. & Veciana, J. (eds.), *Entrepreneurship and Small Business Research in Europe*, Aldershot: Avebury.

Spilling, O.R., 1997, Research on entrepreneurship and small business in Norway, in Landström, H. & Frank, H. & Veciana, J. (eds.), *Entrepreneurship and Small Business Research in Europe*, Aldershot: Avebury.

Wedervang, F., 1964, *Development of a Population of Industrial Firms*, Oslo: Scandinavian University Books.

Central Europe

Klandt, H., 2003, A Study on the State of Entrepreneurship Education and Research at Gman Speaking Universities and Polytechnics, Working Paper, Oestrich-Winkel, Germany.

Schmidt, K-H., 2002, The history of dogma in international research cooperation – as exemplified by the Rencontres de St-Gall, paper at the Rencontres de St-Gall, Hergiswil, Switzerland.

Mediterranean countries

Amatori, F. & Colli, A., 2004, Entrepreneurship: the Italian story, in Corbetta, G. & Huse, M. & Ravasi, D. (eds.), *Crossroad of Entrepreneurship*, Dordrecht: Kluwer.

Cardini, C. & Fumagalli, A., 1997, Patterns of entrepreneurial research in Italy: locational factors, intangible assets and development of new firms, in Landström, H. & Frank, H. & Veciana, J. (eds.), *Entrepreneurship and Small Business Research in Europe*, Aldershot: Avebury.

Jimenez-Moreno, J.J. & Garcia-Villaverde, P.M., 2003, Estado de la cuestión y perspectivas de la investigación en creación de empresas en España: Una revisión de los articulos publicados entre 1996 y 2001, in Genescá, E., *Creación de Empresas – Entrepreneurship. Homage to Professor José Maria Veciana Verges*, Bellaterra, Barcelona: Servei de Publicacions de la Universitat Autónoma de Barcelona, 111-133.

Linz, J.J. & De Miguel, A., 1963-64, Fundadores, Herederos y Directores de las Empresas Españolas, *Revista Internacional de Sociologia*, No 81, 82 and 85.

Veciana, J.M. & Genescà, E., 1997, Entrepreneurship and Small Business Research in Spain, in Landström, H. & Frank, H. & Veciana, J. (eds.), *Entrepreneurship and Small Business Research in Europe*, Aldershot: Avebury.

Transition countries

Catoiu, I. & Veghes, C., 2003, Living to Survive: The Small and Medium Enterprise Sector in Romania after Ten Years of Transition to a Market Economy, in Kirby, D.A. & Watson, A. (eds.), *Small Firms and Economic Development in Developed and Transition Economies: A Reader*, Aldershot: Ashgate.

Mateev, M., 2003, Entrepreneurship and SME Development in Transition Countries, The Case of Bulgaria, in Kirby, D.A. & Watson, A. (eds.), *Small Firms and Economic Development in Developed and Transition Economies: A Reader*, Aldershot: Ashgate.

Mugler, J., 2000, The Climate for Entrepreneurship ub European Countries in Transition, in Sexton, D.L. & Landström, H. (eds.), *The Blackwell Handbook of Entrepreneurship*, Oxford: Blackwell, 150-175.

Smallbone, D. & Welter, F., 2001, The Distinctiveness of Entrepreneurship in Transition Economies, *Small Business Economics*, 16, 249-262.

Welter, F. & Smallbone, D., 2003, Entrepreneurship and enterprise strategies in transition economies: An institutional perspective, in Kirby, D.A. & Watson, A. (eds.), *Small Firms and Economic Development in Developed and Transition Economies: A Reader*, Aldershot: Ashgate.

Australia

Australian Bureau of Statistics, 1999, *Small business in Australia*, Canberra: AGPS.

Bailey, J. & Royston, S., 1980, *Small business education and training in Australia*, Canberra: AGPS.

Beddall Report (House of representatives Standing Committee on Industry, Science and technology), 1990, *Small business in Australia: Challenges, problems and opportunities*, Canberra: AGPS.

Carmichael, L., 1994, *The Shape of Things to Come: Small Business Employment and Skills*, Canberra: Australian Government Publishing Service.

Department of Trade and Industry and Wiltshire Report, 1971, *Report of the Committee of Small Business*, Canberra: Australian Government Publishing Service.

Karpin, D., 1995, *Enterprising Nation: Renewing Australia's Managers to Meet the Challenges of the Asia-Pacific Century*, Canberra: Report of the Industry Task Force on Leadership and Management.

LEK Partners, 1994, *Intelligent Exports*, Sydney: Austrade.

Meredith, G., 1975, Small business policy at national & state levels, *Management Forum*, 1, 3.

Meredith, G., 1984a, *Government & small business*, Institute of Public Affairs Review, 38, 1.

Meredith, G., 1984b, *Small business education & training for Australia*, Canberra: CTEC.

Williams A.J., 1991, *Small business survival: The roles of formal education, management training and advisory services*, Canberra: AGPS.

Chapter 5

PIONEERS – THE INDIVIDUALS WHO CREATED THE FIELD

The previous chapters (Chapters 3 and 4) described the growing interest in entrepreneurship and small firms among international researchers in the late 1970s and especially in the 1980s. A number of scholars observed the prevailing tendencies in society – with an increased focus on industrial renewal, innovation and entrepreneurship – and in various ways these pioneers stimulated an interest in entrepreneurship and small firms among their colleagues around the world. Who then were these pioneers? In this chapter, some of them will be presented. Naturally, views differ concerning the individuals and events that have been influential in the development of the field, and this presentation is a subjective evaluation. However, I have attempted to cover a broad range of topics within the field including the pioneers who built an infrastructure (section 1) as well as those involved in entrepreneurship and small business research (section 2). Since 1996 the Swedish Foundation for Small Business Research (FSF) and the Swedish Business Development Agency (NUTEK) have presented the International Award for Small Business Research to scholars within entrepreneurship and/or small business whose research has contributed substantially to increased knowledge and understanding of entrepreneurship and/or small businesses. The FSF-NUTEK International Award will be presented in section 3 together with a brief overview of the first recipients of the Award – recipients that can all be regarded as pioneers in the field of entrepreneurship and small business research. These pioneers will then be described in Part II and Part III of the book.

1.   INFRASTRUCTURE BUILDERS – SETTING THE STAGE

An academic infrastructure – including education, authors of textbooks, professional organizations, conferences, scientific journals and incumbents of chairs in the field – is central to the development of the field. In the following section some of the milestones and the individuals who prepared the ground for entrepreneurship and small business research will be presented.

1.1   Pioneers in the Area of Education

As has been shown in Chapter 3, the business schools in the US were pioneers in the area of entrepreneurship education. We have to go back to the late 1940s to find the first academic course in entrepreneurship, which was "Management of New Enterprises" offered by Myles Mace at Harvard Business School in 1947. This was followed by New York University with a course in entrepreneurship and innovation in 1953, spearheaded by Peter Drucker (Cooper, 2003). In the 1950s entrepreneurship courses were also offered at the University of Illinois, Stanford University, University of South Dakota, and MIT. In 1967 the first contemporary MBA entrepreneurship courses were introduced at Stanford University and New York University (Katz, 2003). Babson College was the first to offer an undergraduate major in entrepreneurship, which began in 1968, while the University of Southern California (led by Herb Kierulff and Leonard Davis) was the first to offer a major in entrepreneurship at MBA level in 1972. (Cooper, 2003)

Several support programs were launched in the US, for example, the National Science Foundation initiated a couple of innovation centers that introduced courses in entrepreneurship. An important initiative in the development of more broadly based education programs was the Small Business Institute Program in 1972, sponsored by the Small Business Administration (SBA), which provided support to universities initiating courses in which students collaborated with small businesses. Texas Tech University launched the first program under the direction of Robert Justis and Jack Steele. The program was successful and by 1976 as many as 398 universities were participating.

Since then entrepreneurship education has shown remarkable growth (Katz, 2003) and has mainly been concentrated in schools of management and to some extent schools of engineering (Vesper, 1982). According to Vesper (1982; Katz, 2003), in 1970 there were 16 schools in the US offering entrepreneurship courses. By 1975 the number had increased to 104, while in 1986 it was 253. However, it was mainly during the 1990s that an enormous growth in the number of courses and education programs took place. For example, the number of educational institutions with entrepreneurship courses in the US had increased to about 1,600 schools offering more than 2,200 courses (Katz, 2003).

The developments in Europe were similar, although there was a great difference between countries. Great Britain was one of the early countries to offer entrepreneurship and small business courses, and in the 1970s Allan Gibb and Mike Scott at Durham Business School and Stirling University respectively were among the first to become well known in the area. Another early example was Bengt Johannisson who, at the start of the 1970s, introduced entrepreneurship and small business management courses at Växjö University in Sweden.

In Europe, the late 1980s and early 1990s could be characterized by a dramatic increase in the number of PhD students within the field. However, the number of post-graduate courses in entrepreneurship and small business management was rather limited – one of the first PhD courses in Europe was organized by José Veciana at Universitat Autònoma de Barcelona in Spain 1976 on the "Historical Evolution of Entrepreneurship". Even in this respect Bengt Johannisson can be regarded as one of the pioneers in the European context, and in the early 1980s he organized a national PhD course in Sweden on the theme "Perspectives on Small Business". But, as indicated, the number of PhD courses at the national level in Europe was rather sparse. Therefore, an important initiative was the establishment of the European Doctoral Programme in Entrepreneurship and Small Business Management, initiated by the European Council for Small Business (ECSB) in 1990 and originally organized by Durham University in the UK and the Universitat Autònoma de Barcelona in Spain.

The production of textbooks was related to entrepreneurship and small business education, and during the 1970s there was increased production of entrepreneurship and small business textbooks – several of which continued in use at many universities until well into the 1990s. Some of the most widely used early textbooks within the area of entrepreneurship were (Kent & Sexton & Vesper, 1982; Sexton & Smilor, 1986; Katz, 2003):

Broom, H. (and Longnecker, J.), 1961, *Small Business Management*, Cincinnati: Southwestern.

Kilby, P. (ed.), 1971, *Entrepreneurship and Economic Development*, New York: Free Press.

Liles, P. (and Stevenson, H.), 1972, *New Business Ventures and the Entrepreneur*, Homewood, Ill: Irwin.

Baty, G., 1974, *Entrepreneurship: Playing to Win*, Englewood Cliffs, NJ: Prentice-Hall.

Baumback, C.M. & Mancuso, J.R., 1975, *Entrepreneurship and Venture Management*, Englewood Cliffs, NJ: Prentice-Hall.

Timmons, J., 1977, *New Venture Creation*, Boston, MA: Irwin.

1.2   Builders of Social Networks for Entrepreneurship and Small Business Scholars

In the 1970s and 1980s an emerging community of teachers and researchers in entrepreneurship and small business could be identified, and some individual initiatives were taken to stimulate communication within this community – professional organizations, academic conferences, and scientific journals began to emerge (see Cooper et al., 1997; Cooper et al., 2000; McCarthy & Nicholls-Nixon, 2001; Katz, 2003; Cooper, 2003).

Professional organizations were developed in order to organize the individuals within the community. For example, in this respect government officials (especially the Small Business Administration in the US) and practising entrepreneurs played an important role as driving forces in the establishment of the National Council for Small Business Management Development in 1956 (the name was changed to the International Council for Small Business [ICSB] in 1977), and since then the organization has grown and today (2004) has twelve international affiliates and more than 2,000 members. The first conference organized by ICSB was in 1956 when the University of Colorado acted as host to the 40 participants, mainly coordinators of courses and training programs for small businesses from different parts of the US (Brockhaus, 2003). One of the largest affiliates within ICSB is the European Council for Small Business (ECSB) with its 500 members in almost 30 countries. The ECSB was founded in 1988 with Josef Mugler of the Vienna School of Economics and Business Administration as the driving force. The ECSB is however, not the only arena for entrepreneurship and small business scholars in Europe. In this connection the European Foundation for Entrepreneurship Research (EFER) and the European Foundation for Management Development (EFMD) should also be mentioned, as they created an international arena for entrepreneurship and small business researchers at an early stage in the form of conferences and seminars (e.g. the EFMD Small Business Seminars which started in 1971).

At the Academy of Management Meeting in 1974, Karl Vesper organized a meeting for those interested in entrepreneurship, and an Interest Group on Entrepreneurship was formed as a part of the Division of Business Policy and Planning (today Business Policy and Strategy). The Interest Group remained rather small for many years, and the Entrepreneurship Interest Group did not achieve full status as the

Entrepreneurship Division of the Academy of Management until 1987, with John A. Pearce II as the first chairman.

One of the first *academic conferences* on entrepreneurship in the US was held at the newly established Center for Venture Management at Purdue University in 1970. The conference brought together 12 researchers (Arnold Cooper, Victor Danilov, Richard Dooley, Kirk Draheim, Cary Hoffman, Richard Howell, John Komives, Lawrence Lamont, Edward Roberts, Albert Shapero, Karl Vesper, and Jeffrey Susbauer), who met and presented their findings on technical entrepreneurship for the first time. In 1973, the 1st International Conference on Entrepreneurship Research was held in Toronto, Canada. The conference attracted researchers such as Jeffry Timmons, George Kozmetsky, and David Brophy, and in 1975 the International Symposium of Entrepreneurship and Enterprise Development, organized by Jeffrey Susbauer, was held in Cincinnati with more than 230 participants from all over the world, and with Al Shapero, Patrick Lyles, David Berlew and Joseph Stepanek as key-note speakers. The first Babson Research Conference was held in 1981, when Carl Vesper held the Paul T. Babson Chair of Entrepreneurship at Babson College. Together with John Hornaday he organized the first conference, at which 39 papers were presented. Today the Babson Research Conference is one of the leading conferences within the field, and at the 2004 conference there were more than 300 participants from 35 countries who presented a total of 237 papers.

In the European context, internationalization began rather early in entrepreneurship and small business research – maybe due to the limited quantitative basis for researchers at national level, which meant that exchange could virtually only take place on an international basis. As a result, several conferences were held at a relatively early stage in Europe, of which the "Rencontres de St-Gall" in Switzerland was probably the first conference on small business in the world – initiated by Alfred Gutersohn in 1948. Great Britain was also active in this regard at an early stage, and in 1979 Allan Gibb and Terry Webb organised the first Small Firms Policy and Research Conference in the UK, followed by the Nordic Conference on Small Business in 1980 organized by Göran Andersson and Bengt Johannisson at Växjö University in Sweden. The first Workshop on Recent Research in Entrepreneurship – the RENT Conference – initially organized by the European Institute for Advanced Studies in Management (EIASM) but since then co-organized by the ECSB and EIASM, was held in Brussels in 1987 with Rik Donckels as the conference chair.

The first *scientific journal* in entrepreneurship *Explorations in Entrepreneurial History* (later changed to *Explorations in Economic History*) was published by the Research Center in Entrepreneurial History at Harvard University (from 1949 to 1958) and later at the University of Wisconsin (1963-1969). The *Journal of Small Business*

Management (JSBM) started in 1955 under the auspices of the National Council for Small Business Management Development, and the journal became the official publication of the successor organization ICSB in 1977. The *American Journal of Small Business* was launched in 1975 and, in 1988, under the editorship of Ray Bagby, its name was changed to *Entrepreneurship Theory and Practice*. In Europe the first journal within the field of small business was the German language journal *Internationales Gewerbearchive* (today *Zeitschrift für Klein- und Mittelunternehmen*), launched in 1952. Thirty years later, in 1982, the *European Small Business Journal* – later entitled the *International Small Business Journal* was started. During the 1980s there was an increase in the number of entrepreneurship and small business journals, for example: *Journal of Small Business and Entrepreneurship* (1983), *Journal of Business Venturing* (1985), *Piccola Impresa* (1987), *Revue Internationale PME* (1987), *Entrepreneurship and Regional Development* (1989), and *Small Business Economics* (1989).

One important aspect when building an infrastructure is the establishment of *chairs* dedicated to entrepreneurship. In the US, the first endowed position, the Bernard B. and Eugenia A. Ramsey Chair of Private Enterprise at Georgia State University, was created in 1963 (Katz, 2003). In Europe, as mentioned previously, the focus has been more on small businesses than on entrepreneurship. The first chair dedicated to small business in Europe was established as long ago as 1936 at Vienna Business School with W. Bouffier as the first incumbent. However, not much happened in this respect until the 1980s, when the number of chairs started to increase.

2.   RESEARCH PIONEERS – PLAYING THE GAME

Recent years have seen an exponential increase in entrepreneurship and small business research all over the world – which originated in the 1970s and 1980s. Who were the researchers who opened up the research field? In section 2.1. I will present some of the pioneers who focused on macro-level analysis (including the societal, regional and sectorial levels), while in subsection 2.2. pioneers with a micro-level focus will be discussed.

2.1   Pioneers – Macro-level Analysis

For a long time Keynesian economic theory seemed to be working, and the large firms accounted for employment and social dynamics. The Western world experienced a major economic development – there was no need for entrepreneurship and small businesses. In Chapter 3 I discussed the "social turmoil" that characterised much of the 1970s and which was evidenced by social dynamics and transformation of the industrial structure – the industrial landscape was radically transformed, the large corporations lost their attraction while interest in new and small businesses increased, and new political winds began to blow, emphasizing a more market oriented view of industrial development. These changes were also reflected in the academic area, and during the 1970s and early 1980s there were a number of pioneering scientific contributions in the area of "small business economics" from researchers with a background in disciplines such as economics, industrial economics, and economic geography, all of whom focussed on macro-level analysis – society, regional or sectorial levels of analysis.

2.1.1   The Entrepreneurial Function in Society

For the most part, and with few exceptions, researchers in economics have neglected the role of the entrepreneurial function in society. Their models have been formed based on existing firms and focussed on a static world and, in perfect markets, capital and labor are optimal and can produce output in an efficient manner. In 1968 William Baumol made clear that, within the framework of market equilibrium, there was no room for the entrepreneurial function: what is required is management making routine decisions based on rational calculations within known constraints in order to meet defined goals – and a managerial function that is quite different from entrepreneurship. Thus any approach to the study of the economy in a market equilibrium framework will ignore the function of entrepreneurship in modern capitalism (Metcalfe, 2004).

However, we can identify a number of individual economists, who took an interest in entrepreneurship and attempted to relate it to different economic theories. Among the leading economists who took an early interest in entrepreneurship were Israel Kirzner, William Baumol and Mark Casson, whose main contributions to knowledge in the area of entrepreneurship include:

Baumol, W.J., 1968, Entrepreneurship in Economic Theory, *American Economic Review*, 58, 64-71.

Casson, M., 1982, *The Entrepreneur*, Totowa, NJ.: Barnes and Noble Books.

Kirzner, I.M., 1973, *Competition and Entrepreneurship*, Chicago: University of Chicago Press.

Moreover, it should be noted that the Schumpeterian view on entrepreneurship provided a compelling framework for several economists with a special interest in the economics of innovation. Based on Dahmén's (1970) notion of "development blocs" describing how innovations create new complementaries, thereby contributing to the re-allocation of resources in society, Bo Carlsson (1992) later developed the concept to what he called "technological systems", in which technical knowledge plays a critical role in creating productivities at a higher level of aggregation, while the Swedish economist Gunnar Eliasson (1987; 1992; 1996; Eliasson & Eliasson, 1996) developed an Experimentally Organized Economy (EOE) theory and coined the concept "competence bloc", which refers to the total infrastructure needed to create, select, recognize, diffuse and commercially exploit new ideas in clusters of firms.

Another early topic that occupied the interest of economists was the labor market and the high unemployment rate that characterized many countries during the 1970s. The pioneering work in this regard was no doubt David Birch's ground breaking report *The Job Generation Process* in 1979. The report provided economic researchers, not only in the US (e.g. Armington and Odle) but also around the world (e.g. Storey, Gudgin and Johnson in the UK) with an intellectual basis for the inclusion of smaller firms in their analyses.

2.1.2   The Dynamic Development of Industries

We can thus assert that entrepreneurship and economic theory have never been easy travelling companions (Metcalfe, 2004) and that interest in entrepreneurship and small business among more "pure" economists has been relatively limited. On the other hand, interest in industrial dynamics, innovation and the study of the entrepreneurial function increased among researchers within so-called industrial organizations – the field of research in micro economics that comes closest to management studies.

For a long time researchers in industrial organizations were embedded in the idea of mass production and economies of scale. Early industrial organization research was concerned with the complex set of problems associated with economic concentration in the market, and the efficiency of oligopolistic markets. A characteristic of this research was not only the focus on market concentration and oligopoly but also the view that small businesses are sub-optimal in terms of the scale of production, and the research itself was highly static in nature. There was a concern about the existing industrial structures but little attention was paid to the emergence of new structures and the development of old ones (Audretsch, 1997).

However, based on the static view, the researchers identified two puzzles: (i) the persistence of an asymmetric firm-size distribution predominated by small firms and (ii) new firms are not deterred from entering industries where economies of scale play an important role (ibid.). The need for a more dynamic perspective on industrial organization was obvious. A shift in focus can be identified among industrial organization researchers in the 1980s, with the introduction of a more dynamic or evolutionary framework and a stronger emphasis on the role and contribution of small business. In this respect, Richard Nelson and Sidney Winter were among the pioneers due to their application of an evolutionary model of economic development in their seminal book *An Evolutionary Theory of Economic Change* (1982). The evolutionary idea was also adopted by Boyan Jovanovic (1982). In his model, new firms face costs that are not only random but also differ across firms. A new firm does not know what its cost function is, i.e. its relative efficiency, but rather discovers it through the process of learning from its actual post-entry performance. Those entrepreneurs who discover that their ability exceeds their expectations will increase the scale of their business. Jovanovic's model is a theory of "noisy selection", where efficient firms grow and survive, but inefficient firms decline and fail.

There are a number of researchers within industrial organization that can be regarded as pioneers and that started to examine the dynamic process: from the entry of new firms into industrial markets, their survival and growth, or their exit from the industry. Traditionally, the entry of new firms has been regarded as interesting because they have an equilibrating function in the market in that price and profit are restored to a competitive level – new firms are about "business as usual". An alternative explanation was presented by Audretsch (1995) who argued that new firms entering an industry do not simply increase output by being a smaller replica of other firms in the industry but serve as "agents of change" as a result of their innovative activities. This idea is based on the knowledge production function model, formulated by Zvi Griliches (1979), in which the most decisive input is new economic knowledge. The greatest source of new economic knowledge is generally considered to be R&D (Cohen & Klepper, 1991; 1992), and this seems to hold at all levels of aggregation, as the most innovative countries are those with the greatest investment in R&D (Audretsch, 2002). However, the relationship becomes less convincing at the disaggregated microeconomic level of the enterprise. Zoltan Acs and David Audretsch (1990) have shown that small firms can serve as the engine of innovative activity in certain industries as a result of their systematic investigation of the determinants of innovative activities in different industries.

In some industries the new knowledge that generates innovative activities tends to be rather routine and can be managed within the context of incumbent hierarchical bureaucracies, whereas in other industries innovation tends to emerge from knowledge that is not of a routine nature and therefore is rejected by hierarchical bureaucracies. Nelson and Winter (1974; 1978; 1982) described this as two distinct technological regimes: the entrepreneurial and the routinized. The major conclusion of Acs and Audretsch (1990; see also Audretch, 1995) was that the existence of these distinct regimes can be inferred by the extent to which small firms are able to innovate relative to the total amount of innovative activity in an industry, i.e. when the small firm innovation rate is high, the knowledge conditions are more likely to reflect an entrepreneurial regime.

One of the major conclusions from studies about entry is that the process does not end with the entry – industry dynamics depend on what happens to new firms following their entry (Audretsch, 1995). Early studies (e.g. Mansfield, 1962; Audretsch, 1991) indicate that not only is the likelihood of a new entrant surviving quite low but also that the likelihood of survival is positively related to firm size and age. In this respect, what has become known as Gibrat's Law (Gibrat, 1931), or the assumption that growth rate is identical regardless of firm size, has been subject to numerous empirical tests (Hall, 1987). There is evidence that the growth of small and new firms is negatively related to firm size and age (Hall, 1987; Wagner, 1992; 1994) while the growth of larger firms is independent of size and age.

2.1.3   Agglomeration in Space

The early researchers in the field were not only interested in the importance of small businesses for employment and industrical dynamics – during the 1970s their importance for regional development was also identified. This pioneering work was primarily made by a couple of Italian economists, of whom Giacomo Becattini at the University of Florence can be regarded as the most prominent. Another pioneer of research on industrial districts was Sebastiano Brusco at the University of Modena with an empirical base in the Emilia Romagna region, in contrast to Becattini, whose base was in the Tuscan economy.

Most of Becattini's and Brusco's works were written in Italian, and it was not until Michael Piore and Charles Sabel published their book *The Second Industrial Divide* in 1984 that the concept of industrial district received international attention. The research program on industrial districts organized by the International Institute for Labour Studies in Geneva with Werner Sengenberger as co-ordinator also contributed to international interest.

The international recognition of the concept of industrial district has prompted many researchers to draw inspiration from the Italian industrial districts and the experience of the Italian researchers. Of these, Michael Porter of Harvard Business School has exerted the greatest influence, and in his book *The Competitive Advantage of Nations* in 1990, he publicised the cluster concept, and his theory formation was accepted both in main stream economics and in management studies.

The cluster concept has, not least through Porter's seminal contribution, had a major influence not only among researchers but also among politicians and policy-makers. In many cases the focus of the researchers' attention has been the technology oriented regions and clusters – especially Silicon Valley in California – which have symbolized the importance of entrepreneurship. Several attempts have been made to understand the dynamics of these regions by, among others, AnnaLee Saxenian, who is one of the best known researchers in this area and who showed an early interest in these technological clusters.

A similar interest in science parks and technology oriented regions can also be seen among UK researchers, for example Ray Oakey and Doreen Massey. In general, the regional aspects of entrepreneurship have been the focus of great interest among UK researchers – some regions in the UK appear to exhibit a higher rate of new firm formation as well as superior dynamics and development in the area of social welfare compared to other regions. Examples of researchers who focussed on the regional aspects of entrepreneurship at an early stage are David Storey as well as Graham Gudgin and David Keeble.

2.1.4 Summary – Examples of Pioneers with a Macro-level Focus

A conclusion is, thus, that we can identify a number of researchers with a focus on macro-level analysis, who took an early interest in the entrepreneurial function in society, the dynamic development of industries, and the agglomeration of small firms. In Figure 5-1 some of these pioneers are presented. It should be mentioned that the categorization of the researchers has not been entirely easy, as in many cases they have been involved in many different aspects, with the consequence that their research is to a great extent overlapping.

Themes	Examples of pioneers
The entrepreneurial function in society	William Baumol, Mark Casson, Israel Kirzner, Robert Hebert, Albert Link
Economics of innovation	Erik Dahmén, Bo Carlsson, Kenneth Arrow, Gunnar Eliasson, Gerhard Mensch
Job creation and employment	David Birch, David Storey, Steven Johnson, Graham Gudgin, John Atkinson, Catherine Armington, Marjorie Odle, Graham Bannock, David Evans, Charles Brown, James Medoff
The dynamic development of industries	Richard Nelson, Sidney Winter, Boyan Jovanovic, Giovanni Dosi, William Brock, David Evans
Size distribution (large and small firms)	Frederic Scherer, William Brock, David Evans, Gary Loveman, Robert Lucas, Boyan Jovanovic, Lawrence White
Enter – survival – growth – exit	David Evans, Linda Leighton, Bruce Phillips, Bruce Kirchhoff, Paul Reynolds, Boyan Jovanovic, Paul Geroski
Innovation	Zoltan Acs, David Audretsch, Bo Carlsson, Roy Rothwell, Sidney Winter, Richard Nelson
Agglomeration in space	Giacomo Becattini, Sebastiano Brusco, Werner Sengenberger, Michael Piore, Charles Sabel, Michael Porter, Paul Krugman, David Storey, Graham Gudgin, David Keeble, AnnaLee Saxenian, Ray Oakey, Doreen Massey

Figure 5-1. Pioneers - macro-level analysis.

2.2   Pioneers – Micro-level Analysis

It is also possible to identify a number of early researchers with an interest in entrepreneurship and small business but with a stronger focus on micro-level analysis – researchers with their roots in management studies.

2.2.1   Thematic Development

In the early years of entrepreneurship research (see Chapter 3), there were strong links to the behavioral science research of the 1960s on the entrepreneur as an individual. A number of researchers built their work on this research tradition, and some of the best known articles in this area are:

Liles, P.R., 1974, Who Are the Entrepreneurs?, *MSU Business Topics*, Winter, 5-14.

Shapero, A., 1975, The Displaced, Uncomfortable Entrepreneur, *Psychology Today*, November, 83-88.

Stanworth, M.J.K. & Curran, J., 1976, Growth and the Small firm – An Alternative View, *Journal of Management Studies*, May, 95-110.

Ketz de Vries, M.F.R., 1977, The Entrepreneurial Personality: A Person at the Crossroad, *Journal of Management Studies*, 14, 1, 34-57.

Brockhaus Sr, R.H., 1980, Risk Taking Propensity of Entrepreneurs, *Academy of Management Journal*, 23, 509-520.

Carland, J.W. & Hoy, F. & Boulton, W.R. & Carland, J.A., 1984, Differentiating Entrepreneurs from Small Business Owners: A Conceptualization, *Academy of Management Review*, 2, 79-93.

Hence, the focus was on the individual, and researchers very soon realized that entrepreneurs were different from other types of leaders (see for example the comparison between entrepreneurs and managers in the study by Collins, Moore and Unwalla in Chapter 3). Moreover, the group of entrepreneurs was extremely heterogeneous, which led the researchers to focus on specific categories of entrepreneurs who were perceived to possess certain qualities. There was, for example, an interest in women entrepreneurs, and Robert Hisrich in collaboration with Marie O'Brien was one of the pioneers in this area. They presented their studies at the first Babson Conferences in 1981 and 1982 but also in an article "The Woman Entrepreneur: Management Skills and Business Problems", which Hisrich presented together with Candida Brush in the *Journal of Small Business Management* (1984). Another category of entrepreneurs who attracted considerable attention consisted of those who established and managed technology based operations. The researchers were highly interested in the new technology based companies, their development and growth as well as the individuals behind them (see for example studies by Cooper, Roberts and Wainer, Litvak and Maule).

The researchers soon discovered that the venture process was something more than an individual phenomenon – it was a social one – and, consequently, the research on "social networks" in entrepreneurship became prominent at an early stage:

Birley, S., 1985, The role of Network in the Entrepreneurial Process, *Journal of Business Venturing*, 1, 107-117.

Aldrich, H. & Zimmer, C., 1986, Entrepreneurship Through Social Networks, in Sexton, D.L. & Smilor, R.W. (eds.), *The Art and Science of Entrepreneurship*, Cambridge, MA: Balloinger, 3-23.

Johannisson, B., 1987, Anarchists and organisers: Entrepreneurs in a network perspective, *International Studies of Management and Organisation*, XVII, 1, 49-63.

Larson, A., 1988, Networks as social system, unpublished doctoral thesis, Harvard Graduate School of Business Administration, Boston, MA.

Entrepreneurship researchers have long been interested in venture capital, and several researchers have concentrated on issues related to the scope, character and importance of venture capital for new companies, for example Jeffry Timmons, William Wetzel, David Brophy, Albert Bruno, Tyzoon Tyebjee, Ian MacMillan, William Bygrave and William Sahlman. An example of an individual pioneering contribution is William Wetzel's article on business angels "Angels and informal risk capital" in *Sloan Management Review* in 1983. Even if the informal venture capital market had been observed by researchers in the 1970s, Wetzel was the first to shed some light on the significance of the informal investor's market. In the area of formal venture capital, the articles by Tyzoon Tyebjee and Albert Bruno on the venture capital process "A Model of Venture Capital Investment Activity" in *Management Studies* (1984) and Gorman and Sahlman's article "What do venture capitalists do?" in *Journal of Business Venturing* (1989) deserve to be mentioned. Another of the central pioneering works is William Bygrave and Jeffry Timmons' book "*Venture Capital at the Crossroads*" (1992).

For many years there has also been an interest in the study of new innovations – the commercialization of new technologies – technology-based entrepreneurship. As early as the 1940s and 1950s, universities offered programs in "Engineering Business", designed for business students with a future career, that required a background in applied science (Kao et al., 2002), and in 1965 Harry Schrage wrote the first major work on high technology-based entrepreneurship in "The R&D entrepreneur: profile of success" in *Harvard Business Review*. In the 1970s the development of new industries, such as computer technology, semi-conductors, and micro-processors was identified as important for economic development. New firms in these industries were often spin-offs from universities or research institutes, which developed along

Route 128 and in Silicon Valley – a phenomenon observed by researchers such as Edward Roberts at MIT and Arnold Cooper at Purdue University. In Europe David Watkins in the UK was one of the first to recognize the new technology-based firms, and he presented a paper on "technical entrepreneurship" at the Rencontres de St-Gall in Switzerland in the early 1970s (see Watkins, 1973). Some of the first studies on technology-based firms include:

> Roberts, E.B., 1968, Entrepreneurship and technology: a basic study of innovators, *Research Management*, 11, 4, 249-266.

> Cooper, A.C., 1971, The Foundation of Technology-Based Firms, Milwaukee, WI: Center for Venture Management.

Entrepreneurship researchers have also for a long time had close links to strategic management – several of the pioneers of entrepreneurship research were also regarded as pioneers in the area of strategic management – which led to an early interest in "performance", expressed as an interest in finding predictors of success for new ventures, and in some cases also for an investigation of corporate entrepreneurship. The first group of studies attempted to identify predictors of survival and growth (or lack thereof) in either the entrepreneurs' background, the chosen strategy, environmental considerations, or some combination of these (see Cooper & Bruno, 1975; Miller, 1983; Dollinger, 1984). For example, Sandberg and Hofer (1987) found that industry structure and venture strategy constitute more important influences on venture performance than "internal factors", such as the entrepreneur and the founding team. But the interest in predictors of survival and growth also included research by for example Timmons and Bygrave (1986), who attempted to identify predictors of success in new ventures funded by venture capitalists.

The importance of "corporate entrepreneurship" was also recognized at an early stage, and the "intrapreneurship" concept was one of the earliest attempts to apply creativitity and entrepreneurship in the corporate environment. An early contributor was Peter Drucker, who through his book *Innovation and Entrepreneurship* (1985), where he discussed the role of entrepreneurship in management, became very influential in legitimizing entrepreneurship among traditional business schools in the US. In her book *The Change Master* (1983), Rosabeth Moss Kanter described the organizational characteristics of the most innovative companies, and Gifford Pinchot wrote about different phases of the corporate entrepreneurship process in his book *Intrapreneuring* (1985), while Robert Burgelman developed a framework for corporate venturing (1983; 1984). Other researchers with an interest in corporate entrepreneurship who can be regarded as pioneers within the area are: Norman Fast, Ian MacMillan, Zenas Block, Bill Gutz, Hans

Schollhammer, Michael Tushman, Eric von Hippel, and James Brian Quinn.

Finally, there was an early research interest in the management of small firms. An extensive review of our knowledge of small business management is given in the book *Betriebswirtschaftslehre der Klein- und Mittelbetriebe* (1993) by Josef Mugler. Researchers with roots in the field of business administration have tried to apply different management models to small business. However, many of these models were designed for large businesses although some are probably also relevant to the operation of small businesses. These models consist of function oriented models (e.g. marketing, finance, strategy, management control) or models of specific business development situations (such as growth, internationalization and business failures), models applicable to specific categories of small firms such as family firms, firms in the service sector, etc. Small business management appears to be a non-US research theme (even if some US researchers seem to have taken an early interest in small business management). I will not attempt to provide a comprehensive picture but merely mention some of the pioneers who have tried to apply a "management perspective" to small business, such as: Ingolf Bamberger, Geoffrey Meredith, Rik Donckels, Mario Raffa, David Kirby, Josef Mugler, William Sandberg, Frank Hoy, and David Brophy.

2.2.2   Conceptual Development

For a long time the conceptual development of entrepreneurship knowledge was limited, due to the emphasis on discovery-oriented research with its focus on descriptions and normative studies. Some early contributions to the conceptual development of the field were presented by William Gartner, whose work is, in my opinion, of major importance:

- In his conceptual framework based on his thesis (Gartner, 1982), in which he observed the great heterogeneity among entrepreneurs and their ventures, he argued that new venture creation includes four major aspects: (i) characteristics of the individual(s) who start the venture, (ii) the organization which they create, (iii) the environment surrounding the new venture, and (iv) the process by which the new venture is created (see Gartner, W.B., 1985, A framework for describing the phenomenon of new venture creation, *Academy of Management Review*, 10, 4, 696-706).
- Thus, the process was essential in Gartner's reasoning about entrepreneurship, and he was one of the first to claim that entrepreneurship researchers ought to pay more attention to the processual aspects of venture creation, as in his view entrepreneurship is primarily concerned with the creation of new organizations (see Gartner, W.B., 1988, Who is the entrepreneur? Is

the wrong question, *American Journal of Small Business*, 12, 4, 11-32).

Another early contributor to the conceptual development of the field was Howard Stevenson. Stevenson (Stevenson & Gumpert, 1985; Stevenson & Jarillo, 1986) developed an opportunity-based view on entrepreneurship which he defined as a process by which individuals – either on their own or within organizations – pursue and exploit opportunities irrespective of the resources they currently control. According to Stevenson, the entrepreneurial process can take place in any type of organizational context, while in established organizations entrepreneurship is largely a management issue and "entrepreneurial management may be seen as a different 'mode of management' to traditional management" (Stevenson & Jarillo, 1990, p. 25). In this respect Stevenson placed entrepreneurship within a broader management framework and along eight dimensions (strategic orientation, commitment to opportunity, commitment of resources, control of resources, management structure, reward philosophy, growth orientation, and entrepreneurial culture), and he contrasts entrepreneurial behavior (promoter) with administrative behavior (trustee) in an organization.

Thus, both Gartner and Stevenson stress the importance of the venture process rather than a focus on the entrepreneur as an individual. Many scholars with an interest in entrepreneurship had an academic affiliation to management studies, in which the firm was the unit of analysis. A topical question was how business opportunities and companies are established and developed. A central theme is therefore what can be described as "the venture process", and there are many early researchers who took an interest in this theme. This resulted in several "processual models" on the venture creation process and growth, usually strongly normative (examples of such models were presented by Neil Churchill and Virginia Lewis, and Clifford Baumback and Joseph Mancuso). The venture process also includes the growth of the firm. One systematic approach to venture creation and growth was suggested by Jeffry Timmons (1971; 1979; 1980). According to Timmons, a high-potential, growth oriented venture is characterized by: (i) a talented lead entrepreneur with a balanced team, (ii) a technically sound and marketable idea, (ii) a thorough venture anaysis and a complete business plan, and (iv) appropriate financing of the venture.

2.2.3 Summary – Examples of Pioneers with a Micro-level Focus

The pioneers presented in this section have a stronger focus on micro-level analysis – the individual, the process, behavior and performance of the firm – and have generally had a background in management studies. At the risk of being too subjective I will in Figure 5-2 present a number of pioneers with a micro-level focus. As in the case of pioneers with a macro-level focus, the thematic categorization is difficult to make, since several of the pioneers have investigated many different topics in their research.

Themes	Examples of pioneers
Small business management	Josef Mugler, Rik Donckels, Ingolf Bamberger, Horst Albach, Hans Jobst Pleitner, Mario Raffa, Michel Merchesnay, David Kirby, Gerald Hills, William Sandberg, Charles Hofer, Justin Longnecker, Frank Hoy, David Brophy, Dick Ramström, Jonathan Boswell, John Deeks.
Performance	
Survival and growth	Arnold Cooper, William Dunkelberg, Carolyn Woo, Jeffry Timmons, Albert, Bruno, Danny Miller, Marc Dollinger, William Bygrave, Charles Hofer, William Sandberg, Joseph Brüderl, Peter Preisendörfer, Rolf Ziegler
Corporate entrepreneurship	Norman Fast, Rosabeth Moss Kanter, Robert Burgelman, Ian MacMillan, Zenas Block, Gifford Pinchot, Peter Drucker, Bill Gutz, Hans Schollhammer, Michael Tushman, Eric von Hippel, James Brian Quinn, Jeffrey Covin, Dennis Slevin, Danny Miller
Process and behavior	
Venture process	William Gartner, Neil Churchill, Virginia Lewis, Howard Stevenson, Carl Vesper, Clifford Baumback, Joseph Mancuso, Arnold Cooper, William Dunkelberg, Jeffry Timmons, William Bygrave
Social networks	Howard Aldrich, Cathrine Zimmer, Sue Birley, Bengt Johannisson, Andrea Larson
Venture Capital	Jeffry Timmons, William Wetzel, David Brophy, Albert Bruno, Tyzoon Tyebjee, Ian MacMillan, William Bygrave, William Sahlman
Technology-based firms	Harry Schrage, Arnold Cooper, Edward Roberts, David Watkins, Norman Fast, James Utterback, Modesto Maidique, Douglas McQueen, Torkel Wallmark, Robert Kazanjian, William Abernathy
Individual and cognition	
General	Patrick Liles, Manfred Kets de Vries, Albert Shapero, John Stanworth, Jim Curran, Robert Brockhaus, James Carland, Frank Hoy, William Boulton, JoAnn Carland, Elisabeth Chell
Women entrepreneurs	Robert Hisrich, Candida Brush, Marie O'Brien
Technical entrepreneurs	Arnold Cooper, Edward Roberts, Herbert Wainer, Isaiah Litvak, Christopher Maule

Figure 5-2. Pioneers - micro-level analysis.

3.   AND THE WINNER IS ...

In order to stimulate the development of the field and promote scientific work of outstanding quality and importance, the Swedish Foundation for Small Business Research (FSF) instituted an annual award of USD 50,000 in 1995, sponsored by the Swedish Business Development Agency (NUTEK) and the Swedish telecommunications company Telia. This award, known as the FSF-NUTEK International Award, is presented annually to a researcher in entrepreneurship and small business research who has "produced scientific work of outstanding quality and importance, thereby making a significant contribution to theory-building in the area of entrepreneurship and small business development and/or the role and importance of new firm formation and/or SME's role in economic development".

The annual winner is selected by an independent scientific committee, consisting of the leading Swedish scholars in the field. The committee reviews nominations from more than 250 qualified international researchers who are invited to nominate candidates for the Award. The nomination process and the prize money involved make the FSF-NUTEK Award one of the most prestigious within the research field.

Between 1996 and 2002 nine researchers have been awarded the prize, of whom each can be regarded as a pioneer within the field of entrepreneurship and small business research:

1996   David Birch, Cognetics Inc, USA
1997   Arnold Cooper, Purdue University, USA
1998   David Storey, Warwick Business School, UK
1999   Ian MacMillan, Wharton School of Business, USA
2000   Howard Aldrich, University of North Carolina, USA
2001   Zoltan Acs, University of Baltimore, and David Audretsch, Indiana University, USA
2002   Giacomo Becattini, University of Florence, Italy, and Charles Sabel, Columbia Law School, USA

In Part II and Part III of the book these award winners and pioneers in entrepreneurship research will be presented in more detail.

REFERENCES

Aldrich, H. & Zimmer, C., 1986, Entrepreneurship Through Social Networks, in Sexton, D.L. & Smilor, R.W. (eds.), *The Art and Science of Entrepreneurship*, Cambridge, MA: Ballinger, pp 3-23.

Acs, Z.J. & Audretsch, D.B., 1990, *Innovation and Small Firms*, Cambridge, MA: MIT Press.

Audretsch, D.B., 1991, New-Firm Survival and the Technological Regime, *Review of Economics and Statistics*, 73, 3, 441-450.

Audretsch, D.B., 1995, *Innovation and Industry Evolution*, Cambridge: MIT Press.

Audretsch, D.B., 1997, Technological Regimes, Industrial Demography and the Evolution of Industrial Structures, *Industrial and Corporate Change*, 6, 1, 49-82.

Audretsch, D.B., 2001, Research Issues Relating to Structure, Competition, and Performance of Small Technology-Based Firms, *Small Business Economics*, 16, 37-51.

Audretsch, D.B., 2002, The Dynamic Role of Small Firms: Evidence from the US, *Small Business Economics*, 13, 13-40.

Baty, G., 1974, *Entrepreneurship: Playing to Win*, Englewood Cliffs, NJ: Prentice-Hall.

Baumback, C.M. & Mancuso, J.R., 1975, *Entrepreneurship and Venture Management*, Englewood Cliffs, NJ: Prentice-Hall.

Baumol, W.J., 1968, Entrepreneurship in Economic Theory, *American Economic Review*, 58, 64-71.

Birch, D.L., 1979, *The Job Generation Process*, MIT Program on Neighborhood and Regional Change, Cambridge, MA.

Birley, S., 1985, The role of Network in the Entrepreneurial Process, *Journal of Business Venturing*, 1, pp 107-117.

Brock, W.A. & Evans, D.S., 1989, Small Business Economics, *Small Business Economics*, 1, 1, 7-20.

Brockhaus Sr, R.H., 1980, Risk Taking Propensity of Entrepreneurs, *Academy of Management Journal*, 23, 509-520.

Brockhaus, B., 2003, History of the International Council for Small Business, *ICSB Bulletin*, 45, 3-4, 4-5.

Broom, H., 1961, *Small Business Management*, Cincinnati: Southwestern.

Burgelman, R.A., 1983, A Process modell of internal corporate venturing in the diversified major firm, *Administrative Science Quarterly*, 28, 2, 223-244.

Burgelman, R.A., 1984, Design for corporate entrepreneurship in established firms, *California Management Review*, 26, 3, 154-166.

Bygrave, W.E. & Timmons, J.A., 1992, *Venture Capital at the Crossroad*, Boston: Harvard Business School Press.

Carland, J.W. & Hoy, F. & Boulton, W.R. & Carland, J.A., 1984, Differentiating Entrepreneurs from Small Business Owners: A Conceptualization, *Academy of Management Review*, 2, 79-93.

Carlsson, B., 1992, The rise of small business: causes and consequences, in Adams, W.J. (ed.), *Singular Europe, economy and policy of the European community after 1992*, Ann Arbor, MI: University of Michigan Press.

Casson, M., 1982, *The Entrepreneur*, Totowa, NJ.: Barnes and Noble Books.

Churchill, N.C. & Lewis, V.L., 1983, The five stages of small business growth, *Harvard Business Review*, 61, 3, 30-50.

Cohen, W. M. & Klepper, S., 1991, Firm Size Versus Diversity in the Achievement of Technological Advance, in Acs, Z.J. & Audretsch, D.B. (eds.), *Innovation and Technological change: An International Comparison*, Ann Arbor: University of Michigan Press.

Cohen, W. M. & Klepper, S., 1992, The Tradeoff Between Firm Size and Diversity in the Pursuit of Technological Progress, *Small Business Economics*, 4, 1, 1-14.

Cooper, A.C., 1971, *The Foundation of Technology-Based Firms*, Milwaukee, WI: Center for Venture Management.

Cooper, A.C., 2003, Entrepreneurship: The Past, the Present, the Future, in Acs, Z.J. & Audretsch, D.B. (eds.), *Handbook of Entrepreneurship Research*, Dordrecht: Kluwer.

Cooper, A.C. & Bruno, A.V., 1975, Predicting performance in new high-technology firms, proceedings of the 35th Academy of Management Meeting, 426-428.

Cooper, A.C. & Hornaday, J.A. & Vesper, K.H., 1997, The field of entrepreneurship over time, Frontiers of Entrepreneurship, xi-xvii.

Cooper, A.C. & Markman, G.D. & Niss, G., 2000, The Evolution of the Field of Entrepreneurship, in Meyer, G.D. & Heppard, K.A. (eds.), *Entrepreneurship as Strategy. Competing on the Entrepreneurial Edge*, Thousand Oaks: Sage.

Covin, J.G. & Slevin, D.P., 1988, The influence of organization structure on the utility of an entrepreneurial top management style, *Journal of Management Studies*, 25, 217-234.

Covin, J.G. & Slevin, D.P., 1989, Strategic management of small firms in hostile and beign environments, *Strategic Management Journal*, 10, 1, 75-87.

Covin, J.G. & Slevin, D.P., 1991, A Conceptual Model of Entrepreneurship as Firm Behavior, *Entrepreneurship Theory and Practice*, 16, 1, 7-25.

Dahmén, E., 1970, *Entrepreneurial Activity and the Development of Swedish Industry 1919-1939*, Homewood, Ill: Irwin.

Dollinger, M.J., 1984, Environmental boudary spanning and information processing effects on organizational performance, *Academy of Management Journal*, 27, 2, 351-368.

Dosi, G., 1982, Technological Paradigms and Technological Trajectories: a Suggested Interpretation of the Deeerminants and Directions of Technical Change, *Research Policy*, 13, 3-20.

Dosi, G., 1988, Sources, Procedures, and Microeconomic Effects of Innovation, *Journal of Economic Literature*, 26, 3, 112-117.

Drucker, P., 1985, *Innovation and entrepreneurship*, New York: Harper & Row.

Eliasson, G., 1987, Technological Competition and Trade in the Experimentally Organized Economy, Research Report No 32, Stockholm: IUI.

Eliasson, G., 1992, Organizational Learning and Economic Growth: Establishing the Smith-Schumpeter-Wicksell Connection, in Scherer, F.M. & Perlman, M. (eds.), *Entrepreneurship, Technological Innovations, and Economic Growth*, Ann Arbor: University of Michigan Press.

Eliasson, G., 1996, *The Firm, Its Objectives, Its Controls and Its Organization*, Dordrecht: Kluwer.

Eliasson, G. & Eliasson, Å., 1996, The Biotechnological Competence Bloc, *Revue d'Economie Industrielle*, 78-4, Trimestre.

Fothergill, S. & Gudgin, G., 1982, *Unequal Growth*, London: Heinemann.

Gartner, W.B., 1982, An empirical model of the business start-up and eight entreprenurial archtypes, unpublished doctoral thesis, University of Washington, Seattle.

Gartner, W., 1985, A conceptual framework for describing the phenomenon of new venture creation, *Academy of Management Review*, 10, 4, 696-706.

Gartner, W.B., 1988, Who is the entrepreneur? Is the wrong question, *American Journal of Small Business*, 12, 4, 11-32.

Gartner, W.B. & Bird, B.J. & Starr, J.A., 1992, Acting as if: differentiating entrepreneurial from organizational behaviour, *Entrepreneurship Theory and Practice*, 16, 3, 13-31.

Gibrat, R., 1931, *Les Inégalités Economique*, Paris: Libraire de Recueil Sirez.

Gorman, M. & Sahlman, W.A., 1989, What do venture capitalists do?, *Journal of Business Venturing*, 4, 231-248.

Griliches, Z., 1979, Issues in assesing the contribution of R&D to productivity growth, *Bell Journal of Economics*, 10, 92-116.

Gudgin, G., 1978, *Industrial Location Processes and Regional Employment Growth*, Farnborough: Saxon House.

Hall, B.H., 1987, The relationship between firm size and firm growth in the US manufacturing sector, *Journal of Industrial Economics*, 35, 583-605.

Hisrich, R.D. & Brush, C., 1984, The Women Entrepreneur: Management Skills and Business Problems, *Journal of Small Business Management*, January, 30-37.

Jacobs, J., 1969, *The Economy of Cities*, New York: Random House.

Johannisson, B., 1987, Anarchists and organisers: Entrepreneurs in a network perspective, *International Studies of Management and Organisation*, XVII, 1, 49-63.

Jovanovic, B., 1982, Selection and Evolution of Industry, *Econometrica*, 50, 649-670.

Kanter, R.M., 1983, *Change Masters*, New York: Simon and Schuster.

Kao, R.W.Y. & Kao, K.R. & Kao, R.R., 2002, *Entrepreneurism*, London: Imperial College Press.

Katz, J.A., 2003, The Cronology and Intellectual Trajectory of American Entrepreneurship Education, *Journal of Business Venturing*, 18, 283-300.

Kazanjian, R.K., 1988, Relation of dominant problems to stages of growth in technology-based new ventures, *Academy of Management Journal*, 31, 2, 257-279.

Keeble, D., 1978, *Industrial Location and Planning in the United Kingdom*, London: Methuen.

Kent, C.A. & Sexton, D.L. & Vesper, K.H. (eds.), 1982, *Encyclopedia of Entrepreneurship*, Englewood Cliffs, NJ: Prentice-Hall.

Ketz de Vries, M.F.R., 1977, The Entrepreneurial Personality: A Person at the Crossroad, *Journal of Management Studies*, 14, 1, 34-57.

Kilby, P. (ed.), 1971, *Entrepreneurship and Economic Development*, New York: Free Press.

Kirzner, I.M., 1973, *Competition and Entrepreneurship*, Chicago: University of Chicago Press.

Larson, A., 1988, Networks as social system, unpublished doctoral thesis, Harvard Graduate School of Business Administration, Boston, MA.

Liles, P.R., 1972, *New Business Ventures and the Entrepreneur*, Homewood, Ill: Irwin.

Liles, P.R., 1974, Who Are the Entrepreneurs?, *MSU Business Topics*, Winter, 5-14.

Litvak, I.A. & Maule, C.J., 1973, Some characteristics of successful technical entrepreneurs in Canada, *IEEE Transactions on Engineering Management*, 20, 3.

Mansfield, E., 1962, Entry Gibrat's Law, Innovation and the Growth of Firms, *American Economic Review*, 52, 5, 1023-1051.

McCarthy, A.M. & Nicholls-Nixon, C.L., 2001, Arnold Cooper on entrepreneurship and wealth creation, *Academy of Management Executive*, 15, 1, 27-34.

Metcalfe, J.S., 2004, The entrepreneur and the style of modern economics, in Corbetta, G. & Huse, M. & Ravasi, D. (eds.), *Crossroad of Entrepreneurship*, Dordrecht: Kluwer.

Miller, D., 1983, The correlates of entrepreneurship in three types of firms, *Management Science*, 29, 7, 770-791.

Mugler, J., 1993, *Betriebswirtschaftslehre der Klein- und Mittelbetriebe*, Band 1 & Band 2, Wien: Springer.

Nelson, R.R. & Winter, S.G., 1974, Neoclassical vs Evolutionary Theories of Economics Growth: Critique and Prospectus, *Economic Journal*, 84, 886-905.

Nelson, R.R. & Winter, S.G., 1978, Forces Generating and Limiting Concentration under Schumpeterian Competition, *Bell Journal of Economics*, 9, 524-548.

Nelson, R.R. & Winter, S.G., 1982, *An Evolutionary Theory of Economic Change*, Cambridge: Harvard University Press.

Oakey, R.P., 1979, An analysis of the spatial distribution of significant Britisk industrial innovations, CURDS, paper no 25, University of Newcastle upon Tyne.

Pinchot, G., 1985, *Intrapreneuring*, New York: Harper & Row.

Piore, M.J. & Sabel, C.F., 1984, *The Second Industrial Divide. Possibilities for Prosperity*, New York: Basic Books.

Porter, M., 1990, *The Competitive Advantage of Nations*, New York: Free Press.

Roberts, E.B., 1968, Entrepreneurship and technology: a basic study of innovators, *Research Management*, 11, 4, 249-266.

Roberts, E.B. & Wainer, H., 1966, Some Characteristics of the Technical Entrepreneur, Working Paper 195-66, Sloan School of Management, MIT.

Sahlman, W., 1990, The Structure and overnance of Venture Capital Organizations, *Journal of Financial Economics*, 27, 473-521.

Sandberg, W.R. & Hofer, C.W., 1987, Improving new venture performance: the role of strategy, industry structure and the entrepreneur, *Journal of Business Venturing*, 2, 1, 5-28.

Saxenian, A., 1990, Regional networks and the resurgence of Silicon Valley, *California Management Review*, 33, 89-111.

Schollhammer, H., 1982, International Corporate Entrepreneurship, in Kent, C.A. & Sexton, D.L. & Vesper, K.H. (eds.), *Encyclopedia of Entrepreneurship*, Prentice Hall: Englewood Cliffs, NJ.

Schrage, H., 1965, R&D entrepreneur: profile of sucess, *Harvard Business Review*, 43, 6, 56-69.

Sexton, D.L. & Smilor, R. (eds.), 1986, *The Art and Science of Entrepreneurship*, Cambridge, MA: Ballinger.

Shapero, A., 1975, The Displaced Uncomfortable Entrepreneur, *Psychology Today*, 9, 83-88.

Stanworth, M.J.K. & Curran, J., 1976, Growth and the Small firm – An Alternative View, *Journal of Management Studies*, May, 95-110.

Stevenson, H.H. & Gumpert, D., 1985, The Heart of Entrepreneurship, *Harvard Business Review*, March-April, 85, 2, 85-94.

Stevenson, H.H. & Jarillo, J.C., 1986, Preserving entrepreneurship as companies grow, *Journal of Business Strategy*, 6, 10-23.

Stevenson, H.H. & Jarillo, J.C., 1990, A paradigm of entrepreneurship: entrepreneurial management, *Strategic Management Journal*, 11, 17-27.

Timmons, J.A., 1971, Black is Beautiful – Is It Bountiful?, *Harvard Business Review*, Nov-Dec.

Timmons, J., 1977, *New Venture Creation*, Boston, MA: Irwin.

Timmons, J.A., 1979, Careful Analysis and Team Assessment Can Aid Entrepreneurs, *Harvard Business Review*, Nov-Dec.

Timmons, J.A., 1980, A Business Plan Is More than a Financing Device, *Harvard Business Review*, March-April.

Timmons, J.A. & Bygrave, W.D., 1986, Venture capitalist's role in financing innovations for economic growth, *Journal of Business Venturing*, 1, 2, 161-176.

Tyebjee, T.T. & Bruno, A.V., 1984, A Model of Venture Capitalist Investment Activity, *Management Science*, 30, 9, 1051-1066.

Vesper, K.H., 1982, Research on education for entrepreneurship, in Kent, C.A. & Sexton, D.L. & Vesper, K.H. (eds.), *Encyclopedia of Entrepreneurship*, Englewood Cliffs, NJ: Prentice-Hall.

Wagner, J., 1992, Firm Size, Firm Growth and Persistence of Change: Testing Gibrat's Law with Establishment Data from Lower Saxony, 1978-1989, *Small Business Economics*, 4, 2, 125-131.

Wagner, J., 1994, Small Firm Entry in Manufacturing Industries: Lower Saxony, 1979-1989, *Small Business Economics*, 6, 3, 211-224.

Watkins, D.S., 1973, Technical entrepreneurship: a cis-Atlantic view, *R&D Management*, 3, 2, 65-70.

Wetzel, W.E., 1983, Angle and informal risk capital, *Sloan Management Review*, 24, 4, 23-34.

PIONEERS – MACRO-LEVEL ANALYSIS

Chapter 6

DAVID BIRCH

1. DAVID BIRCH – A GENUINE PIONEERING ACHIEVEMENT AND A BREAKTHROUGH FOR ENTREPRENEURSHIP AND SMALL BUSINESS RESEARCH

1.1 The Contributions of David Birch

David Birch presented his report *The Job Generation Process* in 1979 – at a time of transition in American society; the large-scale systems and giant corporations were beginning to be questioned, the structure of industry was undergoing change and new industries were starting to emerge, unemployment was high, and a trend in the economy toward more small businesses could be discerned. Birch observed the prevailing developments in society. In his report he showed that small companies accounted for the majority of new jobs in the US, thereby challenging conventional wisdom about the creation of new jobs in society.

However, Birch's study has been heavily criticized due to the method used and the conclusions drawn, for definitions lacking in rigor, for the difficulty of replicating his results, and weak documentation. However, these critics are guilty of misunderstanding his pioneering effort – Birch's contribution is not his rigor but rather his creativity. David Birch's achievement was that he realized that no data were available to resolve various questions related to job creation. Instead, it was a question of trying to utilize and reshape existing data and to combine them in such a way that they could be used for longitudinal analyses. In this way he pieced together an extremely powerful database that allowed him to study the business dynamics of a large range of businesses and industries in the US.

Even if an emerging research field could be discerned in the 1970s, Birch opened up that field, not least among economists. It was Birch's systematic studies and empirical results that gave small businesses a place on the research map. Even though small businesses accounted for a large part of employment in the US, few economists before Birch had previously studied small businesses in the economy. Birch has had many followers. The results have been refined thanks to improved databases and methodological development, but his main finding that new and small businesses play a significant role in job creation remains valid.

Birch's report not only opened up the research field, it also received considerable attention from politicians and the media, which led to a focus on the situation and on the importance of small companies. The interest reached far beyond the borders of the US, and Birch's results were completely in line with the new market-oriented political winds that had started to blow in Thatcher's UK and Reagan's USA.

1.2   Career

David Birch did not start his academic career as an economist but as an engineer and computer programmer with a degree in applied physics and nuclear reactor design from Harvard University in 1959. Between 1962 and 1966, he combined a position as research engineer at General Dynamics/Astronatics and Jet Propulsion Laboratory with studies in economics at Harvard Business School, where he presented his PhD thesis on the economics of the US space program in 1966. He worked for a couple of years at Harvard Business School, but the burden of teaching became too heavy. In the mid 1970s, he moved to MIT and the Center for Urban Studies. He was appointed Director of the MIT Programme on Jobs, Enterprises and Markets in 1974. Most of the research at the centre was focussed on the changes taking place in US cities. Cities were the big issue in the US in the post-Vietnam era, and there was a substantial amount of research money available to study the dynamics of big cities.

> "Since the end of the 1960s, the large cities were very much a subject of debate. We had race riots going on, we had a lot of disturbances in the cities. I became very interested in the cities and how they changed, they were fast living creatures that nobody seemed to understand, and it was also something computers could help us understand ... and for 6-7 years I worked on building a huge database on every neighborhood in five US cities and analysing what was going on in the cities."

In the studies of large cities, jobs seemed to be of interest. For example, jobs were moving away from the city centers, but no one appeared to know how jobs were created or how important they were for regional development. This led to Birch's research interest being increasingly directed toward job creation rather than to the cities and their neighborhoods.

"I looked at the economy as a physicist looks at it – not as an economist. The economy consists of individual companies doing things ... individual companies that change over time ... we followed a large number of individual companies over time, not using classified data or aggregates of companies, as mainstream economists do. We stumbled across a lot of new questions, of which the main question was: where do jobs come from? But also questions like: where are new jobs located, and which firms are growing?"

The results on job creation – a spin-off from his studies of big cities – were published in 1979 in the seminal report *The Job Generation Process* and they were really surprising, as they showed the importance of new and small firms for job creation. The reactions were enormous, not least in political circles.

"It was a time of economic recession, unemployment, and all politicians needed help – from the President, the US Congress, as well as Governors of different states ... they were all saying 'You know where the jobs are created ... help us'. So my network was mainly made up of politicians, and my context was policy-making, and I had almost no academic context. I was not connected with the academic research community and I had no academic counterpart, I was dealing with people who needed help."

However, it was not only American politicians who took an interest in Birch's results. It also attracted great attention in the UK, where Margaret Thatcher was one of the leading advocates of Birch's study. At the same time, representatives of the major companies started to react and run campaigns against the study. The study was also questioned within the research community. Criticism was levelled at Birch's study for many years, and newspaper articles questioning his results were still appearing more than ten years after its publication.

"I found myself in the middle of a huge goldfish bowl ... I was under enormous pressure all the time, all these people shooting at me. In particular a group of researchers at the Brooking Institute were very critical. And I spent a lot of time listening to their criticism. As I see it, one reason for the differences in the results of our studies was variations over time ... there are differences in the significance of small firm job creation between periods of recession and boom ... but the main results are more or less the same. However, the attacks by the large corporations and the trade unions were even more severe ... they saw the small business part of the economy increasing, while large firms were decreasing."

The database that Birch had created offered great opportunities for analysing data in different ways. Birch understood that not all small businesses were equally important for job creation – it was primarily a small group of fast growing companies. Birch therefore initiated a new project in 1983-1984 to study the distribution of growth among US companies, and the book *Job Creation in America*, based on the project, was published in 1987.

> "I suddenly stumbled on the fact that it was a relatively small group of companies that were very successful. The companies could be divided into two groups – gazelles and mice, and in the book *Job Creation in America* I elaborated on this observation, together with some reasoning about firm location and regional aspects of the job creation process."

In the mid 1980s Birch realized that he could utilize his database to identify patterns in data that conventional statistics could not distinguish, by taking advantage of modern computation methods and new software. This enabled him to help individual companies develop instead of merely studying them. He entered business consultancy in 1983 when he established the consulting firm Cognetics, which is a marketing research company performing customer-specific analyses based on data from more than 10 million business establishments.

> "So I really left the research field in the mid 1980s. Today I am two careers beyond that ... as an entrepreneur for a long period of time and now a new career as a naval architect."

At the age of 63, David Birch sold his company in year 2000 and gradually reduced his involvement in it. His energy is more and more channelled into Birch Boat Works. David Birch works as a naval architect, working with his son, who is a craftsman specialising in restorations.

2.   STREAM OF INTEREST IN DAVID BIRCH'S RESEARCH

David Birch is best known for his seminal work *The Job Generation Process*, and in the first section I will present the report in more detail. The report had an enormous impact on the research community as well as among politicians and policy-makers, and this development will be discussed in section 2.2. David Birch not only took an interest in which companies created new jobs but also in where these jobs were created – the regional effects of enterprise. In section 2.3., the book *Job Creation in America* published in 1987 is presented. He was also among the first to emphasize the importance of the fast growing companies, and he coined the term "gazelles" to describe them (section 2.4.).

2.1   The Report "The Job Generation Process" (1979)

The Job Generation Process represents, as already mentioned, a genuine groundbreaking report and is one of Birch's most cited works. It is a research report comprising 54 pages, published within the framework of the MIT Program on Neighborhood and Regional Change. In the report Birch aimed to develop an "economic microscope" that could reach beyond aggregate statistics in order to explain how the behavior of individual firms caused employment changes in the US. One of the main problems for Birch was to obtain adequate data – existing databases were not well equipped to cope with large longitudinal data. Birch used the Dun & Bradstreet database originally developed for credit ratings. The research group acquired the complete files for the US as per 31 December 1969, 1972, 1974 and 1976 – containing about 12 million records and over 100 reels of magnetic tape. Considerable efforts were made to reduce the files into a compact set, with all four years merged together, which made it possible to analyze changes in each firm between years. Each establishment was assigned a unique identification number, and the files for the four years were matched on a case-by-case basis.

The database had its limitations. Even if Dun & Bradstreet had a strong incentive to ensure high quality information, the database was not developed for the purpose of studying economic change. Firstly, it was never intended to be a census of the corporate population in the US, i.e. it was a sample, and it made no pretence of covering all businesses. For a variety of reasons, Dun & Bradstreet had concentrated their efforts on manufacturing firms, but improvements were made between 1969 and 1976 to expand coverage in the trade and service sectors as well. Contrary to what could be expected, smaller firms were not underrepresented in the database – smaller firms usually pose greater credit risks than larger ones, and therefore they were well represented in the database. Secondly, the data were collected for credit rating purposes. For example, new firms entered the database as credit information was required of them, which probably created a bias in terms of underreporting new firm births. In addition, there were difficulties separating "branches" – branches are an inherent part of the corporation – and, therefore, were less interesting from a credit point of view. Thus, the Dun & Bradstreet data file could be regarded as a unique resource – it contained a large sample of firms that could be analyzed over time on an individual firm basis. But the file was not designed for analytical purposes and, of course, there were several biases in the database.

With these limitations in mind, what did David Birch and his research colleagues find? As mentioned, the study was focussed on employment creation, and it indicated that migration of establishments from one state to another played a virtually negligible role. Much attention was often given in the media to the migration of firms from one region to another, but the symbolic effect seems to be more important than the effect on the job base. In addition, job losses seem to be about the same everywhere – the death and contraction rate varies little from one region to another, despite the rather large range of net change rates between regions. Thus, the variation in net change is mainly due to variation in the rate of replacement, not the rate of loss, i.e. differential rates of job replacement are the crucial determinant of the growth or decline of a region. But who are the major generators of these jobs? What kind of firms play the critical role in job generation? In this respect, some highly interesting results emerged from the study:

– The majority of expansion growth consisted of independent firms, and independent firms played a more important role in industries like farming, trade and service sectors, i.e. growing sectors of the economy during the 1970s.
– On average, about 60% of all jobs in the US were generated by firms with 20 or less employees, and about 50% of all jobs were created by independent small entrepreneurs, whereas large firms (with over 500 employees) generated less than 15% of all net new jobs.
– Not all small firms were job providers. It was the smaller, younger firms that generated jobs – once the firms were over four years old, their job generation powers declined substantially.

It could also be concluded that these results seemed to vary very little across industries and regions, but at the end of the report Birch emphasized the need to conduct deeper studies on why firms locate where they do and on the regional effects of the dynamics of the job creation process. However, the answers were not presented until almost ten years later when Birch presented the book *Job Creation in America* (1987).

2.2   ... and after

The report *The Job Generation Process* was only sold in twelve copies, but its influence was enormous, not least on politicians and policy-makers around the world. The report was in line with the new political winds that had started to blow across the western world with Reagan and Thatcher as the most prominent protagonists. The report alerted both the Congress and the local economic-development officials all over the US, and it interested politicians and policy-makers not only in the US but around the world. Small business was no longer only an economic sideshow – it was the main event.

The report also had an enormous impact on the research community – it provided the intellectual foundation for researchers throughout the world to incorporate smaller firms into the analyses of economic development. However, as with any influential work, it is inevitably subject to intense scrutiny – and so it was with Birch's report. The report has for a long time been a source of considerable controversy, and Birch's methodology of using the underlying data, his way of documenting data, the statistical analyses in the report, and his reluctance to publish his works in refereed economics journals have been discussed and criticized. For example, as a consequence of the remarkable results of the study, the US Small Business Administration (SBA) asked the Brooking Institute in Washington to look at the 1978-1980 period using the same Dun & Bradstreet database as used by Birch. Despite the use of an identical data set, they were unable to replicate the findings. Their results (Armington & Odle, 1982) showed that small firms were growing no faster in terms of employment than other firms in the economy. However, the time period differed – Birch covered the period 1969 to 1976, whereas the Brooking Institute covered the period 1978 - 1980 – which of course could explain the conflicting results. Therefore, SBA provided Birch with a copy of the data set for 1978 - 1980 and asked him to produce an estimate of the job creation contribution of small firms. Based on the identical data set and the same time period, Birch obtained a much higher job contribution compared to Armington and Odle – Armington and Odle found that about 38% of all jobs were created by firms with 100 employees or less, which was approximately proportionate to their share of total employment in the economy, whereas the corresponding figure from Birch was 70% (see discussion in Giaoutzi et al., 1988).

The difference in results was due to confusion between enterprises and establishments but also to the assumptions made about missing data in the Dun & Bradstreet data set. Dun & Bradstreet collected data at both establishment and enterprise level. However, Armington and Odle observed that the sum of establishments was less than the enterprise employment for multi-site enterprises, and they believed the enterprise figure to be "true", whereas Birch based his analyses on the establishment data. Furthermore, the data used by Birch were incomplete with many missing establishments, and assumptions needed to be made about these. Armington and Odle showed that the nature of these assumptions fundamentally affected the number of jobs that could be generated by small firms (Atkinson & Storey, 1994).

Birch's study has been replicated in other countries using different data sources and methods. For example, in the UK, Gallagher and his colleagues (Gallagher et al., 1990; Daly et al., 1991) have made similar analyses based on the Dun & Bradstreet data in the UK. The results indicate that small firms in the UK make a disproportionately large contribution to net job creation, but the contribution is not nearly as high as originally estimated by Birch. It can be concluded that, while Birch's study has been a source of considerable controversy, his qualitative conclusion that the bulk of new jobs emanate from small firms has been largely confirmed – his main findings seem to be very robust and have been verified in many later studies.

2.3   Job Creation in America (1987)

The book *Job Creation in America*, published in 1987, summarizes twelve years of research on job generation (see also Birch, "Who creates jobs" in *Public Interest*, 1989, in which some of the key findings are summarized). In the book, Birch argued against the view of an aggregated description of the economy and posed the question: What do we see when we put these aggregates under the microscope and look at the individual units? Beneath the balanced surface there is a chaotic and turbulent collection of individual companies, all of which are constantly undergoing change. A large number of new firms appear each year, some of which grow rapidly while many mature firms decline, and a large number of them go out of business every year. In addition, every year 20 million Americans leave their jobs, half of them involuntarily – they are either fired or laid off with little warning. But the remarkable thing is that this balance on the aggregate level is maintained. In order to understand the incredible dynamics and job transformation that occur, there is a need for detailed analyses of the economy, which is what Birch tried to provide in this book.

In this chaotic and turbulent context, the small firms seem to be the engine in the economy – they create more jobs than the giant companies, grow more rapidly, run greater risks of failure, and show more adaptability. Firms with 1-19 employees accounted for 88% of all net new jobs during the period 1981 - 1985. However, it could have been expected that there is safety in numbers, i.e. the larger the firm, the more secure it would be in terms of employment. But the results in Birch's study indicate that although smaller firms may close down with greater frequency, they nevertheless offer just about the same job security as the larger ones, and this holds true even over a longer period – over the business cycle. The conclusion could be that "the aggregate, macro stability of an economy flows from its micro instability, the instability of the individual firm" (p. 52).

We often believe that firms behave as human beings – it starts small, grows steadily, and more rapidly during a "growth phase", matures and stabilizes and eventually becomes out-dated and declines. An interesting observation was that, of the firms that experienced high growth during the 1970 - 1972 period, only a small proportion did well in 1973 and 1974, and several of the winners became big losers. Furthermore, almost one fifth of those that suffered major losses came back with large advantages, which would indicate that, if trying to predict the major winners it would make sense to look among the firms that suffered the heaviest losses during the previous period. In addition, the firms that showed little change during previous periods seem to be most at risk of dying. The conclusion is that, instead of a "life cycle model" of business development, we could talk about a "pulsation model" to explain how firms respond to a changing economy and technological developments. Dynamic firms pulsate quite strongly as they grow, and aggregate growth is constructed on massive, continual failure.

The 1980s was a decade of conflicts in US society, as well as a time of military-political conflict with the USSR and economic war against Japan. Moreover, the US was undergoing a transition from a manufacturing economy to one that was increasingly dominated by service-oriented trade and industry. Birch argues that the main problem is that the US is doing quite well in products and services with short half-lives, i.e. the short time that passes before half of the value dissipates, but rather poorly with those with long half-lives. On the other hand, other countries, led by Japan, have become very adept at copying and improving upon products with long half-lives. As a consequence, the growth segments of the US economy were those whose products and services have relatively short half-lives.

In order to sustain competitiveness, not least in relation to Japan, creativity and innovation constitute a central theme in US industry. What, then, characterizes the high-technology segments of the US economy? Firstly, the segment was very small – it represented only 2.8% of all jobs. Secondly, Birch identified a couple of high-innovation sectors in US industry, including for example high-technology manufacturers (e.g. computers, communication equipment, electronic components), information-age firms, leisure time firms (e.g. toys and sporting goods, charter services), baby boom/yuppie/women-in-the-labor-force/aging firms. Thirdly, Birch's results indicated that creativity and innovations in the US economy were not only to be found in the small high-technology sectors – innovative firms can be found in virtually every industry. Entrepreneurial firms in innovative sectors accounted for 2.7% of the firms and 20.8% of replacement jobs, whereas entrepreneurial firms in non-innovative sectors made up 15.4% of the total and provided 65.6% of the jobs. Thus, entrepreneurial firms provided 86.4% of the replacement jobs, which provides strong evidence for the fact that innovative firms, irrespective of industry, were the engine of job generation.

An interesting observation was that every region in the US loses about the same percentage of firms and job bases each year due to firm layoffs and closures – about 7-8% per year – but that there were variations in average loss rates over the business cycle. Relocation of firms is rarely a solution – firms seldom make radical moves from one metropolitan or rural area to another. Many firms move each year but mainly only short distances – the net effect of firm "migration" was rather negligible relative to the job base. Instead, the variation in growth in different areas was mainly attributed to variation in the start-up rate of new firms and the growth rate of existing firms, which compensated for the fixed losses of firms. However, there was a great variation in the formation and growth rate between different geographic areas.

Which areas of the US are doing well? Contrary to earlier days when the key to success was low labor and material costs, many areas exhibiting strong growth were high-cost areas, such as San Fransisco, Phoenix, Denver, Dallas, Boston, Atlanta and Miami. As has been indicated, it is the high-innovation firms that create most of the growth in the US economy, and these firms primarily depend on "brains", not land or raw material. The key to attracting well-educated people is quality, not cheapness, i.e. high-innovation firms will locate in an environment that creative and well-educated people find attractive.

Furthermore, Birch analyzed the propensity of new firms to form and young firms to grow in 239 US metropolitan areas. The results indicated an enormous spread in performance. The best metropolitan areas showed almost ten times greater entrepreneurial activity compared to poorly performing areas – but the entrepreneurial activity was not limited to a few "hot-shot" cities – it emerged everywhere, even in areas considered extremely unlikely. One conclusion may be that some of the elements necessary to create an appealing area for high-innovation firms and workers cannot be created overnight – it may take generations. On the other hand, when compared to industrial firms, high-innovation entrepreneurs are much freer with regard to the location of their firms, although in order to establish attractive locations they need assistance from far-sighted political leaders.

2.4   Gazelles (1994)

As has been shown throughout this chapter, David Birch is one of the leading proponents of the notion that the majority of new jobs are created by small firms. However, as indicated in subsection 2.2., this view has not gone unchallenged. For example, in the book *Employers Large and Small* (1990), Charles Brown, James Hamilton and James Medoff wrote: "Perhaps the most widespread misconception about small businesses in the United States is that they generate the vast majority of jobs and are therefore the key to economic growth ... Small employers do not create a particularly impressive share of jobs in the economy, especially when we focus on jobs that are not short lived" (pp. 1-2).

In the chapter "Gazelles" published in *Labor Markets, Employment Policy, and Job Creation* (1994), edited by Lewis Solomon and Alec Levenson, the two protagonists David Birch and James Medoff collaborated in order to find some common ground in the debate. What could they agree about? Their common efforts resulted in the following:

1. The relative role of smaller firms in generating jobs varies enormously from time to time and from place to place.
2. Most small-firm job creation occurs within a relatively small number of firms – the Gazelles.
3. There is a great and growing instability in the US stock of jobs due to the rapidly changing fates of US firms.

Thus, one conclusion may be that the distinction between small and large firms as job creators is of less importance – most jobs are created by the Gazelles, which are firms that are neither large nor small.

Our knowledge about these Gazelles is limited. However, from Birch's research we know that, in 1993, the average size of a Gazelle firm was 61 employees and that they employed around 20 million people in the whole of the US. Contrary to popular myth, there is no particular sector of the economy that produces Gazelles, they are found in health care, the fishing industry, wholesales, textiles, etc, and only a very small proportion is "high-tech". Furthermore, the Gazelles are extremely volatile and inherently unstable. They are constantly taking risks and making mistakes as well as enjoying great success if everything goes well. This means that the best predictor of decline in these firms is present growth and that the best predictor of growth is present decline. Finally, Gazelles make conscious choices regarding their localization. Gazelles seek places where skilled workforces want to live and where managers can easily commute from home-to-work and try to move away from city centers, locating instead near airports, highways and universities.

3. PERSPECTIVES ON HIGH GROWTH FIRMS (GAZELLES)

In this final section I will present an interview with David Birch in which he talks about his insights in the field of entrepreneurship in general and high-growth firms in particular.

You have been studying the small business sector for a long period, almost three decades, what are your main insights?

I would say that small business is like a thundercloud. From a distance, a thundercloud can present a pretty static image, but the closer you come, the more turbulent it will be. The same goes for small businesses. In the US there are about 15 million of them, and the number is growing slowly and steadily at about the same rate as the overall economy. But come closer and you will find turbulence – every year we see about 8% of new firms, while a similar number go out of business. It is this turmoil that you find when studying small business closely that I would like to capture in my research.

When studying the "Gazelles" it is also interesting to see that some of the fastest-growing firms appear in old, declining manufacturing sectors like steel and textiles ... those sectors are just crawling with specialized companies that are filling the niches left by the dinosaurs who were unable to respond to the market. Many gazelles are operating in rather mundane lines of business.

How about high tech?

Of course, but even at the height of the boom in the late 1990s, the percentage of small business involved in high-tech was very small. There was a conception that everyone was starting high tech companies – but this was not the case – you cannot simply decide to start a high tech business ... you are not going to succeed unless you are very good at what you are doing, and not that many people are good at programming or circuit board design. Most new firms and most growth firms don't come from high tech sectors, they didn't during the boom, and they certainly don't today.

Some twenty years ago you coined the term "gazelles" to describe small fast-growing companies ...

I needed a simple, almost naïve way of explaining what was going on in the economy and I therefore used the metaphors "elephants", "gazelles" and "mice" to help people understand the dynamics of the economy. The big companies, elephants, are slow and not very innovative. Then there are a large number of very small firms – mice – that run around but fail to develop. And then the gazelles ... small firms that grow quickly and create employment.

What then are the characteristics of a gazelle?

There are fundamental differences between those firms that want to grow and those that only want to make a living. But the gazelles are extremely unstable ... the difference between growth and bankruptcy is not particularly great, and the life of an entrepreneur in a gazelle company is a life of almost constant fear. Everything is uncertain. What will happen next? This means that the entrepreneurs must be able to control their fear, which few can. It's like a downhill skier before hurtling down the precipice ... the fear is there but under control.

Nor is the entrepreneur in a gazelle concerned about external economic conditions ... if you have developed something that "everybody" needs, you are not dependent on the external economy, and that's why we find gazelles in all lines of business ... from growth sectors to stagnating lines of business ... most lines of business are teeming with small specialized firms that occupy the niches where the elephants are unable to satisfy market demands.

On the other hand, a prerequisite for creating a gazelle is an entrepreneurial culture ... acknowledgement of the value of the entrepreneur ... a culture where for example young people want to become entrepreneurs in a growing company.

If a young doctoral student came to you asking: What are the most important questions to study within the area of entrepreneurship? What would your answer be?

I always come back to the rock opera Jesus Christ Super Star, and my favourite line is when Christ is hanging there nailed to the cross, questioning his death and having a conversation with God, saying "You're far too hot on what and how, and not so hot on why." It is the "why" that has come to interest me so much, and that is the essence of research.

One thing worth noting is that a business is the work of a single individual and that is interesting – it's people like Bill Gates (Microsoft), Andy Grove (Intel) ... And the interesting question in this respect will be what causes some people to become entrepreneurs, where do they come from, why do some countries and some cities have more of them than others? These questions are really the key questions for the future of any economy.

Another thing that I have noticed during my years as an entrepreneur ... I have talked to a lot of successful entrepreneurs, and my conclusion is that any one who becomes a successful entrepreneur is constantly terrified – you never know if you are going to get the next contract, you never know if .... The people who succeed are people who can tolerate the fear, the fear of awful events, and if you learn to tolerate the fear well, then you can do almost everything. As an entrepreneur you need to learn how to deal with fear – and to understand the psychology of fear and ways of managing fear is an important challenge for future research.

REFERENCES

Armington, C. & Odle, M., 1982, Small businesses – how many jobs?, *Brooking Review*, Winter, 14-17.

Atkinson, J. & Storey, D., 1994, Small firm and employment, in Atkinson, J. & Storey, D.J. (eds.), *Employment, the small firm and the labour market*, London: Routledge, 1-27.

Birch, D.L., 1979, *The Job Generation Process*, MIT Program on Neighborhood and Regional Change, Cambridge, MA.

Birch, D.L., 1987, *Job Creation in America*, New York: Free Press.

Birch, D.L., 1989, Who creates jobs?, *Public Interest*, 65, 3-14.

Birch, D.L. & Medoff., J., 1994, Gazelles, in Solmon, L.C. & Levenson, A.R. (eds.), *Labor Markets, Employment Policy and Job Creation*, Boulder: Westview Press.

Brown, C. & Hamilton, J. & Medoff, J., 1990, *Employers Large and Small*, Cambridge, MA: Harvard University Press.

Daly, M. & Campbell, M. & Robson, G. & Gallagher, C., 1991, Job Creation 1987-89: The Contributions of Small and Large Firms, *Employment Gazette*, November, 589-596.

Gallagher, C. & Daly, M. & Thomason, J.C., 1990, The Growth of the UK Companies 1985-87 and their Contribution to Job Creation, *Employment Gazette*, February, 92-98.

Giaoutzi, M. & Nijkamp, P. & Storey, D.J., 1988, Small is beautiful: The regional importance of small-scale activities, in Giaoutzi, M. & Nijkamp, P. & Storey, D.J. (eds.), *Small and medium sized enterprises and regional development*, London: Routledge, 1-18.

Chapter 7

DAVID STOREY

1. DAVID STOREY – BUILDING BRIDGES BETWEEN RESEARCH AND POLICY MAKING

1.1 The Contributions of David Storey

David Storey is perhaps the most prominent exponent of small business research in Great Britain – research that is strongly policy oriented – and it is primarily David Storey's great interest in and emphasis on policy related knowledge that merits attention. Storey's research consists of robust, high-quality empirical work, which includes detailed literature reviews, a carefully thought out methodology, in-depth reflection and interesting conclusions. In particular, his critical reviews of earlier research deserve attention along with his ability to synthesize knowledge and to make complex phenomena easily understandable. In this way, Storey has provided a more balanced picture of the importance of small businesses for societal development as well as making small business research more credible.

Storey can be regarded as something of a bridge-builder. His research demonstrates his interest in both macro-level analysis – showing the importance of small businesses for society in general and regional development in particular – and micro-level analysis, which involves the development of individual companies. Storey has also created a link between research and policy making in the area. Although his criticism of prevailing small business policy is severe, he exerts an enormous influence on national policy-makers in different European countries, both directly and through bodies such as the EU, OECD, etc. – thus his research impacts on both academic and non-academic audiences.

1.2   Career

At the age of 21 David Storey took his degree in economics at Hull University in 1968. For four years after his graduation, he worked at the Department of Trade and Industry and then for a local authority in Buckinghamshire. In 1974 he obtained a position as a research fellow at the Department of Economics at Newcastle University, and at the same time he studied for a PhD on a part time basis – a thesis on environmental economics – which was completed in 1978.

After his contract with Newcastle expired, he got a job at the Centre for Environmental Studies, an independent research institute in London, but David's work was in Middlesbrough on Teesside (about 50 miles from Newcastle) where he studied economic development in the area. Teesside and Cleveland, in the north east of England, were by almost all measures the least entrepreneurial areas in Britain.

"At the end of the 1970s the British economy was in an absolutely monumental recession, with jobs disappearing, many of them from the manufacturing sector and particularly from the north of England. The Cleveland area had a large number of engineering and chemical companies, and we saw a number of old engineering companies disappear and the misery associated with closedowns. David Birch's results inspired hope – he presented his study in 1979, and it had an incredible impact in the UK – I would say that David Birch created my job – as we needed to look at these people starting businesses with a view to generating jobs.

I was an environmental researcher, I had no research agenda, and I was pitched in to look at economic development ... I knew something about the industry, but I knew very little about economic development. But I literally stumbled across big packing cases full of survey forms of businesses in the municipality from 1965 and also new data that the municipality had collected. So suddenly we thought we could do for Teesside what David Birch had done for the US."

The report, which was published in a book entitled, *Entrepreneurship and the New Firm*, appeared in 1982. The key finding was that new businesses in the manufacturing sector will never generate a sufficient number of jobs to replace those that are being lost from the large firms.

"In 1980 the Institute was closed and I was fired. I had received some research money and went to the Economics department of the University of Durham ... and I actually wrote the book at Durham University. The book came out and people liked it. Nobody had looked at how people start businesses in the UK, nobody looked at their problems and their experiences, nobody had looked at the impact of these businesses ... this was quite new territory."

In 1981 David Storey went back to Newcastle University, this time to the Centre of Urban and Regional Development Studies, where he stayed for almost six years, only on the basis of the research funding that he generated.

"At that time I was almost 40 years old, and I had always been working on short term contracts. My wife and my mother said to me: 'It's time you got a proper job'. But there were no 'proper jobs' for me in Newcastle".

In 1987 David Storey received an offer from the Centre for Small and Medium-sized Enterprises at Warwick Business School. The Centre was run by Ian Watson – Watson died a couple of years later and David Storey assumed responsibility for managing the centre – a position that he still maintained in the early 2000s. At the time of his departure from Newcastle to Warwick, the Economic and Social Research Council (ESRC) initiated a major research program on small businesses in the UK. Over the years, Thatcher had focused on entrepreneurship and small businesses in the economy, and a number of governmental initiatives had been taken. In many cases policy was way in front of research – there was a need for a major research program on small businesses. David Storey was appointed coordinator for the program, with a grant of in total GBP 1.5 million.

"When we announced the program, we received 132 applications, and we made 13 awards. A clear message was that this was a serious area of research ... to influence policy makers at the highest level and to persuade colleagues in various disciplines that the research required academic rigor. In addition, we wanted to attract new researchers who had either a distinguished record outside small business research or who had new ideas, which could be developed in a rigorous framework. What we looked for was academic rigor, relevance and knowledge."

It was a 3-year program, with an additional year to draw conclusions from the different parts of the program. The results were presented in the book *Understanding the Small Business Sector* in 1994. This book is one of the "classics" within small business research and is probably one of the first books that sought to synthesize research on the small business sector in a way that was accessible to policy makers.

"Nobody came to me and said: Storey, you have totally changed the way we look upon things and as a result we have decided to change policy based on your arguments ... but it is interesting that a number of key policy recommendations in the book were either implemented during the research process or have been implemented post 1994 ... it could be a coincidence."

David Storey's interest in policy-relevant questions has continued unabated, and during the 1990s he picked up and elaborated on some central topics of the 1994 book, such as the regional aspects of business formation, technology-based firms, human resource management, and evaluation of policy measures.

"One topic that I find particularly interesting is the regional aspects of business formation, and I have been editor of three state-of-the-art reviews, one in 1984, another in 1994 and the third in 2004. These reviews allowed us to recognize the extent and development of our knowledge at each point in time.

In the 1984 review the aim was to identify regional differences in firm formation – the rate of firm formation and the characteristics of the firms established in different regions. There were no good data, and the question was if it was a subject for research.

In 1994 we knew that there were differences in the rate of business formation between regions in the same country, but we didn't know whether there were differences between countries and if it was the same factors that explained regional differences in different counrties. Interestingly enough, we found that it was the same factors that influenced the firm formation rates ... the growth in demand, a population of businesses dominated by small firms, and an urbanized context ... the same factors explained differences in the formation rates in various regions in different countries. However, factors that seemed to be important for regional variation were very difficult to influence from a policy-making perspective – they were events that took place naturally – easy to explain but difficult to do anything about.

The 2004 review focused on trying to explain the relationship between the firm formation rate and the economic performance of the region. The conclusion was that this relationship seems to be highly complex ... more complex than we expected, and it is not necessarily the case that high entrepreneurial activity in a region creates a high employment rate or wealth in the region."

Another theme of interest in David Storey's research during the 1990s has been technology-based firms, and together with co-authors such as Paul Westhead and Bruce Tether, Storey has discussed the importance of new technology-based firms in a number of articles that also focussed on the policies necessary to stimulate the start-up and survival of technology-based firms.

A third major theme that David Storey developed from the 1994 book was the question of why it appears to be so difficult to promote formal training among managers and employees in small firms.

"This question has attracted a great deal of interest among policy-makers. Policy-makers assume that there is market inefficiency ... an ignorance among small business managers ... and different subsidies have been provided to overcome this ignorance. My argument is that this is not a question of market inefficiency, but a rational decision ... small business managers receive less return on formal education compared to other managers ... and this is of course not what policy-makers want to hear."

One can conclude that, despite his administrative responsibilities as manager of the Centre for Small and Medium-sized Enterprise and later as Associate Dean with responsibility for research at Warwick Business School, David Storey has been influential as a researcher not only among academics in small business research but also among policy-makers at different levels and has actively participated in the policy debate throughout Europe.

2. STREAM OF INTEREST IN DAVID STOREY'S RESEARCH

David Storey first became interested in job creation, especially in less prosperous regions such as northern England. His production primarily consists of books. Section 2.1. presents three books that demonstrate his interest in job creation and the policy implications that may be deduced from these studies. David Storey was also the co-ordinator of a major research program in the UK in the late 1980s and early 1990s, the ESRC Small Business Initiative. The program generated a host of interesting results concerning the development possibilities of small businesses. Storey summarised these results in his book *Understanding the Small Business Sector*, a summary of which is presented in section 2.2. In addition to these studies, David Storey has also taken an interest in several research areas, and his research on new firm formation, job creation and regional development will be summarised in section 2.3., his research on new technology-based firms in section 2.4., and finally on formal training in small firms in section 2.5.

2.1 Job Creation and Regional Development

In this subsection three early books from Storey's research on job creation and regional development will be presented: *Entrepreneurship and the New Firm* from 1982, *Job Generation and Labour Market Change* together with Steven Johnson in 1987, and *The Performance of Small Firms* written together with Kevin Keasey, Robert Watson and Pooran Wynarczyk and also published in 1987.

2.1.1   Entrepreneurship and the New Firm (1982)

The book *Entrepreneurship and the New Firm* was published in 1982. This was a period in Britain when small firms had undergone a remarkable metamorphosis. From the late 1960s the number of small firms had increased, and this trend occurred at a time when the British government was convinced that large corporations were of paramount importance and that economies of scale were the basis for economic development. The Bolton report of 1971 predicted an increase and stabilization of the small business sector – based on higher income levels in society, leading to a demand for more "one-off" goods, which the small firm sector was most suited to supply. This prediction came true, and during the 1970s small firms were responsible for an increasing share of total output and employment in Britain.

In the book *Entrepreneurship and the New Firm,* Storey critically reviewed the evidence for the justification of a growing small business sector and concluded that small firms' role in and contribution to development is more complex than previously assumed. He further argued that large firms still create the majority of new jobs (as well as being responsible for the majority of job losses) and although small manufacturing firms produce an increasing proportion of the total manufacturing output, this is due to a decline in demand for the products of large firms rather than increased demand for the products of small firms. In addition, the majority of new firms disappear within a few years of establishment, and most small firms exhibit a low level of growth. However, this does not detract from the fact that a handful of firms show rapid growth and will be major producers and employers in the future. It may well be that the distinction between small and large firms is less meaningful than that between old and new firms – the poor economic development in Britain since the Second World War is perhaps more attributable to the relatively low birth rate of new firms than to the existing stock of small firms. There is considerable evidence of the contribution of new firms to the local, regional and national economy. However, robust knowledge is hampered by the lack of a recognized definition of small firms and by the absence of databases on non-manufacturing small firms.

Part II of the book is devoted to a comprehensive multi-disciplinary examination of existing theories on new firm formation. It includes a historic review of entrepreneurship in economic thinking as well as non-economic aspects (such as the role of class divisions and education, family background and entrepreneurial personality, etc.). Storey synthesized the reasoning behind various theoretical approaches with reference to new firm formation and outlined some factors that might be expected to influence the number of new firms:

$$NFi = f(Gi, Ci, Ui, Si)$$

where

NFi = totally new firms in industry i
Gi = growth in employment in industry i
Ci = investment required to establish a firm of the minimum efficient
size in industry i
Ui = unemployment rate in industry i
Si = proportion of total employment in industry i in firms with less
than 100 employees.

Part III presents an empirical study of 301 new firms in the county of Cleveland in north-east England. The firms included all sectors of private industry with the exception of retailing. The aim was to describe the process of new firm formation as well as the individuals behind the establishment of new firms. The results can be summarized as follows:
- The analysis of personal characteristics of the entrepreneurs showed differing results when linked to the performance of the firm. Storey concluded that personal characteristics seem to have little influence upon the firm's performance.
- The entrepreneurs showed a reluctance to make use of assisting agencies – an entrepreneur is likely to cherish his/her personal independence and ability to solve his/her own problems. Nevertheless, the number of agencies shows an increase. Thus, it would be important to identify criteria for determining the effectiveness of such agencies.
- Banks and finance houses were important external sources of finance for new firms. However, clearing banks do not seem to be particularly adept at avoiding investments in loss-making companies nor are they "over" represented amongst the companies making the highest rate of profit. The explanation could be that branch managers are not especially skilled at identifying businesses with high growth potential, but also that the banks did not actively market their financial possibilities to entrepreneurs during the 1970s, i.e. they were not given any opportunity to invest in these firms.
- New firms make little contribution to job creation in the short term, and it is a small percentage of small firms that provides most of the jobs.

What policy implications can be drawn from the study? At a regional level, Storey developed an index of latent entrepreneurship based on factors such as the percentage of small firms in the region, the population in managerial groupings, the population with high level degrees, availability of capital in the region, percentage of the population in low entry barrier industries, and regional income distribution. It was shown that regions in Britain differed greatly in their entrepreneurial index ratings, with the south-east of England having the highest rating and the northern regions the lowest score. Storey argued that prosperous regions are more responsive to favorable conditions for new firm formation than less prosperous regions. Thus, policies designed to assist new and small firms are likely to be most successful in the most prosperous regions, and conversely, regions currently experiencing high unemployment are likely to derive very little benefit from such policies (this argument is further elaborated on in Storey & Johnson, 1987).

At governmental level, many policies were introduced during the 1970s to stimulate the small business sector in Britain. Storey argues that there has been a tendency to uncritically accept these policies in the hope that they may provide some benefits – small firms will create new jobs and new wealth. However, Storey argues that this "euphoric" view of the potential contribution of the small business sector is neither supported by fact nor have the various policies always succeeded in their aim of stimulating this sector. Storey questions the tendency among policy makers at that time to positively discriminate in favor of the small business sector. Due to its bureaucratic nature, government is unsuited to assisting entrepreneurs – policy makers should take the interests of all sizes of firms into account and not discriminate in favor of one size of firm.

2.1.2   Job Generation and Labor Market Change (1987)

As discussed in Chapter 3, the 1970s could be characterized as a period of "social turmoil" that included several structural changes in society: (i) oil crises that triggered or coincided with a number of major developments in the world economy, such as a slowdown in economic growth in most of the developed countries, increased competition from countries in South East Asia, a technological revolution, especially the growth of computers and microprocessors, (ii) a change in attitude among young people – "small is beautiful" – large firms were regarded as boring and bureaucratic, while smaller companies were increasingly regarded as dynamic and as providing a more creative environment, and (iii) the late 1970s and early 1980s also saw major political changes with the coming to power of Ronald Reagan and Margaret Thatcher – both elected on the manifesto of reducing the power of the state and providing greater opportunities for the individual to be responsible for themselves. As a consequence it was an environment in which small businesses could grow and make contributions to job creation.

In the book *Job Generation and Labour Market Change* (1987), David Storey and Steven Johnson attempted to describe the changes that had occurred in the labor market since the early 1970s, but also to find explanations as to why these changes took place. The main contribution of the book is, however, the methodological discussions – Storey and

Johnson's critical review of the data and analyses made in previous studies on small firms and job creation, which provide the reader with a more credible and balanced interpretation of the conclusions arrived at in previous studies in the area. The main conclusions of the book can be summarized as follows:

- Storey and Johnson provided a comprehensive critique of Birch's study *The Job Generation Process* (1979) and concluded that Birch overestimated the contribution made by small firms to job creation. Although since the end of the 1960s, small firms have no doubt been significant creators of new jobs in the US – the rate of job creation is fairly high in times of recession and relatively low in periods of prosperity – whereas the large firms showed net job losses. Replications of Birch's study were made in many countries, and the results indicated that (i) the scale of net job creation by small firms is not as significant as that indicated by Birch, and (ii) it is a relatively small number of new and expanding small firms that create a substantial proportion of the new jobs.
- There is no simple or single explanation for the relative growth of small firms in the economy. To illustrate this, Storey and Johnson used three different geographic areas as examples: Birmingham (UK), Boston (USA), and Bologna (Italy). In each of these areas, small firms had become more important but for different reasons. In Bologna the growth of the small business sector stemmed from the system of locating small firms in industrial districts, where they specialized in high-quality products, co-ordinated by merchants with international linkages. In Boston the growth of the small business sector was due to the wealth created by high technology-based firms, stimulated by defense expenditure and the concentration of higher-education institutions, which led to a massive increase in consumer-based demand, which in turn tended to be satisfied by small firms. In Birmingham small firms were "forced" to become more important because of the decline or restructuring of larger firms. In advanced economies there will be elements of the above three models, and it must be borne in mind that policy implications are very different for each of them.

According to Storey and Johnson, the lesson to be learned is that it appears not to be the number of small firms – the quantity of small firms – that determines the performance of the economy – it is the quality of these firms that is crucial, and relatively few firms in an economy are the prime determinants of success. In this respect Storey and Johnson argued that instead of a public policy focusing on the quantity of small firms and the promotion of new firm formation, government should adapt a selective policy, i.e. focusing on the relatively few firms that have the capacity to improve an economy.

2.1.3 The Performance of Small Firms (1987)

Interest in small businesses saw an increase during the 1980s, and Margaret Thatcher introduced a range of measures to stimulate the small business sector in Britain. Some of these initiatives, such as the Enterprise Allowance Scheme, were designed to raise the rate of new business formation, while other measures primarily targeted existing small businesses, for example, the Business Expansion Scheme and the Loan Guarantee Scheme. These initiatives aimed at creating employment and were based on certain fundamental propositions, such as: (i) that the small business sector would thrive if government regulation was reduced, therefore small firms should be exempted from some taxes and regulations, (ii) that small firms are disadvantaged compared to large firms, for example regarding finance and knowledge and that public policy should compensate for these disadvantages, (iii) that there was an ideological justification for the small business sector, and (iv) that an attempt should be made to bring small business or self-employment to the attention of those who perhaps never considered this option. The book *The Performance of Small Firms* (1987), co-authored with Kevin Keasey, Robert Watson and Pooran Wynarczyk, is primarily intended for policy makers and aims to provide a better insight into the process of job creation in smaller businesses, and the conclusions could be summarized as follows:

Small businesses job creation. The book is based on 636 independent single-plant manufacturing companies in Northern England with less than 200 employees. From the results it is obvious that small firms are far from being a scaled down version of a big publicly listed company, indicating that the large body of empirical studies based upon performance of listed companies will be of little relevance to policy-makers. For example, the separation of ownership and control in a small firm is likely to be minimal, management is usually in the hands of the founder(s) and their immediate families, and small firms are more likely to be restricted by a lack of financial and managerial resources and have little market power. Therefore, small firms probably respond differently to stimuli such as reduced taxation and other growth incentives compared to large firms.

A major thrust of British Government policy toward existing small business was to reduce their operational costs and in this way increase their profitability in the hope of creating more jobs. Policy was especially directed at the level of "trading profit" in small firms. However, Storey could find only modest evidence of an association between high trading profits and increased job creation. Instead, those firms that had higher "retained profits" appeared to create more jobs. Thus, public policy should pay more attention to small business profit retention than trade profit. In addition, young firms were not only more profitable but grew faster than older firms – indicating that the age factor is an important aspect for our understanding of the small business sector.

It was also clear that only a handful of firms contributed to the main growth in employment, or as Storey formulated it (p. 152): "In the broadest terms one-third of the jobs are found in less than 4 per cent of those businesses which start to trade." In the light of this fact it would appear to be an attractive strategy to concentrate public resources on the fast growing firms. However, arguments against such a policy are that the public sector has a poor record of "picking winners" – an increase in the total number of new businesses would presumably lead to an increase in the number of winners, and it may be unjust to direct public resources to a small group of firms while excluding the majority. However, Storey's conclusion was that it seems unlikely that "across the board" assistance to all small firms will be effective in terms of new job creation, and he presented a justification for a more selective small business policy – toward those small businesses that have the potential and determination to grow. The reasons behind a selective policy are that significant job creation takes place in only a few firms and, in addition, if policies are to be effective they have to have a significant and clearly visible effect upon the performance of the firms.

Failure prediction. One important characteristic of small firms is their high failure rates – there is an almost tenfold probability of failure compared to large firms. The high failure rate of small businesses makes it important to try to gain an understanding of small business failures in order to develop prediction models that will make it technically possible to identify indicators of impending failure. One major problem for such predictions is that many small firms die early in life, thus there is insufficient data for a satisfactory time series analysis.

Storey and his colleagues conducted a series of analyses based on univariate, multiple discriminant and logit analysis. Three indices of potential failure were examined: profitability, liquidity and gearing. The assumption was that firms more likely to fail would exhibit lower profitability and lower liquidity, but be more highly geared. In the univariate analysis, all these assumptions seemed to be supported. However, the ratios showed a high variance, indicating that they did not constitute a consistently effective prediction measure. To overcome these problems, multiple discriminant analysis was employed, and in this case the "best" prediction models included "cash flow" and "asset structure ratios" rather than liquidity and profitability measures. However, in the logit analysis, the importance of profitability and liquidity was re-emphasized, whereas gearing did not appear to be a powerful factor. Throughout the analyses, two other factors seemed to be important, but difficult to isolate; namely the age of the business – failure rates are higher among young firms of a given size than among older firms – and the existence of possible differences in failure rates between sectors (even within manufacturing). In the study, some qualitative factors were included, and the analysis showed that small firm failure was positively correlated with fewer directors, "qualified" last year's account by auditors, longer account submission lags, and having loans secured by the banks. The "best" predictive model developed in the study correctly classified about 3/4 of the firms, which is significantly better than could be expected if classified by chance. But all predictions of failure must be based on the individual case, and the model could only be considered as supplementary – and not a substitute for – the judgement of the officials at financial institutions.

2.2 Understanding the Small Business Sector (1994)

Understanding the Small Business Sector published in 1994 has its origin in the decision by the Economic and Social Research Council (ESRC) to fund a research program on small businesses. In 1987 David Storey was appointed Program Co-ordinator for the research program. The program was structured in three main research centers, each of which would focus upon a major theme: the center at Kingston Polytechnic (today Kingston University) led by James Curran looked at the role of small firms in the service sector, the center at the University of Cambridge under the leadership of Alan Hughes investigated the economic contribution of small firms, while the center at the Institute of Manpower Studies at Sussex University with John Atkinson as director focussed on small firms and the labor market. In addition, 13 separate research projects on a variety of topics were commissioned. The research was performed between 1989 and 1992. A number of articles were published based on the research program, and three books on key topics were edited: urban and rural issues (Curran & Storey, 1992), employment (Atkinson & Storey, 1993), and finance (Hughes & Storey, 1994).

The book *Understanding the Small Business Sector* is by far David Storey's most frequently cited work. In the book, he synthesizes a large amount of research in the area, not least the projects that formed part of the ESRC Small Business Initiative research program. Based on these syntheses, David Storey draws carefully considered conclusions from a policy perspective. Below, a brief summary of the main conclusions within the different themes covered by the book is presented.

– Small business development in the UK (Chapter 2). Storey concluded that small businesses are important for economic development and that their share of employment and output in manufacturing had risen in the UK since the end of the 1960s. The rise in self-employment in the UK at that time could be attributed to a combination of a higher rate of unemployment, a reduction in the real level of unemployment benefit, government schemes, a lower rate of self-employment than most other comparable countries, and technological changes, especially the increased role of information in the economy.

– Changes in the stock of firms – birth, death and growth (Chapters 3 - 5). The studies showed that new firms had a major influence on the stock of businesses in an economy but that their formation rates varied significantly from one sector to another, from one time period to another, and from one country or region to another. These variations appear to be due to expected profitability and the presence of entry barriers. Thus, these are the key factors for understanding sectorial differences in new firm formation. Similarly, profitability, measured by the level of aggregate demand in the economy, is a key factor for explaining spatial and time series differences in new firm formation, but access to capital and the real interest rate on capital also appear to be important explanatory variables.

Death of firms is an important characteristic of the small business sector – young firms are more likely to fail than old ones, and very small firms are more likely to fail than their larger counterparts. The most powerful influence on the survival of young firms seems to be their ability to grow within a short period of time after start up. The characteristics of the entrepreneur as an individual (e.g. age, gender, education), on the other hand, do not appear to be related to business performance (except for "education"). This indicates that neither the individuals themselves nor other bodies have a clear understanding of which individuals will succeed in business. Only by being an entrepreneur and observing performance can success be identified.

Rapidly growing firms constitute a very small proportion of the small business population – most small firms do not want to grow – but these high-growth firms make a major contribution to job creation. There seem to be three main factors influencing small firm growth: (i) the background/resources of the entrepreneur(s) (e.g. motivation, education and management team), (ii) the nature of the firm itself (e.g. smaller and younger firms grow more quickly, and there are sectorial and locational differences), and (iii) strategic decisions taken by the management (e.g. willingness to share ownership and the ability to identify niches), although the components need to be appropriately combined in order to achieve growth, which indicates the difficulty involved. On the other hand, constraints that hinder growth generally relate to finance, labor market issues and markets.

The first two constraints mentioned above, the role of finance and labor market issues, constitute the basis of chapters 6 – 8 in the book.

– Employment and finance (Chapters 6 and 7). Storey concluded that small firms in the US as well as the UK seem to create jobs at a faster rate than larger firms, even though this contribution is nowhere near as high as originally estimated by David Birch (see chapter 6). Moreover, small firms were also more consistent creators of jobs – they seemed less influenced by macroeconomic conditions – irrespective of the trade cycle. However, the quality of jobs was lower in small firms compared to larger firms in terms of, for example, wages, fringe benefits, and training. On the other hand, there seems to be a considerable degree of workplace harmony in smaller firms.

Since the MacMillan Committee report of 1931 there has been discussion about the financing of small firms. The banks are the major external source of finance for many small firms, but the relationship between banks and small firms has also been the target of a lot of criticism. The conclusion arrived at by Storey was that the problems stem from (i) the nature of the contract – the loan contract involves the bank incurring full downside risk but a fixed upside gain – and (ii) the cost structure of the financial institutions – the relative costs of small amounts of money are high.

The ability of small firms to create employment and the difficulties involved in obtaining access to finance were also two issues usually addressed in government policy. Storey examines government policy toward small firms in Chapter 8, which is perhaps the most interesting in the book. Several conclusions are drawn. Firstly, the magnitude of the small business sector in many countries is such that it is no longer possible to discuss economic policy without recognizing the role of small firms in the economy – public policy toward small firms cannot be formulated with only the interest of the small firms in mind. Secondly, whilst there is a wide range of policy initiatives to assist small firms, policies have often been introduced on a piecemeal basis, in response to pressure from the small firm lobby or to changes in the macro-economy. Governments need to formulate a coherent policy toward the small business sector, including the range of public policies that currently exist, clearly specifying the objectives and targets of each policy in measurable terms, thus making it possible to judge whether or not the policies are effective (this reasoning is further elaborated on in Storey, 2000).

General themes
- Concentrate on creating a suitable macro-economic framework.
- Publish a White Paper on the objectives and targets of small firm policy.
- Continue policy development at local level.
- Treat small firm policy as an integral part of economic, employment and social policy.

Reduce emphasis on:	*Increase emphasis on:*
- Tax	- Selectivity/targeting
- Deregulation	- Technology/science
- Training	- "Special" groups
- Start-ups	- Financial assistance
- Information/advice	- Encouraging dialogue
- Short-term "thinking"	

Figure 7-1. What government should do (source: Storey, 1994, p. 315).

Thirdly, based on several evaluations of public policies, some suggestions on government policy were made in the book (see Figure 7-1).

2.3 New Firm Formation, Job Creation and Regional Development

David Storey's interest in new firm formation, job creation and regional development has been sustained over a long period of time, issues that he discussed not only in books but also in a large number of articles. As we have seen, his interest in these types of issues dates back to David Birch's study published in 1979, which aroused great attention and interest in Great Britain, not least among politicians and policy-makers. However, Storey was in many respects critical of Birch's results, which criticism concerned not only methodology but also the relevance of the results to the UK context (see for example Storey, 1982; Storey & Johnson, 1986; 1987; 1990). David Storey's research in the area of new firm formation, job creation and regional development is on the whole characterized by critical questioning of the existing knowledge in this area.

David Storey's own research in this area was initially based on the studies that he carried out in north east England in the 1980s. In several articles Storey has shown that regional labor market conditions are of great importance when explaining new firm formation rate between regions. For example:

- In earlier research there was an assumption about a relationship between the number of entrants and perceived future profits, but this relationship has seldom been tested. From the empirical studies on Northern England and the East Midlands reported in Storey and Jones (1987), little evidence could be found to support this assumption. Instead, the study showed that a major factor influencing the rate of new firm formation was the rate of job losses in the region, to which self-employment seemed the only alternative. The relationship between unemployment and firm formation can be explained in different ways (Storey, 1991). According to the "pull" hypothesis, it could be argued that new firm formation takes place when an individual perceives an opportunity to enter a market, and this is more likely to happen when demand is high. The converse hypothesis, the "push" hypothesis, suggests that depressed market conditions and high unemployment are more likely to lead to the establishment of new firms – even if the expected income from self-employment is low, it is higher than the expected income from unemployment benefit. There may be a third hypothesis suggesting that the relationship between unemployment and business formation is non-linear – at a low level of unemployment increased job losses will lead to an increase in the rate of new firm formation, but once a "critical" level of unemployment is reached, further increases in unemployment result in a reduction in new firm formation, due for example to less business opportunities in highly depressed market situations.

- The relationship between firm size and performance is also poorly understood and has mainly been examined on populations of relatively large firms. It was assumed that firm growth is independent of firm size, the so-called Gibrat's Law, but Evans (1987) argued that when applied to the small firm sector, Gibrat's Law no longer holds, since growth and size appear to be negatively correlated. In order to explain the performance of the small business sector, it is necessary to introduce both the age of the firm and number of plants as, for example, growth decreases with age in younger firms, but increases with age in older firms. Similar results were obtained by Storey, Keasey, Watson and Wynarczyk (1987) using a sample of manufacturing companies in the north-east of England. Storey (1989) further elaborated on these results, and he explored some of the reasons underlying the differences in performance between small and large firms. He observed that many small business owners of fast growing firms had an ownership interest in at least one other business and that growth was positively associated with the proportion of trading profits which were retained within the business. From these observations Storey speculated that the objective of small business owners is to maximise the time-discounted stream of earnings from a portfolio of business interests. This could explain the fact that owners of more than one business are more likely to have both fast growing firms and companies likely to fail. The portfolio of companies is constantly adjusted through the formation of new firms and the closure of others. However, it also highlights the level of analysis required in the studies of small businesses – statistical data tend to be collected at firm or establishment level whereas the most appropriate unit of analysis seems be the entrepreneur.

David Storey did not only take an interest in regional development in northern England. Together with Paul Reynolds and Paul Westhead, he received an assignment from the European commission (DG XXIII) to co-ordinate a cross-national comparison of new firm formation rates in different countries, including France, Germany, Italy, Sweden, the UK and the US (Reynolds & Storey & Westhead, 1994a; b). The aims of the comparison were to explain why regions in some countries have higher new firm formation rates than others and to discuss what contributions public policy can make to raise the formation rates in a region. The underlying assumption was that new firm formation rates are affected by seven determinants that have a profound influence on new firm formation in a region: (i) demand growth, (ii) urbanization/ agglomeration, (iii) unemployment, (iv) personal/household wealth, (v) proportion of small firms and sectorial specialization, (vi) political ethos, and (vii) government spending/policies. The results showed that the average new firm birth rates are roughly similar across countries and that regional variations in firm formation rates are also similar within all countries – the most fertile regions have annual new firm birth rates that are two to four times higher than the least fertile regions.

How can these differences be explained? Looking at the underlying determinants affecting the establishment of new firms, the explanations appear to be rather uniform across countries (see Table 7-1), indicating that three determinants have a definite and positive effect on firm birth rates, namely growth in demand (population growth and growth in income), a population of businesses dominated by small firms, and a heavily urbanized context reflecting the advantage of agglomerations (access to customers, source of supplies and capital, etc.), whereas unemployment, personal wealth, a liberal political climate and government actions seem to have a weak or mixed impact.

Table 7-1. Determinants of new firm birth (source: modifications of Reynolds & Storey & Westhead, 1994, p. 1092).

Determinant	Relation	Number of countries (a total of 6 countries were included in the study)
Demand growth	Positive	6
Urbanization/agglomeration	Positive	6
Small firms/specialization	Positive	6
Unemployment	Positive	4
Government spendings/policies	None	4
Personal/household wealth	Positive	3
Political ethos	Positive	2

These results lead to the question: What can governments do to encourage firm births? According the Reynolds, Storey and Westhead (1994b), efforts to stimulate firm births can be divided into (i) general efforts to enhance all businesses to function more effectively, i.e. building an infrastructure, and (ii) more direct efforts related to the entrepreneurial process, i.e. reducing the transaction costs for small firms. However, from a regional perspective, these national policies to stimulate firm births seem to favor more prosperous and socially and economically well-endowed regions, that is, non-selective policies with no built in regional targeting may only serve to increase regional differences (see also Storey, 1982).

In addition, Storey questions policies aimed at promoting firm births. Actions to stimulate new firm formation may be less effective in terms of job creation than devoting resources to facilitate the growth of those firms expected to follow a high growth trajectory – the firms that, over time, are responsible for the majority of jobs, sales and exports. This argument is further elaborated on in Storey (1993), where he argues that the impact of public policies promoting start-ups is diffuse – a high proportion of new firms fail in their early years and job creation among surviving firms is heavily concentrated on a small percentage. For policy-makers it is extremely difficult to distinguish between those start-ups that will succeed and those doomed to failure, i.e. policy toward start-ups is a lottery with low odds to win. As a consequence, current policy in many countries has been to make public support available to all start-ups, which may be a less cost effective way of using public funds. Instead policy should target businesses with growth potential. Small firms with growth potential are subject to a number of growth constraints, for example, a shortage of skilled labor, financial constraints, management motivation, etc. However, it seems difficult to identify a single constraint that is relevant to all small firms, as constraints are likely to vary from one geographic region to another. This indicates that policies to overcome growth constraints are best implemented at regional level and should vary according to the firm concerned.

2.4   New Technology-based Firms

Ever since the Arthur D. Little Consulting Group's (Little 1977) path-breaking report comparing new technology-based firms in the US with those in the UK and Germany, the interest in new technology-based firms (NTBFs) has remained high among policy makers in many European countries. This is also true of the UK. David Storey, together with co-authors such as Bruce Tether and Paul Westhead, has in a number of articles discussed the importance of new technology-based firms.

2.4.1   Evolution of Industries – an Analytical Framework

The most well-known model for explaining the evolution of industries is the life cycle model, which states that an industry is expected to pass through a standard evolutionary path over time:

Phase I   *Expansion.* In the early phase of an industry there is a net enry in terms of the number of firms as well as the number of jobs.

Phase II   *Shake-out.* After a while the number of exits will exceed the number of entries, i.e. there is a net exit in terms of the number of units in the industry, although employment in the industry continues to rise

Phase III   *Consolidation.* Later on, the industry stabilizes and then contracg with a decline in both the number of firms and the level of employment

The life cycle model has been powerful in many ways, not least among policy-makers discussing the role of new technology-based firms in industrial renewal. However, the generalizability of the life cycle model has been questioned, and it has been argued that it is best suited to mass markets and does not hold for industries lacking rich opportunities for both product and process innovation. It can also be argued that the model provides an over-optimistic interpretation of the role of NTBFs in industrial regeneration – it predicts that some new firms in high-technology industries will grow into larger firms in the future, leading to the conclusion that the ability of an economy to produce a large number of new technology-based firms is crucial for industrial renewal and future industrial strength.

Together with Bruce Tether, David Storey presented an alternative framework which provides a means for "mapping" the development of industries. The framework (Tether & Storey, 1998; see also Tether & Storey, 1997) comprises four types of industry that are characterized by a two-dimensional change over time: the number of units (enterprises or establishments) active in the industry, and the level of employment (see Figure 7-2).

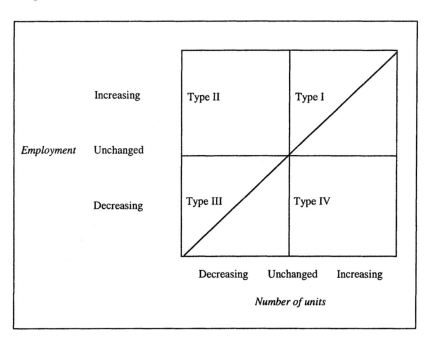

Figure 7-2. Framework for analysis of industries (source: modified from Tether & Storey, 1998, p. 950).

The framework relates to the "life cycle" model of industrial evolution; industries in phase I are found in the top right quarter of the graph (Type I industries), industries in phase II are found in the top left quarter (Type II industries), and industries in phase III are situated at the bottom left quarter of the graph (labelled Type III industries). In addition, a fourth group of industries have been identified. Type IV industries are those that contract in terms of employment but expand in terms of the number of units active in the industry. Along the diagonal line in Figure 7-2, the number of firm units and employment changes will be the same, which means that the average firm size remains unchanged. As a consequence, above the diagonal there is a move toward larger firms, while at points below the diagonal, there is a move toward smaller firms, regardless of whether or not total employment is increasing or decreasing.

Tether and Storey tested the framework on a variety of "high technology" sectors and also compared industrial changes between countries. Their conclusions were that the high technology service sectors (computer services, technical services, and R&D services) in Europe followed an almost universal Type I expansion trend during the 1980s, i.e. growth in both number of units and employment. In contrast, the high technology manufacturing sector (computers and office equipment, electronics, pharmaceuticals, and instruments) in many European countries could be characterized as Type IV industries, i.e. growth in the number of units but contraction in terms of employment. This indicates an increase in the number of small units and a decrease in the number of large units, which changes tend to dominate employment in high technology manufacturing sectors. Given that the high technology sector is expected to be important for future job creation, the findings are highly interesting. The existence of Type IV industries may be less favorable for the role of small firms as a source of economic rejuvenation, which indicates that Type IV industries may be influenced by "negative factors", such as a trend among large firms to "down-size" and focus on core activities. This will result in an increase in the establishment of many new firms due to a "redundancy push" as well as the creation of technology-based firms that are economically marginal and dominated by their larger customers.

2.4.2   The Performance of High Technology Firms

As indicated above, for a long time there has been an increasing concern among policy-makers about the creation of new technology-based firms – technological innovations seem to play a key role in the revitalization of the economy. However, we have limited knowledge of the factors associated with the survival of such firms. Westhead, Storey and Cowling (1995; see also Storey & Strange, 1992) conducted a longitudinal study in order to chart the survival of high-technology based firms from 1986 to 1992 and to identify factors that influence the survival over time of high technology firms based in UK Science Parks in 1986. In total, 284 face-to-face interviews were conducted, of which 183 were with Science Park firms. In 1990 a follow-up study was conducted on the Science Parks firms from the original study. Of the 183 Science Park firms in 1986, only 31 firms could be regarded as failures (defined as businesses no longer identifiable as trading).

The study by Westhead et al. (1995) is to a large degree based on the research by Arnold Cooper, especially Cooper and Gimeno Gascon (1992) and Cooper (1993) – see Chapter 10. The results indicated that few variables seem to explain survival or non-survival of technology-based firms. Although as many as 69 variables – all derived from earlier research – were included in the analysis, only 13 were found to be significantly associated with survival/non-survival. However, most interestingly, among variables associated with survival/non-survival, none of the technology-related variables were significant, which suggests that factors influencing survival/non-survival of technology-based firms are no different from factors influencing other firms.

In order to further elaborate on these results, and especially to explore the importance of informal and formal linkages made by technology-based firms to higher education institutions (HEIs), Westhead and Storey (1995) made an analysis based on the original database complemented by a new sample of 110 firms located in Science Parks in the UK. The results showed that, in 1986, many of the Science Parks were relatively new and that the linkage between industry and HEI were less than anticipated. However, firms located in a Science Park were significantly more likely to have a link with a local HEI than off-Park firms, and more interestingly, technology-based firms with a link to a local HEI, irrespective of location, were significantly more likely to survive. The conclusion is that the co-operation between technology-based firms and a local HEI seems to be important for the survival of the firm, and therefore, Science Park managers and HEI industrial liaison officers have an important role in encouraging and stimulating more formal linkages between technology-based firms and HEIs over time.

Considering the importance of technology-based firms for the economic development of a society, the main question will be: How can technology-based firms be supported? Based on an analysis of public policy measures to support new technology-based firms within the EU, Storey and Tether (1998) concluded that in most countries the support available to new technology based firms is identical to that given to other types of firms. They argued that new technology-based firms are "special": (i) their returns from research and development are likely to be long term and uncertain and, therefore, it is more difficult to make an accurate assessment of their success, but (ii) technology-based firms may also have a short "window of opportunity", i.e. if investments are not made at the appropriate time, all may be lost. Therefore, policy-makers must recognize the special qualities and requirements of new technology-based firms, and policies should focus exclusively upon these firms.

2.5   Management Training in Small Firms

A third theme in David Storey's research that he discusses in his book *Understanding the Small Business Sector* in 1994 concerns the issue of formal management training in small firms. It is a well known fact that small firms are much less likely than larger firms to provide their employees and managers with formal training. In Storey and Westhead (1997) two explanations were given as to why the provision of training is lower in small firms compared to large ones:

- The "ignorance" explanation, i.e. the small firm owner is assumed to underestimate the benefits to the business of providing training for managers and the workforce, and therefore government needs to persuade business owners that more training would enhance firm performance.
- The "market" explanation, i.e. small firms provide less training, not because of a lack of awareness of the benefits, but rather due to the fact that small firm owners face higher training costs and reap less benefits compared to managers of large firms.

Among policy-makers there seems to be a widespread acceptance of the ignorance explanation – small firm owners underestimate the benefits of management training – implying a market failure – which provides justification for public subsidies. However, there are rational arguments as well as empirical indications against the ignorance explanation, which favor a market explanation – thus making the case for governmental subsidies much weaker.

In Storey and Westhead (1997) the authors provide some explanations as to why small firms are less likely than large firms to provide formal training for managers. From a demand perspective there are several reasons: (i) management training results in a long rather than a short term benefit, and the smaller the firm the less likely it is to survive long enough to take advantage of the benefits derived of management training, (ii) small firms are more likely to be at risk of losing managers with formal management training, (iii) there is no internal labor market for individuals with managerial aspirations employed by small firms, and (iv) smaller firms have higher training costs per employee because they cannot spread fixed costs over a larger number of personnel. But there are also arguments from a supply perspective, such as that is is more time consuming and hence costly to train providers to offer courses for small firms, i.e. the contact cost per trainee is higher in small firms. In addition, the heterogeneity of small firms renders the unit cost of supplying training high in cases where the training provider wants to offer customized courses that fulfil the needs of each individual firm. In conclusion, there is evidence of less managerial training among small firms, but this does not necessarily indicate an ignorance-based market imperfection. Instead, it reveals the operation of the market in an entirely predictable manner, i.e. market forces rather than ignorance.

The importance of formal training in small firms is often based on the assumption that there is a broadly linear relationship between management training and firm performance. However, Storey and Westhead (1994) and Westhead and Storey (1996) fail to identify robust studies that have demonstrated a clear relationship between the provision of management training and enhanced small firm performance. Moreover, in a study of medium-sized firms in the UK, Storey (2002) found no direct link between training and firm performance but instead that both "attitudes to" and "practices of" education, and training and development variables were positively linked to firm performance. Thus, the conclusion seems to be that there are rational arguments against, as well as weak empirical evidence for, the ignorance explanation for the low level of formal management training in small firms. This calls into question the existing public programs for small firms, which are often based on the ignorance argument.

What small firm training policies can be found in different countries? In Storey (2004) a comparison was made between six OECD countries (Canada, Finland, Germany, Japan, the US and the UK) regarding their formal small firm training policies. The results show clear differences between countries, reflecting national differences in approach to learning:

- The US is the country that makes the greatest use of independent private sector training providers (e.g. training consultants). The implicit assumption is that entrepreneurship is "endemic" within the culture and that concern about business failure is almost non-existent, i.e. those who are sufficiently entrepreneurial will start a business, after which they will learn from their own mistakes. In many cases they may fail, but will start again.
- The opposite approach was found in Germany, where the chambers of commerce and industry associations play a core role in formal training for small firms.
- The provision of formal training for small firms by state organizations takes place primarily in Japan, which has a long history of public management training for small firms through government-backed organizations like the Small and Medium Enterprise Agency (SMEA) and the Japanese Small Business Corporation (JSBC). A similar situation exists in Finland with the Employment and Economic Development Centers, and to some extent in Canada, which has more than 400 Canada Small Business Service Centers.

Governments tend to favor formal training because it leads to a qualification that is recognized by all employers, and it is easier for government to monitor funding and to ensure that training is actually being provided. On the other hand, small firms do not favor formal training, but are more likely than larger firms to provide the greater part of their training in the form of an "informal" package. Thus, the challenge for government is to consider the US approach, assuming that experience is the most effective learning method for small firms, with perhaps some of it acquired through failure, which also implies another attitude toward business failures and bankruptcy.

3.   PERSPECTIVES ON SMALL BUSINESSES

Finally, an interview with David Storey is presented, in which he discusses his research but also looks to the future and discusses issues that require further research.

If we look at your research on job creation, starting in the 1980s, what do you think are the most interesting insights that you have made in your research?

I have always been interested in what I call "unenterprising areas". I am not convinced that geographic areas need high rates of new firm formation and I am not particularly impressed by the argument that public policy should be devoted to artificially stimulating birth rates. There are a number of reasons for this objection, particularly in unenterprising areas. In "unenterprising areas" with low rates of firm formation, there is a tendency amongst policy-makers to say that we should seek to encourage enterprise, get more people to start businesses, thus leading to higher rates of economic development. I don't agree with that ... I believe that this is particularly untrue in such areas, due to their comparatively low levels of entrepreneurial and human capital. What they do is ... if you encourage, stimulate, subsidize such people into starting businesses, they will start hairdressing, window cleaning, vehicle repair, plumbing businesses ... and these subsidized businesses tend to displace existing hair dressing, vehicle repair, plumbing businesses. I believe that this actually destabilizes the foundation of employment in that area and can lead to even lower rates of employment creation. What I am saying is that I believe there is quite strong evidence to suggest that intervention in the form of stimulating or subsidizing the rate of new firm start-ups could not only have no effect, but may actually have a negative effect.

So, what would your suggestion to government be?

The first thing is that ... as far as areas that traditionally do not have high rates of new firm formation are concerned, you have to look at other factors that influence the level of economic development other than increasing the new firm formation rate. And part of that has to do with education ... in the long term, education is the key to economic development. The second thing is to recognize that economic development in some areas will be stimulated by attracting enterprises from outside, either outside the country, but certainly outside the region ... inward investments can play an important role. Thirdly, I think that in the less prosperous areas of the UK at any rate, there are often higher education institutions that have very strong market skills. If we talk about the regions that I have looked at, there is a University of Teesside that produces a very considerable number of highly talented graduates in film and animation. Now, almost all of these people go and work for the film and animation industry in central London. So, it might be worth trying to devise a way in which they could utilize their skills within the locality, not necessarily start businesses straight away, but you must try to capitalize on overall skills within an area, and I think that exclusively focusing upon stimulating new firm formation is fundamentally misguided.

Another area that you have been interested in is high-growth firms .... what are the most interesting insights from that research?

I think this is an area where I have changed ... or adjusted my interpretation over time. If you look at what I wrote 10 or 15 years ago – while I still believe it is appropriate to devote more attention to businesses that have the willingness and the ability to grow as a means of stimulating job creation – I feel that the policy proposals I made at that time were probably slightly naïve. I thought it was merely a case of ignoring all but a few new firms, as the vast majority are too risky, and providing support for 3-7 year old businesses on the grounds that they have a track record that can be used to forecast their future performance. I think it is more tricky now. I still think it is not appropriate to consider intervention until the businesses are over three years old, but I believe my ability to identify businesses that will grow over the next five or ten years with a tolerable level of accuracy is not as good as I thought it was ten years ago.

Reading your work, you seem to have a tendency to let the empirical data speak ... you don't seem to be afraid to change your mind because you see something new in the empirical data. Why did you change your mind in this respect?

I think it comes from two strands. The first strand is a policy strand, observing the difficulties encountered by the UK government in focusing on businesses with the ability to grow. Broadly speaking, what happened in UK policy was that the 1980s was a decade in which we sought to maximize the number of people starting businesses. That policy changed in the early to mid 1990s, and for most of the remainder of that decade the focus was on established businesses with growth capacity. My observation is that government was actually not very good at implementing such a policy – it failed to pick the right businesses. So, you can offer policy prescriptions that are good in theory but where implementation causes considerable administrative, political and other problems. It might be great in theory but if it doesn't work in practice, then you have to say to yourself ... well, perhaps that is the wrong policy or maybe we have to change the way it is implemented.

The second thing that began to emerge was that the characteristics of growth businesses do not appear to be consistent over long periods of time. There is a very strong, what I would call stochastic component, the firms can be lucky or unlucky ... there is no surefire way guaranteed to achieve growth and job creation. Therefore a selective policy needs to be implemented with caution and monitored as to its effect. It must be evaluated, it must be adjusted if necessary, and it is not a universal solution to problems.

Government must be willing to change the policy, even if the aspirations remain the same. That means that you have to set up a monitoring system, and it is vital to have a willingness and openness on the part of government to evaluate whether the policy is working or whether it requires movements or shifts ... that is quite expensive in terms of money and prestige, because government doesn't like admitting "we didn't get this right".

A third area in your research is the work that you did with the ESRC Small Business Initiative at the end of the 1980s. It was a major achievement in small business research and a project that contributed substantially to existing knowledge. What did you see as the most interesting insights gained from that program?

I think the issue of public policy toward enterprise and enterprise creation was a subject that had received almost no attention from the academic community with regard to serious academic work. I would say that it is probably the chapters in the 1994-book about small business finance and public policy that I find most challenging and interesting and that I was pleased to write.

Another contribution is that small business literature was previously about running a small business, they were "how to do it" books, focussed on MBAs and people who were going to start a business. The title of the book is "Understanding the small business sector" ... it is actually synthesizing research on this whole group of firms, so it's about the birth and death of firms, it's about the environment ... it's not about producing a business plan, it's not about cash flow, it's not about how to market the businesses more efficiently ... so the book was the first book about small businesses.

What influence do you think that the ESRC Small Business Initiative has had on the development of small business research in the UK?

First of all I do think it had some impact on policy, because policy, as I indicated, shifted around the time the book, *Understanding the Small Business Sector*, was published. The politicians and the civil servants knew that the book was coming out. I don't for a minute suggest that the book was responsible for the shift in policy, and no civil servant has ever come up to me and announced that the book had revolutionized their view of the situation ... but, this focus upon growing businesses, moving away from start-ups – I think it was influential.

As far as the research is concerned, I do believe that the research projects in the program set a standard of analytical rigor, which became the norm, and which was not present prior to the ESRC Initiative ... the data sets were larger, there were more time series, less "soft case studies", more econometrics and more statistical analyses in the projects .– that I think was the sort of analytical rigor that the projects contributed.

If we look at the area of small business economics as a research field – what have been the most important research achievements during the last two decades?

The first thing that has happened is that the data sets have become vastly better. The reason for this is that small business research has become important for policy-makers, so if they consider small businesses as a critical component in long-term economic development, then those data sets are necessary in order to monitor that contribution. So the first thing is that data sets have become improved, which implies more time series, they are more accurate, more consistent, and they are not only consistent within countries but between countries as well. As a consequence, it has been possible to do more robust statistical work than was the case twenty years ago.

Secondly, at least from my perspective, statistical techniques have also improved during that period of time, although perhaps we are slower than we should be within the small business research area in incorporating those improved statistical techniques into our research. To give a simple example, if we were interested in the impact of government services upon small firms in a country, we would simply have looked at the recipients of the services and observed what happened ... but now the statistical techniques address the issue of control groups and are increasingly starting to address the issue of sample selection. To be honest, we are probably still behind many areas of labor market economics in terms of the sophistication of the techniques used, but over time our area has improved.

If we look at small business economics from the point of view of a young PhD student interested in small business economics ... are there some path breaking books or articles that you would suggest he/she should read?

The PhD students will probably only read one article that is the most relevant to their area and that they feel they must try to develop or extend. If you were to ask me to name the most interesting book I have read in recent years, I could point you toward two pieces. The first one is an absolutely gripping article by Fairlie in *Journal of Labor Economics* (2002). It follows cohorts of young people through different phases of their lives and concludes that, where all else is equal, an individual is more likely to be self-employed in their thirties if they were convicted of illegal drug dealing in their teens, irrespective of race, gender, education, and other "controls". What this suggests to me is not of course that we should have an entrepreneurial education program on drug dealing, but it is a very interesting case of economists identifying the impact of an entrepreneurial personality, because the type of person who engages in illegal drug dealing clearly has an entrepreneurial disposition that ultimately converts into self-employment later on in life. That is just a very interesting snippet of information. A second article is that by Hamilton in the *Journal of Political Economy* in 2000. What he is doing is really attempting to quantify the extent to which people in entrepreneurship actually obtain non-pecuniary benefits from being entrepreneurs. In other words, it demonstrates that these people could actually earn more in paid employment, but that they have no desire to change. I think ... that epitomizes the essence of entrepreneurship.

If you look at the field as a whole, what developments can you see in small business economic research?

I am really interested in public policy ... and the impact of public policy on the creation and growth of enterprises and its links with long-term economic development. To me there are still many unanswered questions about what does and does not work. I have my prejudices about what works, and I am prepared to place policies into categories of those that I would encourage some governments to study quite closely and others that I would strongly advise against ... but it would be nice to firm that up.

What do you see as the future for entrepreneurship research?

The field of entrepreneurship has experienced a surprising level of growth. The issue for me has always been to make sure that the research meets the necessary academic standards, that the interpretation of the results is justified, and that if issues are unclear, they should be clarified.

I think ... and this is a very personal perspective ... I am one of few people in the book who is not North American, and I think there are specific European perspectives. Whilst I do not lay claim to being the embodiment of the European perspective, I am probably closer to it than the North Americans ... there is a gap, a divide, and I think that is important ... we are not employing the same vocabulary. US researchers talk about entrepreneurship and enterprises, but in the UK the focus is on small business. In a similar way US scholars are interested in successes ... successful entrepreneurs, growth companies, and successful geographic areas, such as Silicon Valley ... and this is miles away culturally from the interest in the UK ... where it is more business as usual themes, less successful businesses ... less exemplary business. And, the word "policy" does not seem to exist in the vocabulary of US researchers.

REFERENCES

Atkinson, J., & Storey, D.J. (eds.), 1993, *Employment, the Small Firm and the Labour Market*, London: Routledge.

Curran, J. & Storey, D.J. (eds.), 1992, *Small Firms in Urban and Rural Locations*, London: Routledge.

Hughes, A. & Storey, D.J. (eds.), 1994, *Finance and the Small Firm*, London: Routledge.

Storey, D.J., 1982, *Entrepreneurship and the New Firm*, London: Routledge.

Storey, D.J., 1994, *Understanding the Small Business Sector*, London: Routledge.

Storey, D., 2000, Six steps to heaven: evaluating the impact of public policies to support small businesses in developed economies, in Sexton, D.L. & Landström, H. (eds.), *The Blackwell Handbook of Entrepreneurship*, Oxford: Blackwell.

Storey, D.J. & Johnson, S., 1987, *Job Generation and Labour Market Change*, Basingstoke, Hants: Macmillan.

Storey, D. & Keasey, K. & Watson, R. & Wynarczyk, P., 1987, *The Performance of Small Firms. Profits, Jobs and Failures*, London: Croom Helm.

New firm formation, job creation and regional development

Evans, D.S., 1987, The Relationship between Firm Growth, Size and Age: Estimates for 100 Manufacturing Industries, *Journal of Industrial Economics*, 35, 567-582.

Gallagher, C.C. & Stewart, H., 1984, Jobs and the business Life Cycle in the UK, Research Report 2, Department of Industrial Management, University of Newcastle upon Tyne.

Giaoutzi, M. & Nijkamp, P. & Storey, D.J., 1988, Small is beautiful: The regional importance of small-scale activities, in Giaoutzi, M. & Nijkamp, P. & Storey, D.J. (eds.), *Small and medium sized enterprises and regional development*, London: Routledge. 1-18.

Reynolds, P. & Storey, D.J. & Westhead, P., 1994a, Cross-national Comparisons of the Variation in New Firm Formation Rates: An Editorial Overview, *Regional Studies*, 28, 4, 343-346.

Reynolds, P. & Storey, D.J. & Westhead, P., 1994b, Cross-national Comparisons of the Variation in New Firm Formation Rates, *Regional Studies*, 28, 4, 443-456.

Storey, D., 1981, New Firm Formation, Employment Change and the Small Firm: The Case of Cleveland County, *Urban Studies*, 18, 335-345.

Storey, D.J., 1989, Firm performance and size: Explanations from the small firm sector, *Small Business Economics*, 1, 3, 175-180.

Storey, D.J., 1991, The Birth of New Firms – Does Unemployment Matter? A Review of the Evidence, *Small Business Economics*, 3, 167-178.

Storey, D.J., 1993, Should we abandon support to start-up businesses?, in Chittenden, F. & Robertson, M. & Watkins, D (eds.), *Small firms: recession and recovery*, London: Chapman. 15-26.

Storey, D.J. & Johnson, S., 1986, Job generation in Britain: a review of recent studies, *International Small Business Journal*, 4, 4, 29-46.

Storey, D.J. & Johnson, S., 1987, Regional Variations in Entrepreneurship in the U.K., *Scottish Journal of Political Economy*, 34, 2, 161-173.

Storey, D.J. & Johnson, S.G., 1990, A Review of Small Business Employment Data Bases in the United Kingdom, *Small Business Economics*, 2, 279-299.

Storey, D.J. & Jones, A.M., 1987, New Firm Formation – A Labout Market Approach to Industrial Entry, *Scottish Journal of Political Economy*, 34, 1, 260-274.

New technology-based firms

Little, A.D., 1977, *New Technology-Based Firms in the United Kingdom and the Federal Republic of Germany*, London: Wilton House.

Storey, D.J. & Strange, A., 1992, Where Are They Now? Some Changes in Firms Located on UK Science Parks in 1986, *New Technology, Work and Employment*, 7, 15-28.

Storey, D.J. & Tether, B.S., 1998, New technology-based firms in the European union: an introduction, *Research Policy*, 26, 933-946.

Tether, B. & Storey, D., 1997, Smaller firms and the evolution of technology-based sectors in Europe, in Arundel, A. & Garrelfs, R. (eds.), *Innovation measurement and policies: conference proceedings*, Luxembourg: Office for Official Publications of the European Communities. 197-203.

Tether, B.S. & Storey, D.J., 1998, Smaller firms and Europe's high technology sectors: a framework for analysis and some statistical evidence, *Research Policy*, 26, 947-971.

Westhead, P. & Storey, D.J., 1995, Links between higher education institutions and high technology firms?, *Omega*, 23, 4, 345-360.

Westhead, P. & Storey, D.J. & Cowling, M. 1995, An exploratory analysis of the factors associated with the survival of independent high-technology firms in Great Britain, in Chittenden, F. & Robertson, M. & Marchall, I. (eds.), *Small firms: partnership for growth*, London: Paul Chapman. 63-99.

Management training in small firms

Storey, D.J., 2002, Education, training and development policies and practices in medium-sized companies in the UK: do they really influence firm performance?, *Omega*, 30, 249-264.

Storey, D.J., 2004, Exploring the link, among small firms, between management training and firm performance: a comparison between the UK and other OECD countries, *International Journal of Human Resource Management*, 15, 1, 112-130.

Storey, D.J. & Westhead, P., 1994, *Management Development in Small and Medium-sized Enterprises with Growth Potential*, London: CBI.

Storey, D.J. & Westhead, P., 1997, Management training in small firms – a case of market failure?, *Human Resource Management Journal*, 7, 2, 61-71.

Westhead, P. & Storey, D.J., 1996, Management training and small firm performance: why is the link so weak?, *International Small Business Journal*, 14, 13-24.

Other references

Fairlie, R.W., 2002, Drug dealing and legitimate self employment, *Journal of Labor Economics*, 20, 3, 538-567.

Hamilton, B.H., 2000, Does entrepreneurship pay? An empirical analysis of the returns to self employment, *Journal of Political Economy*, 108, 3, 604-631.

Chapter 8

ZOLTAN ACS AND DAVID AUDRETSCH

1. ZOLTAN ACS AND DAVID AUDRETSCH – DISCOVERERS OF THE ROLE OF SMALL FIRMS IN INNOVATION AND CREATORS OF THE SMALL BUSINESS ECONOMICS RESEARCH FIELD

1.1 The Contributions of Zoltan Acs and David Audretsch

Zoltan Acs and David Audretsch are two of the most prolific researchers within the entrepreneurship and small business field. Both jointly and individually they have published a considerable amount of scientific articles and books and have made a number of significant contributions in the area of small business economics.

From among their rich production, their joint pioneering collaboration in the 1980s and early 1990s on the innovative role of small firms deserves special mention. In particular, two issues should be highlighted: the systematic analysis of how the role of small firms varies according to the characteristics of the industry of which they form a part and how findings on the innovative role of small firms are sensitive to the type of innovative activity in question. Since their seminal work in the 1980s and early 1990s they have made important contributions on the subject of the evolution of small firms and regional aspects of small business and innovation.

Apart from their own empirical work, Zoltan Acs and David Audretsch have made important contributions to the open and critical assessment and discussion of the role of small firms in the economy, including organizing several high class conferences and editing books.

However, their single most important contribution is the establishment of the *Small Business Economics* journal as a high quality outlet for small business research.

1.2   Career

The following subsection is devoted to a description of the careers of Zoltan Acs and David Audretsch with focus on the period of their pioneering collaboration in the 1980s and early 1990s on the innovative role of small business in society.

1.2.1   Zoltan Acs

Zoltan Acs did not seem destined for an academic career.

"I was born in a refugee camp in Austria of Hungarian parents after the war. My parents emigrated to America in 1952. I was never a very good student. After high school I had various jobs for a couple of years, and I didn't know what to do. I saved some money and went to college in Ohio. I wanted to be an engineer, but didn't do very well ... I thought I could study business, but I didn't like business either ... what I did like was economics ... so, I ended up as an economist."

Acs' research and thinking have to a great extent been influenced by his roots – his roots as an immigrant child in the US during the 1950s, but also his youth in the 1960s, which was coloured by the cultural changes that occurred in the US and Europe during that period. There was an overwhelming belief in large industrial corporations, concentration, etc., and one of the main exponents of this kind of large scale industrial model was John Kenneth Galbraith, as well as authors such as Douglass North. It was a time when the world was divided into communist states with central planning and collectivism, and capitalistic countries. The big debate in the US was about where society was heading.

"When I finished college I really wasn't sure what I was going to do, but I decided to go to graduate school. I was interested in the big social picture ... the issue of capitalism and socialism, and I went to graduate school at the New School for Social Research in New York City. I went there for two reasons. I was interested in social movements and how they affected society, and the other thing was that one of the most prominent thinkers on this issue, Robert Heilbroner, was professor at the New School for Social Research. This intellectual tradition held that socialism would eventually replace capitalism, and a great deal of my time in graduate school was devoted to these social issues ... It was in this context that I began my academic career.

I was a great admirer of John Maynard Keynes. In some sense Keynes' ideas were an attempt to balance private and public interests. He basically said that the private sector, which at that time implied the large corporations, was the driving force in society and that governments needed to deal with the demands of the large corporations. In the large corporations the greatest investment was capital equipment, and therefore, the main policy prescription was the promotion of low interest rates, and the use of monetary and fiscal policies to ensure that the machines operated continuously."

Inflation was one of the big issues in macroeconomics at that time, and many countries managed inflation through different forms of wage and price controls. In order to understand inflation, Acs started to study the price mechanism behavior of large corporations. The steel industry was ideal for such a study – with its well established oligopolistic market and strong unions and where the wages paid set the pattern for other industries.

The thesis *Price Behavior and the Theory of the Firm in Competitive and Corporate Markets* was presented in 1979 at the New School for Social Research. In his thesis Acs examined the price behavior of the large companies in the steel industry. The assumption was that in a corporate market such as the steel industry, the firms could raise prices sufficiently to finance internal growth. Acs concluded that companies in the steel industry had enough money to finance their investments, but as most of it was distributed to workers and shareholders, there was insufficient capital available to finance internal growth.

After graduation from the New School for Social Research, Acs moved to the Department of Economics at Middlebury College in Vermont, where he remained from 1980 to 1982. It was at Middlebury College that he met David Audretsch and they became very good friends. When Acs moved back to New York in 1982 they remained in contact.

"My wife stayed in New York with our baby ... it became complicated, so I went to Columbia University in New York, where I was a part of a large international political economics research group – which was a hotbed of political debate about where the world was going."

This environment changed Acs' thinking about the development of society – from a left-wing Keynesian view toward a market oriented view of economic development. In his thesis he tended to disregard small firms as, theoretically, there was nothing to indicate that small firms might be important. After his dissertation, Acs became more and more aware of the importance of small firms. He discovered that there were some small firms in the steel industry – "mini-mills" – that could compete with the large corporations and the way they did it was through the use of innovative production technologies and innovative ways of organizing their companies. Due to this discovery, Acs re-wrote three chapters of his thesis between 1980 and 1982, and a new book *The Changing Structure of the US Economy: Lessons from the Steel Industry* was subsequently published in 1984. In the book, Acs attempted to use technology and innovation to explain why Keynesian economics could not work and that planning and government intervention was the wrong approach to technical change. He also introduced another perspective on small businesses, when he asserted that small businesses were not in fact inferior copies of large companies but that there was a fundamental difference – they were agents of change in the economy – introducing a type of dynamics that was equally or even more important for societal development than the effeciency of large companies. What the study showed was that small companies could have innovative advantages over large established companies within the steel industry.

"The early 1980s was a period that really influenced my thinking. There was a political movement ... the election of Margaret Thatcher in England and Ronald Reagan in the US, which gave the world a new direction and introduced policies characterized by less government intervention, lower taxes, deregulation, more focus on entrepreneurship ... everything that I had studied before led me to believe that it was wrong ... that this was not the way to go. But at the same time, I had studied the steel industry, and it was clear to me that the old model no longer worked. Several other people had also made similar observations and that influenced my thinking. For example, David Birch, who from a completely different perspective found that small firms created jobs, Michael Piore and Charles Sabel, co-authors of *The Second Industrial Divide*, who argued that the technology that made mass production possible was now evolving toward flexible technologies and new organizational forms, Irwin Toffler's book *The Third Wave* about the technological revolution, as well as Gerhard Mensch, who studied long waves of technological change. These observations just didn't fit the old industrial world ... So, while at the outset I thought of the world as based on the old industrial Galbraithian and Keynesian models, I ended up viewing it as a Schumpeterian dynamic entrepreneurial model ... and as a consequence I had to add three new chapters to my thesis. All of a sudden I gained a totally different perspective on the world. It was no longer the Keynesian left of the center view ... it was more a market oriented view ... that completely changed my thinking."

In 1985 Acs left New York and moved to the University of Illinois and tried to plan his future.

"At that time we had two children, and I couldn't afford to live in New York so I took a job at the University of Illinois. I tried to figure out the next step in my career. I needed a large research project in order to look more closely into the importance of technological change. I wrote a proposal to the Small Business Administration, which, I found out, was also involved in another proposal to study innovations and in the process of compiling a database for that purpose. I received funding from the University of Illinois to buy the SBA Innovation Database. So, I ended up with a database with which to study the change in the structure of the US economy, not only from one industry but from the manufacturing sector as a whole ... and it was data from 1976 to 1986. In addition we bought the US SBA Database ... so, I was able to pool the two databases, one on innovations and the other on small firms. Together with a database on industrial data that David had got from the Federal Trade Commission, we had an incredibly rich data set."

It was thanks to these databases that Acs and Audretsch subsequently accomplished their pioneering work on the importance of small business for innovation and technical development.

1.2.2   David Audretsch

David Audretsch, born 1954, comes from a quite different background – an American middle-class one – and he was more conscious in his choice of professional career.

"When I graduated from college at Drew University in Madison, New Jersey, in 1976 I knew that I wanted to be a professor, so I went to graduate school at the University of Wisconsin. At that time ... the mid 1970s ... one of the biggest problems in the US was high unemployment combined with high inflation. In the public press there were a lot of accusations to the effect that large corporations, especially the oil companies, seemed to exploit their power to the cost of the average American. And the reason why I selected the University of Wisconsin was that there were some researchers who focused on the links between large corporations and the impact they had on performance ... both company performance and for the industry as a whole ... and this was really the core of the field of 'industrial organization' at that point in time ... how much concentration (monopoly and oligopoly) is there in the US, what is the impact and, if negative, what could be done about it. Thus, my early career and my disciplinary training has nothing to do with small business – on the contrary, it was about big business."

This interest in the large corporations was also reflected in David Audretsch's thesis *The Effectiveness of Antitrust Policy Towards Horizontal Mergers* in 1980, which was an evaluation of an anti-trust act from the 1950s which gave the Federal Trade Commission the power to prevent horizontal mergers, which was amended in the early 1970s, and Audretsch empirically calculated the costs and benefits of this policy change.

After graduation Audretsch accepted a position as Assistant Professor at Middlebury College in Vermont – a small college with about 1,500 graduate students.

> "In fact I was not interested in research ... I went to graduate school so that I could be a teacher. I wanted to teach ... I enjoyed the interaction with young people, and I felt that a PhD was something you needed to make this possible. At Middlebury College I lectured in economics ... which was concerned with the big policy issues in the US ... should we break up General Motors, US Steel, IBM, etc."

In 1980 Zoltan Acs arrived at Middlebury College as Assistant Professor in Economics after his graduation at the New School University.

> "Zoltan Acs and I became friends, we talked a lot about economic issues, what was going on in the world ... but most of all we were friends, we hiked in the mountains, played basketball ... we had a great time."

Zoltan Acs left Middlebury College in 1982 but visited the school frequently, while David Audretsch remained until 1985. In 1984 he spent a summer in Washington D.C. to work for the International Trade Commission.

> "When I was in Washington D.C. I met Joanne, my wife ... but she was on her way to Paris. I realized that Vermont was a long way from Paris. It should be added that my thesis advisor, Leonard Weiss, received a request from the International Trade Commission to write a recommendation for me. He quickly sent me a letter pleading me to stay in academia and not leave for government. Instead he suggested that I should go to the International Institute of Management in Berlin, where I could do research. I knew that Berlin was much closer to Paris than Vermont. So, I went to Berlin. It was shocking ... I was 29 years old, had never been outside the US, except for Canada ... and flying over 'enemy territory' ...."

At the International Institute of Management in Berlin they quickly offered Audretsch a two year research contract, and in 1985 he started to work on a project on how concentration and market power influenced performance in mature industries compared to new industries. His stay in Berlin became much longer – he remained for 13 years at the International Institute of Management in Berlin, which was subsequently known as the Wissenschaftszentrum Berlin für Sozialforschung.

1.2.3 Acs and Audretsch's Pioneering Work on Innovation and Small Firms

In 1986 Zoltan Acs visited David Audretsch in Berlin.

"I realized that there was an opportunity for what they called a 'summer fellow' at the Institute in Berlin, and I asked if I could arrange summer fellowship for Zoltan. They said 'sure, that will be fine, but on one condition – that he brings his data with him'. So, Zoltan arrived in the summer of 1986 ... we really began a systematic, empirical and quantitative analysis of the data that Zoltan brought to Berlin." (DA)

The analysis soon provided interesting results.

"Our first intention was not to focus on innovative activities. What we wanted to do was to try to document the extent to which economic activity was shifting from large to small firms. But I knew enough from earlier research in industrial organization that innovation was a big topic in the literature. What we discovered pretty quickly was, contrary to the conventional wisdom at that time, based on researchers like Schumpeter, and Galbraith, who believed that large corporations generate most of the innovative activity ... we found that small firms were just as innovative as their larger counterparts, and when we related it to employment, the small firms were actually more innovative than the large ones. But small firms didn't account for all the innovation, it varied from industry to industry. For example, in industries like aircraft and pharmaceuticals, large corporations were innovative. But what surprised us was that in industries like computers, where IBM was the dominant firm, small firms were very innovative. At first, when we looked at the results, we thought that it was a computational error, but we checked it over, and it seemed to be correct." (DA)

The results led Acs and Audretsch to start systematic analyses, asking the questions: why does innovative activity vary across industries, why does innovative activity vary in relation to size, and how does the industry environment make a difference? Within a short period of time Zoltan Acs and David Audretsch wrote a couple of articles that really led to the discovery of the innovative role of small firms. The findings were published in the book *Innovation and Small Firms* in 1990 as well as in a couple of articles, such as:

Acs, Z.J. & Audretsch, D.B., 1987, Innovation, market-structure, and firm size, *Review of Economics and Statistics*, 69, 4, 567-574.

Acs, Z.J. & Audretsch, D.B, 1988, Innovation in Large and Small Firms: An Empirical Analysis, *American Economic Review*, 78, 4, 678-690.

Acs, Z.J. & Audretsch, D.B., 1989, Small-firm entry in the United States manufacturing, *Economica*, 56, 255-265.

"We can define the essense of our findings in one sentence: Both large and small firms contributed to the innovative process. It sounds very simple, but in the field of industrial organization, the whole focus had been that only large firms are important. Based on a new way of measuring innovation and the databases that we had access to, we broadened our understanding of innovative activties in industry." (ZA)

However, it was not only the research contributions that characterised Acs' and Audretsch's activities during the late 1980s. They were extremely active in organizing this new area of research by means of workshops and conferences, and they established the *Small Business Economics* journal – the first volume of which was published in 1989 – and the journal rapidly became one of the leading outlets within the field of entrepreneurship and small business.

"The late 1980s was characterized by a 'coming together of people'. Scholars anchored in some main discipline, social sciences, management studies, etc., with an interest in small business, seemed to have difficulties gaining attention in their parent discipline. So, we started to meet people from different countries, we organized conferences and seminars in order to get together. We also realized that there were no research outlets for this kind of research ... that gave us the idea of launching the *Small Business Economics* journal in 1989.

There were a couple of things that made this happen. First, the world had changed by the late 1980s and early 1990s ... countries in the West realized that 'entrepreneurship matters', which also resulted in an awareness among scholars in different fields. Secondly, my location in Berlin was important. The International Institute of Management gave me freedom, it was a multidisciplinary research institute, and there were a lot of resources for the organisation of workshops, for travelling, inviting guests, and thus interaction. So, being in Berlin at the Institute was really essential for many things that happened during this period of time." (DA)

1.2.4   David Audretsch – His Later Career

Both David Audretsch and Zoltan Acs have continued as highly active researchers throughout the last decade of the 20th and the early years of the 21st century, both jointly and individually. With regard to David Audretsch's research, we can identify some dominant themes. Such a theme is, for example, the evolutionary process of new firms.

> "I understood that the start-up process was important and that it was people that started firms. Actually, I recall one of the conferences in Berlin with a lot of industrial organization economists, and they kept talking about the entry of firms ... and it became very clear to me that they discussed the firm as if there were no people, and I really felt that this was something that limited the development of industrial organization as a research field. So, I started to attend entrepreneurship conferences – interacting with people who realized that people start firms.

> I became interested in start-up activities and at that point in time we knew that there were a lot of start ups, but we didn't know much about what happened to the firms after their launch. What I found, and what we know today, is that most of the firms don't survive. And that raised a lot of questions, for example, why would somebody start a firm that is going to fail? I started to study patterns of survival and growth using a longitudinal database that I got from the Small Business Administration, which enabled me to track firms in every US manufacturing industry over time from 1976 to 1984.

> What I found was that firms in the most innovative industries had the lowest survival rate, but if they survived they had the highest growth rate. And, I gradually started to develop an interpretation that suggests that people start firms because they think they are going to do something differently but that they are unable to evaluate the chances of success. They gradually learn if it is a good idea and whether or not they are capable of succeeding – if not, the firm will disappear – it is an evolutionary process." (DA)

The results of these studies were presented in one of Audretsch's most important works since his studies on innovations in the 1980s, the book entitled *Innovation and Industry Evolution* (1995) as well as in the article "New firm survival: new results using a hazard function" in *Review of Economics and Statistics* (1995) in collaboration with Talat Mahmood.

Another central theme in David Audretsch's production during the 1990s deals with regional spillovers.

"From our studies in the 1980s we knew that small firms innovate, but on the other hand, small firms don't have a lot of R&D. According to the so called 'knowledge production function' there will be a linkage between knowledge input and innovative output. This seems to hold if we look at the national level – countries with highly educated people, scientists and engineers are also the most innovative countries – and it holds for industries – industries with a lot of R&D such as computers and pharmaceuticals are the most innovative. But when looking at the firm level, the analysis breaks down – small firms are innovative, but they are innovative without the R&D input ... they seem to get something for nothing ... so, the question is: Where do they get the knowledge?

A PhD student, Maryann Feldman, approached Zoltan about our innovation data and said that she would like to look at the geographic dimension of innovations, and Zoltan called me up and together with Maryann we started to look at the data. We soon found that innovative activities are clustered together, and we began to understand where the small firms get their knowledge ... they get it from somebody else ... it is a knowledge spillover from one firm or a research lab, and the small firms either use it or are in fact the result of this spillover, for example, scientists leaving a large pharmaceutical company to start their own company.

In a global market with low information costs, you would expect that anything based on information could be located anywhere ... location doesn't really matter in relation to information. But we found that innovative activity occurs in geographic clusters, especially in knowledge intensive industries, and the reason is the need for tacit knowledge ... which you can't transmit via e-mail ... so, location matters, it is important to be positioned where you have access to this knowledge spillover." (DA)

A third theme of interest in Audretsch's research concerns linking start-up activities to growth, or what Audretsch calls the consequences of entrepreneurship. In this respect he has collaborated with Roy Thurik in the Netherlands to link the entrepreneurship (start ups) rate to the growth rate of the country – similar to the Global Entrepreneurship Monitoring project (Reynolds, 2000), but using OECD data. In common with the GEM project, they found that those countries that implemented different measures to stimulate entrepreneurship activities have grown more and witnessed a drop in unemployment. Hence, the general recommendation for governments would be: if you don't develop an entrepreneurial economy, the country pays a price in terms of a lower growth rate and higher unemployment.

In 1997, David Audretsch moved back to the US and a chair in economics at Georgia State University. Two years later he was offered the Ameritech Chair of Economic Development at Indiana University in Bloomington, and he became Director of the Institute for Development Strategies.

1.2.5   Zoltan Acs – His Later Career

In 1989, Zoltan Acs moved to the University of Baltimore. His research interest changed in more or less the same direction as that of David Audretsch, and during the 1990s he focused his attention on the regional aspects of innovation, and more specifically the importance of cities.

> "What our research in the 1980s failed to answer was: 'How can small firms with no R&D or capital, innovate in an industry alongside competitors such as IBM?' In the 1990s I began to elaborate on this question, and my understanding was that small firms obtain their R&D from knowledge spill-overs, mainly on a regional basis and in this respect the cities play an important role. So, in the 1990s I switched my unit of analysis from industry and became interested in the cities." (ZA)

Acs had two PhD students working on these questions, Maryann Feldman on the geography of innovations (1994) and Attila Varga on innovations at city level (1997). Some of the findings with Feldman and Varga have been developed in a couple of articles, which have subsequently been well-cited:

Acs, Z.J. & Audretsch, D.B. & Feldman, M.P., 1992, Real effects of academic research: comment, *American Economic Review*, 82, 1, 363-367.

Acs, Z.J. & Audretsch, D.B. & Feldman, M.P., 1994, Research development spillovers and recipient firm size, *Review of Economics and Statistics*, 76, 2, 336-340.

Audretsch, D.B. & Feldman, M.P., 1996, R&D spillovers and the geography of innovation and production, *American Economic Review*, 86, 3, 630-640.

Anselin, L. & Varga, A. & Acs, Z., 1997, Local geographic spillovers between university research and high technology innovations, *Journal of Urban Economics*, 42, 3, 422-448.

"In my earlier work, especially my 1984 book, I wrote extensively about the role of technical change, and I spent a lot of time trying to understand what drives technical change in society. The industrial revolution that we are now experiencing began back in the 1980s ... people began to talk about the information economy or the knowledge revolution. Transportation was central in this industrial revolution as in all others. In earlier industrial revolutions we saw the importance of railroads, steam engines, automobiles, airplanes, jet engines ... transportation has always been an important component. In this new industrial revolution, it was a question of the transportation of information ... for example the internet ... and I was interested in this transportation of information and knowledge and how it was connected to the importance of small firms. In the articles written with Maryann Feldman and Attila Varga ... we really found strong evidence to suggest that knowledge spillovers are important for small firms ... a fact that people knew from anecdotal evidence and that we could validate." (ZA)

This research was further examined with Felix FitzRoy and Ian Smith at the University of St. Andrews. They were interested in the effect of R&D spillovers on employment creation, and their results were presented in two articles:

Acs, Z.J. & FitzRoy, F. & Smith, I., 1999, High Technology Employment and University R&D Spillovers: Evidence from U.S. Cities, *Economics of Innovation and New Technology*, 8, 57-78.

Acs, Z.J. & FitzRoy, F. & Smith, I., 2002, High Technology Employment and R&D in Cities: Heterogeneity v.s. Specialization, *Annals of Regional Science*, 36, 373-386.

In the book *Innovation and the Growth of Cities* (2002) Zoltan Acs has collected the bulk of his research dealing with the regional aspects of innovation and technical change. In the concluding chapter of the book, he presents a theoretical framework that can be used to understand technology-led regional economic development and that combines ideas from (i) the new economic geography based on Krugman (1991), which answers the question as to why economic activity is concentrated in certain regions but not in others, (ii) the new growth theory (Romer, 1990) that explains the causes of economic growth, and (iii) the new economics of innovation of which Nelson (1993) is the main exponent and which tries to explain the institutional structure in the innovation process.

This initiative was undertaken with Catherine Armington at the US Bureau of the Census where Zoltan Acs was a research fellow from 1988 to 2001 and had access to microdata of the Longitudinal Establishment and Enterprise Database. Using the database they examined the impact of entrepreneurship and geography on economic growth in a series of studies, while in a forthcoming book they will examine the impact of entrepreneurship in the 1990s.

Acs, Z.J. & Armington, C., 2004, Employment Growth and Entrepreneurial Activity in Cities, *Regional Studies*, October.

Acs, Z.J. & Armington, C., 2004, The Impact of Geographic Differences in Human Capital on Service Firm Formation Rates, *Journal of Urban Economics*, October.

Acs, Z.J. & Armington, C., forthcoming, *Entrepreneurship, Geography and American Economic Growth*, Cambridge: Cambridge University Press.

Since 1992 Zoltan Acs holds the Dorris and Robert McCurdy Distinguished Professorship of Entrepreneurship at Merrick School of Business, University of Baltimore, USA.

2.   STREAM OF INTEREST IN ZOLTAN ACS' AND DAVID AUDRETSCH'S RESEARCH

Since the 1980s, Zoltan Acs and David Audretsch have been two of the most productive researchers in the area of entrepreneurship and small business research. They have published several hundred scientific articles, books and reports jointly, individually or in collaboration with other researchers and it is, therefore, virtually impossible to present their entire research production. For this reason, I have chosen to concentrate on their joint seminal research on innovation and small firms. First, I will present Acs and Audretsch' pioneering work in the book *Innovation and Small Firms*, published in 1990. Then follows a review of some of their research articles during the late 1980s and early 1990, articles that are based on Acs and Audretsch' pioneering work on innovation and small firms.

2.1   Innovation and Small Firms

For a long time most of the ideas on innovation and technological change have been based on the "knowledge production function", originally formulated by Zvi Griliches in the article "Issues in assessing the contribution of R&D to productivity growth" (1979) in which he argues that innovative activities are based on new economic knowledge. The knowledge production function assumes that the majority of industrial R&D is undertaken by the larger companies and according to conventional wisdom, large enterprises are the engine of technological change. There is substantial evidence that investment in R&D is positively related to firm size (Cohen & Levin, 1989).

In the book *Innovation and Small Firms*, Acs and Audretsch base their reasoning on the paradox that small businesses more and more are the drivers of the economy at the same time as technological change appears to demand the investment of large resources in R&D to an increasingly greater extent in order to exploit the global market – something that ought to be the preserve of large companies. This raises the question: What role do small businesses play in innovation and technological change in society? The book concentrates on this issue, which represents the area where these researchers have made their greatest empirical contributions.

Their contributions are twofold: First, a methodological contribution – experience from earlier research showed that innovation is not an easy phenomenon to measure and the research mainly examined the innovative activity of relatively large firms – however, in their studies Zoltan Acs and David Audretsch developed a more direct measure of innovative output and used a new database developed by the US Small Business Administration, which also included data on innovative activities by small firms. Second, they contributed to our understanding of the role of small firms in the changes brought about by innovation and technology in different industries.

2.1.1   Methodology – New Measures of Innovation and a New Database

In order to empirically estimate the knowledge production function, it became evident that measurement issues played a major role, and the state of knowledge within the area has been shaped by the nature of the data available to scholars for analysis and typically involved one of three major aspects of the innovative process – aspects that have evolved over time (Acs & Audretsch, 2003):

- The early attempts to quantify technological change in the late 1950s and early 1960s involved measures of the input into the innovative process, for example, R&D expenditure or share of the labor force involved in R&D activities.
- Intermediate output, for example, number of inventions patented – measures that were publicly available in the mid 1960s.
- In the 1970s attempts were made to provide a direct measure of the innovative output, for example, using a panel of experts who identified innovations representing significant new products and processes that had been successfully commercialized.

These measures were not without limitations. For example, the use of R&D activity as an indicator of technological change merely takes account of the resources devoted to innovation but not the actual amount of innovative output, while the use of patented inventions is also no indicator of innovative output, nor does it reveal whether or not the knowledge generated has a positive economic value – in addition to which, not all innovations are actually patented.

Thus, such measures are associated with a range of problems. Acs and Audretsch's pioneering contribution meant, among other things, the development of a means of measuring innovation that quantifies the number of innovations introduced on the market at a certain point in time.

Another methodological problem encountered in previous research was the lack of data on small businesses. Acs and Audretsch utilised a new database developed in the US during the 1980s. The US Small Business Administration's Innovation Data Base (SBIDB) consists of 8,074 commercial innovations introduced in the US in 1982. The "Futures Group", a private firm, compiled the data for the US Small Business Administration by examining over one hundred technology engineering and trade journals listing innovations and new products. The database made it possible to distinguish between data from large and small businesses (< 500 employees). In their research, Acs and Audretsch have utilized and developed this database in a robust way.

2.1.2   Results

What then was the conclusion arrived at by Acs and Audretsch in the book? In general terms it can be said that, by their systematic research and robust use of methodology, they in many respects clarify and erase a number of question-marks in earlier research. Their results can be summarized as follows:

– The contribution of small businesses to technological change in society is significant but there seems to be no single firm size that is optimum – there is a place for all sizes of business. While large companies are responsible for launching more innovations than smaller ones, when related to the number of employees, the situation is reversed. Moreover, the importance of small and large businesses in terms of innovative activity in different industries appears to differ – in some industries small companies are more innovative, whereas in others large companies account for technological change. Large businesses tend to have some advantages in capital intensive industries characterised by strong concentration.

– In the manufacturing industry the number of small companies varies dramatically between different lines of business. Not surprisingly, there are few small companies in capital intensive lines of business with high R&D intensity and where different economies of scale are present.

- The relation between an industry's level of innovation and new firm formation is complex. Even if the start up rate is high in technological environments that promote the innovative activities of small businesses, the results show that both the total innovative activity and the R&D intensity of an industry have a negative impact on start up frequency, i.e. in industries where innovative activity is dominated by existing companies, the establishment of small businesses is less frequent.
- Several studies have shown that small businesses often exhibit a higher growth rate than larger ones. Is a company's growth dependent on its size? The answer seems to be no, as in at least two thirds of all industries small and large businesses grow at a similar rate. What is the explanation? While small businesses appear to have a higher growth rate, they also have a tendency to exit the industry more rapidly – in most industries these two tendencies offset each other, which is why small businesses do not exhibit a higher growth rate than large companies at an aggregate level.
- What are the factors that determine the dynamics within and between industries? The study indicates that the knowledge on which innovations are based is of great importance for the dynamics of an industry. If the innovative activities are primarily dependent on knowledge accumulated through experience within the industry, established companies will have an advantage in terms of innovation, thus making the industry less attractive to new and independent companies. When few companies are established in the industry, relatively few companies will fail or exit, leading to low level dynamics. On the other hand, if knowledge is mainly generated outside the industry, the industry will be accessible to new companies. However, this does not mean that these new companies will survive within the industry. Innovation is an ongoing activity and learning is critical for its success.

What conclusions can be drawn from these results? We can firstly establish that small businesses are important for technological change in society as well as for much of the dynamics within or between different industries. Consequently, there is every reason for politicians and policy-makers to stimulate the innovative activities of small businesses.

2.2 Acs and Audretsch's Production During the Late 1980s and Early 1990s

Zoltan Acs and David Audretsch's results have also been published in a number of journal articles. Some of the most often cited works in their joint production are summarized below. It should be mentioned that the majority of these works are based on the same empirical data material as the above-mentioned book. In some cases the contents are similar, while in other cases the articles constitute a development of the reasoning presented in the book.

Schumpeter (1942) argued that large companies are primarily responsible for the innovative activities in a society and even more so in industries where competition is limited – where high entry barriers can be expected. In their article "Innovation, market-structure, and firm-size" (1987), Acs and Audretsch attempt to test these two assumptions. In contrast to Schumpeter's first assumption, the results show that, generally speaking, large companies are not more innovative than smaller ones – in some industries large companies are more innovative while in others it is the small companies. Hence, the question is not which firm size is the most innovative but "Under what conditions have small and large companies an innovative advantage?" The authors concluded that within the manufacturing industry, large companies appear to have some innovative advantages in sectors where competition is limited, while small companies enjoy similar advantages in sectors more exposed to competition – which supports Schumpeter's second assumption.

In another frequently cited article "Innovation in large and small firms" (1988), Acs and Audretsch continue the discussion on the impact of industry structure on innovative activity. The results show, among other things, that the total number of innovations in an industry is negatively related to industry concentration but positively related to the intensity of R&D, the ratio of skilled employees and the proportion of large companies. An interesting observation is that industries with a high share of large companies exhibit more innovative activity despite the fact that it is mainly the small businesses that are responsible for this activity. A possible explanation is that where an industry is dominated by large companies, the small companies will have to be innovative in order to survive.

The majority of start ups are very small – in most cases too small to survive within the industry. Another question that Acs and Audretsch were interested in was: Why are companies started, whose size is disadvantageous? How can they survive? Audretsch and Acs' (1990; Audretsch, 1991) results indicate that the technological preconditions prevailing within an industry determine the ease with which external companies can innovate and establish themselves within the industry. In situations where experience of the industry is crucial for the innovative activity, few firms will enter and few of the existing companies will therefore be squeezed out – resulting in limited industry dynamics – or what Audretsch and Acs define as a "routinized regime". Conversely, when external knowledge is crucial, more new start ups take place, leading to an increase in industry dynamics – which the authors term an "entrepreneurial regime". This indicates that many firms whose size is disadvantageous are set up in cases when innovations can be generated based on external knowledge.

A reason for the survival of these firms can be found in their learning strategy. Even if the companies tend to be below optimum size, they can survive and grow by continuous learning and adaptation. Many of the new firms will of course fail – resulting in comparatively high industry dynamics. The results indicate that industry dynamics are positively related to the possibility for new entrants to become successful at the same time as less successful companies are forced to wind up. Another finding was that the dynamics of small firms – as opposed to large firms – is greater in capital intensive industries. Small firms that are successful tend to flourish and grow, whereas less successful small companies are usually squeezed out. On the other hand, the dynamics in large companies are low, in most cases due to a greater accumulation of experience in these companies.

The entry of new companies into an industry often leads to increased dynamics and growth. What is it, then, that encourages new companies to enter an industry? In a number of articles (Acs & Audretsch, 1989a; 1989f), Acs and Audretsch have described how the start up differs in some respects between large and small businesses. All companies, irrespective of size, appear to be attracted by a high growth rate in an industry. However, contrary to what one might expect, high capital intensity does not deter companies from entering an industry whereas high R&D intensity and market concentration tend to do so in the case of small firms. On the other hand, small businesses tend to establish themselves in industries that are not dominated by small firms.

In subsequent studies (Audretsch & Acs, 1994), Audretsch and Acs focus on start ups in different industries, which they believe are largely influenced by both macro economic and industry specific conditions. For example, macro economic growth appears to act as a catalyst for the establishment of new firms, and starts-ups are also stimulated by low capital costs and a high rate of unemployment. The results also indicate the importance of universities for new firm formation, as industries where academic research is important and where small firms in general tend to be innovative constitute a good breeding ground for start ups. The authors conclude that new businesses mainly fulfil the requirements of the "creative destruction" described by Schumpeter (1942), where start ups introduce new products as a result of a high level of innovative activites as well as reemploying people who had become redundant in the former companies.

3. PERSPECTIVES ON SMALL BUSINESS ECONOMICS

In this section I will present an interview with Zoltan Acs and David Audretsch in which they give their views on small business economics research and its future development.

What were the most interesting findings in your research?

Acs: It can actually be summarized very simply ... we noticed in the 1980s that small firms were starting to innovate, and we didn't know how this actually functioned. It was interesting because everybody had said that only large firms innovate. But by using a new database and a new measure of innovative activity we observed that small firms were innovative alongside large firms in progressive, technology oriented industries that placed great emphasis on R&D. My favourite example was the computer industry ... this was an industry that was one of the most progressive, IBM was one of the most important companies in the world with a huge amount of R&D, they had the best scientists, laboratories, etc., and yet within this industry there was a great deal of innovation by new companies and entrepreneurs.

Audretsch: Yes, but I would say that interesting findings evolve over time. What seem to be the most interesting findings early on later become less interesting as the idea spreads and gains acceptance and recognition. That is probably true of the world of ideas in general ... the most interesting findings always change over time.

As Zoltan mentioned, the first interesting finding was that small firms were innovative, whereas according to conventional wisdom they were not. And there was empirical evidence for this, based on measures such as the amount of R&D, the number of scientists and engineers, or R&D investment ... they all appeared to indicate that large firms were the ones who were responsible for the majority of innovative activities. The conventional wisdom in the US was that small firms were actually ineffecient and that they really could not exist without some kind of state support. So, the notion that they were more innovative was very surprising – it was really something that went against conventional wisdom. Ten years later however, the results were accepted and thus less controversial.

A second interesting finding was that the most innovative industries tended to be those in which small firms were particularly innovative ... industries like computers, software, etc. – with the exception of pharmaceuticals and aircraft. Over time this finding turned out to be particularly important, as it seems to suggest that the industries in which small firms assume an important role are knowledge based.

A third interesting result was ... I remember Zoltan said: small firms are innovative in an environment that also includes large firms. That indicated for the first time that there are complementarities between small and large firms. Small versus large firms was really the wrong perspective to adopt ... but rather the complementarities between the contribution of the larger firms and the small firms.

These results seemed important initially, in the 1980s, when they really contradicted conventional wisdom. I think that a second set of results started to emerge, and we began to ask: why is it that small firms are more innovative, and in what way are they innovative? In this respect we really went against the most common model in innovation literature, the knowledge production function, according to which the input to innovation is knowledge, which most scholars considered had something to do with R&D and human capital. Small firms generally don't have a lot of R&D, despite the fact that some of them are R&D intensive. Our findings seemed to contradict the knowledge production function, and this made us think about where the firms obtained their input. The answer was: "from somewhere else". At the same time an interest in economic geography developed, with people like Paul Krugman, so we started to introduce the geographic dimension, and several interesting findings emerged. One was that, spatially, innovation clusters are not just concentrated in a few areas, but also linked to knowledge input. The results indicated that it was important to include the geographic dimension in order to understand innovation. We found that the knowledge production function is more valid for regions and countries than for the firm and that small firms obtained their knowledge from other firms or universities – through knowledge spillovers – that was a very important finding.

You are both pioneers in the area of small business economics. Why did you discover something that many other researchers failed to recognize?

Audretsch: One reason, I believe ... I have always considered it important to study questions that matter to people ... the idea of making the world a better place to live in. When I went to Germany, I became aware of European policy-makers' strong orientation toward Servan-Schreiber's "American challenge" of the large US corporations that European companies have to compete against. I realized that what was different about the US was not General Motors or IBM, but rather the new firms, the Silicon Valley phenomenon, etc., and I noticed when I lectured at Middlebury College that the students were less interested in large corporations and more interested in starting their own company ... so, at the beginning of the 1980s you could really feel this change in US society.

But that is not all. You've got to figure out how this fits into the world of academic ideas – you have to make a scientific contribution. Zoltan and I was part of an established field – industrial organization – a field that had ignored small businesses for a long time. There was an assumption that small firms were more or less unimportant, they didn't contribute to employment, they were not innovative, etc. ... small business was off the map. When we saw the innovation data, we realized that we had found something interesting ... something that went against conventional wisdom within the field – and we knew how to speak the language of the field. And this shows how important it is to have something to "push against" ... to have a strong discipline base.

I learned a saying: "The greatest thing a father can give his son is roots ... where he comes from ... and the second greatest thing is wings to escape them". I think this is great. Most of our generation of researchers come from a discipline, and it is important to have roots in a discipline – it gives you something to challenge in your research. But you also need ways to escape. In Berlin, in order to "escape" my roots, I felt a combination of "isolation" and "interaction" that I think was important. Berlin was far from the US ... in a way I was really isolated. But the distance really helped me to see the US in another perspective. On the other hand, the Institute in Berlin gave me great opportunities to interact with others – it was a multidisiplinary research institute, it gave a lot of freedom to interact with others, organize workshops, attend conferences ... by listening to people from other disciplines, you learn ... that has guided my career.

If we talk about the development of small business economics as a research area ... how would you describe its emergence?

Acs: For a long time people have studied big firms. "Why did they study big firms?" For two reasons: Large companies were considered to be the most important type of firm, and we had data on them. Small firms always existed, but we didn't really have any data. It was believed that small firms were inefficient because they failed to innovate or do much of anything, and the small business sector was shrinking, whereas the large firm sector was growing – it was really "big business economics" – it was the study of monopoly, of concentration, of capital intensity, of unions, and the role of public policy was mainly to facilitate and manage the growth of big business.

Then, several things happened. An important factor was that we started to obtain data and the cheap computing power necessary to really study small firms. Without these data and until computer power was cheap enough to analyse large data sets, you really couldn't do this. And you could hear economists and econometricians say: "Ooh, thousands of observations ... this is really fantastic. I can do something with this". Suddenly we had these data ... and some interesting results emerged. We discovered the role of small firms in innovation, David Birch discovered the job creation potential, and Michael Piore and Charles Sabel discovered the regional aspect, David Evans and Linda Leighton discovered the shift to self-employment, etc. So, a group of researchers discovered pieces of this development. Thus, small business economics began to develop as people in different fields of economics started to look at the various aspects, such as innovation, job creation and firm growth ... and policies toward SMEs emerged.

The development of these databases and computers allowed the economists to start thinking about small firms, and William Brock and David Evans were among the leaders in the theoretical understanding of this phenomenon. They wrote the book *The Economics of Small Business* in 1986, in which they described the field, and all of this led to the question: can we understand what is happening in the economy by looking at these large samples ... a lot of economists from different research areas became interested, and new insights were developed by researchers like Boyan Jovanovic, Linda Leighton ... a whole set of people that were looking at the question of small firms.

When I look at what we have learned over the last couple of decades, we can say that we have a much better understanding of the role of small firms than we had a mere 10 or 15 years ago ... we have put many pieces together ... from different fields of economics, sociology, regional studies, policy, etc. ... and today we have a reasonably good understanding of small firms. Of course, it is hard to state exactly what we have learned, but I think David Storey's book *Understanding the Small Business Sector* in 1994 is a good summary of our knowledge. He studied small business economics in a very interesting way ... the definition, the entry and exit, growth and survival of, as well as training and financing in small firms ... thus providing a composite picture of the small business sector. Since the publication of Storey's book we have refined our knowledge ... a refinement that to a great extent consists of empirical observations, although today there is a trend toward more and more theoretical work within the area.

Audretsch: As I see it, there are two areas of achievements – intellectual achievements and achievements in terms of career and legitimization ... although of course the two are related. I would say that what distinguishes "small business economics" from other entrepreneurship areas is that the focus isn't on managing small business, but more on addressing the implications of small firms, as well as their impact on the economy and society, which provides a different perspective to that of classic management. Small business economics research creates an understanding of what small firms are, how they differ from large firms, the connections between large and small firms, their contributions, their role in the economy, and how their roles changed ... it has taken years of research to develop this, but it has been successful when one compares our present knowledge to that available back in the late 1970s and early 1980s. Regarding the more professional contributions ... we have also been successful in the sense of becoming a much more legitimate area of research, people can now get tenured ... the field of small business economics exists ... which has given legitimacy to a younger generation of researchers and to the area itself as well as an understanding of why it is valuable to do research in this area.

What do you see as the strengths within the field of small business economics?

Audretsch: One of the strengths is that it is a relatively interdisciplinary issue ... a field that appeals to researchers in social science as well as management disciplines. This leads to a lot of diversity, a lot of new ideas ... it is an open field. In addition, if you deal with large organiziations the problems are very complex, and it is very difficult, for example, to link strategies, organization and investment to performance. The great thing about small firms is their size and the fact that they are relatively non-diversified ... so when things don't go well they fail ... it actually makes research much easier in the sense that you have large numbers and you can make inferences that if a firm fails the performance will be negative ... the observations are much clearer ... that is one of the econometrical and statistical attractions. But also, the field addresses an area of interest to policy makers ... pretty much worldwide. That has brought a lot of life to the area.

You are so positive in your view of the development of the research area. Haven't there been any disappointments?

Acs: Of course, for example, when we got the idea about launching the journal ... we were looking for cross-fertilization between business and economics scholars. When we originally set up the journal the people we brought in were from entrepreneurship, business and economics. The big disappointment was that these two groups wouldn't talk to each other, either because they didn't have the same interests or the motivation was lacking ... thus both the journal and the field drifted so that you basically ended up studying economics as opposed to the relationship between business and economics. I think over the last few years we began to notice that a change has taken place ... it has taken 15 years, but I think we are now seeing the development of a greater synergy. One reason behind this development is that the number of people who are interested in this topic has increased. They see that this topic is really interesting, but in order to understand it you need to draw from many different disciplines ... thus we have people with a background in geography, sociology, psychology, strategy ... and they are all interested in this topical issue. We are starting to get more cross-fertilization ... but it didn't happen as quickly as I thought it would.

What do we not know about small business economics? What will the future topics in small business economics be?

Audretsch: As I see it, an important topic will be the process by which individuals become entrepreneurs, which involves tracking individuals over a period of time, not just when they start a firm but also in their careers. I think we feel that entrepreneurship is not merely a question of the distinction between an entrepreneur and a non-entrepreneur, as individuals may have entrepreneurial episodes during their careers. This is important for the topic as it really summarizes the question: Where do firms come from? To answer this question we will see a convergence between researchers focusing on firms, and researchers that focus on individuals ... and this is interesting because in a knowledge based economy, the individuals ... their decision making capabilities, their function ... are much more important than previously, where individuals were basically unskilled workers, and therefore the individual the most important unit of observation.

Another topic of importance is the link between entrepreneurship and growth, which in a way is the real justification for promoting entrepreneurship. David Birch's studies were really about the firms ... small firms created more jobs ... it was the same for me and Zoltan with innovation – our unit of observation was the firms. But I think in this more recent research, the unit of observation is really the country or region. If you make that link between entrepreneurship and growth ... where more entrepreneurship leads to increased growth, more jobs, greater wealth ... the jobs don't have to be in a small entrepreurial firm, they can be anywhere, even in larger firms.

Another of the research challenges for small business economics is the issue of heterogeneity. You can't state with any degree of certainty that some small businesses are innovative and others are not ... this heterogeneity ... in the future we are going to find more and more different types of small business ... different kinds of small firms, small firms with varying roles. We all started to look at this as a kind of homogeneous concept, and now we find that it is more differentiated, a heterogeneous phenomenon.

Acs: I would like to add ... one of the topics that we have completely neglected is the study of public policy on both small business and entrepreneurship. If small business and entrepreneurship are important, there must be public policy issues. The traditional subjects in public policy schools were defense, security, health ... and now they include transportation policies, mergers and acquisition, and concentration policies. In the public policy arena, entrepreneurship and small business are not on the agenda ... nowhere, neither in the US nor in Europe. I think this is a disappointment and a huge challenge, because governments aren't going to take this issue seriously until people come out of public policy schools trained to think about this issue ... that is what we need to see in the future.

I think we also need to define what an entrepreneurial society is ... that is a big issue ... we have no idea of what an entrepreneurial society really is. So, I think it would be really interesting for a new PhD student to explore this topic. What is an entrepreneurial society? What is an entrepreneurial economy? What is an entrepreneurial policy? What do you have to do to make people more entrepreneurial? How should the education system change? How should the regulatory system change? There is a whole set of questions. Many researchers have written about why people choose self-employment over waged work, gender issues, ethical entrepreneurship ... but these are not the fundamental issues ... all these topics are sort of playing around because they are easy to study, but in my opinion the really big issues are the roles of an entrepreneurial society and wealth creation.

Talking about PhD students: What advice would you give to a PhD student interested in small business economics?

Acs: My advice would be that, as you cannot get a PhD in small business, you need to obtain your doctorate in some other discipline and then focus on small business. When you look at the scholars in the area of entrepreneurship and small business, they all come from different backgrounds, yet collectively they understand small business because they all contribute something to it. So, my advice would be to get a good grounding in some discipline – get a good disciplinary training, and then focus on entrepreneurship or small business as an area for either empirical or theoretical inquiry if that is what interests you.

Audretsch: I agree, but I also think that every researcher, whether in this or any other area, has their own special identity or "voice" ... and the real challenge is how a young researcher can find his/her voice in research – by which I mean his/her own style. I have always considered it essential to have one eye focussed on the issues that seem to be important among policy-makers, in politics, in the media ... in other words trying to answer the questions that everybody cares about ... addressing issues that are relevant at this point in time. The other eye has been on the literature ... there is earlier research in all areas, which indicates the importance of certain topics, and which also provides certain answers. Irrespective of the research area, you have to bring competence to the issue ... but you also have to explain, make the case, why your research adds value to the existing body of knowledge.

It is also important ... in developing one's voice ... for young researchers to walk the thin line between answering questions that they are interested in, that they consider important, while at the same time connecting to the body of literature that will get them into small business economics journals. So, while it is very important that they feel a passion about what they are doing, if they can't connect it to something that has already been done, it will not qualify as a contribution.

Based on your small business economics research, what policy recommendations would you like to make to policy-makers in a region, in order to improve entrepreneurship and small business in society?

Audretsch: I think each region is unique. I think the current state of the art would say that there are some best practices including a certain kind of culture that rewards entrepreneurship and the people who start new businesses ... and that seems to make a difference. For example, having financial support – not necessarily venture capital, because most small businesses don't use venture capital – but to have the kind of institutions that provide loans to small business seems to be very important. But there are a lot of more subtle aspects that involve individual mobility, how easy it is to start a firm – the lack of restrictions, regulations, bureaucracy – but there is really no formulas, so my answer is rather vague in this respect.

Acs: I would also like to emphasize the complexity. If we look at it historically ... in the old Keynesian model ... if you went to talk to the government about how to promote economic growth you would talk about lowering interest rates, subsidies, making it cheaper to build a plant – and that was the main issue, the role of education and knowledge were secondary ... In the 1980s, however, there was a view that the government was actually avoiding the policy issue ... there were deregulation, lower taxes, and you could argue that the government was not receptive to economic issues. But today there has been a shift in emphasis from national policies toward regional policies, because the regional environment has become the cutting edge in terms of development. In this new world it is all about how do we make it easier for small firms to start, grow, survive, prosper ... and how can governments facilitate the creation and growth of firms in different regions?

And in this respect there is a whole set of important issues, and of course if you raise the tax rate to a point that makes it impossible to start a business, if you make the regulations too strict, if the licensing process is complicated, if you educate everyone to get a public service job, if you make financing difficult, nobody will start a business ... there is a myriad of issues. Even to this day most regional governments are much more interested in attracting a business or a plant than growing a firm.

Governments really haven't got into the business of growing a high tech economy ... certain places have ... and they have done a lot of things that have helped their small firms ... everything from incubators, science parks, to ... a whole set of measures.

What does the future look like for small business economics research?

Acs: I think that will depend on what role small firms and entrepreneurship will play in the economy in the future. To me the interesting question is: Does entrepreneurship play a fundamental role in the creation of wealth? In the 20th century, along with Keynesian economics, it was all about limiting the ability of individuals to create wealth ... and to me the whole Reagan and Thatcher revolution was basically saying that we were unhappy with that model, because it failed to create wealth. So, wealth creation is important, and we know that individuals play a fundamental role in that ... individuals have always played an important role in this regard, be it Rockefeller, Ford, or Gates ... and if they play an important role, then entrepreneurship is important. What we have done is to open up this box, focusing on the role of entrepreneurs and small firms in society. And if economic growth and wealth creation are to become even more important in the future, research on entrepreneurship and small firms will remain important.

REFERENCES

Books

Acs, Z.J., 1979, *Price Behavior and the Theory of the Firm in Competitive and Corporate Markets*, PhD thesis, New York: New School University.

Acs, Z.J., 1984, *The Changing Structure of the US Economy: Lessons from the Steel Industry*, New York: Praeger.

Acs, Z.J. (ed.), 1996, *Small firm and economic growth*, vol 1, Cheltenham: Elgar Edwards.

Acs, Z.J. (ed.), 1996, *Small firms and economic growth*, vol 2, Cheltenham: Elgar Edwards.

Acs, Z.J., 2002, *Innovation and the Growth of the Cities*, Cheltenham: Elgar Edwards.

Acs, Z.J. & Armington, C., forthcoming, *Entrepreneurship, Geography and American Economic Growth*, Cambridge: Cambridge University Press.

Acs, Z.J. & Audretsch, D.B., 1990, *Innovation and Small Firms*, Cambridge, MA: MIT University Press.

Acs, Z.J. & Audretsch, D.B. (eds.), 1990, *The economics of small firms. A European challenge*, Dordrecht: Kluwer.

Acs, Z.J. & Audretsch, D.B. (eds.), 1991, *Innovation and technological change: An International comparison*, New York: Harvester Wheatsheaf.

Acs, Z.J. & Audretsch, D.B. (eds.), 1993, *Small firms and entrepreneurship: An East-West perspective*, Camridge: Cambridge University Press.

Acs, Z.J. & Audretsch, D.B. (eds.), 2003, *Handbook of Entrepreneurship Research*, Dordrecht: Klüwer.

Audretsch, D.B., 1980, *The Effectiveness of Antitrust Policy Towards Horizontal Merger*, PhD thesis, University of Wisconsin: UMI Research Press.

Audretsch, D.B., 1995, *Innovation and industry evolution*, Cambridge: MA: MIT Press.

Chapters in books

Acs, Z.J. & Audretsch, D.B., 1991, Innovation as a means of entry, in Geroski, P.A. & Schwalbach (eds.), *Entry and market contestability*, Oxford: Blackwell, 222-243.

Acs, Z.J. & Audretsch, D.B., 1991, Small firm turbulence under the entrepreneurial and routinized regimes, in Davies, L.G. & Gibb, A.A. (eds.), *Recent research in entrepreneurship*, Aldershot: Avebury, 11-28.

Acs, Z.J. & Audretsch, D.B., 1992, Entrepreneurship and economic development, in Sexton, D.L. & Kasarda, J.D. (eds.), *The state of the art of entrepreneurship*, Boston: PWS Kent, 45-67.

Acs, Z.J. & Audretsch, D.B., 1992, Technological regimes, learning and industry turbulence, in Scherer, F.M. & Perlman, M. (eds.), *Entrepreneurship, techological innovation, and economic growth: studies in the Schumpeterian tradition*, Ann Arbor: University of Michigan Press, 305-320.

Acs, Z.J. & Audretsch, D.B., 1993, Analysing innovation output indicators: the US experience, in Kleinknecht, A. & Bain, D. (eds.), *New concepts in innovation output measurement*, Basingstoke: Macmillan, 10-41.

Acs, Z.J. & Audretsch, D.B., 1993, Innovation and technical change, the new learning, in Libecap, G.D. (ed.), *Advances in the study of entrepreneurship, innovation and economic growth: A research annual*, vol 6, Greenwich, Conn: JAI Press, 109-142.

Acs, Z.J. & Audretsch, D.B., 1994, Entrepreneurial activity, innovation, and macroeconomic fluctuations, in Shionoya, Y. & Perlman, M. (eds.), *Innovation in tehncology, industries, and institutions: studies in Schumpeterian perspectives*, Ann Arbor: University of Michigan Press, 173-183.

Acs, Z.J. & Audretsch, D.B., 2003, Innovation and Technology Change, in Acs, Z.J. & Audretsch, D.B. (eds.), *Handbook of Entrepreneurship Researcher*, Dordrecht: Kluwer, 55-79.

Journal articles

Acs, Z.J., 1988, Innovation and technial change in the US steel industry, *Techovation*, 7, 3, 181-195.

Acs, Z.J. & Armington, C., 2004, Employment Growth and Entrepreneurial Activity in Cities, *Regional Studies*, October.

Acs, Z.J. & Armington, C., 2004, The Impact of Geographic Differences in Human Capital on Service Firm Formation Rates, *Journal of Urban Economics*, October.

Acs, Z.J. & Audretch, D.B., 1987a, Innovation and large and small firms, *Economic letters*, 23, 1, 109-112.

Acs, Z.J. & Audretsch, D.B., 1987b, Innovation, market-structure, and firm size, *Review of Economics and Statistics*, 69, 4, 567-574.

Acs, Z.J. & Audretsch, D.B., 1988a, Innovation and firm size in manufacturing, *Technovation*, 7, 3, 197-210.

Acs, Z.J. & Audretsch, D.B, 1988b, Innovation in Large and Small Firms: An Empirical Analysis, *American Economic Review*, 78, 4, 678-690.

Acs, Z.J. & Audretsch, D.B., 1988c, Small-firm mobility: A first report, *Economics letters*, 26, 3, 281-284.

Acs, Z.J. & Audretsch, D.B., 1988d, Testing the Schumpeterian hypothesis, *Eastern Economic Journal*, 14, 2, 129-140.

Acs, Z.J. & Audretch, D.B., 1989a, Births and firm size, *Southern Economic Journal*, 56, 2, 467-475.

Acs, Z.J. & Audretsch, D.B., 1989b, Entrepreneurial strategy and th presence of small firms, *Small Business Economics*, 1, 3, 193-213.

Acs, Z.J. & Audretsch, D.B., 1989c, Job creation and firm size in the US and West Germany, *International Small Business Journal*, 7, 4, 9-22.

Acs, Z.J. & Audretch, D.B., 1989d, Patent as a measure of innovative activity, *Kyklos*, 42, 2, 171-180.

Acs, Z.J. & Audretsch, D.B., 1989e, Patents innovative activity, *Eastern Economic Journal*, 14, 4, 373-376.

Acs, Z.J. & Audretsch, D.B., 1989f, Small-firm entry in the United States manufacturing, *Economica*, 56, 255-265.

Acs, Z.J. & Audretsch, D.B., 1989g, Small firms in US manufacturing: A first report, *Economics letters*, 31, 4, 399-402.

Acs, Z.J. & Audretsch, D.B., 1990, The determinants of small-firm growth in US manufacturing, *Applied Economics*, 22, 2, 143-153.

Acs, Z.J. & Audretsch, D.B., 1991, Innovation and size at the firm level, *Southern Economic Journal*, 57, 3, 739-744.

Acs, Z.J. & Audretch, D.B., 1994, New firm startups, technology, and macroeconomic fluctuation, *Small Business Economics*, 6, 6, 439-449.

Acs, Z.J. & Audretsch, D.B. & Feldman, M.P., 1992, Real effects of academic research – comment, *American Economic Review*, 82, 1, 363-367.

Acs, Z.J. & Audretch, D.B. & Feldman, M.P., 1994, Research and development spillovers and recipient firm size, *Review of Economic and statistics*, 76, 2, 336-340.

Acs, Z.J. & FitzRoy, F. & Smith, I., 1999, High Technology Employment and University R&D Spillovers: Evidence from U.S. Cities, *Economics of Innovation and New Technology*, 8, 57-78.

Acs, Z.J. & FitzRoy, F. & Smith, I., 2002, High Technology Employment and R&D in Cities: Heterogeneity v.s. Specialization, *Annals of Regional Science*, 36, 373-386.

Anselin, L. & Varga, A. & Acs, Z., 1997, Local geographic spillovers between university research and high technology innovations, *Journal of Urban Economics*, 42, 3, 422-448.

Audretsch, D.B., 1991, New firm survival and the technology regime, *Review of Economics and Statistics*, 73, 3, 441-450.

Audretsch, D.B. & Acs, Z.J., 1990, The entrepreneurial regime, learning, and industry turbulence, *Small Business Economics*, 2, 2, 119-128.

Audretsch, D.B. & Feldman, M.P., 1996, R&D spillovers and the geography of innovation and production, *American Economic Review*.

Audretsch, D.B. & Mahmood, T., 1995, New firm survival: new results using a hazard function, *Review of Economics and Statistics*, 77, 1, 97-103.

Other references

Brock, W.A. & Evans, D.S, 1986, *The Economics of Small Business: Their Role and Regulation in the US Economy*, New York, Holmes and Meier.

Cohen, W.M. & Levin, R.C., 1989, Empirical studies of innovation and market structure, in Schmalansee, R. & Willig, R. (eds.), *Handbook of Industrial Organization*, Amsterdam: North-Holland.

Feldman, M., 1994, *The Spacial Determinants of Innovative Activity*, PhD thesis, Carnegie-Mellon University.

Griliches, Z., 1979, Issues in assessing the contribution of R&D to productivity growth, *Bell Journal of Economics*, 10, 92-116.

Krugman, P., 1991, Increasing returns and economic geography, *Journal of Political Economy*, 99, 3, 483-499.

Nelson, R. (ed.), 1993, *National Innovation Systems*, New York: Oxford, University Press.

Reynolds, P.D., 2000, Nationl panel study of US business start-ups: Background and methodology, in Katz, J.A. (ed.), *Advances in Entrepreneurship, Firm Emergence, and Growth*, Vol 4, Stanford, CT: JAI Press.

Romer, P.M., 1990, Endogenous technical change, *Journal of Political Economy*, 98, 72-102.

Schumpeter, J.A., 1942, *Capitalism, Socialism and Democracy*, New York: Harper and Row.

Storey, D.J., 1994, *Understanding the Small Business Sector*, London: Routledge.

Varga, A., 1997, *Universities and the Spacial Patterns of Innovative Activity in US Manufacturing*, PhD thesis, West Virginia University.

Chapter 9

GIACOMO BECATTINI

1. GIACOMO BECATTINI – REDISCOVERY OF THE MARSHALLIAN INDUSTRIAL DISTRICTS

1.1 The Contributions of Giacomo Becattini

Giacomo Becattini has made several important contributions to our knowledge about "industrial districts" based on Marshall's reasoning in his works *Economics of Industry* (1879), *Principle of Economics* in 1890 and *Industry and Trade* published in 1921, all of which focus on the importance of proximity for small firms in order to achieve external economies of scale. In his seminal article "From the industrial 'sector' to the industrial 'district'", published in Italian in 1979 and in English 1989, he introduced the concept of "industrial districts" and re-discovered the Marshallian concept in an Italian context. A major contribution to the understanding of industrial districts was Becattini's strong emphasis on the role of the cultural and historical background of the districts, and he was the first to point out that a skill that appears abundant in a specific area may be scarce on the world market – for example, people who have been manufacturing clothes for centuries tend to possess a kind of "clothing culture and knowledge" that is of great significance. Thus, Becattini extended Marshall's analysis of the purely economic effects of agglomeration to a broader perspective, to include the social, cultural and institutional foundations of local industrial growth. He also introduced the idea of "embeddedness" of the local industrial structure as a key analytical concept in understanding industrial districts. However, Becattini is more interested in using the concept of "sense of belonging", which is a more active concept. In order to have a sense of belonging you not only have to share a vision of the future but also act accordingly – as opposed to "embeddedness", which implies a more passive approach.

As research on industrial districts mainly originates from Italy, most of the publications on the subject are therefore in Italian. There have been many attempts to make industrial districts an internationally well-known phenomenon. The single most important contribution in this respect is the book *The Second Industrial Divide* written by Charles Sabel, together with Michael Piore in 1984, using the Italian industrial districts as the main example for their macro-historical analysis. The book created a great deal of interest in the industrial districts, which in recent decades has extended to academia as well as to the political debate, both at national and regional level. Interest in industrial development and renewal, especially at regional level, has been inspired by Italy and the Italian industrial districts, and new concepts have been introduced, such as Castell's "technology districts" (Castell & Hall, 1984), the Silicon Valley model developed among others by Saxenian (Saxenian, 1990; 1994) and, of course, Porter's "clusters" (Porter, 1990). Research on industrial districts has also had an enormous impact on regional development policies. The Italian experience of industrial districts has become a major point of reference in the international debate on regional policy aimed at promoting endogenous development.

1.2   Career

Giacomo Becattini, born 1927 in Florence, Italy, became professor of Economics at the University of Florence in 1968. He devoted his whole academic career to the University of Florence. After his retirement in the late 1990s he has remained very active as a researcher with a whole range of international publications also into the 21st century.

In 1962 he presented his book *Il concetto d'industria e la teoria del valore* (The concept of industry and the theory of value), a methodological critique of mainstream economic theory. Throughout his career, Becattini has been interested in two different but related areas of research: (i) theory and history of economic thought, and (ii) applied economics with a special interest in the Tuscan economy and industrial districts.

In his theoretical studies, Becattini has mainly explored the limits of mainstream economics in explaining social phenomena such as labor, consumption and their environmental impact. In Becattini's research on the history of economic thought he has been especially interested in the ideas of Alfred Marshall and the Cambridge School of economics in the 19th century. In 1963 Becattini spent time at the National Institute of Economic and Social Research in London, under Christopher Freeman. This was a turning point in Becattini's research – it was here that he gained support for his fundamental scientific conviction that, since economics is concerned with real life questions, rigorous economics research should not be confined to the drawing board or the development of abstract models of the world, but requires empirical knowledge. According to Becattini, economists must concentrate on real life, how economies and societies function and try to avoid decline and unemployment – economists must be useful in the concrete world, otherwise their discipline is pointless. Becattini's second stream of research therefore consists of more "applied" research focusing on the industrial development of the Tuscan economy – the Tuscan post-war industrialization and especially the industrial development around the town of Prato.

Becattini was born in Florence, and throughout his life he has been strongly committed to the development of the region – as an active left-wing debater and member of the City Council of Florence between 1980 and 1985.

"My father was a salesman and travelled a lot around Tuscany, and when I was young I accompanied him, and over the years I visited all the towns in Tuscany ... I experienced and got to know the region. Of course this has influenced me as a researcher. If you study a reality, for example Prato or Tuscany, and your knowledge is not only based on books or statistical data, you will have a different kind of understanding ... you will feel it. When I looked at statistics it was not simply data, but I could see beyond the data ... the reality of people, of relationships, of experiences, of failures and successes. To me this kind of knowledge is much more valid than the knowledge one can achieve through figures and data only.

I started to write about the Tuscan economy as far back as 1954. I collaborated with a journal *La Regione*, and for several years I examined different aspects of the region ... simultaneously I studied economic theory. In 1962 I wrote my book on the theory of value *Il concetto d'industria e la teoria del valore*, in which I devoted a long chapter to Alfred Marshall. So when I had the opportunity to become director of the Regional Institute for Economic Planning in Tuscany (IRPET) in 1968, it was quite natural to study Tuscany in the light of Marshall's ideas and "external economies" ... it was more or less unconscious – part of my own biography.

For many years my interpretation of the Tuscan economy and development was heavily criticized, not only by the scientific community, but also by the Tuscan politicians ... even within the left to which I belonged ... you may be sure that I had to face many difficulties. Fortunately, after some decades of confirmation of my interpretations, the situation changed ... in the end I succeeded."

In 1968 he founded and became the first Director of the Regional Institute for Economic Planning in Tuscany (IRPET). The first paper written within the research center was "Lo sviluppo economico della

Toscana: un'ipotesi di lavoro" (The economic development of Tuscany: A working hypothesis) in 1969, in which Becattini used Alfred Marshall's concept of external territorial economies to explain the industrial development of the region, and in a way, he rediscovered the localized Marshallian external economies, which are needed to formulate properly the concept of "industrial district". However, both scholars and politicians were extremely doubtful about and critical of Becattini's interpretation of the Tuscan development.

Therefore, in 1975 IRPET published a book, edited by Becattini and entitled *Lo sviluppo economico della Toscana, con particolare attenzione per l'industrializzazione leggera* (The economic development of Tuscany with special focus on light industry), where Becattini retracted one step, being much more cautious in his use of Marshall's reasoning and in his interpretation of Tuscan industrial development. In this report he uses the term "campagna urbanizzata" (urbanized countryside) as a synonym and substitute for the "industrial district" concept.

However Becattini reverted to using the term "industrial district" for the first time in a paper on "Italian regional development" at a meeting of the Italian Economic Association in Pisa in 1977, which was later published in English under the title "The development of light industry in Tuscany: an interpretation" in *Economic Notes* 1978. But it is not this paper that is regarded as the starting point for the research on industrial districts but another of Becattini's reports, namely the essay "Dal 'settore' industriale al 'distretto' industriale" (From the industrial 'sector' to the industrial 'district'), which appeared in the journal *Revista di economia e politica industriale* in 1979. The English translation of the article can be found in Goodman and Bamford (eds.) *Small firms and industrial districts in Italy* (1989).

Since the 1980s Becattini has produced several works on "industrial districts", of which some have been translated into English, for example:

Becattini, G., 1990, The Marshallian industrial district as a socio-economic notion, in Pyke, F. & Becattini, G. & Sengenberger, W. (eds.), *Industrial Districts and Inter-firm Co-operation in Italy*, Geneva: IILS.

Becattini, G., 1991, The industrial district as a creative milieu, in Benko, G. & Dunford, M. (eds.), *Industrial change and regional development: the transformation of new industrial spaces*, London: Belhaven Press.

Becattini, G. & Rullani, E., 1996, Local systems and global connections: The role of knowledge, in Cossentino, F. & Pyke, F. & Sengenberger, W. (eds.), *Local and regional response to global pressure: The case of Italy and its industrial districts*, Geneva: IILS.

Becattini, G., 2002, From Marshall's to the Italian "Industrial Districts". A Brief Critical Recontruction, in Curzio, A.Q. & Fortis, M. (eds.), *Complexity and Industrial Cluster. Dynamics and Models in Theory and Practice*, Heidelberg: Physica-Verlag.

Becattini, G. & Bellandi, M. & Dei Ottati, G. & Sforzi, F., 2003, *From Industrial Districts to Local Development. An Itinerary of Research*, Cheltenham: Edward Elgar.

To this should be added a large number of important publications on the Tuscan economy and Tuscan society published in Italian, and some of these articles have recently been collected in the book *L'industrializzazione leggera della Toscana* (The light industrialization of Tuscany) published in 1999. In these studies Becattini looked at the development of light industrial sectors in Tuscany (e.g. textiles, clothing, shoes and furniture). Becattini, contrary to the prevailing opinion at that time, considered the development of Tuscany's light industrial sectors as a positive development, and in his studies he paid special attention to the relationship between the efficiency and competitiveness of production, and the socio-cultural conditions underlying local society.

It is important to mention that in 1986 the International Institute for Labour Studies (IILS) in Geneva started an international research program on industrial districts, *The New Industrial Organization*, and this was the first time that Giacomo Becattini and Charles Sabel met. The IILS program generated several books that gave international recognition to the concept of industrial districts. Some of the publications within the program were:

Sengenberger, W. & Loveman, G.W. & Piore, M. (eds.) 1990, *The re-emergence of small enterprises. Industrial restructuring in industrialised countries*, Geneva: IILS.

Pyke, F. & Becattini, G. & Sengenberger, W. (eds.), 1990, *Industrial Districts and Inter-firm Co-operation in Italy*, Geneva: IILS.

Cossentino, F. & Pyke, F. & Sengenberger, W. (eds.), 1996, *Local and regional response to global pressure: The case of Italy and its industrial districts*, Geneva: IILS.

An understanding of industrial districts could, according to Becattini, only come from an in-depth study of the phenomenon in action over a longer period of time. He identified Prato as an industrial district – perhaps an archetype – and concluded that an intensive study of the Prato district would yield significant insights into the development of industrial districts. Becattini's research is dominated by longitudinal in-depth studies of the Prato district, were the historical analyses of the development are central to Becattini's findings and conclusions.

During the 1980s, Becattini and his research group at the University of Florence intensified their research on the textile district of Prato. Under the leadership of the French historian Fernand Braudel, they tried to decipher the extraordinary economic performance of the industrial town of Prato. The results were published in a four-volume work *Prato. Storia di una città* (Prato. History of a city) in 1997. Becattini edited the fourth volume and contributed to it with an essay entitled *Prato in un mondo che cambia, 1954-1993* (Prato in a changing world, 1954-1993). This essay was subsequently translated into English in a book entitled *The caterpillar and the butterfly. An exemplary case of development in the Italy of the industrial districts*, published in 2001. In Becattini's work on the Prato case he emphasizes the importance of the adaptation between the purely economic and technical aspects of local development and the local system of values and institutions – the interplay between the economic reactions to external conjuncture and their effects on the continuous redefining of local institutions and, in the end, the character of the people in the local community.

> "We started our study on Prato, and we continued for eighteen years. I remember the different volumes of the history of Prato from medieval to modern to contemporary to my own volume during and after world war II, which was number four in the series. In a sense I saw Prato developing over the course of one thousand years in a continuous line. It was fascinating ... there were changes but also great continuity."

Parallel to the studies of Prato and its history, Becattini and his colleagues (among others Fabio Sforzi) started a summer school on local development, in which an expanding group of scholars, local administrators, entrepreneurs, etc. could exchange views and discuss topics related to local development. In addition, Giacomo Becattini together with Fabio Sforzi and some other colleagues founded a journal, *Sviluppo Locale*, in 1994 as an international forum for ideas on local development.

2.   STREAM OF INTEREST IN GIACOMO BECATTINI'S RESEARCH

Giacomo Becattini is thus one of the leading exponents of research on industrial districts. In this chapter, I will first describe the background of the research (section 2.1.), after which I will present the two articles in which he introduced the concept of "industrial districts" (section 2.2.). In section 2.3. some of Becattini's contributions to the knowledge about industrial districts are summarized (the material is limited to publictations in English). Finally, in section 2.4. Becattini's research on the Prato industrial district is presented.

2.1   Research on Industrial Districts

During the early years of industrialisation in the 19th century, the dominant view among economists was that the factory system was most efficient where the manufacturing processes were concentrated under one roof with a high degree of vertical integration. The first researcher to challenge this assumption was Alfred Marshall, who expressed a different view in his writings as far back as 1870. Through his observations of English industry, for example, the cutlery works in Sheffield and metal trade in Birmingham, he came to the conclusion that for certain types of production, there were two efficient manufacturing systems: (i) the established method, based on large, vertically integrated production units and (ii) production based on the concentration of many small factories specializing in different phases of the production process and located in the same geographic area (Becattini, 2002). In their work *The Economics of Industry* in 1879, Alfred and Mary Marshall wrote:

> "We shall find that some of the advantages of division of labor can be obtained only in very large factories, but that many of them, more than at first sight appears, can be secured by small factories and workshops, provided there are a very great number of them in the same trade. ... The manufacture of commodity often consists of several distinct stages, to each of which a separate room in the factory is devoted. But if the total amount of the commodity produced is very large, it may be profitable to devote separate small factories to each of the steps." (2nd ed, 1881, p. 52)

> "But small factories, whatever their number, will be at a great disadvantage relative to large unless many of them are collected together in the same district. ... in these districts a further division of specialisation has grown up, and separate trades have sought separate localities. ... Those that work in wool do not generally live among the Lancashire cotton workers, but are collected together in Yorkshire; and they themselves are divided into the "woollen trade" and the "worsted trade". (2nd ed, 1881, p. 47)

As opposed to more dogmatic economists, who were blinded by the economies of scale and the factory system, Marshall used concrete examples to show that there was one alternative to the traditional manufacturing system. In these early descriptions and lines of reasoning, it is possible to discern a predecessor of the framework that Marshall later called "external and internal economies" (Marshall, 1890; 1921), i.e. the rationale for industrial districts rests on the creation of agglomeration economies – economies that are external to the firm but internal to the area, for groups of firms. External economies concern the productivity of the individual firm, obtained through an external division of labor between firms, which can be secured by the concentration of small firms of similar character in particular localities, thus providing an alternative to the internal economies of scale of large corporations.

Marshall's influence on economic thinking in these areas was limited. Most of the 20th century was dominated by a belief in large-scale systems and internal economies of scale. It was not until the 1970s that a couple of Italian economists discovered some interesting phenomena in the Italian economy. In several Italian regions, both the agricultural sector and large firms were declining, but parts of the industries were growing, and the structures of these growing industries were agglomerations of small firms strongly connected to international markets. The researchers realized that high productivity in a manufacturing process could not only be achieved by investing in means of production but was related to the physical contiguity of firms – economies that were external to any one firm, but internal to an industrial sector or territorial group of firms.

Among these Italian economists, Giacomo Becattini can be considered as the most prominent researcher and he revitalized and developed Alfred Marshall's century-old idea of external economies of scale and industrial districts. At around the same time, the late 1970s and early 1980s, Sebastiano Brusco, professor at the University of Modena, made similar observations, but from quite a different theoretical basis. Brusco's stance was based on the thoughts of the Italian economist Piero Sraffa (1898-1983) – one of the most prominent critics of Marshall's reasoning about external economies of scale – and Brusco refused to accept that the advantages of localized division of labor derived from external economies of scale. Instead he recognized that small firms with modern technology could be as efficient as large firms – it is only a question of numbers – and due to the social conventions of the local community, one can have low transaction costs which may replace the internal economies of scale of the large companies. Furthermore, Brusco's empirical studies were based on the Emilia Romagna Region in the North-East of Italy. Becattini's and Brusco's conclusions were rather provocative for those who believed in the theory of internal economies of scale.

What did they find? In certain places or localities where large private and public-sector companies were showing clear signs of weakness, there was a "strange" flowering of small manufacturing businesses specializing in different products, resulting in increased local income, jobs and exports. These regions were, for example, Sassuolo (ceramic tiles) and Cento (mechanical engineering) in Emilia Romagna, Prato (textiles) in Tuscany, Montegranaro (shoes) in Marche, and Nogara (wooden furniture) in Veneto. The new companies in these regions were not created inside the industrial cities and across the full range of industrial sectors. Instead, they were established across a vast geographic area, between the traditional industrial regions of the north of Italy and the economically depressed areas in the south (i.e. the Central and North-Eastern regions of Italy) – and have been labelled the Third Italy. The firms were concentrated in relatively small areas. In addition, they were involved in industries that were considered "mature" with less growth potential (e.g. textiles, garments, footwear, leather goods, furniture) and obsolete forms of organization – primarily family-owned small firms (Becattini, 2002).

However, the community of economists has not always been supportive, and for many years Becattini and Brusco's observations were disregarded in the scientific and political debate. Most economists were uninterested in the concepts of "industrial districts" and "external economies of scale" and more fascinated by large-scale internal economies and Taylorism, as a result of a solid positivist distrust of vague concepts such as "industrial atmosphere", "belonging", and "reputation", concepts that have been regarded as both complex and fuzzy (Becattini & Musotti, 2003).

In addition, the greater part of the Italian economists' works on industrial districts were written in Italian and, consequently, dissemination of the reasoning outside Italy was limited. Not until Michael Piore and Charles Sabel published their book *The Second Industrial Divide* in 1984 did the concept gain international recognition. Piore and Sabel were inspired by the Italian industrial districts and in the book they used these districts as one main example in their macro-historical analysis of the societal transformation from the Fordist mass production model to the flexible specialization of production in the industrial districts. The book not only changed the attitude of the international academic community but also that of politicians and policy-makers.

The recognition of the usefulness of the concept of industrial districts and the existence of such districts that could be analyzed with conceptual tools were followed by a terminological explosion from the notion of "industrial districts" to concepts like local production systems, technological districts, clusters, etc. – concepts that partly overlap but that focus on different aspects of the reality (Becattini, 2002). In the early 1990s, a major research project was carried out by Michael Porter and his research group at Harvard Business School and it was due to Porter's book *The Competitive Advantage of Nations* (1990) that international interest grew still further. Porter's concept of clusters originates in Marshall and is inspired by the Italian industrial districts. Porter's clusters consist of contiguous lines of business, customers, networks, organizations, such as universities, regulatory bodies and other institutions that facilitate development in a region. He proposed four factors to explain what makes a cluster dynamic and what provides it with the potential to grow, namely access to specialist competence in the labor market, quality of local demand, access to specialized subcontractors, and the existence of competing companies that forces a productive rivalry. Porter's analyses and lines of reasoning gained a large audience and paved the way for acceptance of the concept of business cluster both in mainstream economics and management studies.

2.2   The Introduction of the "Industrial District" Concept

Becattini's article "The economic development of Tuscany: an interpretation" (1978, see also 2003a) in which he first introduced the term "industrial district", is a historical overview and description of the origin of the Tuscan industrial districts in Italy.

Becattini argues that the emergence of the industrial districts can be explained historically and he retraces their development over time. As long ago as the first half of the 19th century, the Tuscany region appeared a suitable site for industrialization, based on the region's considerable mineral resources, its financial structure, and its long history as a centre of trade. But Tuscany failed to live up to its potential. Up to the Second World War, Tuscany had not succeeded in building a modern industrial structure. There are several reasons for this, including "exogenous factors", such as the way in which Italian unification was achieved and the relative isolation of Tuscany in terms of the construction of roads and railways. But there were also "endogenous factors", the most important of which was anti-industrialism and the maintenance of a status quo ensuring ample economic rewards for the landowners and the partly overlapping group of coupon-clippers, who first appeared in the Tuscany of the grand-dukes and continued in the Kingdom of Italy.

However, during the interwar period, some changes in the industrial development could be observed. For example, some public support for heavy industries (e.g. engineering, metal and chemicals) slowed down the stagnation in the Tuscan economy, but compared to many other regions of Italy, the improvements in Tuscany were fairly modest. Instead, an increase in specialization in the "light" sectors of industry started to emerge. This development was accompanied by a gradual modernization of Tuscan society and a growing diversification in its means of production. From the perspective of communication, the period was characterized by a steady improvement in both the road system and the region's links with the outside world. But in terms of commerce, education and degree of illiteracy (especially in the countryside) at the end of the Second World War, Tuscany clearly lagged behind many other regions of Italy.

From an industrial point of view, Tuscany was highly differentiated –
a vast agricultural area virtually without manufacturing industry,
although with some important mining units. In the central valleys there
was a more or less unbroken string of towns and villages (not least in the
Prato area) with considerable industrial concentration – different types of
productive activities coexisted and the enterprises differed considerably
in size. This mix of enterprises gave rise to a social environment in
which wage-laborers lived side by side with independent craftsmen. This
was the economic and socio-cultural context in which the development
took place and which Becattini related to Marshall's concept of
industrial districts.

> "To employ a concept much used by Alfred Marshall, the course of
> Tuscan history leads to a form, still incomplete but already clear in
> outline, of "industrial district" ... which produces economies external
> to the single firm and even to the industrial sector defined by
> technology, but internal to the "sectorial-social-territorial" network".
> (Becattini, 2003a, p. 17)

Becattini has reflected on the emergence of these industrial districts
and argues that there are three main socio-cultural assumptions behind
this development in Tuscany: (i) there was a peasant protest, particularly
among women and young people against the rigidity within families and
their close economic dependence on older male members, (ii) a work
ethic that held a "mastery of the craft" in high esteem and that is
intimately linked to the first assumption, and (iii) the cultural-touristic
open-mindedness of the region – a long tradition of export trade and a
great influx of foreigners, tourists, merchants and artists.

But there were also certain factors during and immediately after the
Second World War that acted as a "priming mechanism" for the
development in Tuscany, such as the damage caused by the war and the
subsequent intensive rebuilding of the region. The high rate of
destruction led to a high rate of public expenditure as well as the renewal
of industrial and civic structures. However, according to Becattini, the
logical and historical starting-point for the development in Tuscany must
be sought in the labor market situation, consisting of a large pool of
underemployed farm workers, who were anxious to escape the life
associated with the "family farm". It was the mass of farm laborers who
rejected the paternalism and subordination of earlier times but not the
belief in the proverbial connection between effort and reward, or job
commitment and social success. Of course, this surplus of peasants on
the local labor market had also existed previously, resulting in mass
emigration. The fact that this failed to occur on this occasion may be due
to the influence of the exceptional expansion of international trade in the
post-war period. For twenty years Tuscany was involved in a very
rapidly expanding "external" market – a boom in light industry
reinforced by Italian government currency exchange measures to

encourage exports – and without this "exogenous" market expansion, this development would not have occurred but there was also an emerging structure that could handle this expansion. In Tuscany, there already existed a "sectorial-territorial-social network" of industrial activities – more or less developed "integrated industrial areas", arranged in a non-random way across the region, and these areas were capable of benefiting from the expansion in world markets.

However, it is not this article in *Economic Notes* 1978 that is regarded as the starting point for the research on industrial districts, but rather an article that appeared in the journal *Rivista di economia e politica industriale* in 1979 under the title "Dal 'settore' industriale al 'distretto' industriale". The English translation of this article was entitled "Sectors and/or districts: some remarks on the conceptual foundations of industrial economics" and was published in a book edited by Edward Goodman and Julia Bamford (1989).

In this article Becattini discussed various ways of aggregating productive units and, in his opinion, economists who study industrial activity at an intermediate level between the system as a whole and the single firm are faced with the problem of defining an industry or sector – to determine the boundaries of what should be regarded as internal as well as what remains external to the industry or sector. Even if it were possible to determine these boundaries, the fact that industries and sectors undergo constant change would very quickly make such demarcation obsolete.

An alternative way of aggregating productive units is, according to Becattini, to use Marshall's concepts of external and internal economies of scale as the point of departure. In the article, Becattini discusses the criticism levelled at Marshall's reasoning, especially by Becattini's fellow countryman Piero Straffa, which criticism is based among other things on the fact that economies of scale external to the individual business but internal to the industry as a whole are extremely rare, almost non-existent in reality. Becattini considers that Straffa's interpretation of Marshall focusses too strongly on a single industry, whereas external economies of scale, according to Marshall, develop in such a way that they do not fit the boundaries of any single industry but are attracted to groups of correlated industries. Marshall believed that, in at least some manufacturing sectors, the advantages of large scale production could be equally well attained by an aggregation of a large number of small firms located in a district – a precondition being, however, that it is possible to divide the process of production into several stages, each of which can be performed with the maximum of economy in a small establishment. Becattini concludes his article by pointing out that the Marshallian type of external economies of scale is found in certain areas of Italy.

"What I should like to stress here is that the unit to which Marshall referred even then is not that of technologically defined industries but that of an industrial district or area. The conditions of population density, presence of infrastructure, industrial atmosphere, which are both the source and the result, the cause and the effect, of those returns that cannot be explained either by internal economies of scale or by R&D apply to the industrial district. It is this extra-element of productivity that made Lancashire, the Ruhr and Lombardy yesterday, and the so-called Third Italy today, stand out against the rest." (Becattini, 1989, p. 132)

The industrial district tends to be multisectorial, but on the other hand reasonably stable over time, a stability that a single industry lacks, thus making it possible to study the industrial district in order to ascertain its permanent characteristics as well as the laws that govern its formation, development and decline.

2.3 Becattini's Contributions to Our Knowledge of Industrial Districts

2.3.1 Prerequisites of Industrial Districts – an Outline of Postwar Italian Industrial Development

Becattini has studied the development of industrial districts in Tuscany, placing this development in a historical perspective and focusing on the social context out of which the industrial districts emerged.

As in most industrialized countries we can find a shift in the industrial structure during the 1970s and early 1980s from a focus on large scale companies toward a growing small business sector, which also applies in Italy. The importance of small businesses increased in the Italian economy during the 1970s, and the proportion of self-employed was atypically high. In a book chapter focusing on Italy in Sengenberger, Loveman and Piore, Becattini (1990a) discusses the historical mechanisms behind the changes in the Italian economy. He maintains that the war, the reconstruction, the revival of political life, and the renewed participation in the international market could be seen as main events that gave an initial impetus to post-war industrial development in Italy.

Italian industrialization developed very rapidly in the 1950s and early 1960s (what is often called the "Italian miracle") but slowing down from 1963 to 1966. The first phase (1945 to 1951) of the Italian miracle period was devoted to the material reconstruction of the country after the war, whereas the second phase (1951 to 1963) was characterized by the take-off of the Italian economy. The annual rate of GNP growth was 5.4%.

The second period between 1963 and 1973 could be considered as a "stop-and-go" period with annual GNP growth of 4.7%. Initially this period was characterized by an extensive restructuring of industry, but it ended with the intense social turmoil of the early 1970s. Italian industry followed the same pattern as many western economies – small firms were seen as a remnant of the past. In addition, in Italy the regions squeezed between the "Industrial Triangle" in the North-West and the subsidized South were seen as a weak point. The third period started with the 1973 rise in oil prices. The fluctuation in industrial activity became greater, and the GNP declined to 1.9% per year (1973-1975). The whole post-war period represented a real "structural evolution" of Italian industry: the agricultural sector decreased from 48% of total employment in 1951 to 15% in 1981. The corresponding figure for industry was an increase from 26% to 35%, while the service sector showed an increase from 26% to 50% in 1981 leading to an accentuation of the regional skewness between the north and south of Italy.

The industrial change outlined above also corresponded with a social transformation – a multifaceted and complex development that is difficult to understand, but some main indicators are (Becattini, 1990a; 2002):

– The disappearance of the *metayage* system of land tenure (share-cropping) that prevailed for centuries in many regions. The fading-out of the system produced a host of workers ready to be employed by the many small firms that required general rather than specific skills, in order to produce rather unsophisticated goods.
– General demand conditions; including a higher standard of living for large segments of the middle class. Progress beyond the normal standard creates the conditions for the emergence of new sets of needs that produce a highly variable demand for differentiated and personalized goods.
– The special role played by the Italian Communist Party (PCI) in social development. Despite its official Marxist ideology, the party showed an interclass character, for example allowing local administrators belonging to the party to comply with industrialization needs while ignoring Marxist class orthodoxy.
– A change in world market demand. After the Second World War the Western world was characterized by a long and unequal increase in income that concentrated wealth in the pockets of a large segment of the middle class, who sought increasingly differentiated and personalized goods and services in order to achieve "new sensations" and social prestige. This change in the world market was channeled to Italy, where there was a tradition of formal and informal links with foreign markets, for example through "culture-tourism-external trade, in many Italian regions".

Thus, the emergence of the Italian industrial districts should be considered in the light of this development and context. Becattini hereby maintains that the industrial districts that primarily emerged in the North-East-Centre (NEC) regions of Italy should be seen as a stage toward the industrialization of a region. The path of the NEC-regions leads from an artisan-agricultural stage to an industrial one, through intermediate stages characterized by high territorial short-range mobility of population, the subdivision of production tasks between territorially grouped firms, and a gradual organization around a particular sector – the development of industrial districts. But beyond the industrial districts we find, for example, specialized industrial areas merged into a more complex urban structure.

2.3.2   The Characteristics of the Italian Industrial Districts

Becattini (1990b) has defined the industrial district as "a socio-territorial entity which is characterized by the active presence of both a community of people and a population of firms in one natural and historically bounded area. In the district unlike in other environments, such as manufacturing towns, community and firms tend to merge." (p. 38) To elaborate on the characteristics of an industrial district, Becattini (1990b; 2002) argues that industrial districts have certain characteristic traits:

- A population of families and businesses interacting with each other in various ways within one natural and historically well-defined area – there is a deep merger between productive activities and the daily life of the district.
- The businesses can be broken down into different populations working on different phases of the production process (e.g. spinning, weaving, dyeing, finishing) organized in flexible teams often headed by a finished goods manufacturer who interacts with the external market (the so called *impannatore*, whose special function is to translate the capabilities of the district into products that can be sold on the market).
- The most important trait of the local community is its relatively homogeneous value system, expressed for example, in an ethic of work, family and reciprocity. At the same time a system of institutions and rules (e.g. the firm, the family, the church, local government, the local branches of political parties, associations of different kinds, etc.) must develop in order to spread these values throughout the district.
- There is a process of learning and utilization of knowledge in the industrial districts that includes an integration of, on the one hand, "contextual knowledge" that is essentially tacit and deeply rooted in personal experience, and which can be socialized only through a long process of context and experience sharing and, on the other, "codified knowledge" that makes it possible to transfer knowledge from one context to another. This process of interaction from contextual to

codified knowledge is complex and involves the use of metaphors and analogies which are particularly suitable for personal experiences and culturally homogenous areas such as industrial districts (Becattini, 1996).

- There is a continuum of job possibilities from home-based work, part-time waged work, and self-employment, and the district has an inner tendency to constantly reallocate its human resources. The importance of homeworkers and part-time workers must be kept in mind – these categories of workers constitute the link between the firm and the families and are important for increasing the income of the family beyond the bare minimum.

- A balance between competition – a struggle to improve one's own position and to satisfy market demands outside the district – and co-operation, for example, expressed in strong personal relationships between the principals of firms engaged in the different phases of production.

- A local credit system – the local bank is an organism born and bred in the district, and closely linked with the small business community, but also deeply involved in local life, which gives it an excellent grasp of the economic conditions of small firms.

However, there are critics of the concept of industrial districts who, for example, have raised the question about their innovative ability and how functional they are in promoting innovations and introducing new technologies. The GREMI group (Groupement de Recherche Européenne sur les Milieux Innovateurs) among others has criticized industrial districts for being static as their firms enter into local relationships in order to enhance local efficiency (Camagni, 1991). GREMI introduced an alternative concept "innovative milieu", i.e. a complex network of mainly informal social relationships in a limited geographic area, aimed at enhancing the local innovative capacity through synergetic and collective learning processes – creativity and innovation are the result of a collective learning process based on factors such as intergenerational transfer of know-how, imitation of best-practice, tacit circulation of innovation, etc.

However, innovative milieus do not represent any alternative or new perspective on the industrial district. In his book chapter "The industrial district as a creative milieu" (1991) Becattini argues that industrial districts could be regarded as a "creative milieu". In order to be a source of creative processes in a territorially defined environment, different competencies have to coexist – the coexistence of divergent approaches creates the conditions for a number of challenges in the formulation of a given problem. But that is not enough – there is a need for "a linking primer" – different institutions that act as links between competencies, making them interact dynamically and promoting the dialogue between actors. Thus, the coexistence of competencies and the existence of catalysts that link them will define a "creative milieu".

The main question will then be: "Can the industrial districts be regarded as a creative milieu?" One critical argument may be that, since a single sector (e.g. textile, furniture, etc.) often dominates the district, coexistence of different competences is difficult to achieve – for example, a "textile culture" may dominate the local culture. But according to Becattini, this is only partly true, one has to consider the concrete production process – the phases of production in a textile district involve many different competencies (e.g. chemical for dying, mechanical for repairing, etc.) and different "cultures" exist – thus the coexistence of different competencies is therefore common within industrial districts, even those dominated by a single sector. In addition, the role of catalyst in an industrial district is often played by middlemen (*impannatore* in Prato), i.e. actors whose job is to link external markets and the internal production capabilities of the district – to earn a living they must divide and continuously recombine the production process of the district in new ways. Thus, there are grounds for regarding the industrial district as a "creative milieu".

2.4 The Development of Prato as an Industrial District

Becattini and his co-workers under the leadership of the French historian Fernand Braudel studied the textile district of Prato for a period of 18 years. The results of the studies were presented in a four-volume work in 1997. Becattini's contribution was the final volume, which was subsequently published in English in the book *The Caterpillar and the Butterfly* (2001). In the book, Becattini provides an economic-historical analysis of the development of the Prato district, where the social and historical aspects are emphasized.

The Prato-district on the outskirts of Florence has a long history of textile manufacturing. In 1927 this sector employed around 11,500 people, the majority of whom worked in the big textile companies. This situation was drastically altered in the 1930s when the big companies were forced to shed labor. However, they showed social responsibility by assisting some of the workers in starting up their own businesses as sub-suppliers. This pattern was repeated during the deep textile industry crisis of the 1950s – when these companies once again had to reduce the workforce but on this occasion former textile workers established new sub supplier firms, sometimes with the help of the big textile companies. This development during the crisis in the 1950s led to a dramatic increase in the number of companies, and in 1965 the number of companies in the district approached 6,000.

In his analysis of the Prato district, Becattini divides its development into three periods:

Period 1: The "metamorphosis" phase (1945-1954)

A "massacre" of the small industries located in the South of Italy took place, leading to a strong concentration of the industry to the north. At the same time, Italian industry, and especially the textile sector, was exposed to greater international competition primarily from Far-Eastern countries. However, Italy emerged fairly unscathed from this competition, exhibiting a high and steady share of world export in sectors such as textile, furniture, ceramic tiles, but also in mechanical engineering.

During this period, the Prato district was transformed, from a traditional industrial region with scores of large, dominant companies and their many sub suppliers, to an industrial district. Small companies replaced the big companies, most of which had less than 10 employees. One factor behind this development can be found in the invention of nylon during the 1930s and its significant entry into the carded woollen production in Prato during the post-war period – the use of nylon made it possible to achieve a much wider range of goods, made from lighter, stronger fabrics which could be made in a wide range of colours and textures. This had considerable effects on the way firms were organized: articles were more numerous, had a wider range of types and colors, the series were shorter, and this situation became unmanageable for individual large companies. It was better to specialize in only one phase of production.

Period 2: The phase of "classical development" of the Marshallian industrial district (1954-1975)

In Italy during this period there was a process of "spontaneous" proliferation of clusters of small firms, grouped together in areas and engaged in different stages of the production of certain types of products, for which demand was fragmented and variable – the development of industrial districts. Thus, the formation of industrial districts is intimately linked to the process which leads to the creation of small firms in general. The development of the Prato-district remained very positive – there was a trend toward increased production, the number of companies continued to grow as did employment figures – this was the golden age of the industrial districts and not least for Prato.

Period 3: Restructuring (1975-1993)

During the 1980s and early 1990s there was a great deal of fluctuation in the world economy and upturns were followed by periods of deep stagnation with strong negative consequences for the Italien export industry. The unemployment rate soared, especially among younger people in the South of Italy. Since textile production in Prato was intimately linked to the increasingly turbulent world market, the district was subject to a whole series of external changes. During this phase the product range increased from comparatively standardized woollen products to include various knitted products. Many companies were established that provided peripheral services to the textile industry. The number of companies and the level of employment within purely textile operations gradually declined. In 1982 the textile and fashion market changed radically: fashion suddenly abandoned wool and turned to different materials such as cotton, linen and silk – overnight the basic manufacturing capacity of Prato was sidelined, and between 1985 and 1990 the industrial district of Prato was hit by a severe economic crisis. The recovery was much helped by a devaluation of the lira (September 1992), which provided a substantial price advantage for Italian textile products.

The crisis of the late 1980s also meant a transformation of Prato – the district emerged "slimmed down" and "impoverished" in relation to early production – as well as exhibiting remarkable adaptability. This phase can therefore be described as "restructuring". Accelerated by the deep worldwide recession in the mid 1990s, this restructuring was manifested in different ways, such as a shift toward high-quality products resulting in shorter series and more market oriented production.

3. PIORE AND SABEL "THE SECOND INDUSTRIAL DIVIDE" (1984)

The research on the Italian industrial districts failed to attract international attention until Michael Piore and Charles Sabel published their book *The Second Industrial Divide* in 1984. The book, which was written in the wake of the mid 1970s crisis, gives a macro-historical review of industrial development from the beginning of the extensive mechanization in the early nineteenth century to the crisis during the 1970s. In this historical review, the authors concentrate on the US development although the development in other countries, e.g. West Germany, France, Italy and Japan, is also analyzed.

In the book Piore and Sabel argue that political interventions in the economy (e.g. formation of oil cartels, and the operation of the welfare state) aggravated the crisis, but the crisis had deeper causes – resulting from the limits of the industrial development model founded on mass production. Seen from the perspective of hundreds of years of economic development, we find that breakthroughs in the use of labor and machines are followed by periods of expansion, which culminate in crises that reveal the limits of existing arrangements. In this respect we can identify two kinds of crisis. The first is characterized by the realization that existing institutions no longer succeed in securing a match between the production and the consumption of goods, while the second concerns the choice of technology itself – and it is these movements when the path of technological development itself is at issue that Piore and Sabel call "industrial divides".

The first industrial divide occurred in the 19th century with the introduction of mass production – initially in Great Britain and then in the US – and when the first Model T Ford rolled out of the factory at Highland Park, Michigan, in 1913 it could be regarded as the culmination of a century long mass production experience. Mass production followed on from a technology characterized by craftsmanship, where skilled workers used their tools in a flexible manner, allowing them to adapt to changes in the market. Business success was based in equal measure on cooperation and competition. However, the introduction of mass production presupposed market stabilisation and homogenization, which is a prerequisite for large production volumes. This type of production required large investments in highly specialized equipment – conditions that formed the very basis for the establishment of large companies. Thus, it is possible to observe a dramatic development of large companies during the period between 1870 and 1920. Subsequently, Keynes' ideas regarding the possibilities of the State to control supply and demand in society had a great impact on the financial policy in many countries, thus further strengthening the preconditions for mass production.

The central point in Piore and Sabel's book is that the 1970s and early 1980s were characterized by the second industrial divide. Their line of argument is, among other things, that mass production, large systems and state regulation have gradually hindered industrial investment and development. These problems began in the late 1960s but continued during the whole of the 1970s. The crisis began with the social unrest of the late 1960s – in the US the problem was associated with student protests against the war in Vietnam and with the civil-rights movement, whereas in Western Europe social unrest was more diffuse. That was followed by a crisis in the international monetary system in 1971 – the abandonment of fixed exchange rates and the shift to a system of floating currencies. The crisis of the 1970s were further exacerbated by the two oil shocks in 1973 (based on the Arab oil embargo as a political reaction by the Arab states to Western support for Israel in the Arab-Israeli war in 1973) and in 1979 (initiated by the Iranian revolution). During these crises the interest rates increased, and the industrial world was finally driven into a prolonged recession characterized by rapid inflation and rising unemployment. The result was that Keynesian logic began to be questioned and new political winds started to blow – and not only in the US.

The authors point to two competing strategies at company level for dealing with the situation at hand. The first strategy is based on the principles of mass production and consists of linking the production facilities as well as the markets of the advanced countries with the fastest-growing third-world countries. This presupposes multinational operations in order to be able to stabilise world markets in a way that individual countries cannot. The second company level strategy is a return to the methods of craftmanship that were lost during the first industrial divide. Piore and Sabel use the term "flexible specialization", which is characterized by technically sophisticated and specialized companies, which nevertheless create great flexibility by means of network co-operation. The authors especially highlight Emilia Romagna in Italy as a model in this respect – the industrial districts were, according to Piore and Sabel, distinguished by flexibility, skilled labor and a society that places a premium on cooperation between specialized companies.

In the final chapters of the book, Piore and Sabel place these two company-level strategies in the context of their national economies. They argue that whether firms drift toward flexible specialization or maintain the mass production model depends on their country's adaptation to mass production, where Piore and Sabel's interpretation and prognosis were that the US and France can be expected to follow a mass production path, whereas Italy, West Germany and Japan, with a strong craft tradition, seem to favor a shift in the direction of flexible specialization.

4. PERSPECTIVES ON INDUSTRIAL DISTRICTS

In this final section I will present an interview with Giacomo Becattini, in which he talks about his insights in the field of industrial districts.

You have studied "industrial districts" since the 1950s, what are the most interesting insights you have had in your research?

I would like to mention a couple of aspects. One aspect is the interactive relationship between productive structure and the normal life of the people. Marshall defined economics as a study of man in the ordinary business of life, thus a study of business but also, and even perhaps principally, a study of man. It is at the crossroads of technical and sociological studies and in the districts that you find everyday examples, very important in my opinion, of the interaction between everyday life and industrial activity at a local level. This is, I think, the main result of my research, because it describes the district as a complex socio-economic entity.

The second aspect is methodological. We are accustomed to discussing the modern world ... for example capitalism in general terms, but you cannot test the theories of capitalism anywhere because capitalism is everywhere, and the empirical equivalent of the theory is the world in its complexity and entirety. So, everybody can say different things about capitalism, but there is no way to test them. But, in a micro cosmos, like the district, where all the capitalistic relationships are present and functioning on a regular basis, you can try to understand how it operates as you can test your hypotheses. I believe that we grasped many aspects of post-Fordist capitalism in our studies of the Prato phenomenon. We found some aspects of the Prato district that were interesting. For example, the idea that the market must be rooted in society ... you can see it at work in the district ... because market and society are two sides of the same coin. So I found the study of the districts a very useful tool to understand how the world works.

If we look at the research on industrial districts, most of your research has been published in Italian. What influence do you think that Piore and Sabel's book The Second Industrial Divide had on the research on industrial districts?

The book by Piore and Sabel was very important because, in Italy, only Sebastiano Brusco from Modena, myself, and a few other economists such as Garofoli and Prodi devoted their attention to the phenomenon of industrial districts. Brusco had good contacts with Charles Sabel, and Sabel was writing down his reflections on the changes in American industry partly in the light of his experience in Emilia Romagna together with Brusco, and he published the book in cooperation with Piore, and that book was important mainly because it was an American book.

I don't agree completely with their idea of flexible specialization – in my view we should be talking about flexible integration ... instead of specialization, because what is typical is the fact that there is flexible integration between the firms at the local level. Nevertheless, we share many ideas on the theme of industrial districts.

In addition, there was a development in Japanese industry at that time which was important. Despite the fact that there were a lot of large firms in Japan ... there was an aspect that helped us to develop the ideas about industrial districts, because when trying to explain the success of Japanese industry, there was an indication that the cultural background was a reason for success. So, you see, we in Tuscany discovered a phenomenon that had a certain kind of equivalent in the US and another kind in Japan. So, there could be different ways of being efficient, of being competitive ... and the Tuscan way was one.

Since then the ideas seem to have been diversified and during the 1990s there has been a lot of different concepts ... you have Castell's concept of "technology districts", Michael Porter's concept of "cluster" ... to me it is a mess of different concepts ...

I met Porter in Venice some years ago, and we had a very friendly discussion. We came to the conclusion that there is not much difference between the concepts of "industrial districts" and "clusters", but there is one point, a fundamental point of difference ... I start from the community itself to examine its productive activities, the effect of the way in which the community develops based on its productive structure. Porter approaches the issue from the opposite direction; he highlights the population of firms and pays comparatively little attention to the relationship between the population of firms and the social background. Methodologically speaking it is a big difference, even if our practical conclusions are not so different.

If we look at the research on industrial districts today, how would you characterize the research in a general sense?

The research has developed greatly over the last few years. Now, we have the traditional approach, which we may call the monographic approach, you take a concrete district and you study it in depth comparing it, when possible, with other districts ... this is a kind of socio-economic study. But recently, in the last few years, econometrical studies have been introduced. In Italy, the Institute of Statistics defines the districts, giving us the statistical data for the districts and non-districts areas, so you can easily compare the characteristics and the performances of two categories of local systems in different econometrical studies. The third approach ... the concept of district became more and more refined, and a growing number of "young lions" of economic theory tried to formulate theoretical models of the industrial district. I receive numerous studies from many different places trying to discribe and interpret this particular entity ... so, thirdly the theoretical attempts at modeling districts.

If a young doctoral student, coming to you for advice, and he or she wants to carry out research on industrial districts ... what advice would you give him or her?

I would give this advice ... If you are a brilliant theoretician you should try to theorize the industrial districts. I have reviewed a lot of papers in which the authors have tried to extract a theory about industrial districts based on existing knowledge .. and that is in my opinion the first point.

Second, if you are a PhD student, I would say ... why not study the theory of the firm from the new perspective suggested by industrial district studies. I don't agree with the poor representation of the firm given by the economists. I think that future theoretization should take account of the fact that the firm ... I put it roughly ... is not only a knot of private interest but also an engine of the local (and national) community and a social factor. This is a different perspective from the prevailing one.

Based on your research on industrial districts, what policy recommendations would you make?

I do not have any complete or ready answer. I can only give some hints about what one should do and not do. What should you not do? If as usual you build your industrial policy on the needs of the big firms ... you can severely damage the industrial districts. For instance, the needs of the populations of small firms working for big ones are completely different from, and frequently opposite to, the needs of the small firms in the districts. So, you should consider that there are two different engines driving development ... your policy must be compatible with the needs of both and not only conceived to meet the needs of the bigger firms and/or their satellites.

Industrial districts in Italy face many difficulties, and some districts may be gone in ten years time ... I don't believe it myself, but maybe ... what is certain is that the incubator activity within the district is crucial, you need to create an atmosphere in the district that makes people want to try ... This atmosphere involves a "sense of belonging" – an active approach where you not only share a vision of the future, but also actively act upon that vision ... and this is a crucial point ... only where you can create such feelings can you speak about a social entity that goes beyond more individualistic approaches. My main point is that it is very difficult to achieve this "sense of belonging" due to the modern philosophy of life ... which is terribly individualistic and atomistic ... so, the maintenance and the development of a sense of belonging requires a cultural fight. The theory of industrial districts is part of it.

It is important to promote a "sense of belonging", but another crucial point is the necessity of having access to the world market. You need to be in touch with the world market, even a tiny part thereof. In Italy we had early experience of buyouts ... American and German and English buyouts ... they helped a great deal at the start but that is not the case now because distribution is monopolized by a few firms, which is an obstacle. So, perhaps it is not so easy.

REFERENCES

Asheim, B.T., 2000, Industrial Districts: The Contributions of Marshall and Beyond, in Clark, G.L. & Feldman, M.P. & Gertler, M.S. (eds.), The *Oxford Handbook of Economic Geography*, New York: Oxford University Press.

Becattini, G., 1989, From the industrial 'sector' to the industrial 'district', in Goodman, E. & Bamford, J. (eds.), *Small firms and industrial districts in Italy*, London: Routledge.

Becattini, G., 1990a, Italy, in Sengenberger, W. & Loveman, G. & Piore, M. (eds.), *The re-emergence of small enterprises. Industrial restructuring in industrialized countries*, Geneva: IILS.

Becattini, G., 1990b, The Marshallian industrial district as a socio-economic notion, in Pyke, F. & Becattini, G. & Sengenberger, W. (eds.), *Industrial Districts and Interfirm Co-operation in Italy*, Geneva: IILS.

Becattini, G., 1991, The industrial district as a creative milieu, in Benko, G. & Dunford, M. (eds.), *Industrial change and regional development: the transformation of new industrial spaces*, London: Belhaven Press.

Becattini, G., 2001, *The caterpillar and the butterfly*, Firenze: Le Monnier.

Becattini, G., 2002, From Marshall's to the Italian "Industrial Districts". A Brief Critical Recontruction, in Curzio, A.Q. & Fortis, M. (eds.), *Complexity and Industrial Cluster. Dynamics and Models in Theory and Practice*, Heidelberg: Physica-Verlag.

Becattini, G., 2003a, Industrial districts in the development of Tuscany, in Becattini, G. & Bellandi, M. & Dei Ottati, G. & Sforzi, F., *From Industrial Districts to Local Development. An Itinerary of Research*, Cheltenham: Edward Elgar. Reprint of the article Becattini, G., 1978, The development of light industry in Tuscany: an interpretation, *Economic Notes*,1978.

PIONEERS – MICRO-LEVEL ANALYSIS

Chapter 10

ARNOLD COOPER

1. ARNOLD COOPER – COMBINING INTERESTING RESEARCH QUESTIONS WITH SCIENTIFIC RIGOR

1.1 The Contributions of Arnold Cooper

Since the 1960s, Arnold Cooper has been one of the leading entrepreneurship scholars and can be considered as a pioneer in strategic management as well as in entrepreneurship research. His pioneering work on spin-offs in Silicon Valley and new technology-based firms has significantly enhanced our understanding of entrepreneurial phenomena. Cooper can also be said to be the archetype of an entrepreneurship researcher, as his research is wide-ranging, and for having attempted to answer many of the fundamental questions that define the research field. His contributions are not merely empirical but also methodological – he was for example one of the first researchers to carry out longitudinal studies of a large number of companies – and he has also made a whole range of theoretical contributions. Arnold Cooper's strength is his ability to combine a strong theoretical base with good empirical research. Furthermore, he was one of the first entrepreneurship researchers to have his work published in the leading management journals, which is an indication of the quality of his research.

Arnold Cooper has, unquestionably, been instrumental in elevating entrepreneurship research to a higher academic level, not only through his own research but also due to being one of the first to organise the research field, his participation in conferences, synthesizing of research reviews, and not least as a mentor and supervisor of young entrepreneurship researchers.

1.2   Career

Arnold Cooper, born 1933, obtained his first degree in chemical engineering in 1955 at Purdue University, and in 1957 he was among the first batch of students from the Krannert School of Management at Purdue University to obtain a Master of Science in Industrial Management. Having left the university, he worked for a year at Procter & Gamble. In 1958 he went to Harvard Business School as a doctoral student. At Harvard, Arnold Cooper was influenced by W. Arnold Hosmer, who had developed a new course entitled "Small Manufacturing Enterprises", and Arnold Cooper duly became his research assistant. Hosmer was interested in the dynamics of growth oriented small firms – firms that could be found around Route 128 in Boston – and by studying these firms a great deal could be learned about wealth and new job creation. In 1962, Arnold Cooper presented his thesis *Practices and Problems in the Development of Technically Advanced Products in Small Manufacturing Firms* under the supervision of Arnold Hosmer. In keeping with the tradition of the Harvard Business School, the thesis was based on a number of case studies concerning the practices and problems of product development in small manufacturing companies.

Some of the ideas on which the thesis was based were published in two *Harvard Business Review* articles in 1964 and 1966.

"At the time the prevailing view was that large companies enjoyed many advantages, not least in R&D where they benefited from advantages of scale. I went out and identified small companies, many of which competed directly against large companies with highly successful R&D. Many of the people that I interviewed in small companies said 'we were able to develop this product at much lower cost than we could have done in some of the larger companies where we used to work' ... That led me to investigate the comparative costs of R&D in small and large companies ... The two articles in *Harvard Business Review* challenged some of these prevailing assumptions.

The article I published in *Harvard Business Review* in 1964 was the first I ever wrote. I was surprised that there was so much interest in it. I received letters, people contacted me, and I testified before a senate subcommittee. It developed some ideas that were contrary to what was generally assumed at the time – a time when many considered that large companies were especially suited for the development of innovations."

In 1963 Arnold Cooper went back to Purdue University – a university that he has remained true to ever since, although he has often lectured as a visiting professor in other universities such as Stanford, Manchester

Business School, IMEDE in Lausanne, and at the Wharton School in Philadelphia.

> "Purdue University has a strong engineering and science orientation, and when I went back I expected to find a lot of technically-oriented new firms around the university – but that was not the case. I wondered why, and I began to study the phenomenon of new technology-based firms. In my studies I tried to understand why it is that particular kinds of growth oriented companies are started in some places and not in others, and why they are started at certain periods and not at others – general questions with real implications for economic development."

Arnold Cooper was given the opportunity to go to Stanford University as visiting professor during 1967 and 1968. At Stanford he could empirically study the dynamics of new technology-based firms, and his research interest shifted to a focus on the process of new firm formation – an interest that he has maintained ever since. The study was based on some 250 firms in the San Francisco area.

> "What I noticed was that even if the area was characterized by active entrepreneurship, the entrepreneurs tended to come from certain organizations and not from others. So, there was more to it than just geographic location. Therefore, I asked myself, what are the characteristics that make some organizations more likely to function as incubators for entrepreneurs while others do not? Does the strategy or the nature of the business have any influence?"

Cooper found that the spin-off rate in smaller firms was approximately 10 times greater than for larger companies. There may be several reasons for this. People who work for small firms typically develop broadly based skills that are valuable for potential entrepreneurs as well as learning about products and markets that can be exploited by small firms. These small firms go through periods of turmoil – sometimes growing and sometimes experiencing severe difficulties, and this creates incentives to leave the organization. Finally, those who opt to work for small firms are perhaps more inclined to become entrepreneurs compared to those who choose to work for large firms – thus there is an element of self selection.

In the 1970s Arnold Cooper published a large number of articles based on the spin-off study. Some of the articles were co-authored with one of his former students, Albert Bruno. One of the most cited articles appeared in *Business Horizons* in 1977 and was entitled "Success Among High-Technology Firms". The article focused on the fact that the discontinuance rate among high-tech firms was very low, and successful firms were very similar to the organization in which the founder(s) had previously been employed. It was also one of the early studies that showed that businesses started by a team were more successful – which is something that has been found many times since then.

It is also worth mentioning that Arnold Cooper organized one of the first entrepreneurship research conferences in the US, called the Technical Entrepreneurship Symposium, at Purdue University in 1970, at which a number of pioneers in entrepreneurship research, such as Karl Vesper, Edward Roberts and Albert Shapero, presented their work.

> "The Symposium was the first time that a group of entrepreneurship researchers really came together to present their research to each other. At the time, the first research projects on entrepreneurship in the US were being conducted. So there was something to discuss ... and there was a foundation, the Center for Venture Management which supported my research and the symposium. I contacted a couple of people to come to Purdue. We met for two days ... it was a very intense and stimulating meeting."

In the 1970s Arnold Cooper also did a lot of work in strategic management. Strategic management was developing at the same time as entrepreneurship, and Arnold Cooper was deeply involved in the scientific development of both fields, as one of the pioneers in entrepreneurship research as well as of strategic management. Arnold Cooper lectured a great deal within the area of strategic management, and due to the focus of the PhD program at Purdue, many of Arnold Cooper's doctoral students wrote their theses on strategic management. In addition, some of Cooper's most frequently cited articles were written on the subject of strategic management and published in more general management journals, such as *Academy of Management Journal* and *Strategic Management Journal*.

In 1980 Arnold Cooper became involved in a research project initiated by the Small Business Administration in the US, in which each region of the country was required to present a report on small business development. In this project Arnold Cooper worked with William Dunkelberg, who at that time was a colleague at Purdue as well as chief economist of the National Federation of Independent Business (NFIB), which is the largest trade association of small businesses in the US. Together they conducted the study about small business development in the American Mid West. One of the most well-known parts of the study concerns a discussion about the robustness of the typologies used to classify entrepreneurs. The interest in typologies that classified entrepreneurs in various ways started at Michigan State University in the 1960s, with Norman Smith's classical distinction between "opportunistic entrepreneurs" and "craftsman entrepreneurs" being an important example. The idea was that different kinds of entrepreneurs start different kinds of firms.

"We looked at how stable or robust these typologies were and discovered that they were very sensitive to the variables used in forming these typologies ... even if they used the same categories, they often used different variables to form the categories, and if you changed the variables just a little, it would often change the classification of firms quite significantly ... This meant that while the same thing had been discussed in several studies, there were major differences depending on what variables were used to establish the different categories."

Through their contacts with NFIB, Arnold Cooper and William Dunkelberg were asked by William Dennis at NFIB to conduct a large-scale longitudinal study to track new firms' development over time. The NFIB study generated an enormous amount of data. Arnold Cooper and his colleagues have made many interesting analyses based on these data, and the study has been reported in various forms throughout the 1980s and 1990s. In these analyses, Carolyn Woo, who was a member of the faculty at Purdue and who joined the study at an early stage, was a key figure, as were a number of doctoral students who became involved in different parts of the program. The analyses have mainly been focused on the entrepreneurial process and the performance of new firms. There are a substantial number of publications that have emerged from the program, and some of the most frequently cited are:

Cooper, A.C. & Folta, T.B. & Woo, C., 1995, Entrepreneurial Information Search, *Journal of Business Venturing*, 10, 107-120.

Cooper, A.C. & Gimeno-Gascon, F.J. & Woo, C.Y., 1994, Initial Human and Financial Capital as Predictors of New Venture Performance, *Journal of Business Venturing*, 9, 371-395

Cooper, A.C. & Woo, C.Y. & Dunkelberg, W.C., 1988, Entrepreneurs' Perceived Chances of Success, *Journal of Business Venturing*, 3, 97-108.

Gimeno, J. & Folta, T.B. & Cooper, A.C. & Woo, C.Y., 1997, Survival of the Fittest? Entrepreneurial Human Capital and the Persistence of Underperforming Firms, *Administrative Science Quarterly*, 42, 750-783.

McCarthy, A.M. & Schoorman, F.D. & Cooper, A.C., 1993, Reinvestment Decisions by Entrepreneurs: Rational Decision-making or Escalation of Commitment?, *Journal of Business Venturing*, 8, 9-24.

"One reflection is that my earlier work during the 1960s and 1970s was primarily focused upon growth oriented and usually high-technology new firms. Later, when I began to work with the NFIB, my research focused on new firms of all kinds, because the typical member of the NFIB was a privately owned retail or service firm – very representative of small firms in the US. It was an opportunity, and I think when you have the opportunity to develop a lot of interesting data, it often opens the door and allows you to pursue research in a new direction – it changed my emphasis, looking at venture creation in small firms in general, not just in high-technology firms.

In addition, in the analyses we draw upon theory to a much greater extent than I have done in my earlier work ... in many cases we used theoretical frameworks from many different areas, such as psychology, information technology, etc. The fact that I received a very broad education at Harvard Business School has proved both a strength and a weakness in my own career ... and the doctoral students that I worked with ... my co-authors ... were a tremendous asset in this respect – they were getting the most advanced training available in many areas, which meant that they could apply these theories in the program."

2.   STREAM OF INTEREST IN ARNOLD COOPER'S RESEARCH

In this section I will present some of Arnold Cooper's extensive research. I will divide the section into four areas: R&D in small manufacturing firms (section 2.1.), technical entrepreneurship (section 2.2.), entrepreneurial diversity (section 2.3.), and entrepreneurship and performance (section 2.4.).

2.1   R&D in Small Manufacturing Firms

The first stream of interest in Arnold Cooper's research focuses on R&D in small manufacturing firms. His thoughts were expressed in an early article in *Harvard Business Review* "R&D Is More Efficient in Small Companies" (Cooper, 1964), in which he raises the question "Is there a substantial difference in the cost of developing particular products among companies of different sizes?". The study was based on interviews and case studies of "parallel development projects" in which both a large and a small company had independently developed the same product. The case studies clearly showed differences in the way large and small companies undertook product development and also in the effects on development costs. Larger companies tended to spend substantially more time and money on the development of a particular product than did small firms.

Cooper argued that there are three major factors that may explain the advantages enjoyed by small firms. The first is the ability of the individual(s) responsible for product development – ability in terms of technical knowledge, creativity and the ability to see the "core of a problem". The average capabilities of technical staff are higher in small firms than in larger ones, which may be explained by the fact that many small research-based firms are able to attract outstanding technicians and that larger companies often hire a great number of inexperienced young engineers, whereas small firms typically employ people that have already demonstrated their technical competence in larger firms. The second factor concerns the attitude of technical staff. In small firms the staff members are more concerned about how much a project costs than is the case with their counterparts in larger companies. The reasons may be that the cost of a single project is more important in a small firm than in a larger one and that it is easier for technical people in small firms to relate to and have an awareness of the development of the business as a whole. Finally, communication and coordination tend to be easier and less costly in small firms. The results were controversial at that time, and the editors of the journal asked the readers for their opinion on the conclusions of the article. The responses were extensive and mainly in favour of the conclusions.

However, few small firms are involved in R&D work, and many people were pessimistic about the ability of small firms to develop significantly advanced new products – pioneering should be left to the large companies. In a follow-up article "Small Companies can Pioneer New Products" in *Harvard Business Review* (Cooper, 1966), Arnold Cooper addressed some of these issues. This article was more directly based on his doctoral thesis. He summarised the major problems facing small firms when trying to develop technically advanced new products in the following way: (i) small firms have difficulties in recruiting and retaining people with considerable education and unusual abilities, (ii) even when a small firm attracts good engineers, they lack the benefits of "team research" and tend to be distracted by continuously having to solve everyday problems, (iii) even if small firms are able to develop a new product, they do not have the resources to exploit it, (iv) the risks of R&D in small firms are enormous – small firms can seldom afford to support more than a few R&D projects and almost always lack the resources to survive a "run of bad luck", and (v) even if a small firm is successful in developing and exploiting a new product, it is very likely to face heavy competition from larger companies. The conclusion that Cooper makes is that not every small manufacturing firm should be involved in the development of advanced new products. Essential for such a strategy is the presence of at least one highly creative technical person in the firm, a company culture that emphasizes product development and a willingness to take risks.

2.2   Technical Entrepreneurship

In the 1960s, a large number of new technology-based firms emerged in different regions in the US, such as the areas around Boston, Palo Alto, and Los Angeles. These firms seemed to be important in that they developed a significant number of technological innovations, creating new jobs as well as providing career satisfaction for individuals who preferred the small firm context. Thus, it was essential to gain more understanding about how they came into being, and the key questions raised were: What leads to the birth of these firms? In what way do the established firms in an area influence the birth of new technology-based firms?

In a couple of seminal articles, Arnold Cooper elaborated on these questions (Cooper 1970; 1971; 1972). The research was based on a research project in the San Fransisco area, around Palo Alto, and included three phases; (i) interviews with 30 entrepreneurs, (ii) telephone interviews with (or published data on) 250 new technology-based firms that had been created in the San Fransisco Peninsula area since 1960, and finally (iii) interviews with executives from established organizations. Some of the main results of the study can be summarized as follows:

2.2.1   Characteristics of Spin-off Companies

The decision to establish a new technology-based firm is influenced by three major factors:
1. The entrepreneur himself, his motivation, his perception, his skills and knowledge.
2. External factors, for example, the availability of capital, the accessibility of suppliers, and the collective attitude toward entrepreneurship.
3. The established organizations ("incubator organization") in which the founder(s) had previously worked.

Cooper was mainly interested in the third factor – the incubator organizations. He found that the incubator organizations had a major influence on the location of new firms. New firms are closely related to the established organizations in a given region. For example, new firms are typically founded by entrepreneurs who are employed by organizations already located in the area, which means that if there are no such incubator organizations in a region, it is unlikely that any new technology-based firms will be established. Secondly, an entrepreneur typically starts his firm to exploit his own knowledge, and this knowledge is usually related to the market and technical knowledge developed at the incubation organization. This indicates that the new firm will serve the same general market or technology as the incubator organization. Finally, the incubator organization may influence the motivation of the entrepreneur to start a new firm – the entrepreneurs were especially motivated by events they perceived taking place within the incubator organization. In many cases the entrepreneurs felt frustrated in their previous position, due to "a lack of confidence in management", "a feeling that poor decisions were made", etc., indicating that a high spin-off rate is indicative of poor morale and frustration within the organization.

2.2.2 Incubator Organizations

As we have seen, new technology-based firms are dependent upon local incubator organizations that hire, train and motivate potential entrepreneurs. This is reflected by the spin-off rates of different organizations. In the study, spin-off rates were calculated for 325 technology-based organizations in the Palo Alto area. The results indicated a wide variation in the rate of spin-offs from established firms. Most organizations (237 organizations) had no spin-offs. Among the few that had three or more spin-offs, the spin-off rate varied from 1 out of 3,100 employees to 1/14 (measured as the number of spin offs between 1 January 1960 to 1 July 1969, in relation to the average number of employees during the same period). The spin-off rate for the total group was 237/77,600 or 1/306. This indicates that even if the Palo Alto area in general could be regarded as a region favorable for entrepreneurship, organizations varied widely in the extent to which they functioned as incubators for new firms.

Why then do some organizations have higher spin-off rates than others? The characteristics of the incubator organization and the industry in which they operate may provide some explanations. In his literature review "Technical entrepreneurship: what do we know?" (1973), Cooper summarized some of the industrial and organizational attributes associated with the birth rate of new firms (see Figure 10-1).

Low birth-rate	High birth-rate
Characteristics of industry	
Slow industry growth	Rapid industry growth
Honogeneous markets	Opportunities to segment markets
Heavey capital investment required	Low capital investment required
Substantial economies of scale	Minor economies of scale
Characteristics of established incubator organization	
Large number of employees	Small number of employees
Organized by function	Product-decentralized organization
Recruits average people	Recruits very capable, ambitious people
Relatively well-managed	Afflicted by periodic crises
Located in geographic areas with little entrepreneurship	Located in geographic areas of high entrepreneurship

Figure 10-1. Characteristics of incubator organizations and industries (source: Cooper, 1985, p. 79, see also Cooper, 1973, p. 63).

Arnold Cooper's research in the Palo Alto area (Cooper, 1970; 1971; 1972) indicated that industries varied widely in the extent to which there were attractive opportunities that could be exploited by new firms. Fast growing industries and industries characterized by a high rate of technical change will offer many opportunities for new firms. On the other hand, industries with heavy capital investments or with competition from large organizations will have lower spin-off rates.

Spin-off rates also varied between small and large firms – the spin-off rate of smaller firms was about ten times that of large firms. The explanation could be that (i) large firms are often engaged in activities that require heavy capital investments, i.e. economies of scale are important, (ii) professional employees in small firms develop rather broad backgrounds, i.e. small firms constitute a valuable education for potential entrepreneurs, (iii) there is self-selection biases, i.e. those who choose to work in small firms may be more entrepreneurially inclined, and (iv) large firms probably employ a higher percentage of non-professional employees.

Finally, the results indicated that the spin-off rate for universities and non-profit research institutes is about the same as for large companies as a group, whereas the rate for government laboratories seems to be very low, which may be explained by the fact that the work done in these organizations does not have much commercial applicability and, in addition, the employees in general are more scientifically oriented and less entrepreneurial than their industrial counterparts.

2.2.3   Development and Performance Patterns

The firms included in the study were analyzed in a longitudinal study for about a decade – Albert Bruno, a former student of Arnold Cooper, went back to Silicon Valley and made follow-up studies in 1973, 1976 and 1980. The main interest was to identify development patterns of new technology-based firms and essentially to what extent these firms were closed down, acquired or achieved above average growth. The study was presented in Cooper and Bruno (1977) and in Bruno and Cooper (1982).

The results show that the discontinuance rate was very low. By 1976, the median firm was ten years old and, despite a nation-wide recession, the percentage of discontinued firms totalled only 29%, and by 1980 this figure stood at 37%. A comparison between the characteristics of "discontinued" and "high-growth" firms indicated that high-growth firms were more often started by multiple founders, the firms were more similar in terms of technology and/or markets to the organizations that the founders had left and, finally, the founders of high-tech firms were to a higher extent from a larger organization. Many larger incubator organizations had experienced high growth, and the spin-offs from these firms were often positioned in the same high-growth markets.

An interesting finding was that the rate of acquisition or merger among the firms was high – which could also explain the low discontinuance rate, i.e. unsuccessful firms were acquired instead of being closed down. By 1976 as many as 21% of the firms were acquired or merged. The corresponding number for 1980 was about 32%. The peak acquisition period involves just the start-up period, and a second peak seems to occur 4 to 7 years after establishment. The attraction of acquiring a firm just after start up could be the expertise of the founders and/or the product lines on which the firm was based. After 4 to 7 years the firms may have shown a growth rate that makes it necessary to replace the initial founders, who often came from an engineering background, by more professional managers.

2.2.4   An Extension of the Incubator Phenomenon

Cooper carried out his research on incubator organizations in the 1960s and early 1970s, mainly focusing on high-technology firms. But there was no systematic examination of whether the influence of incubator organizations varies across industries and over time. In a broader, cross sectional study, including 161 firms in different industries, Cooper (1984; 1985) found that most new firms did start geographically close to their incubator organizations, which reinforces the knowledge that entrepreneurship within a region is largely dependent on the existing pool of people. In general, new firms were also related to their incubator organization in terms of business. However, there were variations across industries. The linkages were most pronounced for electronics/computers, whereas the majority (54%) of non-technical firms were unrelated to the incubator organization – indicating that the necessary knowledge for these industries could be learned from other sources.

Regarding the type of incubator organization, industrial firms were the incubator for 77% of the new firms, while software firms were more likely to be spin-offs from universities, and biotechnology/medical firms came mainly from universities or hospitals – indicating that software and, particularly in the case of biotechnology, the state-of-the-art technology is mainly found in universities and hospitals.

The conclusions seem to be that entrepreneurs in most industries do not move geographically and usually start firms related to what they did before and that prospective founders of non-technical firms appear to be less tied to the knowledge gained in an incubator organization. The implication for regional development is that the opportunity for high-technology start-ups may be very limited in many geographic regions, and the role of universities seems to be less significant than is often assumed. With the exception of software and biotechnology/medical firms, it is mainly industrial firms that have served as incubators.

2.2.5   Location and Technological Clusters

As indicated, the incubator organizations affect the location of new firms. At the same time, new technology-based firms often seem to start in clusters of related firms, which leads to concentrations of new technology-based firms such as in Silicon Valley, Seattle, Boston and San Diego in the US, Cambridge in the UK, and Kista and Lund in Sweden. In a state-of-the-art chapter, Cooper and Folta (2000) discussed the questions "Why do new technology-based firms start where they do?" and "How does location make a difference?"

Clusters, i.e. sets of related firms in close geographic proximity, are not a purely high-technology phenomenon. For example, we can find clusters in the textile industry in Carolina and Georgia in the US, fashion goods in Milan, Italy, and diamond cutting in Belgium. Although location in a cluster may be important for all firms, it appears to be particularly important for technology-based start-ups due to their newness and hence lack of credibility.

There seems to be strong empirical evidence that entrepreneurship, and not only high-technology entrepreneurship, is concentrated in particular geographic regions and that new technology-based firms are found in certain regions or geographic clusters. What are the benefits and costs of locating in a cluster? Cooper and Folta presented a couple of factors that may influence the location decision of firms:

– Access to specialized labor, specialized inputs, and capital.
– Knowledge spillovers – knowledge spillovers occur more frequently if there are well-developed networks among people in different organizations and if there is substantial mobility in the workforce, i.e. geographic proximity may be vital for knowledge spillovers.
– Proximity to customers and support – location within a cluster could lead to lower search costs to find customers – and in many cases sales are made to other firms in the cluster.

Considering the above mentioned factors, it would appear that the benefits inherent in clusters should encourage entrepreneurs to locate in clusters. On the other hand, there is evidence that suggests that this is not the case – technical entrepreneurs tend to start their firms within commuting distance of their homes and previous places of employment. This indicates that they are relatively restricted in their decision about where to locate their start-ups. However, in view of the importance of spillover effects, location in a cluster may be of special importance for firms trying to compete on differentiation strategies, for firms that make a high percentage of their sales to other firms in the cluster, and for firms in industries experiencing rapid change.

2.3   Entrepreneurial Diversity

The entrepreneurial process is complex, and entrepreneurship involves many different kinds of people. However, most of the research on entrepreneurship during the 1970s studied main tendencies, and many studies used rather narrow samples of entrepreneurs. Of course, there is much to learn from general characteristics, but "average" tends to disregard the wide differences in the phenomenon – relatively little attention was devoted to entrepreneurial diversity, and there were few researchers who systematically used broadly based samples, including many industries, different time periods and geographic areas, etc. The study that Cooper conducted with William Dunkelberg is based on a random sample of members of the National Federation of Independent Business (NFIB). The questionnaire was mailed to 6,225 NFIB members in 1979, and 1,805 responses were received, i.e. a response rate of about 29%. The sample represented virtually all industries and all parts of the US. However, compared to the US business population as a whole, the sample seems to underrepresent very small firms and businesses in the service industry. Nevertheless, the survey represents one of the largest and most diverse samples of small business owners studied at that time.

2.3.1   Typologies of Business Owners

Business owners differ in a number of ways. Differences involve not only their background, but also their motivation and expectations for their firms. Typologies are extremely useful for our understanding of entrepreneurship because they capture frequently occuring combinations that are qualitatively different from each other, in addition to reducing the large number of potential profiles of entrepreneurs to a manageable few. Thus, while typologies may give a less detailed description of entrepreneurs – they provide a way of organizing diversity that makes it possible to identify patterns in a complex phenomenon. In addition, better predictions of entrepreneurial behavior and performance can be made, based on specific typologies.

A number of entrepreneur or small business owner typologies have been presented. Of these, Smith's (1967) "craftsman entrepreneurs" and "opportunistic entrepreneurs" classification may be the best known. The craftsman entrepreneurs came from blue-collar backgrounds and had a relatively narrow education. As managers they were paternalistic, utilized personal relationships and followed a rather rigid business strategy. On the other hand, opportunistic entrepreneurs had a middle class background, broader education and a previous association with top management. They were more proactive in marketing their firm and developed more innovative and diverse competitive strategies. In addition, Filley and Aldag (1978) classified business owners as craftsman, promotion and administrator types. Craftsmen were less adaptive, inclined to avoid risk, concentrated on making a comfortable living, and their firms were stable. Promotion businesses were organized informally to exploit some type of unique competitive advantage, the firms were centrally controlled and often short-lived and transactional in nature. Finally, administrative businesses could be described as formalized and professional, larger in size and less dependent on the personal leadership of the business owner.

In their study, Dunkelberg and Cooper (1982) identified three types of business owners, who seemed to differ with respect to their background and prior experience:

- Growth-oriented owners, who were driven by a desire for substantial growth whose line of business was changing rapidly. They indicated a desire for growth over the following five-year period of more than 30%.
- Independence-oriented owners, who were strongly driven to avoid working for others. These business owners were more often found in agriculture and professional practice (such as dentists, engineers, and accountants). Compared to the other groups of business owners, they more often purchased their firms.
- Craftsman-oriented owners, who were strongly drawn toward doing a particular type of job. They tended to have the least formal education and were more likely to have started their firm themselves.

Compared to previous typologies (e.g. Smith, 1967; Filley & Aldag, 1978), only the independence-oriented owners seem to be distinct from earlier studies. It is interesting to note that 74% of the 1,805 owners were classified into one of the three groups and that none of the three groups were concentrated in any one industry, indicating that these types of business owners could be found in all kinds of business activity.

2.3.2   Critics of Typologies

As indicated, one of the most well-known typologies is the distinction between "craftsman entrepreneurs" and "opportunistic entrepreneurs" developed by Smith (1967). The support for these two types of entrepreneurs has been strong and consistent in several studies (see e.g. Filley & Aldag, 1978; Dunkelberg & Cooper, 1982). However, there may be inconsistencies behind these results, based on differences and limitations in research designs and the samples used in different studies and also due to the dimensions used to make the categorization. A closer examination of previous studies showed that craftsman and opportunistic entrepreneurs were identified on the basis of two criteria in one study, whereas in another study, no less than 50 criteria were employed. Based on this uncertainty, Arnold Cooper together with Carolyn Woo and William Dunkelberg (Woo & Cooper & Dunkelberg, 1988; 1991) posed the question "How sensitive is the derivation of generic entrepreneurial types to the choice of classification criteria?", or put in another way "How likely are we to obtain the same grouping of entrepreneurs from different classification schemes?" If the grouping of entrepreneurs is robust and not sensitive to the choice of dimensions, then prior studies are consistent, and we can find knowledge accumulation within the field.

Cooper and his colleagues tested the consistency of the craftsman-opportunistic typologies on a large sample of manufacturing and retail start-ups, using different dimensions of entrepreneurial classification such as: (i) goals, (ii) goals and entrepreneurial background, and (iii) goals, entrepreneurial background and management style. The results showed that different dimensions produced different groupings. When using only "goals" as an entrepreneurial dimension, no clear-cut difference between craftsman and opportunistic types could be identified. Instead, two other groups of entrepreneurs emerged, which could be described as "independent entrepreneurs" versus "organization builders". When the background dimension was added to the analyses, the entrepreneurs were reclassified into two new groups – "craftsman entrepreneurs" versus "administrative entrepreneurs". A similar categorization was found when the management style dimension was included. Furthermore, individual entrepreneurs often shifted group membership as classification dimensions were added.

It was thus concluded that the derivation of entrepreneurial types is not robust with respect to the choice of entrepreneurial dimensions used. This makes the like hood of obtaining similar entrepreneurial types across studies using different dimensions extremely unlikely and the convergence of earlier studies questionable. It may be that the craftsman or opportunistic types of entrepreneurs only show partial correspondence between different studies. This indicates that the impact of entrepreneurial types cannot be generalized across studies and that the conceptual and theoretical extension of the research can be questioned. Thus, caution must be exercised when interpreting findings on entrepreneurial types, a close inspection must be made of the process, by which the entrepreneurial types were constructed, and there is a need for consistency and careful consideration of the definition of types before validated entrepreneurial descriptions can be developed.

2.4 The Entrepreneurial Process and Performance

Knowledge of predictors of new firm performance is unquestionably of interest to entrepreneurs, to those who provide advice to entrepreneurs as well as to investors in new ventures. The main question is: Why do some new firms succeed whereas others fail? In 1985, Arnold Cooper, William Dunkelberg, William Dennis, and later Carolyn Woo started a large-scale, longitudinal study of entrepreneurs and their firms. The study was jointly initiated with the National Federation of Independent Business (NFIB). The focus of the research program was to examine the start-up process of new firms and the determinants of performance in these firms. The theoretical and methodological framework of the program is to some extent presented in Cooper (1993) and summarized in Figure 10-2. The variables included in the framework are the characteristics of entrepreneurs, the founding process, initial firm characteristics, environmental characteristics and performance.

The research program consisted of a three-year longitudinal study of new businesses. Questionnaires were sent out in May 1985 to 13,000 members of the NFIB, all of whom were believed to have recently started a new firm. 4,884 responses were received.

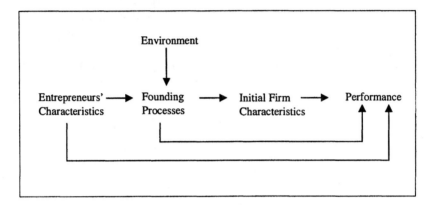

Figure 10-2. Research framework (source: Cooper, 1993, p. 243).

However, as many of the respondents had been in business for many years, the study focused on respondents who had become business owners in the 17 months prior to the survey, i.e. in 1984 and the first five months of 1985, which limited the number of usable responses to 2,994.

The sample represented all geographic areas and all sectors of the US economy. Compared to the US economy, retail businesses and businesses in the western part of the US seemed to be somewhat overrepresented in the sample but in broad terms the sample appeared to be representative of new businesses in the US. The respondents in the first survey were mailed follow-up questionnaires in May 1986 and May 1987 – 629 respondents replied in year two, and 877 in year three. The non-respondents were followed up carefully, which enabled Cooper to determine the survival or failure status of almost all 2,994 businesses in the first survey. Findings from the research program have been reported at a number of conferences and in scientific journals throughout the 1980s and 1990s. In general, the research program can be considered very well thought out, both conceptually and methodologically. Some of the main findings from the program will be summarized below.

2.4.1   The Entrepreneurial Process

Entrepreneurs involved in starting firms must engage in a process of assessing the prerequisites for success. In this respect the following questions may be of interest: How do entrepreneurs perceive their chances of success? Do they see themselves as undertaking risky ventures with marginal prospects, or are they confident that they will succeed? In cases of over-optimism there is as possibility that entrepreneurs may underestimate the difficulties associated with the start-up and fail to make the necessary preparations. On the other hand, pessimistic entrepreneurs may focus on the short-term problems and have less inclination to continue when start-up difficulties arise. Cooper, Woo and Dunkelberg (1988) found that entrepreneurs who have made the decision to become business owners show a remarkable degree of optimism. They see their own odds for success as extremely high (81% perceived the odds of 7 out of 10 or better, of which 33% regarded their chances as "certain" or 10 out of 10). This extreme tendency toward optimism may be explained by a "cognitive dissonance", which leads the entrepreneur to exaggerate the attractiveness of an option after it has been chosen, although a psychological trait involving a propensity to take risks and strong internal locus-of-control beliefs may also play a role. The study also showed that those entrepreneurs who were well prepared and those who were poorly prepared seemed equally optimistic. This may indicate that entrepreneurs are unable to assess their own strengths and weaknesses and the early progress of their firms, but also that all entrepreneurs, whether prepared or not, experience "entrepreneurial euphoria" in which they feel that success is certain.

Information is a key resource for new ventures and a critical factor for the entrepreneur. It may be that entrepreneurs expressing a high degree of confidence in the chances of success of their new firms will seek less information, but it could also be hypothesized that entrepreneurs with previous entrepreneurial experience and entrepreneurs operating in familiar domains will seek more information because of their richer "schema" and greater awareness of what is required. Cooper, Folta and Woo (1995; see also Woo, Folta & Cooper, 1992) supported the relationship between confidence and the search for information and between those entrepreneurs operating within familiar fields and the search for information. But entrepreneurs with no prior entrepreneurial experience sought more, not less, information, and this was especially significant when they entered a field they knew – in such situations the novice entrepreneurs engaged in a more intensive search. Experienced entrepreneurs, on the other hand, seemed to search with about the same intensity, regardless of whether they were familiar with the field or not. One explanation may be that experienced entrepreneurs had developed a richer "schema" but were also more confident and that they may have developed more fixed routines – having become prisoners of their past success. In Cooper, Folta and Woo (1991), it was also found that entrepreneurs utilized personal and professional sources of information to a greater extent than public sources of information, which can be explained by the fact that entrepreneurs perform better in richly connected, flexible and accessible networks.

2.4.2   Entrepreneurial Satisfaction

How satisfied then are the entrepreneurs with their businesses after three years of business ownership? Entrepreneurial satisfaction could in this respect be regarded as a basic measure of performance. In Cooper and Artz (1993; 1995), the authors suggest that individual satisfaction is determined, in part, by whether there is a "gap" between actual rewards (or performance) and the individual goals (or expectations). It was hypothesized that (i) entrepreneurs emphasizing primarily non-economic goals (such as doing the work they wanted to do) would show a higher degree of satisfaction when the business performance was poor, whereas (ii) the satisfaction of those emphasizing economic goals would vary in relation to economic performance. In addition, it was hypothesized that when controlling for performance, entrepreneurs with higher initial expectations would have a lower level of satisfaction because of the greater expectation-performance gap.

The study shows that among firms experiencing marginal performance, those entrepreneurs emphasizing non-economic goals expressed higher levels of satisfaction. Interestingly, and contrary to expectations, those who were initially optimistic were more satisfied later on, even when controlling for performance, and those who had a positive view of the initial process later viewed the experience of business ownership more favorably. The explanation may lie in the benchmark that entrepreneurs use to measure their performance, i.e. as their experience increases, their expectations also evolve to different degrees after three years of operation.

McCarthy, Schoorman and Cooper (1993) also showed that the entrepreneur who starts a business and expresses overconfidence about its chances for success will exhibit an escalation bias in future decisions regarding the expansion of the business. That is, when entrepreneurs express overconfidence, it may be a strong indication that a significant psychological commitment has been made and that the entrepreneur may take the risk of escalation bias in subsequent decisions. Thus, the entrepreneur's initial expectations are associated with subsequent satisfaction and may thus influence whether or not the entrepreneur decides to invest more time and money or to exit their businesses.

2.4.3   The Performance of Different Categories of New Firms

Several studies prior to those of Arnold Cooper and colleagues have examined the discontinuance rate of new firms. The research presented in Cooper, Dunkelberg and Woo (1988) showed that the discontinuance rate among new firms was lower than expected – only 11% of the firms went out of business during the first year, and an additional 8% during the second year. There were also systematic differences in the characteristics of surviving firms compared to those that failed. For example, entrepreneurs associated with surviving firms tended to be older, better educated, had industry experience (although managerial experience was not associated with better chances of survival), and their firms were closely related to their previous work as well as larger in size, compared to those entrepreneurs who failed.

Thus, the initial size of the new firms seems to be associated with performance, although the characteristics of the entrepreneurs and the process of starting the firm also seem to differ. Initial size is related to the financial and human resources that must be assembled and to the ability of the firm to survive and grow. In Cooper, Woo and Dunkelberg (1989) it was shown that entrepreneurs starting larger firms had the necessary backgrounds to assemble substantial resources – better education, greater management experience, and goals that were more managerial in nature. They tended to rely more upon external investors and utilized professional advisors to a greater extent than those starting smaller ventures, and the venture was more closely linked to their previous jobs.

There were minor differences in performance between larger and smaller ventures. The smaller ventures showed somewhat higher discontinuance rates (14% versus 7% of the initial sample after the second year of operation). Both groups of surviving firms reported a low level of serious problems as well as few changes in the direction of the firms, except that smaller ventures were likely to lose partners and larger ventures more likely to add branches or locations. Finally, both groups reported high mean growth rates, although they both included firms that grew substantially whereas others scaled down – indicating the fluidity and experimental character of new firms. The conclusion seems to be that there is no optimal initial size – such decisions must be based upon the particular circumstances confronting each individual entrepreneur.

The study indicated that women seem to start smaller ventures than men. This issue was further elaborated on in Srinivasan, Woo and Cooper (1994), and the main question was "Are there any differences in performance between firms started by male and female entrepreneurs?" The results provided clear evidence that female-owned ventures were less successful, both in terms of survival and growth, in comparison to male-owned businesses. Looking at the determinants of survival, female-owned businesses were more likely to survive if they were similar to the incubator organization that the entrepreneur left and, somewhat surprisingly, less likely to survive if the entrepreneur emphasized the goal of building a successful organization. It may be that those who aspired to growth and experienced only marginal performance could have concluded that they were not achieving the required "threshold level of performance" that would justify the continued existence of the firm. The determinants for growth seem to be influenced by other factors – indicating that survival and growth are two distinct processes. Female-owned ventures were more likely to grow if the entrepreneur emphasized the goal of doing the work they wanted to do, if they quit their previous employment with definite plans for the new venture, and if their ventures were similar to their earlier organizations.

2.4.4   Human and Financial Capital as Predictors of Performance

The initial resources at the time of start-up may be of significant importance as a predictor of performance. Cooper, Gimeno-Gascon and Woo (1994) examined the extent to which the initial human and financial resources can be used to predict the probabilities of different performance outcomes, such as failure, marginal survival and high growth. Four categories of human and financial capital were considered in the study: (i) general human capital (education, gender and race), (ii) management know-how, embodied in the entrepreneur or available through advisors or partners, (iii) specific industry know-how, i.e. previous experience of the same or a similar business, and (iv) initial financial capital raised in the firm.

The results indicate that it should be possible to predict the performance of new firms with some degree of confidence. Interestingly, "survival" and "growth" seem to be governed by similar processes – only a few variables show a strongly different impact. For example, several measures of general human capital influenced both survival and growth. The exception was gender – female-owned ventures were less likely to grow, but just as likely to survive. Similarly, industry-specific know-how and financial capital contributed to both survival and growth.

In a further analysis Cooper and his colleagues argue that new venture survival is not strictly a function of economic performance but also dependent on a firm's own "threshold of performance", determined by the entrepreneur's human capital characteristics, such as alternative employment opportunities, psychic income from entrepreneurship, and cost of switching to other occupations, i.e. new firm survival is influenced by both the determinants of performance and thresholds (Gimeno & Folta & Cooper & Woo, 1997).

In prior studies it has frequently been argued that, in the long run, well-performing firms survive while poorly performing ones disappear as a consequence of a natural selection – the firms that make profits are selected or "adapted" by the environment, while others are rejected and disappear. This argument is based on a relationship between performance and survival – the worst performing firms are also the least likely to survive. In contrast, Cooper et al. argue that firms differ in their thresholds of performance, and exit or survival is determined by whether economic performance falls below or remains above that firm-specific threshold. This in turn is dependent on the entrepreneur – the willingness to withstand poor performance is partly determined by the mobility of the resources controlled by the entrepreneur. This argumentation is developed in a "threshold model of entrepreneurial exit" (see Figure 10-3).

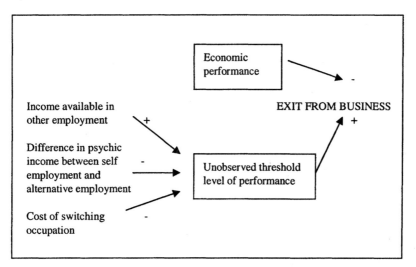

Figure 10-3. Threshold model of entrepreneurial exit (source: modified from Gimeno & Folta & Cooper & Woo, 1997, p. 757)

The empirical analysis provides strong support for the threshold model. Survival of the venture will be influenced by the switching costs for the entrepreneur (i.e. the costs of switching to a new employment) and by the psychic income from entrepreneurship (i.e. the personal satisfaction the entrepreneur derives from self-employment). Previous research has shown that entry into entrepreneurship may be more likely for those with reduced options elsewhere, and this study shows that those entrepreneurs are also more likely to survive, independent of performance. In order to understand the entrepreneurial process, it is of importance to include the threshold of the entrepreneur. The contribution of the study is that it helps us explain the inconsistencies in earlier studies. Furthermore, the threshold of performance concept develops our knowledge about the determinants influencing performance and survival of new firms.

3.   PERSPECTIVES ON HIGH-TECH FIRMS

This final section is devoted to an interview with Arnold Cooper in which he gives his views on research within the field and also shares his thoughts about the future development of entrepreneurship research.

If we focus on your research on technical entrepreneurship, new technology-based firms and incubator organizations that you began to study in the 1960s, what was the most interesting insight that you made in your research?

This research comes from the time when I went to Stanford University as a Visiting Professor in the 1960s, and two things surprised me. I had expected that the typical entrepreneur would have spent a long period of time preparing to leave his previous organization and to have laid the ground work, raising the capital, finding partners, and so on, before leaving the previous organization. I was surprised at how often they left their previous organization with no specific plans for the future and that they often left because of strong pushes – the organization was closing down or failing and the situation became such that they quit their job. And I remember the words of one entrepreneur; as he drove home he thought: "What am I going to do now?" I was surprised that there were a great many that proceeded in that way.

The second area that surprised me was when I was gathering information about the organizations that the entrepreneurs had come from, what I called the incubator organizations. Silicon Valley was an area in which there was a high rate of entrepreneurship, but I was surprised to discover that the spin-off rates, the extent to which employees would leave organizations to become entrepreneurs, varied greatly across organizations, even within an area of overall high entrepreneurial activity. Some organizations, such as Lockheed Aircraft, very rarely had any entrepreneurs leaving, and those who did, did not start businesses that became very visible, at least during that time. There were other organizations such as Fairchild Semiconductor, which had wave after wave of entrepreneurs emerging. So that surprised me and seemed to me to be interesting, and it led to my trying to look at the characteristics of organizations that have high and low spin-off rates.

You are one of the pioneers in research on new technology-based firms. What are the main achievements that have been made in the area during the last two decades?

First of all, I think technology-based firms are very interesting to study. They have some interesting features. For example, they often use strategies that seek to develop a competitive advantage based upon a new technology, which gives them the opportunity to build a business that has substantial impact. So, the average technology-based firm probably has more upside potential, more opportunity to generate employment and substantial wealth, compared to the small firms in general.

Technology-based firms are also interesting because they are often larger in scale than the typical small business, which means that they usually have to raise capital from outside sources. The typical mom and pops start up that is very widespread in all countries is not going to utilize professional venture capital, but many of the most promising high-tech firms do. Everything that has been happening in terms of looking at venture capital in the sense of formal and informal venture capital is very relevant.

Because of their scale, they are often started in teams, and teams raise all kinds of interesting questions. Not only some of the work on the background of teams is of interest, but the functioning of the teams, the ways they do or don't work together, their problem solving style, the dynamics of teams, etc. Over the years there have been a lot of fine contributions in this area, for instance Eisenhardt and Schoonhoven's work on the characteristics of funding teams and the relationship to the subsequent performance. But there are still a lot of interesting questions to explore.

In terms of the founding process of technology-based firms, much attention has been devoted to geography ... to the economics of location. The consideration of how location, whether in a cluster or not, influences not only the founding processes but also the subsequent competitive position. That is one area where there has been clear knowledge development. The work on networks is in this respect quite relevant. There has been some good work in showing ways in which networks influence the perceived legitimacy of the start-up status, which may influence the costs of acquiring certain resources and the ability to tap into those resources. The network also functions as an information exchange, and this is very important for high-tech firms where information is right at the heart of the competitive advantage. So, work in the area of both geographic clusters and networks that looks at the extent to which new technology information diffuses or flows to different geographic areas is relevant. That research suggests that geographic location does make a difference, and I think there is clearly an opportunity for using network concepts when trying to understand more fully how information flows.

Another interesting feature of technology-based firms is that new such firms often seek to operate in industry settings that are changing, they often position themselves in newly developing markets, newly developing industries ... this presents both problems, challenges and opportunities, because things are changing. It is often possible to compete against established organizations because new technology, new market needs create new possibilities, but there is also the challenge that things don't stay the same ... you may develop a competitive advantage, you may have a product which is the leader for a while, but maybe in a short time it is displaced by still newer technology, or the market evolves and other things become important for competing. For instance, costs and price may become much more important as the market matures. So, there are challenges, and firms have to be able to change their strategies and develop new capabilities and that presents very interesting questions of how to do that ... and since these capabilities are often built around individuals, it raises the question as to whether the same people can continue to play a prominent role, and of course the answer seems to vary a lot.

There is a great deal of research on new technology-based firms, what are the questions still to be researched within the area?

I believe that there are still many opportunities to do research in this area. I think that everything we have talked about can be studied in much greater depth. I don't think it is possible to point to a single question and say that everything that could be done has been done here. I think there is often an opportunity to expand on earlier work and to do so in a more sophisticated way that is more fully linked to theory, that may use more appropriate measures, etc.

In many cases researchers have focused upon things that can be measured easily, on things on which we have data. For example, look at the research on managerial teams, work has been done which examines the relative size of the team or background of team members, but no research has really looked at the processes by which these teams interact. There has not been very much work that really looks in a detailed and fine grained way at management styles or the background of team members, e.g. work involving psychological measures or management style, or more specific and detailed measures of the skills and capabilities of the people. All of that remains to be done. To cite just one example.

Generalizing from that, I would say that in almost every area we have looked at, one could take what has been done and find that quite often the work has looked at something that could be measured fairly easily. Now, if you then go beyond the basics and try to get more detailed measures and maybe draw on theoretical frameworks which let you explore more deeply ... what you will find is an empirical question, and whether that will add to the understanding of the first level of knowledge remains to be seen, but I think we can learn a great deal more, even our best research explains a relatively small percentage of performance.

Does this indicate that we need to research new technology-based firms using other methodological approaches?

I believe that a variety of approaches lead to greater understanding, and I believe in looking at interesting questions and drawing from them whatever relevant theory one can find rather than restricting one's consideration to those questions that might emerge from particular theoretical frameworks. I think that as more well-trained young people come into the field, they will have different strengths, some will have a background in sociology, others in economics, others in cognitive psychology, etc., and all of these people contribute their particular strengths. They will look at questions and provide insights that those of us who do not have the same background in these disciplines maybe never thought of.

But in general, I think that entrepreneurship researchers should devote more care to the measurement of variables and the reliability of these variables. It is important to consider the interesting questions, but to do so in a more scientifically rigorous way ... research has to become much more systematic and scientific, but that does not mean that we cannot ask the interesting questions.

Based on your research on technology-based firms, what policy recommendations would you like to give to governments?

I am personally not very supportive of the idea that the government should follow an industrial policy of investing government funds in selected businesses. There might be certain technologies that form a part of a national strategy that government might choose to support ... as occurred indirectly in the US through the defence department expenditures, which for instance supported much of the early work on semiconductors ... but I am not sure that government is very good at picking winners or losers.

I think government should try to ensure that it is not putting up barriers to entrepreneurship. What I really would like to see is a medical attitude among policy-makers – first, do no harm – and those who are entrepreneurs in particular countries are in the best position to provide advice about what government policy may be doing harm. Of course, sometimes there are trade-offs, because these policies may be in place as a part of a social legislation ... thus, implemented for good reasons, but they may have the unintended consequence of greatly increasing the barriers to entry in particular fields.

However, I think government can probably do something useful in the area. A lot of policies are more useful at regional level rather than national level. Some regions are much more favorable than others, and if the region has high unemployment and maybe low levels of human capital it may be very difficult ... entrepreneurship is most likely to occur where there are high levels of human capital and the infrastructure is well developed. The government must therefore ensure that the infrastructure is well developed for instance regarding information systems, transportation systems, education, etc. Thus, infrastructure investments are important – but it is hard to predict where entrepreneurs will find opportunities, but if the environment is reasonably supportive that will make it easier for the entrepreneur to exploit his or her opportunity. For example, on the educational side there is a lot to be done ... to allow educational institutions at the secondary level, at university level, etc. to create education programs that are oriented toward entrepreneurship – that could be very beneficial. The same applies to the intellectual property rights in a country ... it is important to have a legal system that provides stability, that protects property rights, including intellectual property rights.

Thus, what I would recommend relates to the provision of an infrastructure for providing a conducive legal climate, trying to remove barriers ... maybe making some investments in programs that promote education. But I would hesitate to advise government to get into the business of investing directly into ventures.

Entrepreneurship research has developed exponentially during the last two decades, and you have been one of the key researchers in this development. As you see it, what will the future look like for entrepreneurship research?

Howard Aldrich wrote a chapter in the book *Entrepreneurship 2000* entitled "Blinded by the Cites", and he argued that there are different ways in which the field could develop. One way would be the so-called "normal science" with a growing body of research that builds upon specific empirical and theoretical work and that develops as a separate and distinct field with its own literature and its own journals. He noted that an alternative approach to development could be a "multiple-paradigm" field, in which related fields such as sociology, finance, economics and organizational behavior might bring the methodologies and the frameworks of their fields to bear on questions regarding new firms or innovative ventures in established companies. And research might be published in the journals of those disciplines and it would thus become a multidisciplinary field. He then noted a third alternative – a "pragmatic approach" field – which would be perhaps less theoretical.

Now this is interesting, as entrepreneurship has become a hot and attractive area not only in American business schools, but all over the world. Governments are interested in the field; there is money to support work. Fellow scholars in related fields have discovered this fact and are starting to take an interest in entrepreneurship. I consider this to be a very positive development. If people in allied disciplines begin to work within the field ... the economists will bring many of their powerful methods and frameworks and look at some of these questions, and we can but benefit and learn. It is still a young field and it has been developing and will continue to develop in a variety of ways. I think all three avenues described by Aldrich are relevant. I think the entrepreneurship field as such will continue to develop in terms of an increasingly sophisticated and respected research area. I think the multidisciplinary aspect in particular will develop as people in allied fields see the possibilities.

You are also one of the pioneers in the strategic management field, and today there is an intensive discussion about the interface between entrepreneurship and strategic management ... if you are making a comparison between these two areas of research, how would you describe the difference between entrepreneurship and strategic management research?

I think one of the striking things about entrepreneurship is that it has in my opinion evolved in a similar way to the strategic management field, but not to the same degree. Both entrepreneurship and strategic management, or "business policy and strategy", as it was called, emerged about the same time during the 1970s.

Strategic management has probably developed in a way that Howard Aldrich would describe as a normal science ... developing its distinctive literature, the type of research questions that it tends to focus upon, relying more and more upon certain theoretical frameworks to drive and raise questions, etc. In many ways you could say that the research in that field has become a great deal more sophisticated, and in terms of the number of researchers there has been an enormous growth. On the other hand, there are critics who say that the emphasis upon rigor and the requirement of certain underlying disciplinary frameworks used drive the questions, while others raise the question as to whether that tends to exclude interesting questions that might lead to questions that we haven't even thought about.

In many ways this development has gone much faster compared to the development of entrepreneurship, and there are several reasons for this. For example, from an early stage, strategic management was tied to core courses at the universities that were often required in the curricula of both undergraduate and MBA programs. As a consequence, schools had a need for a faculty to teach ... it led to opportunities for people to work completely in that area ... and in order to be up to date, you need to do research, which resulted in full time careers and the development of groups of faculty members. In the late 1970s and early 1980s a theoretical framework was also developed ... the work of Michael Porter for instance played a key role there.

Entrepreneurship on the other hand, developed more slowly in number of courses, often elective courses, and many schools met their needs by using part-time adjunct faculty ... in many cases good teachers but they were not doing any research ... there were very few schools with more than one or two faculties working in the area. So, all of this meant that entrepreneurship developed less rapidly than it otherwise might.

I think entrepreneurship has been very eclectic, very open to a variety of questions, a variety of approaches and has tended to be supportive of many aspects. I hope that with entrepreneurship, even as we move toward greater rigor and concern for the careful application of scientific methods ... I hope we can also, at the same time, remain open to the person who maybe raises interesting questions upon the basis of limited evidence or to less rigorous methods of analysis yet still pose questions that are of practical significance and will open up new avenues of topics within the field.

When we talk about entrepreneurship research of the future. What will entrepreneurship research look like?

I think that in entrepreneurship journals and at conferences you can see that a lot of development and an increase in sophistication have taken place over the last 10 years. I suspect that this will continue. Some are concerned and say "well let's squeeze out the interesting and innovative work and everybody will be so concerned about methodology that it will make things less creative – less interesting". I don't know about that – I hope we will see both more sophistication work, but also researchers who are innovative and who present interesting work within the field. I also think we will probably see more work related to entrepreneurship appearing in the journals of allied fields such as finance and marketing. I think that's excellent. And the people doing that work may well be people who bring a great deal to it, and if they publish in those journals it will help their careers but in the end it will contribute to the overall development of entrepreneurship. So, I am very optimistic about the future development of the field.

REFERENCES

State-of-the-art articles

Cooper, A.C., 1973, Technical entrepreneurship: what do we know?, *R&D Management*, 3, 2, 59-64.

Cooper, A.C., 1982, The entrepreneurship – small business interface, in Kent, C.A. & Sexton, D.L. & Vesper, K.H. (eds.), *Encyclopedia of Entrepreneurship*, Englewood Cliffs, NJ: Prentice-Hall, 193-208.

Cooper, A.C., 1986, Entrepreneurship and high technology, in Sexton, D.L. & Smilor, R.W. (eds.), *The Art and Science of Entrepreneurship*, Cambridge, MA: Ballinger, 153-168.

Cooper, A.C., 1995, Challenges in predicting new firm performance, in Bull, I. & Thomas, H. & Willard, G. (eds.), *Entrepreneurship. Perspectives on Theory Building*, Oxford, UK: Elsevier, 109-127.

Cooper, A.C. 1998, Strategic Management: New Ventures and Small Business, in Birley, S. (ed.), *Entrepreneurship*, Aldershot: Dartmouth.

Cooper, A.C. & Daily, C.M., 1997, Entrepreneurial Teams, in Sexton, D.L. & Smilor, R.W. (eds.), *Entrepreneurship 2000*, Chicago: Uppstart, 127-150.

Cooper, A.C. & Folta, T., 2000, Entrepreneurship and High-technology Clusters, in Sexton, D.L. & Landström, H. (eds.), *The Blackwell Handbook of Entrepreneurship*, Oxford, UK: Blackwell Publishers.

Cooper, A.C. & Gimeno-Gascón, F.J., 1992, Entrepreneurs, Processes of Founding and New-Firm Performance, in Sexton, D.L. & Kasarda, J.D. (eds.), *The State of the Art of Entrepreneurship*, Boston: PWS-Kent Publ, 301-340.

Entrepreneurship research

Cooper, A.C., 2003, Entrepreneurship; The Past, the Present, the Future, in Azs, Z. & Audretsch, D. (eds.), *Handbook of Entrepreneurship*, Dordrecht: Kluwer.

Cooper, A.C. & Dunkelberg, W.C., 1987, Entrepreneurial Research: Old Questions, New Answers and Methodological Issues, *American Journal of Small Business*, 11, 3, 11-23.

Cooper, A.C. & Hornaday, J.A. & Vesper, K.H., 1997, The field of entrepreneurship over time, Frontiers of Entrepreneurship Research, xi-xvii.

Cooper, A.C. & Markman, G.D. & Niss, G., 2000, The Evolution of the Field of Entrepreneurship, in Meyer, G.D. & Heppard, K.A. (eds.), *Entrepreneurship as Strategy. Competing on the Entrepreneurial Edge*, Thousand Oaks: Sage.

McCarthy, A.M. & Nicholls-Nixon, C.L., 2001, Arnold Cooper on entrepreneurship and wealth creation, *Academy of Management Executive*, 15, 1, 27-34.

R&D in small manufacturing companies

Cooper, A.C., 1964, R&D Is More Efficient in Small Companies, *Harvard Business Review*, May-June, 75-83.

Cooper, A.C., 1966, Small companies can Pioneer New Products, *Harvard Business Review*, September-October, 162-179.

Technical entrepreneurship

Bruno, A.V. & Cooper, A.C., 1982, Patterns of Development and Acquisitions for Silicon Valley Startups, *Technovation*, 1, 275-290.

Cooper, A.C., 1970, The Palo Alto Experience, *Industrial Research*, May, 58-60.

Cooper, A.C., 1971, Spin-Offs and Technical Entrepreneurship, *IEEE Transactions on Engineering Management*, 18, 1, 2-6.

Cooper, A.C., 1972, Incubator Organizations & Technical Entrepreneurship, in Cooper, A.C. & Komives, J.L. (eds.), Technical Entrepreneurship: A Symposium, Center for Venture Management, Milwaukee, Wisconsin, 108-125.

Cooper, A.C., 1973, Technical entrepreneurship: what do we know?, *R&D Management*, 3, 2, 59-64.

Cooper, A.C., 1984, Contrasts in the role of incubator organizations in the founding of growth-oriented firms, in Frontiers of Entrepreneurship Research, 159-174.

Cooper, A.C., 1985, The Role of Incubator Organizations in the Founding of Growth-Oriented Firms, *Journal of Business Venturing*, 1, 1, 75-86.

Cooper, A.C. & Bruno, A.V., 1977, Success Among High-Technology Firms, *Business Horizons*, April, 16-22.

Cooper, A.C. & Folta, T., 2000, Entrepreneurship and High-technology Clusters, in Sexton, D.L. & Landström, H. (eds.), *The Blackwell Handbook of Entrepreneurship*, Oxford, UK: Blackwell Publishers.

Entrepreneurial diversity

Cooper, A.C. & Dunkelberg, W.C., 1981, A new look at business entry: Experiences of 1805 entrepreneurs, Frontiers of Entrepreneurship Research, 1-20.

Cooper, A.C. & Dunkelberg, W.C., 1986, Entrepreneurship and Paths to Business Ownership, *Strategic Management Journal*, 7, 53-68.

Dunkelberg, W.C. & Cooper, A.C., 1982, Entrepreneurial Typologies: An Empirical Study, Frontiers of Entrepreneurship Research, 1-15.

Filley, A.C. & Aldag, R.J., 1978, Characteristics and Measurement of an Organizational Typology, *Academy of Management Journal*, 21, 4, 578-591.

Smith, N.R., 1967, *The Entrepreneur and His Firm: The Relationship Between Type of Man and Type of Company*, East Lansing, Michigan: Michigan State University Press.

Woo, C.Y. & Cooper, A.C. & Dunkelberg, W.C., 1988, Entrepreneurial Typologies: Definitions and Implications, Frontiers of Entrepreneurship Research, 165-176.

Woo, C.Y. & Cooper, A.C. & Dunkelberg, W.C., 1991, The Development and Interpretation of Entrepreneurial Typologies, *Journal of Business Venturing*, 6, 93-114.

Entrepreneurship, process and performance

Cooper, A.C., 1993, Challenges in Predicting New Firm Performance, *Journal of Business Venturing*, 8, 241-253.

Cooper, A.C., 1998, Findings on Predictives of Performance from a Large-Scale Research Program, *Small Enterprise Research*, 6, 1, 3-9.

Cooper, A.C. & Artz, K.W., 1993, Determinants of Satisfaction for Entrepreneurs, Frontiers of Entrepreneurship Research, 221-233.

Cooper, A.C. & Artz, K.W., 1995, Determinants of Satisfaction for Entrepreneurs, *Journal of Business Venturing*, 10, 439-457.

Cooper, A.C. & Dunkelberg, W.C. & Woo, C.Y., 1988, Survival and failure: A longitudinal study, Frontiers of Entrepreneurship Research, 225-237.

Cooper, A.C. & Folta, T. & Woo, C., 1991, Information Acquisition and Performance by Start-up Firms, Frontiers of Entrepreneurship Research, 276-290.

Cooper, A.C. & Folta, T.B. & Woo, C., 1995, Entrepreneurial Information Search, *Journal of Business Venturing*, 10, 107-120.

Cooper, A.C. & Gimeno-Gascon, F.J., 1992, Entrepreneurs, Processes of Founding and New-Firm Performance, in Sexton, D.L. & Kasarda, J.D. (eds.), *The State of the Art of Entrepreneurship*, Boston: PWS-Kent Publ, 301-340.

Cooper, A.C. & Gimeno-Gascon, F.J. & Woo, C.Y., 1994, Initial Human and Financial Capital as Predictors of New Venture Performance, *Journal of Business Venturing*, 9, 371-395.

Cooper, A.C. & Woo, C.Y. & Dunkelberg, W.C., 1988, Entrepreneurs' Perceived Chances of Success, *Journal of Business Venturing*, 3, 97-108.

Cooper, A.C. & Woo, C.Y. & Dunkelberg, W.C., 1989, Entrepreneurship and the initial size of firms, *Journal of Business Venturing*, 4, 317-332.

Gimeno, J. & Folta, T.B. & Cooper, A.C. & Woo, C.Y., 1997, Survival of the Fittest? Entrepreneurial Human Capital and the Persistence of Underperforming Firms, *Administrative Science Quarterly*, 42, 750-783.

McCarthy, A.M. & Schoorman, F.D. & Cooper, A.C., 1993, Reinvestment Decisions by Entrepreneurs: Rational Decision-making or Escalation of Commitment?, *Journal of Business Venturing*, 8, 9-24.

Srinivasan, R. & Woo, C.Y. & Cooper, A.C., 1994, Performance determinants for male and female entrepreneurs, Frontiers of Entrepreneurship Research, 43-56.

Woo, C. & Folta, T. & Cooper, A.C., 1992, Entrepreneurial Search: Alternative Theories of Behavior, Frontiers of Entrepreneurship Research, 31-41.

Chapter 11

IAN MACMILLAN

1. IAN MACMILLAN – ACADEMIC LEGITIMIZER, ORGANIZER OF ENTREPRENEURSHIP RESEARCH AND A RESEARCHER DEVOTED TO "ACTIONABLE" RESEARCH

1.1 The Contributions of Ian MacMillan

Ian MacMillan has given legitimacy to the field of entrepreneurship. With the establishment of entrepreneurship as an academic subject at a renowned business school such as Wharton School of Business, the research field acquired the necessary legitimacy, thus making it possible for other universities and business schools in the US to follow suit. This attracted a number of talented young researchers and research students to the field, and especially to Ian MacMillan's Snider Entrepreneurial Center at Wharton School of Business in Philadelphia, where MacMillan has created an international research environment within the field of entrepreneurship.

MacMillan has also been instrumental in the organization of the research field. Here, the establishment of the *Journal of Business Venturing* deserves particular mention, as he developed it into one of the leading journals in the field. Another noteworthy achievement is The Global Entrepreneurship Conference, in partnership with Sue Birley at the Imperial College in London, a conference that has contributed to a broad network and methodological understanding among young scholars around the world.

His own research covers a range of topics within entrepreneurship, but his groundbreaking work on corporate entrepreneurship deserves special attention – a topic that has interested him throughout his academic career. His major contribution in this respect has been the integration of the fields of entrepreneurship and strategic management. His research is characterized by a strong management perspective and an interest in achieving "actionable" research, i.e. the research findings should provide the basis for some kind of achievement in reality.

1.2   Career

Ian MacMillan was born in South Africa in 1940. After graduating in Chemical Engineering in 1963, he worked in the South African atomic energy industry and later on in the oil refining industry. He attended courses in Organizational Politics at the University of South Africa. In 1970 he became a lecturer and graduated from the MBA program in 1972. However, MacMillan was also involved in entrepreneurial activities. Together with his uncle he created a global travel agency specializing in adventure tourists and elderly tourists with an interest in exotic places. MacMillan did his DBA at the University of South Africa and presented a thesis entitled *Aspects of Manipulative and Accommodative Behaviour by Graduate Middle Managers* in 1975.

> "At the time I was doing my thesis, I worked at a company building an oil refinery in South Africa. I noticed that top management decisions were often repackaged by middle managers, so that the outcome was more in line with middle management interests. In this particular case we were building a new refinery and the issue was whether to retain or shut down the old refinery. Top management wanted to build an entirely new refinery and close down the old one. Because of the ways in which the middle managers repackaged the problem, the outcome was to build a somewhat smaller refinery and keep the existing refinery ... the original refinery used a lot more methodology that required middle management skills ... their expertise was much more important in the old refinery than in the more automated new refinery. I was intrigued by the fact that senior management make key strategic decisions that are in a way subverted by middle managers."

The University of South Africa used to invite a number of American professors to the University. Two of them were Larry Cummings and Andrew Van de Ven. They looked at the work that Ian MacMillan was doing and became interested in it. As a result they asked him to visit the US where he received an offer to lecture at Northwestern University in Boston. In 1975 MacMillan arrived at Northwestern University as a visiting professor.

> "When I first came over to the US I really knew very little about the traditional US style of research and during my first year at

Northwestern I spent a lot of time catching up on research methodologies and the way of doing research in the US. I must admit that my early works were not eminent in a methodological sense, and the statistical analyses in the studies were relatively intuitive.

At Northwestern I also met Chuck Hofer ... very well known in entrepreneurship research, and through Hofer I got involved in Dan Schendel's work on strategic management. I was especially intrigued by the PIMS database, Profit Impact of Market Strategy ... a large sample study including data from 3,000 business units, in which I saw a great potential.

Chuck Hofer was teaching a course on entrepreneurship. The course was oversubscribed, so he asked me if I knew anything about entrepreneurship. I said that I had been an entrepreneur ... that seemed to please him, so I started to teach the course. I was lucky, the course was a success.

While I was at Northwestern, Hofer was interviewed for a position at Columbia University in New York and he said to me: 'Why don't you apply too?' What happened was that Hofer decided to go to Stanford, and I got the job at Columbia."

In 1976 Ian MacMillan became Associate Professor in policy at Columbia University, a position that he held until 1983. A lot of MacMillan's research during this period was focussed on strategic management topics.

"I was lucky ... Donald Hambrick had also joined Columbia, and he discovered my interest in the PIMS database, and together we started to make analyses based on the database. We used PIMS to test some of the strategic management theories about company performance. For example, I had been concerned with the Boston Consulting Group Matrix ... I felt that it was an over-simplification. What Hambrick and I decided to do was to use the PIMS database to test the BCG Matrix. We looked at companies in each of the four categories in the matrix and analyzed the extent to which their predictions about cash flow and profitability in those four categories were validated."

At the same time Ian MacMillan became more and more interested in entrepreneurship, and he also became involved in teaching entrepreneurship courses at Columbia.

"At Columbia a guy teaching a course in entrepreneurship died of a heart attack one night, and there was no one to teach the course. I said: 'Well, you know ... I taught an entrepreneurship course at Northwestern, so I could step in and do it'."

MacMillan received a lot of attention for his educational efforts. The *Fortune Magazine* produced a series of articles, which they called "the ten best university business school professors in the country", in which Ian MacMillan and his entrepreneurship courses at Columbia received wide coverage.

"When I started to teach entrepreneurship at Columbia I was intrigued by entrepreneurs and the extent to which they were able to manipulate their environment in order to accomplish their purposes, and I started to take an interest in entrepreneurship research. My first article in entrepreneurship was 'The Politics of New Venture Management' published in *Harvard Business Review* in 1983. In the article I tried to find common patterns of manipulative behavior among entrepreneurs as they tried to start their businesses. What I learned from that simple case analysis was that a lot of the work in entrepreneurship at that time looked at the characteristics of the entrepreneur. I felt that we could not learn much by just looking at who they were ... we couldn't do much with that knowledge. Perhaps I didn't realize it then, but the article was the seed of the idea that it may be more important to study entrepreneurial behaviors than to study the characteristics of the entrepreneurs. But my main research was still focussed on strategic management in established businesses ... entrepreneurship was more a side line."

In the early 1980s a decision had been taken by New York University (NYU) to launch a Center for Entrepreneurship, and they approached MacMillan and offered him the position of Professor and Director of the Center, and it was at NYU that MacMillan's interest in entrepreneurship gained momentum. Ian MacMillan was Professor and Director of the Center for Entrepreneurship Research at New York University between 1984 and 1986.

At the Center for Entrepreneurship Research, MacMillan met Zenas Block, a practician with a long-standing experience of corporate ventures. The collaboration with Block led to a number of important initiatives. One of these initiatives was a large international comparative research project focusing on entrepreneurial drivers in different countries (see for example, McGrath & MacMillan, 1992; McGrath & MacMillan & Scheinberg, 1992; McGrath & MacMillan & Yang & Tsai, 1992).

"Zenas Block and I had a meeting at the Center for Entrepreneurship Research with a couple of colleagues from abroad. My observation was that entrepreneurship seemed to be more difficult in Europe than in the US, and these cultural differences really intrigued us. Block suggested that if we measured culture and variables related to the entrepreneur in different countries we might be able to identify common patterns of entrepreneurial behavior that were independent of culture ... and then the project just grew and in the end included a large number of countries."

Another initiative together with Block was the book *Corporate Venturing* published in 1990.

"We were intrigued by the fact that it seemed so difficult for companies to engage in venturing. In the book we tried to condense our experiences of corporate entrepreneurship ... the work that I had done, and his experience in a number of corporate venturing projects in industry. We tried to write a book in which we could provide some kind of road map for anybody who wanted to do corporate venturing. It is not an academic book but we drew on a lot of research findings ... over the years I have always tried to make research ideas manageable and relevant to people in industry."

A third initiative taken during MacMillan's time at New York University, and also encouraged by Zenas Block, was the launch of *Journal of Business Venturing* in 1985 – a journal which is today regarded as one of the leading journals in entrepreneurship research.

"We were frustrated at the time by the fact that there was no place where people who were interested in writing academic articles in entrepreneurship could find a home that would be, let's say, user friendly. The original idea was to have a mix of practice-oriented and research-oriented articles. However, we found this mix difficult to achieve and fairly soon we decided to have a stronger research focus in the journal."

In 1986 Ian MacMillan was recruited by Wharton School of Business at the University of Pennsylvania in Philadelphia. The condition on the part of MacMillan was not only to pursue education but also to build a research environment focusing on entrepreneurship – and MacMillan became Director of the Snider Entrepreneurial Center at Wharton. He began to recruit people to the center, and by the late 1980s he had built a powerful research group consisting of young talented researchers such as Sankaran Venkataraman, Scott Shane and Rita McGrath. At the same time the Center became a hotbed for a number of visiting young scholars from all over the world, who spent some time at the Center or wrote their theses at the Center.

"This was one of the most interesting and productive periods in my career ... all these young researchers really learned how to do entrepreneurship research ... and I learned a lot from them. The combination of the theoretical and intellectual capacity of Venkataraman, Shane and McGrath and my own more practical insights made our Center attractive to young talented PhD students from all over the world ... together with the fact that is was the right time for entrepreneurship research."

Ian MacMillan's international interest resulted in the creation of the Global Entrepreneurship Conference initiated together with Sue Birley at Imperial College in London in 1990.

"Sue Birley and I have known each other for years, and at a conference we got into a discussion about the different research styles in Europe and in the US. We decided to try to bring young people from all over the world together and let them share each other's research. The basic idea was to develop an understanding that there are different ways of doing research. At the Global Conference we asked professors from different countries to bring a doctoral student along to the conference. Today, there is a large network of scholars all over the world that have participated in the conferences ... all understand each other's perspective, maybe they don't agree with it, but they understand it."

Since the mid 1990s Ian MacMillan's research has developed into the area of corporate entrepreneurship, in which he has worked closely with Rita McGrath, one of the former key researchers at the Snider Entrepreneurial Center at Wharton but now at Columbia University Graduate School of Business in New York. One of the explicit results of this collaboration is the book *The Entrepreneurial Mindset,* which they wrote together and which was published in year 2000.

"One of the biggest problems that corporations face today is their ability to continuously innovate and adapt to environmental changes ... as competition and the turbulence of the environment increase, the traditional concept of strategy becomes obsolete, and it has become much more essential to involve the whole work force in the process. Corporate entrepreneurship is no longer only a question for company managers. In order to mobilize the work force you need tools, and these tools must be simple ... because simplicity is power ... and the aim of the book is to provide such a set of tools.

I felt for some time that there is a need for strongly theoretically-based work that at the same time provides guidelines for practice. In *The Entrepreneurial Mindset* we drew on a lot of the work that has been done within the resource based view of the firm ... if you try to be innovative and adaptive in your organization you need to make use of your basic skills and capabilities. But the book also draws heavily on Rita McGrath's theoretical strengths and the real option reasonings."

It is hard to present a comprehensive picture of Ian MacMillan's extensive research production but an attempt at presenting the most central parts is made in the following section. However, a central theme of his research is that it should be relevant to society as well as to companies. Throughout his research career, he has focussed strongly on the management perspective and the need for "actionable" research, i.e. the findings should provide the basis for some kind of achievement in reality.

2. STREAM OF INTEREST IN IAN MACMILLAN'S RESEARCH

Ian MacMillan has an extensive research production within a variety of entrepreneurship topics. It should be noted that his most well-cited work is within the area of strategic management, which will not be treated in this book. An adjacent research area is corporate entrepreneurship, in which MacMillan incorporates the fields of strategic management and entrepreneurship. This research will be presented in section 2.1. Other areas of entrepreneurship research that will be presented in this section are MacMillan's research on cross-cultural entrepreneurship (section 2.2.) and venture capital (section 2.3.).

2.1 Corporate Entrepreneurship

2.1.1 A Corporate Entrepreneurship Framework

Corporate entrepreneurship involves studies of the creation of new business within existing firms and can be defined as "the process by which members of an existing firm bring into existence products and markets which do not currently exist within the repertoire of the firm" (Venkataraman et al., 1992, p. 488). MacMillan takes a managerial standpoint in his corporate entrepreneurship research, which he believes distinguishes the study of corporate entrepreneurship from the study of other forms of entrepreneurship.

Corporate entrepreneurship is a complex phenomenon, involving numerous actions and decisions. In order to review the research on corporate entrepreneurship, MacMillan and his colleagues (Venkataraman et al., 1992) developed a framework based on the evolutionary process of new business. In corporate entrepreneurship, managers face three distinct challenges: (i) the challenge of business founding, which deals with the issue of creating and developing the competencies and infrastructure required to develop, manufacture and market the product, (ii) the challenge of managing the hierarchical process, i.e. to foster new venture initiatives within the firm, for example, gaining political support and acquiring the necessary resources, and (iii) the challenge of managing the institutional context within which founding and fostering take place, which includes a repertoire of organizational strategies such as incentives, infrastructural support, etc.

The three challenges are continually changing, since business creation is an evolutionary process, consisting of four stages: definition, penetration, contagion, and institutionalization. The framework developed by MacMillan and his colleagues is shown in Figure 11-1.

Process	Definition: clarifying the position of a new idea – attempts to define product/ market and the fit between new business and the company	Penetration: taking the idea to reality – attempts to force market entry, break down barriers, and develop an infrastructure for start-up	Contagion: coping with growth – attempts to cope with escalating resource require- ments and increasing trans- actions due to growth	Institutionalization: integrating the new initiative with the mainstream activities of the firm – attempts to legitimize and socialize
Founding processes	Ideating	Forcing	Roller-coasting	Revitalizing
Fostering processes	Championing ideas	Championing opportunistic behavior – against the firm's routines	Championing resources – to en- sure that suffi- cient resources are released	Championing incorporation – to "fit" the norms and routines of the rest of the organization
Managing processes	Production of variants – to ensure a contin- uous flow of new opportunities	Managing selection: pathclearing – external selection	Managing selection: autonomy and control – internal selection	Managing retention: legitimizing

Figure 11-1. Framework for a review of studies in corporate entrepreneurship (source: modified from Venkataraman & MacMillan & McGrath, 1992, p. 491).

As indicated in Figure 11-1, corporate entrepreneurship includes the processes involved in fostering new ventures (including culture, corporate support and venture efforts to stimulate corporate entrepreneurship) as well as the processes related to managing new ventures (e.g. planning and monitoring, strategy formulation, etc.). In MacMillan's extensive research production on corporate entrepreneur- ship we can find significant contributions in both areas.

2.1.2   Fostering Processes

Competitive advantage is of limited duration. The pursuit of new advantages is therefore a critical strategic responsibility, and the main mechanism through which firms develop competitive advantage is through the pursuit of new initiatives – thus, it is important for general managers to foster corporate entrepreneurship. However, this is not always an easy task – there may be many obstacles to corporate entrepreneurship, especially in the corporate start-up situation. Based on a multistage Delphi study, MacMillan, Block and SubbaNarasimha (1984) found that corporate start-ups encountered more obstacles compared to alternative modes of venturing, such as joint ventures and acquisition. The major problems with start-ups appear to be: (a) imperfect market analysis, (b) impatience for results at corporate level, (c) refusal by corporate managers to acknowledge the venture's weaknesses, (d) underestimation of competitors, and (e) underestimation of the risks inherent in the venture. It is also interesting to note that experience seems to lead to significant benefits, i.e. companies that have attempted several ventures show a substantial improvement in effectiveness. Moreover, there seem to be distinct areas of learning, for example, firms appear to be capable of learning from experience in terms of reading the market and becoming more realistic in their expectations regarding the venture. On the other hand, it seems to be more difficult to learn from past inadequacies in planning and to provide adequate support for the venture. A key problem for general managers seems to be the development of new sources of advantage to replace those that are no longer able to yield rents to the firm.

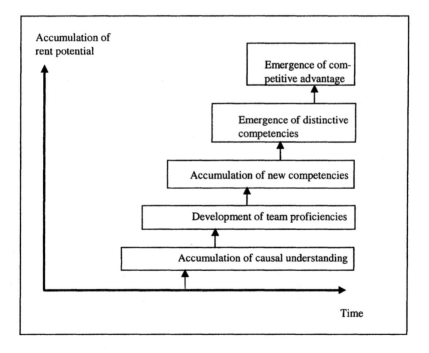

Figure 11-2. Advantage chain for rents from new ventures (source: modified from McGrath & Venkataraman & MacMillan, 1994, p. 363).

McGrath, Venkataraman and MacMillan (1994) developed the "advantage chain" model, grounded on resource-based reasoning, which explores the conditions for gaining insights about, and access to, firm-specific resources with a potential for future economic outcomes (rent). They identified five antecedent conditions, which are sequential and cumulative (see Figure 11-2.): causal understanding, team proficiency, new competencies, distinctive competencies, and competitive advantage.

Firstly, there must be a causal understanding among the venture team members regarding the drivers of the venture's performance, i.e. the team must grasp the relationship between antecedents and consequences of concern to the venture. By definition, this is no easy task in the early stages of a new venture – decisions must be made under conditions of uncertainty (absence of information) as well as ambiguity (lack of clarity about the meaning of data). But as causal understanding develops, the team develops insights into the future, from which new ways of combining resources may emerge. Secondly, causal understanding is not enough – new ideas must be translated into action, and this is the responsibility of the venture team. The venture team creates durable sources of uniqueness by establishing new "bundles" of assets. As the causal understanding improves and team proficiency increases, the firm becomes capable of meeting new objectives in a reliable and predictable manner. It is likely that the resource allocation that led to this outcome will be repeated, i.e. the venture team "learns" what patterns of resource deployment will lead to desired outcomes, and the organization begins to exploit competencies created by the new venture – mobilization of new competencies is the third necessary antecedent for a venture to yield rent. However, the emergence of new competencies does not automatically confer advantages on a firm in competitive markets. A fourth antecedent is therefore that the firm must have some firm-specific competencies that give it distinctiveness in comparison with competitors, i.e. firm-specific competencies that competitors cannot easily match or imitate. Finally, in order to yield rents for the firm, the offerings of the venture must be different from those of competing firms, but they must also be the choice of sufficiently large populations of customers in order to generate adequate revenues. In summary, "new competencies" is determined in relation to the firm's past experience and "distinctive competencies" in relation to competition. The fifth antecedent "competitive advantage" relates to superior product attributes in the eyes of customers. As can be seen from Figure 11-2, the five antecedents are sequential and accumulative in order to create a competitive advantage that will generate rent from the corporate venture.

MacMillan and his colleagues developed this reasoning further and, in McGrath, MacMillan and Venkataraman (1995), they emphasize the role of the venture team in defining and developing competencies necessary to create a competitive advantage. MacMillan et al. argued that competitive advantages cannot emerge unless the venture team can develop competence in what they are doing. Of course, many factors may underlie the success of developing competence, but two processes seem to be important at venture team level if such convergence should occur: "comprehension", i.e. the process of understanding what combinations of resources are necessary to achieve fixed objectives, and "deftness", i.e. the process involved in creating working relations that allow the venture team to perform effectively. Comprehension and deftness are necessary but complex requirements (due to the uncertainty and ambiguous character of the new venture) for the emergence of competencies, and it could be proposed that the degree of competence developed, measured by the ability to achieve objectives, will be positively associated with the venture team's level of comprehension and deftness. This proposition was tested on data from a convenience sample of 160 ongoing projects in 40 different corporations in 16 countries. The results offered only moderate support for a correlation between comprehension and emerging competence. However, strong support was found for a correlation between deftness and the ability of the venture team to become competent, which indicates that deftness is fundamentally important for the development of competence – it is difficult to become competent as a group if the group processes are clumsy or awkward. It may be that the processes that create deftness are to some degree dependent on the degree to which comprehension emerges – comprehension may be a necessary antecedent to deftness, but deftness has a greater influence upon competence.

To further elaborate on the relationships between team comprehension, team deftness, and team performance, Nerkar, McGrath and MacMillan (1996; see also Nerkar et al., 1997) argued that job satisfaction could constitute a mediating variable in explaining the performance of venture teams. A distinction was made between "instrumental satisfaction", which has to do with the way the task is progressing, "social satisfaction", i.e. the way the team members interact with each other, and "egocentric satisfaction" indicating the individuals' perceived personal benefits. The same empirical data as used in the above analysis have shown that the effects of deftness and comprehension on performance appear to be mediated differentially and by different aspects of job satisfaction. Social satisfaction seems to be critical to the innovation process as well as a key mediator between deftness and venture performance, whereas instrumental dissatisfaction appears to obstruct the ability of the venture team to deploy its comprehension to achieve progress in the project. In this situation there is a real need for a methodology that allows the team to discover the underlying reasons why progress is not being made (see for example the reasoning about milestone planning and discovery-driven planning below). Surprisingly, the results show that egocentric satisfaction seems to have no mediating effect between deftness and performance – it may be that participants are willing to accept fewer short-term benefits in anticipation of future prestige and/or rewards.

2.1.3   Managing Processes

Much has been written on how to foster new ventures as well as creating an entrepreneurial climate in corporations. The main focus of interest in Ian MacMillan's research is, however, on the processes of managing new ventures. MacMillan has focused upon several topics, for example, market entry strategies for new corporate ventures, management planning in turbulent situations, and the resource acquisition problems, which new venture managers have to overcome.

Market entry strategies. In MacMillan and Day (1987) it was shown that, in many cases, firms base their strategies on the assumption that a high market share will be quickly achieved and that the performance (measured as both market share and ROI) will be superior compared to those firms that enter with less aggressive share aspirations. As a consequence, large corporations that have the necessary resources and that can afford the cost of failure as well as make significant front-end investments in marketing and production will have significant advantages. The study was based on the so-called PIMS (Profit Impact of Market Strategies) start-up database. This database included 161 corporate ventures that marketed a service or product that the parent company had not previously marketed, and the ventures were mainly divisions or profit centers within larger corporations. Success in obtaining market shares seems to be strongly associated with market entry early in the product life cycle as well as with avoiding fragmented markets and markets upon which the largest competitor is highly dependent. It is interesting to note that it may be less desirable to enter high growth markets due to the fact that many others may be trying to enter the market simultaneously. On the other hand, entering markets that are dominated by a small number of well-entrenched firms may be advantageous because this enables the new entrants to position themselves clearly.

What lessons can be drawn from launching a new product or a new venture from an existing corporate base? This question was discussed in Block and MacMillan (1994), especially in relation to strategic aggressiveness to enter the market (power and degree of effort and amount of resources committed) and the focus of the entry efforts (extent to which the efforts are sharply focused or broader in nature). Management often face some real dilemmas as to whether to be aggressive and/or focussed in their entry strategy, because different combinations of aggressiveness and focus have their particular advantages and disadvantages. However, by looking at the characteristics of the market environment in terms of "munificence", i.e.

degree of richness or sparseness of the niche being entered, and "hostility", i.e. the fierceness of competition that the firm encounters when entering the market (see also Tsai et al., 1991), the managers could obtain some clues as to what might be the most appropriate entry strategy. Based on aggressiveness and market entry focus, four strategies can be identified:

The Blitzkrieg – a highly aggressive and broad-fronted strategy, using all forces over wide ranging geographic and market segments. This strategy requires rapid market penetration and would probably not be appropriate in situations where the market is not munificent.

The Cavalry Charge – a highly aggressive but focussed strategy concentrated on a market segment and/or limited geographic area. This strategy requires a market that is munificent but not so hostile that deferred market segments are swallowed up by the competition.

The Strike Force Approach – is a non-aggressive and focussed strategy. It uses relatively small resources and demands less commitment from the firm. It is a strategy that might be appropriate for a hostile and sparse market. The venture can quietly enter the market, laying the groundwork for further expansion, without alarming competitors.

Guerrilla Tactics – a non-aggressive mode of entry but a wide scope used for striking where they can be most effective in establishing a market position. A guerrilla tactic may be appropriate in a market that is munificent but hostile – the breadth of market will support a broad entry, but the presence of major competitors calls for a less aggressive approach.

Of course, the above market dimensions (hostility and munificence) are important indicators of which market entry strategy should be used, but other dimensions may play a crucial moderating role in the final determination of entry strategy. For example, salience to the venture firm and fit to existing business will affect the extent to which the entry will be supported as well as the corporation's interest in committing resources to the new venture. Other dimensions that affect the decision may be resource availability, corporate culture, etc. It is recommended that managers should first identify an ideal strategy based on market hostility and munificence. Then methods should be sought for putting it into practise, not forgetting the other factors that must be considered, as well as choosing a strategy that makes the risks acceptable and for which the necessary know-how is available.

Management planning. New ventures take place in conditions where information is either missing or difficult to interpret, i.e. decisions and actions must be pursued in the face of uncertainty and ambiguity. In such situations traditional planning of the ventures seems to be inappropriate. Rather than trying to force new ventures into a traditional planning methodology developed for existing, well-understood businesses, a different approach to new venture planning based on a milestone-triggered process might be appropriate. After establishing objectives for the venture, significant milestones required to reach each objective are defined, and planning will focus on getting from milestone to milestone. In this way venture managers, senior corporate managers and investors can learn in an evolutionary way. This milestone planning is further explained in Block and MacMillan (1985), in which they identify ten typical milestones that new ventures have to pass:

Milestone 1: Completion of concept and product testing
Milestone 2: Completion of prototype
Milestone 3: First financing
Milestone 4: Completion of initial plant test
Milestone 5: Market testing
Milestone 6: Production start-up
Milestone 7: Bellweather sale
Milestone 8: First competitive action
Milestone 9: First redesign or redirection
Milestone 10: First significant price change

These thoughts regarding "milestone planning" were further developed together with Rita McGrath in what they called "discovery-driven planning" (McGrath & MacMillan, 1995), which converts unclear assumptions into knowledge as the venture develops. That is, when new data are uncovered, they are incorporated into the evolving plan (see reasoning above about "the advantage chain"). Discovery-driven planning offers a systematic method for uncovering uncertain assumptions that might otherwise pass unnoticed. The process is captured in four related documents:

1. A reverse income statement, which models the basic economics of the business. It starts with the bottom line – "required profits" – and works its way up to determine how much revenue it will take to deliver the required level of profit.
2. Pro forma operation specifications, which set out the operations needed to run the business – these activities comprise the venture's allowable costs.
3. A key assumptions checklist, which will ensure that assumptions are discussed and checked.
4. A milestone planning chart, which specifies the assumptions to be tested at each project milestone.

When new data are uncovered, each of the documents is updated. It is a question of successively transforming uncertain assumptions into knowledge.

Resource acquisition in new ventures. A new venture is by definition uncertain, and there are many types of start-up problems in the corporate context that new venture managers have to overcome. These problems can be summarized as (i) venture managers have to overcome problems of legitimacy – both inside and outside the firm, (ii) the ventures are often desperately short of resources – they must compete internally against powerful established departments, and (iii) venture managers frequently find themselves facing organizational resistance and inertia. How can new venture managers handle this situation?

According to Starr and MacMillan (1990; see also Starr & MacMillan, 1991), new venture managers must attempt what is termed "asset parsimony", i.e. deploying the minimum amount of assets needed at minimum cost. As a result, corporate entrepreneurs seem to employ a high level of cooperative strategies, primarily by utilizing social transactions – rather than economic exchanges – to secure the instrumental results they seek. The entrepreneurs have a tendency to steal personal time, conceal development activities, curry favor, etc. to secure the resources needed for the development of the new venture. In this respect, Starr and MacMillan differentiate between two types of venture managers:

– Administrative venture managers – who favor economic exchanges at full fare.
– Social transaction-oriented managers – who favor social exchanges that capture resources at reduced fare.

In order to gain access to necessary resources that otherwise have to be secured by economic exchange at much greater cost, the social transaction-oriented managers will use "cooptation" by employing four different strategies: borrowing, begging, scavenging and amplifying (the capacity to leverage more value out of an asset than was perceived by the original owner of the asset). This kind of resource cooptation is closely linked to social transactions, whereby the venture managers exploit certain "social assets" in their possession, i.e. a set of obligations, expectations and mutually developed norms and sanctions, which evolved from social interactions. Furthermore, the venture managers build a "social contract" in which he/she "cashes in" on the expectations, norms and governance structures that have been built from past relationships. The social assets used by the social transaction-oriented managers can be described along a spectrum related to the formality of the recognition of a social "debt" by both parties and the cost of "maintaining" the asset. At one extreme, we find "friendship", i.e. a social asset that can be used over and over again without exhausting the relationship or leading to a sense of indebtedness. "Liking" and "gratitude" are less intense than friendship, whereas "trust" can be regarded as a neutral point in terms of the granting of favors. However, these favors are more formally recognized and must be returned some day. At the other extreme we find "obligations" in which there is a mutually clear perceived understanding that a debt is being incurred and that a return of the favor is required to release the debtor from his/her obligation. When social transaction-oriented managers develop a new venture, it can be assumed that they will build and make more use of social assets to procure resources than administrative managers. The latter spend more time on detailed budgeting and à priori estimates of specific resource needs, monitoring for resource utilization, etc.

However, to pursue a more social transaction-oriented strategy is not an easy task. Corporate venture managers may have more difficulties in using resource cooptation compared to independent entrepreneurs due to corporate constraints. For example, established organizations do not have a mindset characterized by asset parsimony (these organizations are often too slow, overplan and are overstaffed, which can be hazardous to fragile new ventures), management techniques for established businesses are inappropriately enforced on new ventures, corporate entrepreneurs are not allowed to bend and break rules, and they do not have the time to develop social assets and build networks.

2.2   Cross-cultural Entrepreneurship

For many years, countries have been exploring and developing policies and programs aimed at stimulating entrepreneurship. The starting point of these programs has in most cases been knowledge about the motivation of the individual to become an entrepreneur, often developed in an American context. The main question is therefore: Are these results valid and relevant outside the US? But there are also other questions of interest, such as: Is there some basic set of beliefs that entrepreneurs hold about themselves and others that transcend cultures? Are entrepreneurs different from other people? Are there any underlying patterns of beliefs among entrepreneurs that differentiate them from others despite cultural diversity?

In an extensive international study, Ian MacMillan, together with Sari Scheinberg and Rita McGrath, among others, tried to find evidence for the argument that entrepreneurs show significant differences in values compared to others in society and that these differences transcend different cultures, i.e. that some general entrepreneurial values are core values, which could be the seeds of entrepreneurial behavior.

Earlier studies in entrepreneurship (see chapter 3) have attempted to isolate those aspects that differentiate entrepreneurs from what is not entrepreneurial in terms of variables such as need for achievement, internal locus of control, propensity for risk-taking, etc. MacMillan's approach is to put the entrepreneur in the context of society in general. In this respect MacMillan and his colleagues utilized Hofstede's (1980) four cultural dimensions; "power distance" which concerns the inequality within society, "individualism" indicating the relationship between individuals and collectives, "uncertainty avoidance", i.e. the stance toward the future, and "masculinity", which concerns the allocation of roles between the sexes. Furthermore, MacMillan put forward the idea that, in many societies, entrepreneurship is regarded as a deviation from usual behavior and entrepreneurs who object to the perception of being different act as deviants. The implication of this would be that entrepreneurs as a group, regardless of culture, tend to view others in society as an "out-group" of sorts.

The results are based on a large survey of entrepreneurs carried out in 13 countries (Australia, Canada, China, Denmark, England, Finland, Italy, Kenya, Norway, Portugal, Sweden, Taiwan, and the US) in 1987. The inclusion criteria for entrepreneurs were as follows: (i) to have founded their own business (in partnership or alone) between 1979 and 1986, (ii) having at least one other person working for them, and (iii) the business was their primary means of livelihood. The selection processes of entrepreneurs differed somewhat from country to country, as did data collection methods and response rates (from 64% in Finland to 3% in the UK). The database contains over 3,000 responses.

A number of publications have been based on different parts of the study, and some of the main results can be summarized as follows:

- The results agree with US stereotypes. The US scored higher than any other country for the factor "need for independence", while their interest in "communitarianism" was lower than that of the other countries (Scheinberg & MacMillan, 1988).
- The Scandinavian countries (Sweden, Denmark and Norway) differed from other countries in that they placed less emphasis on financial aspects as a means of achieving their objectives as well as little interest in investing in their community (maybe as a result of the high tax rates in these countries). Another group of countries includes Portugal, China, Puerto Rico and Italy, which favored "communitarianism" (which may be explained by their similar level of economic development and the inherent cultural orientation that values the family. Finally, a group consisting of some Anglo-Saxon countries (Australia, England, the US) and Finland seems to have a stronger tendency to see money as a means to achieving their objectives but at the same time have stronger interest in investing in their communities or supporting their relatives (Scheinberg & MacMillan, 1988).
- In order to discover which aspects of culture are enduring and which are changeable, an analysis was made comparing China, Taiwan and the US. China and Taiwan share an ancient cultural heritage (in which individuals are unimportant and people are expected to conform to well-defined roles and are bound by the obligations inherent in those roles, etc.), which is fundamentally different from the Western cultural heritage of the US. However, for the past 50 years, Taiwan has embraced a radically different western style capitalistic ideology, whereas China has pursued a communist ideology. One would assume that if culture predominates and endures, the Chinese and the US entrepreneurs would show different patterns of response, while the Taiwanese response patterns would be similar to those of the Chinese entrepreneurs. But if culture can be eroded by ideological forces and is thus relatively changeable, the US

and Taiwanese entrepreneurs should show similar response patterns. It was found that, despite 50 years of ideological pressure, there has been little shift in the basic collectivistic values and in attitudes to work in the two groups of Chinese entrepreneurs (China and Taiwan), whereas some of the Taiwanese entrepreneurs' values have changed – they have accepted a higher power distance and moved toward a recognition and acknowledgement of the risks associated with starting a business to a larger extent than their Chinese counterparts (McGrath & MacMillan & Yang & Tsai, 1992).

- Based on an analysis of three widely differing cultural regions; Anglo-Saxon (Australia, England and the US), Chinese (China and Taiwan), and Nordic (Denmark, Finland, Norway and Sweden), it was found that there seems to be a couple of common "beliefs" among entrepreneurs, irrespective of culture. For example, entrepreneurs believe that there is a link between social benefits, freedom and individual effort and that others in society are unwilling to take charge of their own destiny, unwilling to work hard to earn social rewards as well as less likely to enjoy what they are doing (McGrath & MacMillan, 1992).

- In an analysis contrasting the beliefs of entrepreneurs (business founders) and career professionals (school teachers, bank branch managers, and government employees), it was found that entrepreneurship was, not surprisingly, associated with higher individualism (in favor of individual rather than collective action). Entrepreneurs seem to exhibit higher power distance, reflecting an acceptance of inequality, a lower level of uncertainty avoidance – which indicates that they are prepared to take risks – and more pronounced masculinity, in which success is associated with recognition and wealth (McGrath & MacMillan & Scheinberg, 1992).

- The US entrepreneurial culture is based on values such as independent actions, taking personal risks and self-reliance. Based on the findings of MacMillan and his colleagues, programs funded to foster entrepreneurship in collectivistic cultures may run a serious risk of failure – it is difficult to infuse individualistic values into a collectivistic culture.

The conclusions are that the entrepreneurial culture differs between countries, which difference may explain the fact that business formation rates vary from society to society and that different cultures have different entrepreneurial beliefs. But some underlying patterns of belief seem to exist among entrepreneurs, despite cultural differences, and these can be regarded as core entrepreneurial values.

2.3   Venture Capitalists' Evaluation of New Venture Proposals

Venture capital seems to be an important source of capital and knowledge in the establishment of new businesses, and many dynamic regions are characterized by an ample flow of venture capital. In several of his early studies, Ian MacMillan focussed on the activities of the venture capitalist. One of the research questions he attempted to answer was: What criteria do venture capitalists use when evaluating venture proposals? In a study together with Siegel and SubbaNarasimha, Ian MacMillan elaborated on this question (MacMillan & Siegel & SubbaNarasimha, 1985a; 1985b). They identified 27 different evaluation criteria on the basis of 14 interviews with venture capitalists. These criteria were used in a questionnaire distributed to 150 venture capitalists, where the response rate was 68%. The results of the study confirm the position taken by many experienced venture capitalists, which is that the quality of the entrepreneur – his or her experience and personality – determines whether or not they will invest. If the entrepreneur is so essential, why then is so much emphasis placed on the business plan?

The business plan seems to be a key factor in determining whether or not entrepreneurs will obtain funding from a venture capitalist, although the business plan normally says very little about the entrepreneur – it is generally devoted to detailed descriptions of the product/service, the market, and the competition. MacMillan and SubbaNarasimha (1986) analysed 55 unfunded and 27 funded business plans and concluded that there is a "credibility window" of values that venture capitalists find acceptable. Excessively optimistic performance forecasts can create credibility problems – showing evidence of business naïveté on the part of the proposers. On the other hand, business plans predicting performance below the lower threshold of this window are obviously not worth the risk to the venture capitalist. In addition, the business plan needs to show a balance between key functions (marketing, finance, management, etc.). Business plans where any one function had either too much or too little influence tended to remain unfunded. MacMillan and his colleagues argued that, while the business plan is necessary, it is not the sole reason why venture capitalists decide to invest. However, the business plan must show that the entrepreneur will fit the business, which indicates that the entrepreneur has staying power, a track record, can react well to risk, and is familiar with the target market.

Furthermore, MacMillan, Siegel and SubbaNarasimha (1985a; 1985b) indicated that venture capitalists systematically evaluate ventures in terms of six risk categories: (i) competitive risk (little threat of competition and an existing clearly competitively insulated market, (ii) risk of being unable to bail out if necessary, (iii) risk of losing the entire investment (whether or not the venture is run by a meticulous entrepreneur with a sound track record, etc.), (iv) risk of management failure (whether the entrepreneur is capable of intense sustained effort and knows the market thoroughly), (v) risk of failure to implement the venture idea (whether the entrepreneur has a clear idea of what s/he is doing and whether the product has demonstrated market potential), and (vi) risk of leadership failure (whether the entrepreneur has leadership qualities). Furthermore, three clusters of venture capitalists could be identified from the study. The first cluster representing about 40% of the venture capitalists in the sample can be called "purposeful risk managers", indicating that they tried to ensure that various risks (see above) were well managed. The venture capitalists in this group seek entrepreneurs with demonstrated leadership skills and a product and market with characteristics that clearly reduce risk to manageable levels. The second cluster, termed "determined eclectics", comprised 33% of the venture capitalists and is made up those who showed openness and were prepared to consider any deal. The third cluster – "parachutists" – (about 25% of the venture capitalists in the sample) consisted of venture capitalists willing to support most ventures as long as they felt that they would have an easy way out if things went wrong.

The study by MacMillan, Siegel and SubbaNarasimha (1985), as well as many other similar studies, determined which criteria are used by venture capitalists to evaluate venture proposals. However, these studies do not address the question of whether or not these criteria are actually helpful in distinguishing successful from unsuccessful ventures. Therefore, in a follow-up study, MacMillan, Zemann and SubbaNarasimha (1987) tried to determine the extent to which criteria are useful predictors of performance. The results indicated that it was possible to identify three classes of unsuccessful ventures. In the first cluster (19% of failures) – "well qualified dropouts" – the ventures were characterized by an entrepreneurial team that was highly familiar with the market and had a well-established track-record but was, however, incapable of sustaining intense efforts against their competitors. The second cluster – "arrow-catchers" – (32% of unsuccessful ventures) was characterized by a good entrepreneurial team but that had nevertheless failed to protect the product. Thus, as soon as the entrepreneurs had opened up the market, other companies invaded and occupied it. Finally, the third cluster – "hopeless amateurs" – (almost 50% of the ventures) comprised ventures lacking all desired criteria. They were not capable of sustained effort, had no track record and were not familiar with the market. On the other hand, MacMillan and his colleagues identified four clusters of successful ventures:

Cluster 1 (52% of successes) – "high-tech sure bets" – involves high-tech products and a strong entrepreneurial team.

Cluster 2 (13% of successes) – "distribution players" – involves distinctly low-tech products with well-established distribution channels.

Cluster 3 (18% of successes) – "market makers" – employs articulateness and perseverance to create a market, which can subsequently be defended against competitive attacks.

Cluster 4 (about 25% of successes) – "lucky dilettantes" – has a poor entrepreneurial team and low market acceptance – their only redeeming feature being high product protection.

The results indicate the difficulty that venture capitalists face when evaluating new proposals. Each cluster of unsuccessful ventures has a look-alike cluster among the successful ventures. In each case, the major difference between a winner and a loser seems to be some "difficult-to-define" entrepreneurial team characteristics. Thus, it is not surprising that the evaluation of venture capital proposals can be defined as an "art". As a result, it seems rather difficult to find major criteria that are predictors of venture success.

However, further analysis of the data showed that only two criteria consistently and pervasively predicted performance, namely (1) the extent to which the venture is initially insulated from competition and (2) the degree to which there is demonstrated market acceptance of the product. Interestingly, of all criteria identified in early studies, these two seem to be the most essential, yet neither was rated as essential in the early study (MacMillan & Siegel & SubbaNarasimha, 1985). These two criteria are market related rather than product or entrepreneur related. Why were not criteria related to the entrepreneurial team (capacity for sustained effort, demonstrated leadership, track-record, etc.), which has been emphasized as important by venture capitalists? In this respect, MacMillan et al. make a distinction between necessary and sufficient conditions for success. Venture capitalists will not back ventures with a bad entrepreneurial team. Success and failure have to do with what happens to those ventures that receive funding, i.e. the evaluation of the entrepreneurial team is essential in order to obtain financial backing from venture capitalists, whereas the two criteria – competitive threat and market acceptance of product – are predictors of success for firms already financed by venture capitalists.

One conclusion that can be drawn from the above-mentioned studies is that the entrepreneurial qualities and the entrepreneurial team seem to have a higher impact on venture capitalists' evaluation process than any product and market considerations. In addition, when a venture proposal is presented to a venture capitalist, the product and market can be considered as given – for a specific venture proposal there is little the venture capitalist can do about the product and the market. Thus, the evaluation of the entrepreneur and entrepreneurial team is of paramount importance, and the fundamental issue is whether the characteristics of the entrepreneurial team fit the product and market environment.

In a project in collaboration with Paola Dubini, using the database developed by MacMillan, Zemann and SubbaNarasimha (1987), Ian MacMillan elaborated on the question "Which entrepreneurial team characteristics are useful predictors of performance, given the product and market characteristics of the new venture? (Dubini & MacMillan, 1988). Different groups (clusters) of firms were identified:

Cluster 1: High Powered Followers (21% of the ventures)

This group of ventures entered a well-developed market with established distribution systems and significant competition, but they had high market acceptance in addition to high distribution acceptance. In this group of ventures, the capacity for sustained and intense effort was the entrepreneurial team trait that strongly predicted performance, but also the team's familiarity with the market had a major positive effect.

Cluster 2: High Tech Inventors (42% of the ventures)

These are the "darlings" of the venture capital industry – high-tech firms with strong product protection coupled with new market potential. The entrepreneurial team's ability to manage risk and their capacity to pay attention to detail seem to be pervasive predictors of success for these firms.

Cluster 3: Low Tech Distribution Players (14% of the ventures)

The firms in this group have access to well-developed distributors – otherwise these ventures would be rather unexciting. They are low-tech ventures, with low protection and a high risk of competitive action. In this situation, shrewd, carefully evaluated, yet decisive leadership is essential for success.

Cluster 4: Dream Merchants (20% of the ventures)

This group consists of high-tech firms with high product protection and uncertain long-term profits. For this cluster the strongest predictor of success is the entrepreneurial team's familiarity with the target market, which is not surprising due to the tenuous nature of the project and low market acceptance.

In conclusion, it was shown that different entrepreneurial team characteristics are important for each cluster of firms and they predict the performance of the various clusters, thus supporting the conventional wisdom that some skills are more important than others in different contexts.

3. PERSPECTIVES ON CORPORATE ENTREPRENEURSHIP

What are the developments in the research on corporate entrepreneurship and entrepreneurship research in general? What can be learnt from Ian MacMillan's research? These and other questions related to the research field will be discussed in the following interview with Ian MacMillan.

If we focus on your research on corporate entrepreneurship, what was your most interesting insight?

When looking at companies attempting corporate entrepreneurship, I think that we have come to realise that their processes are very different and in many cases in conflict with the conventional processes of an ongoing business ... and companies just don't seem to be able to cope with the management of corporate entrepreneurship.

Rita McGrath and I are working on the use of option reasoning in relation to corporate entrepreneurship. The problem that we keep coming up against is people who start options but never closed them down, and an intriguing question is: "How do you reward someone who attempts to do something, but doesn't succeed?" If you don't reward them, how would you get the next round of people to even think of trying? But it is not only the reward process that needs to be changed – also the selection processes and the planning processes have to be fundamentally different in corporate entrepreneurship. In this respect we talk about the "pruning problem". We have deliberately used the term "pruning" because you prune trees to obtain a better harvest of fruits ... so you have to cut away. In an organization it is very difficult once they have started something to "cut" something away – products will continue. It is a tough decision to cut something away, especially in cases where things are going well but not well enough, what the venture capitalists call "living dead". To me one of the big challenges that we are going to encounter in corporate entrepreneurship is how organizations get to grips with this problem of pruning.

What are the main achievements that have been made in the area of corporate entrepreneurship over the last two decades?

I find that the number of researchers within the field is fairly small but there are a couple of researchers that have made major contributions. I think if we look at the work that has been done in the innovation field, which overlaps corporate entrepreneurship, there is plenty of good work, and I will mention a few of the researchers:

I like the work of Clayton Christensen and his book *The Innovator's Dilemma* and the most recent one *The Innovator's Solution*. The thing that struck me when reading his case study on Hewlett Packard was that there is a huge opportunity cost in taking a group of very talented people and putting them on a project. In this case a project that appeared at all times as if success was just around the corner, and they kept saying: "Just a few more months ...", and finally they shut down the project ... a tough decision. Christensen has described this case with a great deal of insight.

I must also mention Rita McGrath with whom I have worked a lot. Her ideas about real option reasoning are really fruitful in the corporate entrepreneurship context. She is now looking at the concept of interactivity among options ... I can take out an option here and another there, but there is also a possibility that these options interact with one another. The way that she phrases it is that options can "hunt in packs" ... when you start to take out multiple options and if they are somewhat related to one another, you can find that opportunities grow geometrically ... nobody really looked at that ... and the real option reasoning will be a major direction for corporate entrepreneurship research in the future.

Another scholar with a lot of insight is William Baumol. In his book *The Free-Market Innovation Machine,* he basically argues that the major reason why we have seen such an enormous growth in the advanced economies of the world is not so much entrepreneurship as the partnering of the entrepreneurial process with big companies and that one of the most fundamental mechanisms that makes this possible is the rule of law. If you do not have a law that protects the person who develops a new technology or innovation from having their invention taken away from them, there is no incentive to invest in research and development. Baumol states that this is absolutely critical because, as the pace of technology increases, people are increasingly reluctant to invest in new technology if they feel that they are unable to reap some of the benefits of the rent deriving from it. You need a legal structure that allows big firms to license from small firms ... it is this kind of teamwork between small firms and big firms that creates growth. Small firms are no doubt better innovators than big firms but they need to have the innovation disseminated ... and to share the jackpot. This book is brilliant and full of insight. Baumol got his hands on something that nobody really thought about ... and I found it hard to disagree with him.

What will the future areas of corporate entrepreneurship research look like? What will the next phase of research be?

We need to have more research focusing on important, relevant questions. I am working on several big ideas, all of which have a low probability of success, but if they succeed they will have a profound impact. One area is to develop a methodology that allows companies that get a patent to identify applications for that patent far quicker than they ever did before ... and the reverse of that problem, that is to find a solution to a problem that I have today, where the solution might be somewhere else. The problem was originally raised in a chapter that I wrote in the book *Wharton on Technology* a couple of years ago. Someone pointed out to me in one of my executive education courses that it took his company 15 years to find an application for one of their patents, and we looked at all patents that were issued every year and how few of them were actually commercialized ... we realized that there is a need to find a methodology that can make this process easier.

A second area is the work that I have done in collaboration with Rita McGrath, where we have been intrigued by the question: "How do you create an organization that is continuously innovative?" "What are the systems and processes necessary for that kind of work?" In this respect we have focussed our attention on what we call "market busting" – firms that make moves that basically transform the market. We believe that what is really missing is a deep understanding of how you go about looking at a market and systematically thinking about how you change the rules of the game in that market space. And if you could find a possible mechanism for transforming your market, how do you implement it? I think a lot would have been gained by more work in these areas.

The third area is that I think we can use entrepreneurship as a weapon to solve social problems. So, I am now looking at social wealth creating entrepreneurship, and the question is: "Can we find new emerging methodologies and techniques that entrepreneurs can deploy to tackle social wealth problems?" The methodology that I have used is called "fuzzy logic regression" to derive hypotheses about causal effects in very complex environments ... you specify a number of outputs and inputs, a number of possible links between inputs and outputs are identified in the regression, and these links are formulated into hypotheses. The system learns by testing these hypotheses and becomes increasingly confident in the results. We have commenced a number of experiments to solve different social problems, from medical treatment problems to techniques for accessing retired people and using their experience without employing them.

A fourth area where I think we can do a lot more research is the use of simulation models. You can use simulations to let a lot of things happen without having to wait for them to occur in reality. For example, we can run a simulation to analyze why some countries are more entrepreneurial than others ... it has to do with things like to what extent entrepreneurship is rewarded, to what extent society protects the ideas, etc. ... and we can look at the impact of different governmental policies ... we don't need to wait for the government to do it. In general, I think we have failed to make sufficient use of simulation techniques in corporate entrepreneurship and entrepreneurship research in general.

You have been very prolific and successful in your research, both individually and in collaboration with others. But I suppose not everything has been successful. What have been the major learning experiences over the years?

Looking back, I think more attention should have been devoted to the underlying theoretical structure. I tend to be a lot more driven by the phenomenon than by the theory. We could have done a lot more on theory ... although I have been pushed to do more and more of that with the people with whom I have been working, and I think we can see more and more theoretical work in entrepreneurship research in general.

In our cross-cultural study of entrepreneurship in different countries we made a couple of major mistakes, and learned a couple of lessons. First, we went out and collected a huge amount of data on what motivated entrepreneurs in different countries, but we did not have any dependent variable. When we analysed the data I said to myself: "If we had only been able to capture something about performance". The lesson is: you need to have clearly defined dependent variables, and you need to have "actionable" independent variables ... that you can do something about it ... the most powerful research has that quality. Secondly, without a dependent variable, the results can easily become trivial. So, all doctoral students that I work with today must go through my "six-people-test": If you are going to do research you need to do something that couldn't be solved by six smart people in a two-hour discussion. If they come to the same conclusion as you do from research, then why do the research? Why not talk to six smart people? Research must go beyond what is self-evident.

What would your advice be to a young doctoral student interested in corporate entrepreneurship?

This is perhaps one of the most difficult questions to answer. I have spent many years trying to tell my doctoral students to think in terms of relevance ... to think in terms of the impact of their research. It must be of relevance and importance to society. Therefore, it is really important for us to better understand the social wealth creation process, and I think a lot of that will come from corporate entrepreneurship. It is the wide adaptation of innovations in society, a process in which the large corporations will play a major role, which really makes the big difference for wealth creation.

The problem is that corporate entrepreneurship research needs to be interactable, and it is seldom possible to obtain large samples and numbers that can be analysed statistically, which means that you will have problems getting published. So, I find it difficult to advise young researchers, who have a strong urge to be published, to go out and try to perform relevant research in corporate entrepreneurship. When you have tenure, you can start doing relevant work within the field. I can afford to have my papers rejected ... but it is difficult to encourage young researchers to go out and do it, with little chance of getting published, because journals are more interested in statistical robust results than in relevance.

This is also a signal to young European researchers. Europeans seem to go too far in adopting the American research model – including a lot of empirical work, large samples, and advanced statistical analysis. I'm seeing the downside ... there is a small number of people who can do excellent methodological studies and still do relevant work. The difficulty is that if you have to make a trade off between generalizability, replicability and relevance, there is a tendency to take the easy way ... to replicate existing work with a few minor variations, but nothing really novel or exciting comes out of it ... it is methodologically excellent but it tells us nothing new. Europeans shouldn't do that.

What will the future look like for entrepreneurship research?

The kind of questions that people are asking in the entrepreneurship field in general are not very exciting, and I would not like to see another study on gender differences in entrepreneurship, another study on the lending practices of banks toward minority entrepreneurs – that has all been done. We need to start asking important questions ... powerful questions ... questions that have an impact on society and social wealth creation. In corporate entrepreneurship for example, questions like how do you value real options, how do you infuse real option thinking, how do we shut down things gracefully, so that when something is shut down, the people will still feel proud that they tried and not ashamed that they failed. If you don't change the way organizations think about these things we will never achieve innovative organizations and wealth creation in society. In entrepreneurship in general, we must get away from "nose counting" and get down to what is meaningful. For example, I don't care about mom and pop shops ... they will always be there ... let us pay attention to the ones that have an impact ... such as the Bill Gates of this world ... entrepreneurs that have a major impact.

REFERENCES

State-of-the-art articles

Low, M.B. & MacMillan, I.C., 1988, Entrepreneurship: Past Research and Future Challenges, *Journal of Management*, 14, 2, 139-161.

MacMillan, I.C. 1986, Progress in research on corporate venturing, in Sexton, D.L. & Smilor, R.W. (eds.), *The art and science of entrepreneurship*, Cambridge, MA: Ballinger, 241-263.

MacMillan, I.C. & Katz, J.A., 1992, Idiosyncratic milieus of entrepreneurial research: the need for comprehensive theories, *Journal of Business Venturing*, 7, 1-8.

Venkataraman, S. & MacMillan, I.C., 1997, Choice of organizational mode in new business development: theory and propositions, in Sexton, D.L. & Smilor, R.W. (eds.), *Entrepreneurship 2000*, Chicago: Upstart Publ, 151-166.

Venkataraman, S. & MacMillan, I.C. & McGrath, R.G., 1992, Progress in research on corporate venturing, in Sexton, D.L. & Kasarda, J.D. (eds.), *The state of the art of entrepreneurship*, Boston: PWS-Kent, 487-519.

Textbooks

Block, Z. & MacMillan, I.C., 1993, *Corporate venturing; creating new businesses within the firm*, Boston, MA: Harvard Business School Press.

McGrath, R.G. & MacMillan, I.C., 2000, *The entrepreneurial mindset: strategies for continuously creating opportunities in an age of uncertainty*, Boston, MA: Harvard Business School Press.

Corporate entrepreneurship

Block, Z. & MacMillan, I.C., 1985, Milestones for Successful Venture Planning, *Harvard Business Review*, September-October, 184-197.

Block, Z. & MacMillan, I.C., 1994, Market Entry Strategies for New Corporate Ventures, in Hills, G.E. (ed.), *Marketing and Entrepreneurship*, Westport: Quorum.

MacMillan, I.C. & Block, Z. & SubbaNarasimha, P.N., 1984, Obstacles and experience in corporate ventures, Frontiers of Entrepreneurship Research, 280-293.

MacMillan, I.C. & Day, D.L., 1987, Corporate ventures into industrial markets: dynamics of aggressive entry, *Journal of Business Venturing*, 2, 29-39.

MacMillan, I.C. & George, R., 1985, Corporate venturing: Challenges for senior managers, *Journal of Business Strategy*, 5, 3, 34-44.

McGrath, R.G. & MacMillan, I.C., 1995, Discovery-Driven Planning, *Harvard Business Review*, July-August.

McGrath, R.G. & MacMillan, I.C. & Venkataraman, S., 1995, Defining and developing competence: A strategic process paradigm, *Strategic Management Journal*, 26, 251-275.

McGrath, R.G. & Venkataraman, S. & MacMillan, I.C., 1994, The advantage chain: Antecedents to rents from internal corporate ventures, *Journal of Business Venturing*, 9, 351-369.

Nerkar, A.A. & McGrath, R.G. & MacMillan, I.C., 1996, Three facets of satisfaction and their influence on the performance of innovation teams, *Journal of Business Venturing*, 11, 167-188.

Nerkar, A.A. & McGrath, R.G. & MacMillan, I.C., 1997, Team processes and progress in innovation. The role of job satisfaction at project level, in Birley, S. & MacMillan, I.C. (eds.): *Entrepreneurship in a global context*, London: Routledge.

Starr, J.A. & MacMIllan, I.C., 1990, Resource cooptation via social contracting: Resource acquisition strategies for new ventures, *Strategic Management Journal*, 11, 79-92.

Starr, J.A. & MacMillan, I.C., 1991, Entrepreneurship, Resource Cooptation, and Social Contracting, in Etzioni, A. & Lawrence, P.R. (eds.), *Socio-Economics: Toward a New Synthesis*, Armonk, NY: Sharpe.

Tsai, W. M-H. & MacMillan, I.C. & Low, M.B., 1991, Effects of strategy and environment on corporate venture success in industrial markets, *Journal of Business Venturing*, 6, 9-28.

Entrepreneurship

MacMillan, I.C., 1983, The Politics of New Venture Management, *Harvard Business Review*, 61, 6, 8-16.

Cross-cultural entrepreneurship

Hofstede, G., 1980, *Culture's Consequences: International Differences in Work Related Values*, Beverly Hills, CA: Sage.

McGrath, R.G. & MacMillan, I.C., 1992, More like each other than anyone else? A cross-cultural study of entrepreneurial perceptions, *Journal of Business Venturing*, 7, 419-429.

McGrath, R.G. & MacMillan, I.C. & Scheinberg, S., 1992, Elitists, risk-takers, and rugged individualists? An exploratory analysis of cultural differences between entrepreneurs and non-entrepreneurs, *Journal of Business Venturing*, 7, 115-135.

McGrath, R.G. & MacMillan, I.C. & Yang, E.A. & Tsai, W., 1992, Does culture endure, or is it malleable? Issues for entrepreneurial economic development, *Journal of Business Venturing*, 7, 441-458.

Scheinberg, S. & MacMillan, I.C., 1988, An 11 country study of motivations to start a business, Frontiers of Entrepreneurship Research, 669-687.

Venture capital evaluation

Dubini, P. & MacMillan, I.C., 1988, Entrepreneurial prerequisites in Venture Capital backed projects, Frontiers of Entrepreneurship Research, 46-58.

MacMillan, I.C. & Kulow, D.M. & Khoylian, R., 1988a, Venture Capitalists' involvement in their investments: Extent and performance, *Journal of Business Venturing*, 4, 27-47.

MacMillan, I.C. & Kulow, D.M. & Khoylian, R., 1988b, Venture Capitalists' involvement in their investments: Extent and performance, Frontiers of Entrepreneurship Research, 303-323.

MacMillan, I.C. & Siegel, R. & SubbaNarasimha, P.N., 1985a, Criteria used by venture capitalists to evaluate new venture proposals, *Journal of Business Venturing*, 1, 119-128.

MacMillan, I.C. & Siegel, R. & SubbaNarasimha, P.N., 1985b, Criteria used by venture capitalists to evaluate new venture proposals, Frontiers of Entrepreneurship Research, 126-141.

MacMillan, I.C. & SubbaNarasimha, P.N., 1985, Characteristics distinguishing funded from unfunded business plans evaluated by venture capitalists, Frontiers of Entrepreneurship Research, 404-413.

MacMillan, I.C. & Zemann, L. & SubbaNarasimha, P.N., 1987, Criteria distinguishing successful from unsuccessful ventures in the venture screening process, *Journal of Business Venturing*, 2, 123-137.

Chapter 12

HOWARD ALDRICH

1. HOWARD ALDRICH – THEORIST AND LEGITIMIZER OF THE FIELD

1.1 The Contributions of Howard Aldrich

Howard Aldrich's work is characterized by true scientific curiosity and a theoretical strength that is unique in entrepreneurship research. Aldrich has been true to his theoretical framework ever since he started to develop his thoughts around the evolutionary approach, an approach that, for many years, has underpinned most of his research and demonstrated the potential of a strong conceptual framework in the area of entrepreneurship and small business issues. He has proved that it is possible to achieve a far-reaching understanding of entrepreneurship by means of a consistent theoretical language. Based on the evolutionary approach, Howard Aldrich has not only made significant contributions in the area of formation and development of new firms, but also in other sub-topics of entrepreneurship such as the role of ethnicity, networks, and gender in the formation and growth of organizations.

Howard Aldrich is an internationally recognized organizational sociologist, who has highlighted entrepreneurship. He has demonstrated how a researcher from a core scientific discipline can contribute important insights into the field of entrepreneurship – in that respect he has been an important role model and legitimizer of the field. It should equally be pointed out that Howard Aldrich has been one of the main critics of the methodology used in entrepreneurship research as well as highlighting the importance of methodological rigour in the research. This has had a positive influence on the development and legitimacy of the research field.

1.2   Career

Howard Aldrich is an internationally well-recognized sociologist who became interested in entrepreneurship and introduced a strong theoretical framework into the field.

"In fact the entrepreneurship field caught up with me in the mid 1980s. I was invited by Donald Sexton – as a substitute for Albert Shapiro – to Sexton's second state-of-the-art conference, prior to the publication of the book *Art and Science of Entrepreneurship* in 1986. Donald Sexton phoned me one Friday and gave me four days to write the paper "Entrepreneurship Through Social Networks" in collaboration with Catherine Zimmer. I went to the conference and found the community of entrepreneurship scholars quite pleasant. This was a really critical event, I met all these people ... Neil Churchill, Alan Carsrud, Karl Vesper, Arnold Cooper ... scholars who were passionate and enthusiastic about the topic. The following year I attended the Babson Conference for the first time, and afterwards I was invited to a lot of entrepreneurship conferences and seminars."

However, the interest in new business creation had been there ever since Aldrich's thesis work in the 1960s. His thesis *Organizations in a hostile environment* was presented in 1969 at the University of Michigan and was based on a panel study of 600 businesses in three American cities. In his thesis Aldrich studied the turbulence and change in the business population, and how this population was affected by the civil disorders in the cities in the late 1960s.

"During my graduate work I was very interested in human ecology ... and I was influenced by researchers like Donald Campbell and Walter Buckley, but also social psychologists such as Katz and Kahn. At the graduate course we read their famous book *Social psychology of organizations* in manuscript form. My interest was in change and turnover, and in my thesis I tried to understand populations from an evolutionary point of view."

After Aldrich's dissertation in 1969, he moved from the University of Michigan to Cornell University in New York, which gave him an opportunity to work in a more interdisciplinary environment, and he remained at Cornell until 1982. Howard Aldrich was appointed Professor of Sociology at Cornell University in 1979. It was during his time at Cornell that Aldrich developed his evolutionary theory. One example of his evolutionary reasoning can be found in his influential book *Organizations and Environments,* published in 1979, in which he looked at organizations and how they changed over time. To a large extent this book summarizes Aldrich's thoughts during the 1970s.

"The book received positive reviews and has been widely cited – it is a convenient book to cite when researchers want to emphasize the importance of the environment and go beyond the rather narrow interpretation of population ecology reasoning. I didn't talk about population ecology until after Hannan and Freeman's article was published in 1977. Before that I called it the natural selection process or the population perspective. In my 1979 book I switched the terms back and forth ... looking back I really regret that I used the word population ecology, because I think it confuses people ... most of the work I did was rather different from Hannan and Freeman's population ecology reasoning."

Thus, the 1970s was a decade in which Aldrich developed his evolutionary reasoning as well as his thoughts on ethnicity and entrepreneurship. This was an interest that dated back to the 1960s and a line of reasoning that appeared in his thesis. It was theoretically rooted in his interest in human ecology and empirically rooted in the mass of re-locations in American cities a result of civil unrest, due to the migration of black people from the American south to the northern cities after the Second World War. However, the main part of Aldrich's research on ethnicity and entrepreneurship was carried out together with a research group in the UK, including John Cater, Trevor Jones and David McEvoy. This collaboration was initiated during Aldrich's sabbatical in the UK in 1975 and 1976. Aldrich wanted to make a comparison between the changes and turnovers in the small business population in British cities and those that occurred in US cities during the 1960s. In England, the New Commonwealth brought with it migration from the Caribbean, India, Pakistan and Bangladesh to larger cities in England.

"My sabbatical in Europe in 1975 and 1976 was extremely important for my work. I used the year to do a lot of reading, especially deepening my knowledge of history. I would say that the year in Europe gave me an understanding of the importance of historical analysis, but also the importance of the political dimension – Europeans had a much more political approach to sociology – both the historical analysis and the political dimension later became very important themes in my work, for example, in my 1979 book."

In 1982 Aldrich moved to the University of North Carolina at Chapel Hill as Kenan Professor of Sociology, where he had access to a larger pool of graduate students, with whom he has often worked in collaboration. Pat Reese was the first, followed by Ted Baker, Ellen Auster, Cathrine Zimmer, Linda Renzulli, and today Amy Davis, Philip Kim, Amanda Elam, Stephen Lippmann, Monika Drake, and Ana Teixeira.

"In the 1970s I didn't have a very big pool of graduate students, but when I came to Chapel Hill I found more and more students interested in entrepreneurship, and quite a few of my co-authors in my articles have been my students, or people that I have met and talked to and enjoyed working with. When you have PhD students you can leverage your interests, accomplish more than you could ever manage by yourself ... I would say that that was a major factor in my ability to be more productive in the 1980s.

From the point of view of my thinking during the 1980s, I was reading more evolutionary theory. In my 1979 book I was unclear as to my position toward the ecological approach ... and all through the 1980s I really struggled to differentiate between my evolutionary approach and the ecological approach that people associated me with."

The real interest in entrepreneurship also emerged in Aldrich's research during the 1980s. Entrepreneurship related topics in Aldrich's research dealt with business formation but also with the role of networks in the entrepreneurial process. Some of his more well-cited articles on business formation and networks are:

Aldrich, H.E. & Mueller, S., 1981, The Evolution of Organizational Forms: Technology, Coordination and Control, in Staw, B. & Cummings, L.L. (eds.), *Research in Organizational Behavior*, Vol IV, JAI Press, 33-87.

Aldrich, H. & Zimmer, C., 1986, Entrepreneurship Through Social Networks, in Sexton, D.L. & Smilor, R.W. (eds.), *The Art and Science of Entrepreneurship*, Cambridge, MA: Ballinger, 3-23.

Aldrich, H. & Auster, E.R., 1986, Even dwarfs started small: Liabilities of age and size and their strategic implications, *Research in Organizational Behavior*, 8, 165-198.

Dubini, P. & Aldrich, H.E., 1991, Personal and extended networks are central to the entrepreneurial process, *Journal of Business Venturing*, 6, 5, 305-313.

Aldrich, H.E. & Fiol, C.M., 1994, Fools rush in? The institutional context of industry creation, *Academy of Management Review*, 19, 4, 645-670.

"The collaboration with Marlene Fiol was really important for me ... in the paper 'Fools rush in?' published in *Academy of Management Review* 1994, I started to describe my ideas in multi-level terms – see more clearly that I could look at entirely new industries at individual, group, organizational and population level."

The multi-level approach is a key characteristic of Aldrich's book *Organizations Evolving* (1999), but many of the ideas in the book date back to a piece that Aldrich wrote in the early 1980s together with Bill McKelvey. In this article "Populations, Natural Selection and Applied Organizational Science" published in *Administrative Science Quarterly* in 1983, they argued that the use of taxonomies and typologies is a blind alley in terms of understanding change. In populations of organizations in which there is a great heterogeneity, there will be no organization representing the central tendency in the population – the organizations will differ from each other, and this variation will pave the way for evolution due to selective elimination, and those organizations that will survive will be copied. The idea about populations being composed of heterogeneous organizations was a breakthrough, and this line of reasoning also formed the basis of the 1999 book. However, it took a while for Howard Aldrich to finish the book. He signed the contract with the publisher in 1992 but was not eager to write the book, and by 1995 only four chapters had been written.

"I wasn't in a great hurry to write the book. Gradually over time I tried to figure out how to minimize the work necessary to write it ... I realized that I had some raw material, previously written pieces, but I was so occupied with other activities and projects that I didn't concentrate on the work for the book. It wasn't until I had a conversation with a couple of colleagues about what would be an appropriate last chapter in the book that I decided to finish it. But in August 1998 it was still not finished ... I was still trying to figure out how to bring everything together, and it was not until the final twelve months of the work that I really realized that I could make something significant out of it."

The book *Organizations Evolving* was published by Sage Publications in 1999 and was very well received by both graduate students and academia in general. Howard Aldrich has received several awards for the book, not least the prestigious Weber Award from the American Sociological Association, and the George R. Terry Award from the Academy of Management.

Howard Aldrich is today chair at the Department of Sociology at Chapel Hill, which limits his research productivity but he is still one of the most productive researchers within the field. He has taken a special interest in the Panel Study of Entrepreneurial Dynamics (PSED) database in the US, and in recent years he has presented a wide range of different studies based on the PSED data set.

"I will try to get maximum intellectual value out of the PSED, I think it's a good dataset and it's a good project. So with my students I want to develop some good empirical papers out of the PSED, and then advance evolutionary thinking. I believe that evolutionary thinking is starting to establish itself more strongly, so I feel that within 20 years I could write a book that would use a great deal more evolutionary studies, in contrast to what I did in the 1999 book, which was a reinterpretation of stuff that people wrote from a different point of view."

2.   STREAM OF INTEREST IN HOWARD ALDRICH'S RESEARCH

The creation of evolutionary models exploded during the 1970s, mainly as a result of the open-system revolution in organization theory. Within a short period of time, scholars in different disciplines presented evolutionary theories, inspired by the seminal work of Donald Campbell (1969) to explain phenomena ranging from the micro to the macro levels of organization (see history of evolutionary thoughts in Murmann et al., 2003). For example, on the individual level, Karl Weick (1979) developed a social psychology theory of how individuals coordinate their actions, which drew on the variation, selection, and retention reasoning developed by Campbell. What Weick did on an individual level, Howard Aldrich (1979) did on an organizational level, when looking at the entire organization and how organizations change over time. Aldrich argued that organizations flourish or fail because they are more or less suited to the particular environment in which they operate.

In the area of industry development, Michael Hannan and John Freeman (1977; 1984) also used a selection-based explanation in their work on the population ecology of organizations, in which they emphasized the founding and closure of organizations in populations relative to the distribution of available environmental resources. On the macro level, Richard Nelson and Sidney Winter (1982) were pioneers in the application of evolutionary models of economic change. However, Nelson and Winter were less inspired by Donald Campbell. Their explanations were more influenced by the Carnegie School of routine-based models of organizational action (Herbert Simon, James March, and Richard Cyert) as well as by Joseph Schumpeter who, in the middle of the century, was a prominent exponent of the idea that economic change could be conceptualized as an evolutionary process, despite rejecting Darwinian evolutionary reasoning.

It is within this tradition that Howard Aldrich builds his reasoning, and it is interesting to note the consistency of his research – even if the topics have changed, the evolutionary approach has always constituted the basis. On the other hand, Howard Aldrich has struggled to describe his approach for a long period of time, and he has been rather inconsistent in his use of concepts to describe his reasoning. For example, in the early 1970s he argued that an "organization-environment perspective" was suitable for describing organizations and their suitability in diverse organizational environments. In his work during the 1970s he talked about the "natural selection model", while in his 1979 book he referred to the approach alternately as "population ecology" and the "natural selection model". During the 1980s he increasingly used the concept "population perspective", but in the book *Organizations Evolving* he adopted the concept "evolutionary perspective" or "evolutionary approach".

2.1 Organizations Evolving (1999) – Toward an Evolutionary Approach

The book *Organizations Evolving* published in 1999 can in many ways be regarded as a framework in which Howard Aldrich chose to position the evolutionary approach in relation to the population ecology approach, whose proponents include Glenn Carroll and Michael Hannan. Briefly, the population ecology approach concerns, "the skeleton" in a population of companies – the structure – it deals with the "births" and "deaths" of firms, which makes it possible to calculate a survival curve within a population of companies. It is assumed that population growth is rapid at first and proceeds exponentially, but will then decrease, thus forming an S-shaped curve. Population ecology research has produced several sets of strong empirical results, which have been successfully replicated within a number of lines of business and in different countries. The strength is that is it possible to calculate, by means of relatively simple parameters, how many companies there are in a specific line of business and the composition in terms of size and age as well as being able to explain the trends in a particular line. However, theory has become more and more mathematically complex, and the trend within research is to use different simulation models.

Howard Aldrich's evolutionary approach is developing in a different direction – it is more a question of the "flesh and blood" of the system. Aldrich attempts to explain why the structure emerges in the first place and why the development takes place. The point of departure in Aldrich's reasoning is the evolutionary process (developed by Donald Campbell in the 1960s). Thus, the four generic processes mentioned below, which are necessary for and which allow evolution, form the point of departure in Aldrich's framework:

- Variation, i.e. a change in current routines, competencies or organizational forms must occur, which can result from deliberate attempts to generate alternatives, or from blind variations generated by chance, mistakes or curiosity.
- Selection – some variations are then selected, while others are rejected, a selection that arises based on market forces, competitive pressure or within-organization selection forces (e.g. pressure to

achieve stability and homogeneity in the organization, and the persistence of previous selection criteria that are no longer relevant in a new environment).

- Retention – the positively selected variation must be retained, preserved, duplicated or reproduced through, for example, a specialization and standardization of roles within the organization or through an institutionalization of practices, cultural beliefs and values – otherwise there will be no organizational continuity or memory.
- The struggle of competing to obtain scarce resources. Organizations are not passive entities and they may have to struggle for time, legitimacy, capital, etc.

The book includes five sections. In the first three chapters Aldrich introduces his evolutionary approach and also summarizes the contributions that a multi-disciplinary framework can make in increasing the understanding of the evolutionary approach, including institutional theory, population ecology, the interpretative approach, research in organizational learning, resource dependence, and transaction cost economies. In the remainder of the book, Aldrich examines the evolutionary processes at different levels of analysis – a multi-level analysis – from organizational level to community level, whereby, in an elegant way, he creates a linkage between micro- and macro processes, i.e. the interplay between the large and the small.

- Chapters 4 to 6 use an organization level of analysis and concern the process by which organizations are created and achieve coherence as entities. These chapters provide a rich description of the role of individuals and groups in the organizational founding process. Aldrich argues that the vast majority of entrepreneurs could be regarded as reproducers rather than starting innovative organizations. Truly innovative start-ups are often the result of creative experimentation with new ideas by outsiders, whereas previous work experience and network ties seem to hinder entrepreneurs within the population from creating radical breakthroughs – indifference and ignorance of population routines and competencies may give outsiders the freedom to break free of the cognitive and cultural constraints of the insiders.
- Chapters 7 and 8 take the existence of organizations as given and examine the transformation of organizations over time, as well as discussing how change occurs in three dimensions: goals, boundaries, and activities.
- Chapters 9 and 10 focus on the population level of analysis and explore how new populations emerge. They include an interesting discussion about the problems of legitimacy that new entrepreneurs face when starting new populations of firms (a discussion based on the article co-authored with Marlene Fiol in 1994 – see subsection 2.2.3.). Chapter 10 includes, among other things, a discussion about how entrepreneurial intentions and access to resources affect

organizational founding and failure (see article co-authored with Gabriele Wiedenmayer in subsection 2.2.1.).

- Chapter 11 involves the community level, and in this chapter Aldrich discusses how entrepreneurship and relations between populations affect the dynamics of communities – activities that cut across populations – for example, discontinuities of existing populations and communities caused by technical and regulatory innovations that are exploited by entrepreneurs, resulting in the extinction of some populations or the emergence of new ones.

In the final chapter (Chapter 12) Aldrich highlights some theoretical issues for further research – a research agenda within the evolutionary approach. Aldrich emphasizes the need for paying greater attention to issues of emergence at different levels of analysis, and especially within three areas of research: the role of nascent entrepreneurs, resource management practices of emerging organizations, and the importance of collective actions by individuals and organizations in emerging industries.

In the book, Aldrich emphasizes the need to read the chapters in chronological order, which shows the applicability of the evolutionary approach to multiple levels of analysis – where communities are built on populations that are constructed on organizations, which have emerged as a result of the actions of entrepreneurs. It is also interesting to note that throughout the book Aldrich highlights the importance of new organizations as a source of variation in society. Therefore, the book has a true entrepreneurship focus, and Aldrich devotes special attention to entrepreneurial issues.

2.2 An Evolutionary Approach to Business Formation

In a number of articles, Howard Aldrich uses the evolutionary approach to understand the set of problems associated with business formation – all of which are frequently cited within entrepreneurship research. Below is a summary of some of these articles.

2.2.1 From a Trait Approach to an Ecological Perspective on Organizational Foundings

For many years entrepreneurship research was occupied with the question: "Why do some people become entrepreneurs, while most people do not?", and researchers argued that there must be something distinctive about an individual's background or personality that made them entrepreneurs. In Aldrich and Wiedenmayer (1993; see also Aldrich, 1990) the authors present a complementary approach – what they term the "rate" approach – based on evolutionary reasoning. In contrast to the "trait" approach, which implies a micro-level analysis, the "rate" approach involves a macro-evolutionary focus, and Aldrich and Wiedenmayer concentrated their reasoning on the founding rates at population level, i.e. examining conditions that affect the rate at which organizations are added to an existing population. The founding of new organizations and the closure of existing ones are, according to the authors, dependent on:

- Intrapopulation processes (i.e. prior foundings, closures, density of firms, and factors associated with density), and it is the environmental resources, or what is known as an environment's carrying capacity, that sets the limit on population density. At the beginning, when density is low, and there are adequate environmental resources for exploitation, the founding rate is high, whereas closure rates are low. When a high density has been achieved, the situation will be reversed, which leads to fewer net additions.
- Inter-population processes, including the nature of the relations between populations. For example, competitive relations between populations may depress founding rates, whereas other interpopulation relations may actually facilitate foundings in other populations (e.g. car manufacturers create a supply industry).
- Societal-level factors, such as cultural norms, government policies and political events. It seems that institutional forces probably have the greatest impact when a new population is emerging, as established foundings within an organizational population respond more to inter- and intrapopulation processes than to institutional forces.

Aldrich and Wiedenmayer argue that previous deaths within the population may affect founding rates in two ways: (i) resources are often tied up by existing organizations, indicating that new firms will only obtain access to them when deaths occur and (ii) potential founders may be frightened by high death rates. However, the importance of previous deaths may differ depending on the population's position in the life cycle. For example, in the early growth stage, deaths will have a lesser impact on the availability of resources, whereas in later stages, when carrying capacity is reached, deaths may be important for freeing resources for new ventures – in this situation previous deaths may have contradictory effects; on the one hand, freeing resources for new ventures, while on the other, sending negative signals to entrepreneurs of the likelihood of failure for new ventures.

In a similar way, previous foundings may have two possible effects on the subsequent founding of new ventures: (i) high levels of foundings may signal to potential entrepreneurs that opportunities are growing within a population, and (ii) that resources and the pool of potential entrepreneurs will soon be exhausted, leading to a diminishing return.

In addition, we can assume that when organizational density increases, there will be a rise in legitimacy and institutionalization –

spreading the knowledge and skills required to achieve a viable organization – which may lead to an increase in foundings. At a later stage, with high levels of density, factors inhibiting foundings become dominant, such as increased concentration, smaller potential gains and diminishing returns. These processes have led to the conclusion that there will be an inverse U-shaped pattern between organizational density and the rate of foundings (Hannan, 1986).

2.2.2   Liability of Aging, Newness and Smallness

Within a population there are processes of metamorphosis that transform the composition of whole populations of organizations so that they become better suited to their environments. This metamorphosis is affected by the age and size of the firms. In their article "Even dwarfs started small: Liabilities of age and size and their strategic implications" (1986), Howard Aldrich and Ellen Auster argue that large, aging organizations face a number of constraints which limit their ability to adapt to changing conditions but, on the other hand, new organizations and especially small ones also face problems, but of a different kind.

The *liability of aging* facing old and large organizations can be summarized by a couple of internal conditions that inhibit adaptability to change, such as: (i) retention of control by the original founders or members of their families, (ii) pressure for internal consistency as a basis for coordination and control, (iii) and a hardening of vested interests where suggestions pertaining to change may be viewed primarily as mechanisms to gain power, and finally, (iv) increased forces to induce a homogeneity of perception within the organization, for example, through recruitment and socialization of new members. But there are also external conditions facing larger and older organizations that create resistance to change, such as interorganizational arrangements, which may become a stabilizing force. However, different entry barriers (scale-economy and product differentiation barriers) will also exert less pressure for change on the aging organization. Thus, large and aging organizations face a number of constraints that limit their prospects for adaptation – liabilities of aging.

However, small and new organizations often experience a *liability of newness*. Even if the organizational population is growing at an aggregate level, there is underlying population volatility – organizations die and are replaced by other organizations. What causes liability of newness? What are the obstacles that hinder the survival of new organizations? Aldrich and Auster identified external as well as internal liabilities of newness. Externally, new organizations face many barriers that make movement into a new domain difficult. For example, lack of legitimacy and fierce competition from established organizations, brand recognition and market acceptance of established products, etc. endanger the survival of new organizations. But new organizations also face internal liabilities of newness, which mainly concern the creation and classification of roles and structures consistent with external constraints and the ability to attract qualified employees.

In addition, many young organizations face the *liability of smallness*, which is an effect of size. Empirical results (see e.g. Birch, 1979) indicate that small size does affect survival. Usually smallness is related to newness, but not all organizations are born small, for example new affiliates of larger companies. Factors that make survival problematic for small organizations – regardless of age – may be related to the problem of raising capital and the administrative burden of handling government regulations, in addition to which, small organizations face major disadvantages in competing for labor compared to larger ones.

The conclusion is that older and larger organizations as well as younger and smaller ones face a number of constraints that make metamorphosis difficult. For older organizations it is a problem of strategic transformation whereas young and small organizations experience a problem of survival. And there seems to be some form of symmetry in these constraints in that the obstacles faced by new and small firms can be easily overcome by larger, more established organizations and vice versa. In order to survive, newer and smaller organizations need to become closely linked to large organizations, for example through franchising, long-term contracts, and mergers or acquisitions. It is through such strong ties that smaller and newer organizations can gain access to resources that are not otherwise available. Paradoxically, older and larger organizations will reduce their liability of aging by forming loosely coupled arrangements with young and small organizations. This may take the form of emulating younger organizations, i.e. by imitating them through internal restructuring in order to create conditions that generate and facilitate innovation and risk-taking, or by exploiting the smaller organization through boundary-crossing strategies – contracting arrangements which will exploit the flexibility and dynamism of younger organizations, while keeping them at arms length.

2.2.3   Early Ventures in New Industries

Small and new organizations always seem to experience a liability of newness. However, such pressures are especially severe when an industry is in its formative years – when entrepreneurs have few precedents for the kind of activities they want to engage in. In another well cited article "Fools Rush In? The Institutional Context of Industry Creation" (1994), Howard Aldrich and Marlene Fiol discuss the challenges faced by early ventures in the formative years of a new industry compared to those that carry on a tradition of many predecessors within the same industry. Of course, many factors are involved in achieving success in a new industry, but one of the most critical problems facing innovative entrepreneurs is their relative lack of legitimacy, and a reasonable conclusion seems to be: founders of new activities, by definition, lack the familiarity and credibility that constitute the basis for interaction.

As an industry develops, the organizations within the industry increase their *cognitive legitimation*, i.e. the spread of knowledge about the new activity and what is needed to succeed in the industry, as well as their *socio-political legitimation*. The latter concerns the value placed on an activity by cultural norms and political authorities. Different strategies may be used by emerging organizations to promote the development of a new industry, as summarized in Figure 12-1. Aldrich and Fiol propose four levels of social context – organizational, intra-industry, inter-industry and institutional – in which entrepreneurs can gradually develop trust, reliability, reputation, and finally institutional legitimacy.

	Type of Legitimacy	
Level of analysis	*Cognitive*	*Socio-political*
Organizational	Develop knowledge base via symbolic language and behaviors	Develop trust in the new activity by maintaining internally consistent stories
Intra-industry	Develop knowledge base by encouraging convergence around a dominant design	Develop perceptions of reliability by mobilizing for collective action
Inter-industry	Develop knowledge base by promoting activity through third-party actors	Develop the reputation of a new activity by negotiating and collaborating with other industries
Institutional	Develop knowledge base by creating linkages with established educational curricula	Develop legitimacy by organizing collective marketing and lobbying activities

Figure 12-1. Entrepreneurial strategies to promote new industry development (source: Aldrich & Fiol, 1994, p. 649).

Entrepreneurs in emerging industries have to interact with extremely skeptical external resource holders (suppliers, creditors, customers, etc.), and the entrepreneurs need strategies for building trust, but this initial trust-building cannot be based on objective evidence. Instead, innovative entrepreneurs must concentrate on framing the unknown in a credible way, and one strategy for achieving this is to simplify, symbolize or give ritual expression, i.e. conventional coding, to the issues in question or, alternatively, the entrepreneur can "act as if" (Gartner et al., 1992) – as if the activity were already a reality. In addition, due to attacks from "conventional" industries, innovative entrepreneurs in emerging industries may need institutional support (sociopolitical approval), and entrepreneurs must build a knowledge base that outsiders will accept as valid. The lack of externally valid arguments makes alternative forms of communication necessary, for example through narratives – to make a case showing that the new ventures are comparable with more established activities. In this respect, the validity of the stories is not dependent on a set of external criteria, but on internal consistency and lack of contradiction.

Once innovative entrepreneurs have developed a basis for understanding and trust at organizational level, they must find strategies for interacting with other organizations in their emerging industry – intra-industry processes. The lack of convergence on dominant standards (designs) within the new industry limits the perceived reliability and increases confusion about what standards should be followed. Such convergence is facilitated if new ventures choose to imitate and borrow from pioneers rather than introducing new innovations of their own. In this way knowledge of new activities will be spread, thus adding to the convergence on a dominant standard. Furthermore, even if collective actions are difficult to organize in the early stages of industry development, it is important to find avenues for collaborative actions within an industry to achieve socio-political approval.

The relation between industries – inter-industry processes – affects the distribution of resources in the environment. Established industries that feel threatened by a newcomer are sometimes able to change the terms on which resources are available to emerging industries, for example, by questioning their efficacy or their conformity with the established order. Therefore, entrepreneurs in emerging industries must build a reputation for the new industry that conveys the idea that it is a reality – something that is taken for granted by others. This process can be facilitated by interfirm linkages such as trade associations, i.e. through third-party actors, and on the socio-political level by reliable relationships with other, more established industries.

Finally, there may be institutional conditions that will constrain the growth rate of the industry by affecting the diffusion of knowledge about the new activities and the extent to which the activities will be publicly tolerated. At this level, entrepreneurs are no longer working as isolated individuals, but using industry councils, cooperative alliances, trade associations, etc, as vehicles for collective action in order to achieve institutional legitimacy. In emerging industries there is a need to raise the level of cognitive legitimacy – mass media may be unfamiliar with the industry, and their reporting may be inaccurate, while the lack of a general understanding about the emerging industry also makes it difficult to recruit and retain employees. This understanding may be facilitated by institutionalized diffusion of knowledge, for example through established educational institutions, but also through collective marketing and lobbying efforts that will gain sociopolitical approval.

To summarize, in the article Howard Aldrich and Marlene Fiol pursue strategies on different levels of analysis – organizational, intra-industry, inter-industry, and institutional – that will generate and sustain trust, reliability, reputation, and finally, culminate in legitimating the industry at institutional level. Thus, as indicated, there is a hierarchical process involved; gaining trust within and around the organization provides a basis from which it is possible to build cooperative exchanges with other similar organizations (intra-industry reliability). Such interactions make it easier to organize collectively and build a broader reputation for the industry as an enduring reality, and finally, an established reputation facilitates the co-optation of institutional actors, leading to institutional legitimation.

2.3   Ethnicity and Entrepreneurship

Ethnicity and entrepreneurship was an early interest of Howard Aldrich, which goes back to his thesis in the 1960s. But it was during the late 1970s and early 1980s when Aldrich started to work with David McEvoy, Trevor Jones and John Cater in the UK that this research issue became clearer and more visible. Some of the results of this research collaboration were presented in the book *Ethnic Entrepreneurs* (1990), edited together with Roger Waldinger and Robin Ward. The book is based on two conferences held in 1985 and 1986 and summarizes much of the knowledge within the area at that point in time.

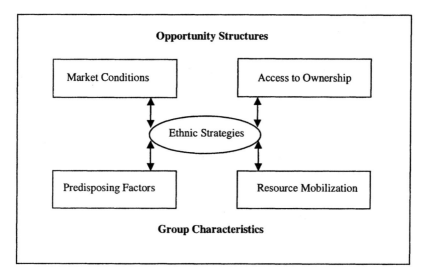

Figure 12-2. An interactive model of ethnic business development (source: modified from Waldinger & Aldrich & Ward, 1990a, p. 22).

But Howard Aldrich has also published several articles on the issue of ethnic differences in entrepreneurship. In the article "Ethnicity and Entrepreneurship" (1990; see also Waldinger & Aldrich & Ward, 1990b), Howard Aldrich and Roger Waldinger summarized their research on ethnicity and entrepreneurship using a framework based on three dimensions: an ethnic group's access to opportunities, the characteristics of a group, and emergent strategies in ethnic firms (see Figure 12-2).

2.3.1   Opportunity Structures

According to the authors, ethnic firms have become more and more heterogeneous and are faced with many different *market conditions*. However, there is one dominant assumption – formulated by Light (1972) as the "protected market hypothesis" – that the initial market for ethnic entrepreneurs typically arises within the ethnic community itself. Thus, if ethnic communities have special needs and preferences, they will best be identified and served by those who know them intimately – namely by the members of the immigrant community itself. Producers who quickly find a niche in the immigrant community are therefore purveyors of culinary products – tropical fruits or oriental specialities – but also "cultural products" like newspapers, books, and clothes, i.e. products with a direct connection with the immigrant's homeland and based on the knowledge of tastes and buying preferences (Aldrich et al., 1985). However, if ethnic firms confine themselves to the ethnic market, their potential growth is severely restricted due to limitations in market size and buying power. This may not always be the case – many ethnic firms find access to customers beyond the ethnic community – and there seem to be certain circumstances under which small ethnic firms can grow in the open market, for example: (i) markets that are underserved or abandoned by large mass-marketing organizations, such as the core areas of urban centers that are abandoned by the large food retailers, (ii) markets where economies of scale are low, (iii) markets affected by instability or uncertainty, in which industries may be segmented into one branch dominated by larger firms, handling staple products, and another composed of small-scale firms catering to fluctuating patterns of demand, and (iv) market for exotic goods.

Given the existence of a market, the potential ethnic entrepreneur still needs *access to ownership* opportunities, which is to a large extent dependent on the number of vacant business-ownership positions and government policies toward immigrants. The likelihood of ethnic entrepreneurs starting a new venture is greatly affected by the level and nature of interethnic competition for jobs and business opportunities. For example, it has been shown that when competition is high, ethnic groups tend to be concentrated in a limited range of industries and, at very high levels of competition, they may be forced out of more lucrative businesses and even pushed out of business altogether. However, residential segregation appears to reduce interethnic competition for business vacancies. In addition, access to ownership is also affected by government policies affecting the ease and terms on which immigrants can start their own business. In most societies, immigrants are free to settle wherever they want – where job opportunities are best – although government often attempts to influence where immigrants settle. Moreover, western societies also maintain policies that impede ethnic business development, for example through "trade licenses" and "residence permits".

2.3.2   Group Characteristics

Why do some ethnic groups start more new ventures than other groups? Historically, considerable disparities in self-employment among various immigrant populations have occurred. For example, US Jews have been far more successful in business than the Irish, and Italians have achieved higher rates of self-employment than the Poles. These differences between ethnic groups can probably be explained based on the complex interaction between conditions such as pre-migration characteristics, the circumstances under which integration took place, the group's subsequent evolution, and post-migration characteristics (Waldinger & Aldrich & Ward, 1990b). Pre-migration characteristics are an individual's skills and experience that can be useful for business success. This predisposition could be based on the selective nature of migration, which means that only individuals with substantial education, business experience and capital migrate. For example, at the beginning of the 20th century, Russian Jews emigrating to the US had prior experience of tailoring, a high level of literacy and a historical orientation toward trading, and they moved rapidly into entrepreneurial positions in the garment industry. The circumstances of migration also influence the conditions under which the immigrants move. For example, individuals arriving as temporary immigrants – with the intention of returning to the home country – are mainly concerned with the accumulation of capital and not with the attainment of social mobility in the societies to which they have migrated. Finally, resource mobilization, which concerns the ethnic social structures such as the network of kinship and friendship around which ethnic communities are built, constitutes a central source of resources, out of which ethnic entrepreneurship may arise. For example, the family is important both for the provision of capital and as the core workforce for small businesses. However, a strong family structure may not be sufficient or necessary for ethnic entrepreneurs' success. For example, Zimmer and Aldrich (1987) found few differences between South Asian and white shopkeepers in their use of family labor. Finally, the post-migration characteristics reflect the immigrant group's position in the economy –

certain environments are more supportive of self-employment than others. For example, immigrant groups concentrated in industries where small firms are the prevailing form will have access to better information about business opportunities and opportunities to acquire relevant skills than immigrant groups concentrated in large scale industries.

2.3.3   Ethnic Strategies

The concept of strategy reflects the positioning of oneself in relation to others in order to accomplish one's goals and involves both the opportunity structure within which ethnic business operates, and the characteristics of the ethnic group. Ethnic entrepreneurs need distinctive strategies in order to exploit distinctive socio-cultural resources and to compensate for the typical background deficits of their group in respect of wealth, political power, etc. In their study of seven groups of minority entrepreneurs in Britain, France, the US, West Germany and the Netherlands, Aldrich and Waldinger (1990) concluded that what was most remarkable was not the differences among ethnic groups in their formation of new firms but how very similar their strategies were. For example, information is typically obtained through the owners' personal networks as well as various ties specifically linked to their ethnic communities. Training and skills are acquired on the job, often while the individual is an employee in a co-ethnic or family member's business. In addition, family and co-ethnic labor are critical to most small ethnic businesses (Waldinger & Aldrich & Ward, 1990b).

2.4   Networks and the Entrepreneurial Process

Entrepreneurs are embedded in a social context and must establish connections to resources within their social networks. The importance of the social network for the entrepreneurial process is a central theme within entrepreneurship research. Howard Aldrich took an early interest in this issue, not least in the book chapter co-authored with Cathrine Zimmer in 1986, which is one of the most widely cited pieces regarding the role of networks in business formation.

2.4.1   The Characteristics of Entrepreneurial Social Networks

In the evolutionary process (variation, selection, retention and struggle) there will be a struggle for resources and opportunities. Sometimes resources will be abundant, and a high proportion of entrepreneurs will be successful in attracting resources, whereas in other situations, especially in evolving industries, resources become scarcer and competition increases, leading to a higher mortality rate and a decline in the population. In order to attract the resources needed, entrepreneurs may use their social networks. The network approach could be applied to the study of entrepreneurship in several different ways, and Aldrich and Zimmer (1986) discuss four different applications:

1. Social forces that increase the density of networks. The likelihood of entrepreneurial success will increase in situations where conditions increase the salience of group boundaries and identity, leading to a greater density in the network, i.e. extensiveness of ties between individuals within the group.

2. "Brokers" who promote access in social networks. In order to reduce transaction costs, "brokers" such as trade associations, technical experts, management consultants, etc. who facilitate the interests of individuals not directly connected to one another will have central positions in networks.

3. The diversity of the network that increases the production of entrepreneurs. Based on Granovetter's (1973) reasoning, which links the type of ties (weak and strong ties) to the scope of opportunities available to the individual, it follows that entrepreneurs are more likely to be found in positions whose centrality is high and which are connected to many diverse sources of information. In addition, entrepreneurs activate their weak ties in order to gain access to business information (e.g. new business locations, potential markets, potential investors, etc.) and also to attract customers.

4. Social resources embedded in the entrepreneurs' network. In combination with the reasoning of strong and weak ties it can be argued that all weak ties are not equally useful for acquiring social resources. In this respect, weak ties to contacts with a leading position in the social hierarchy will provide the greatest access to social resources. Accordingly, we will find successful entrepreneurs with weak ties to individuals who are well placed to provide timely and accurate information as well as to people with different kinds of resources.

Elaborating on the social networks of entrepreneurs, Dubini and Aldrich (1991) distinguish between "personal networks" (centered on a focal individual) and "extended networks" (focussing on collectives). A *personal network* consists of all those individuals with whom an entrepreneur has direct relations, including for example partners, suppliers, customers, bankers and family members. "Networking" as a verb is often seen as something apart from ordinary business behavior – based on pure market-mediated transactions, one-of-a-kind and non-sustaining transactions between people who never expect to see each other again – a transaction form that includes opportunism potential, especially under conditions of uncertainty and when problems occur, as the other party may simply exit the situation. In contrast, networking refers to situations where both parties expect to see each other frequently and where they invest in long-term relations. The benefits may be an increase in trust and predictability as a result of the establishment of long-term relations – and while the uncertainty of a situation is not reduced the other party's reactions to a situation are more predictable. Equally, the individuals concerned are more likely to use "voice", i.e. making their complaints known and negotiating over them, rather than exiting in response to problems. Thus, networking with one's direct ties is a way of overcoming some of the liabilities inherent in purely market-like transactions with other parties.

Extended networks are the collective result when interconnected personal networks are examined. The shift from personal networks, with a focus on direct ties, to extended networks, including indirect ties to individuals and organizations with whom there is no form of direct contact, may enable entrepreneurs and firms to substantially increase their access to information and resources compared to what may be available through their direct ties. Networking is a process – initially in a business process the firm does not exist, and the entrepreneur as an individual will gather the necessary resources, but when the first exchange takes place, the focus may shift from the entrepreneur to the company itself. The use of extended network concepts applied to firms as opposed to individuals enables us to study organizations that otherwise would not have been taken into consideration. Thus, extended networks are associated with organizations, whereas informal personal networks are associated with individuals. Using the "personal network" and "extended network" concepts, two general principles linking network behavior and entrepreneurial success were formulated:

- Effective entrepreneurs are more likely to systematically plan and monitor network activities. For example, they are able to chart their network and discriminate between productive and symbolic ties, they regard networks as crucial for the success of their firm, and they are able to stabilize and maintain networks in order to increase their effectiveness.
- Effective entrepreneurs are more likely to undertake actions to increase the density and diversity of their network. For example, effective entrepreneurs set aside time for purely "random" activities (i.e. with no specific problem in mind) and are able to check their network density in order to avoid too many overlaps that may affect network efficiency.

2.4.2　　The Impact of Social Networks on Business Start-ups and Performance

It can thus be expected that an extensive social network rich in resources is important for the entrepreneur's start-up possibilities but also for the success of an already established company. However, our knowledge of this relationship is very poor. In a longitudinal panel study of 165 prospective and active entrepreneurs in the Research Triangle Area of North Carolina, Howard Aldrich and his colleagues collected data on two occasions. The first study was conducted in February 1986 and the follow-up study was performed in December 1986, which means that the entrepreneurs were followed during a nine-month period. A similar panel study was conducted in 1990 with a follow-up two years later based on the firms that participated in 1990. In all, 281 responses were included in this second study.

Based on the first data collection in 1986, Aldrich, Rosen and Woodward (1987) found some general characteristics. As expected, the results showed that network variables had a significant impact on business foundings and profitability in newly formed companies. Three variables seemed to be of particular importance for the founding of businesses: business founders reported a higher than average number of contacts per week with core network members, they spent more time developing contacts and had networks that were more closely linked, than those individuals who did not start businesses. For newly founded businesses (three years old or less), the results of the study indicated that entrepreneurs who maintain high levels of contact with networks, whose members are inter-connected, are more likely to make a profit. However, some unexpected findings emerged. It was found that successful entrepreneurs had networks with diverse resources and that diversity was greater when network members were not tightly linked. The opposite was found – only 48% of the entrepreneurs who had networks with higher proportions of weak ties made a profit compared to 80% of those entrepreneurs with strong tie networks.

The conclusion seems to be that social networks allow founding entrepreneurs to expand their range of action and gain access to resources and opportunities that would not otherwise be available. In Aldrich and Reese (1993; see also Reese & Aldrich, 1995), a question based on the second panel study from 1990 to 1992 was to see if networks are equally important in ongoing businesses. Interestingly, and to some extent surprisingly, the study showed no evidence that networking activities (measured as the size of an entrepreneur's personal network and time spent on developing and maintaining business contacts) affect business survival and performance – business survival and performance were not related to an entrepreneur's network size or direct effort.

The data from the Research Triangle Area of North Carolina was also used for an international comparison, reported in Aldrich and Sakano (1998), of the make up of personal networks in five countries: Italy, Japan, Northern Ireland, Sweden and the US. The comparisons were based on two different models of how the entrepreneurs' networks are formed:

– Embeddedness model – networks are products of strong ties and long-lasting relationships. The assumption is that the social relationships of entrepreneurs resemble those of other people, with a core of close personal contacts built on ties of reciprocal interdependence and a periphery of weaker ties assembled on a more haphazard basis. For entrepreneurs, strong ties and close friendships can provide the social support needed to weather crises and hardships, i.e. entrepreneurs will turn for business advice to people with whom they have relatively long-standing relations and whom they trust.

– Instrumental model – networks are pragmatic, instrumental tools consisting of weak ties of a short duration. The assumption is that entrepreneurs have different kinds of social relationships than other people, with a core of weak ties assembled on a pragmatic basis – they pick members of their inner circle on an instrumental basis. In this case entrepreneurs may well segregate their relationships into business and non-business, with a special group of people selected as business advisors – on the basis of their expertise rather than social similarities to the entrepreneur.

Entrepreneurs' personal networks seem to be rather similar in all five countries. The networks are composed of four major groupings: a small group of family members where very few have a business relationship with the entrepreneur, a large group of business associates who are defined in strictly business terms, a smaller group of business associates who are also regarded as "friends", and finally a group who are strictly defined as "friends" without an apparent business tie to the entrepreneur. Little support was found for the instrumental model of personal networking. Entrepreneurship is associated with uncertainty, and strong ties of intimate friendship with people they have known for many years provide the social support needed for the development of the company. In accordance with the embeddedness model, entrepreneurs seek people they can trust, although trustworthiness is not always easy to recognise.

2.5   Women Entrepreneurs

Over the past thirty years the number of businesses owned by women has grown rapidly, and the number of female owned firms has also increased in Europe, although the proportion of firms is not as high as in the US. Howard Aldrich has treated the role of gender in the business formation process in several studies. Networks are also a central feature in his reasoning in these studies.

The study by Baker, Aldrich and Liou (1997) is a review of earlier findings regarding differences between women and men's business practices. It was concluded that very few systematic differences were identified in earlier research – the strongest differences involve demographics rather than style. For example, women's businesses tend to be smaller and are more likely to be in retail or service industries. As owners, women tend to have less experience in their firm's industry and as managers are more likely to start businesses to gain flexibility. However, in psychological and demographic aspects, women entrepreneurs are more similar than different from men. The results are not surprising. In a market based perspective all entrepreneurs, men and women alike, operate in a business environment structured by laws, standard practices, a set of institutional contingencies to which owners have to adapt if their businesses are to survive. Accordingly, we could predict that women entrepreneurs behave much like men – differences among women and men are secondary to economic and institutional requirements.

On the other hand, there is extensive research on sex and gender roles providing arguments that even though men and women operate under the same institutional and economic rules, the business world is largely constructed and dominated by men. This makes it reasonable to believe that women and men belong to different types of networks that influence their entrepreneurship – women inhabit a "female world" that only partially overlaps the "male world" (Aldrich, 1989; Aldrich et al., 1989; Baker et al., 1997). First, there is overwhelming evidence that gender has a major impact on the choice of career, in terms of for example college, occupation and the level of authority in a firm. It is during these formative years as an employee that the future entrepreneur accumulates experience and becomes embedded in networks that can subsequently be drawn upon when starting their own business. Women may be at a disadvantage when it comes to building a personal and social network (Aldrich, 1989; Aldrich et al., 1989). Second, most women entrepreneurs have to balance family and work responsibilities in a way that men do not. The critical period for entrepreneurs is around the age of 30, when they accumulate resources and networks that might be important for the establishment of their business. However, in these years women are disadvantaged – their networks are mainly constructed around their husbands' business associates instead of their own (ibid.). Finally, women entrepreneurs often lack full access to informal networks, such as work-related after-hours socializing and voluntary association activities. Thus, key life events connected to work, marriage, family and organized social life could be expected to have substantial effects on the social networks of women entrepreneurs and make an important difference in terms of the possibility of running their own business compared to the situation of men.

Based on these arguments: Are women and men embedded in networks different enough to affect the rates and types of entrepreneurship? Do women differ from men in how they use networks to obtain resources and assistance for their businesses? Based on the two longitudinal panel studies in the Research Triangle Area of North Carolina carried out in 1986 and 1990 - 1992, Howard Aldrich and his colleagues presented some interesting findings. First, in Aldrich and Sakano (1995) it was shown that men do not include women in their network of business advisors (strong-tie network) – women made up only 10% of the advisor networks of male business owners – a fact that may indicate women's position in the existing distribution of economic resources and power in society. In contrast, there were a higher proportion of cross-sex ties among female networks. Thus, men were mainly involved in same-sex networks, whereas women were involved in mainly cross-sex networks. Second, Aldrich, Elam and Reese (1997) examined entrepreneurs' networking activities in their search for legal and financial assistance, business loans, and expert assistance for their businesses. It was found that

- women were as active as men in networking activities (except for legal assistance),
- men and women used similar channels (i.e. friends and business associates) to locate people who could help them,
- pre-existing ties were the main channel of resource acquisition for both men and women, and
- the quality of the assistance obtained via the network favored women – women seem to pay slightly less than market rates for legal and loan assistance, although they receive the same quality of advice as men.

Thus, the results indicate that women's networking – in pattern and outcome – did not differ from men's networking in any major respect – which is in contrast to what could be expected based on research on sex and gender roles. In conclusion, as reported in Aldrich and Sakano (1995), there is evidence of a sex bias in the composition of women's networks, but obviously not in how they use them.

3.   PERSPECTIVES ON THE EVOLUTION OF NEW FIRMS

In this final section I will present an interview with Howard Aldrich in which he gives his views on the evolution of new firms but also the future development of entrepreneurship research.

Your evolutionary theory seems to have a great potential when applied to entrepreneurship research. Based on your evolutionary theory, what have been the most interesting insights in your research on entrepreneurship?

I think one of the most interesting aspects is the legitimacy issue ... and in this respect it is really important to distinguish between being a founder in an established industry and being a founder in a new industry. I think the book by Clayton Christensen *The Innovator's Dilemma* is really superb in illustrating my view. He is not an evolutionary theorist but he uses evolutionary arguments. He makes a distinction between what he calls "sustaining innovations", "normal innovations", and "radical innovations" and argues that in some industries you have certain firms developing radical disruptive innovations, for example, General Electric and Hewlett Packard, but in most industries there are a lot of sustaining kinds of firms that don't understand what is happening when radical disruptive innovations occur, and many of these firms will disappear because they have underestimated the power of the innovations. In this respect he raises the question: "Why aren't established firms that are able to create radical innovations the ones to pioneer entirely new industries?" and "Why are new industries almost always started by firms that no one has ever heard of?" Christensen argues that this is not a technological problem – it is essentially a social problem ... it has to do with the relationship between the established firm and the customers that it currently serves and the way that investors and suppliers think of the firm – it is a matter of legitimacy and identity – "we could do it, but we shouldn't do it". It is the embedded nature of the firm, the relationship to other actors, its identity and legitimacy that can explain why radical disruptive innovations typically come from outsiders. Christensen's arguments are good examples of the underlying sociological or social process orientation that I would like to bring to entrepreneurship research.

What direction do you think future entrepreneurship research based on evolutionary theory will take?

I will give you a few of what I call "analytical dilemmas", which I think can illustrate the possibilities offered to entrepreneurship research by a strong analytical perspective like the evolutionary approach.

I am working on a study of entrepreneurial teams – most entrepreneurship takes place in organized groups, not by solo entrepreneurs. The question we are asking is "what principles govern the creation and composition of teams?" We are using the dataset of the Panel Study of Entrepreneurial Dynamics in the US. From the study we know that about half of the people trying to start a business are doing it solo, while the other half are doing it in a team. We know that of those starters consisting of more than one person, about half of them are husband and wife teams and half of them are other combinations. The question is: "How much 'homophily' is there in the teams?" The results indicate that if we exclude husband and wife teams, there is an overwhelming tendency toward single sex teams, teams with a similar ethnic background, occupational homophily, etc. So, there seems to be a strong principle of homophily operating in entrepreneurship. If you present these results to sociologists, they will say: "Oh yes, that makes sense ... homophily is a very strong principle that seems to operate in society generally". But if we look at the way we teach entrepreneurship, we teach the rational planning model ... when you pick a team you select people based on competence, functional contribution, complementary skills ... which implies that homophily is not a major consideration. On the other hand, it appears that teams that are formed in reality emerge from already existing social structures that generate homophilic teams. This shows that a more general social theory or principle could be used to explain team building in entrepreneurship.

A second "analytical dilemma" is that if we look at the literature on women entrepreneurs and management, you will find that there is no empirical evidence that suggests a difference between the way women manage in comparison to men. If a difference is found, it appears to be quite small. On the other hand, there seems to be a huge discrepancy in start-up rates between men and women ... women just don't try to start businesses at the same rate as men. Why? They apparently have the same skills as men. If the skills were lacking, it would certainly be revealed in the way they managed. So, there must be some institutional reasons, the way in which the labor market is organized, or the family is organized ... it is not the individuals themselves, it is something about the institutional structures, and we have to look at relationships between the individual and the institutional context.

Third, it is interesting to note that the human being seems to be a creative, problem solving creature ... especially when young, and if you look at some institutional sectors of society, for example art and culture, you can find incredibly creative products, but then if you look at typical start-up entrepreneurs, it seems quite vain ... very imitative behavior. So, the question is: "Why aren't there more radical discontinuous organizations?" Again the dilemma is that the literature presents the human as a creative creature, and on the other hand the data that we have on start-ups show that they are not terribly innovative. In the evolutionary approach, it is not surprising that what we see is mostly incremental changes. The nature of evolution is such that it is very difficult for any new activity to succeed if it is not closely tied to what has already worked. When evolutionary theorists, working with animals other than humans ... it is obvious that when we look over time and generations we can see that there is a stabilizing selection ... you have behaviors that are pretty well adapted to the environment. The difference with humans is that they are pretty good at reconstructing their environment ... but the principle still exists ... we are in a situation in which we can't predict the future, we can't see around the corner, we are aware of our immediate environment, and we know what has worked in the past. So, there is a strong continuity, things that worked yesterday are working today and will work tomorrow, and the most sensible change is to do things just a little bit differently but not very differently from what was done in the past. My point is that humans are creative, but in a rather local sense ... creativity is local ... humans can't easily start new industries, or start businesses in existing industries that radically differ from other firms ... the environment has already eliminated things that don't work ... and if you try to break away from the model you have to recognize that it is highly risky.

Finally, if you look at the ethnic business literature, a main point is that it highlights the fact that some ethnic groups noted for their level of entrepreneurial activity today were no different from the normal population in terms of entrepreneurial activities at other times or in other societies. So, people with the same cultural background seem to behave very differently, depending on what country they emigrated to and when. For example, the Chinese and Japanese who came to America in the late 19th or early 20th century first came as railroad workers, as laborers, and it was later on that Chinese immigrants started their own businesses in certain lines of work, like laundries and restaurants. This again indicates that the reasons couldn't come from those people as a unique cultural group – there is nothing special in the Chinese culture that makes them entrepreneurs ... it has to do with the institutional context ... and put into an evolutionary perspective, it is a very contingency-related problem, and we wouldn't be aware of it except through historical analysis.

If we look at the research topic of firm formation in general terms, what have we learned over the last few decades?

Of course, we know a lot more today about the demographics of entrepreneurship, we have a better idea of the volatility of firms in a business population, and we have a better understanding of the huge moving into and out of the firm creation process. Thus, in entrepreneurship research we have come to the point where we recognize volatility at population level and we see that there is tremendous variability within the population of entrepreneurs – entrepreneurs are not one and the same.

But we don't have an underlying understanding of this volatility ... more knowledge is needed about the topics raised by Scott Shane in the area of opportunity recognition: "Why do some people recognize opportunities that other people fail to notice?" There is a tremendous variability across individuals, how they perceive their environment and what they are willing to do next. The problem I think with the way opportunity recognition has been approached is that it is often related to a situation of what we can call "arbitrage" – the case where a person recognizes an opportunity by making inferences from an already familiar situation, for example, from one market, to another situation that is known ... another market ... and recognizes that there is a niche that is not filled. That makes sense.

But in entrepreneurship we are not saying that we are looking at "arbitrage" entrepreneurship, and we don't see entrepreneurship as an analytical and rational process ... it is more a question of new solutions and being at the leading edge ... to me that seems like magic. In some respects I will revert to evolutionary theory and Donald Campbell saying that it is mostly a matter of being at the right place at the right time ... and if you can show me à priori how to identify the right place and the right time, which would be fantastic but unlikely. I think that will also explain what we talked about before, that it is more likely that most people who start businesses are engaged in fairly mundane behavior because they are transferring an idea from one situation to another. It is a question of understanding the limits of human cognition, and such understanding will I think make us a little humbler about what we are doing in terms of opportunity recognition claims.

Has there been any path-breaking research on new firm formation that has changed the research within the field?

I would say that in order to understand entrepreneurship we have to tie entrepreneurship research more closely to other social sciences ... psychology, sociology, social anthropology ... and to the extent that these fields can give us ideas about the understanding of entrepreneurship as a normal human activity. And therefore, talking about path-breaking research, I would look at the disciplines and ask: "What have we learnt from the disciplines?" and "What innovative ideas have psychologists and sociologists come up with?" For example, there has been some really good original thinking going on in evolutionary social psychology, and I thoroughly recommend the book by Jeffry Simpson and Douglas Kenrick with the title *Evolutionary Social Psychology* (1997). For example, there is an interesting chapter on groups and human sociability that I have used in my research on teams, and it gives a theoretical basis for saying that there are distinct grounds for human group behavior ... humans are predisposed to follow others, to fight for status within the group, etc. ... which helps us explain their behavior on entrepreneurial teams.

Based on your experience in entrepreneurship research, what would your advice be to a young doctoral student interested in entrepreneurship?

First, I would say that the basis for understanding entrepreneurship is the disciplines, and therefore you have to set your roots in a discipline ... psychology, sociology, anthropology, or whatever ... and then you can focus on a topic like entrepreneurship. A doctoral student will need in-depth theoretical and methodological training, and the rewards will probably come from discipline-based theorizing, not cross-discipline theorizing.

Second, and as a consequence, you would probably be able to find pretty much all of the concepts that you need within the different disciplines. I am pretty certain that a PhD student who came up with a topical question and spent time in the library looking over the literature published in the last decade would probably find some really good applications of powerful research that he or she could adapt to his/her own research question.

Based on your research on the formation of new ventures, what policy recommendations would you suggest?

I don't believe that this is a simple human capital problem ... we do not create more firms by setting up more training programs ... our network studies show that there are a lot of social capital issues involved. So, to community leaders I would say: "Create voluntary associations in which people have a chance to 'mingle' with people they would otherwise never meet". We know that in personal relationships people have a tendency to find people very much like themselves, and we need associations that offer incentives and thus bring people together, creating heterogeneous role sets, etc.

At national level, one thing that the Global Entrepreneurship Monitoring project has shown is the large differences across societies and angel investments. It is really extraordinary ... in some societies up to 8% of the population are making angel investments, whereas in other societies the figure is less than 1%. The implication in the GEM report is that this is a function of tax policies. We know that informal investors are much more important than formal investors, at least in the start-up phase. So, one suggestion would be to look closely at incentives for people to act as informal investors.

What will the future look like for entrepreneurship research in general?

I wrote a paper for the *Organization and Management Theory* (OMT) at the Academy of Management called "Who Wants to Be an Evolutionary Theorist" (2001) in which I discussed what is missing in OMT research, and in many respects the same discussion can be applied to entrepreneurship research.

What we do in entrepreneurship research and what we have done in the past is to pick those people who succeeded, often the few notable radical successes, and attribute their success to something about their special characteristics or their behavior. But most entrepreneurship is gradual and incremental, not terribly radical. Therefore, let us look at entrepreneurship in the same way as other human behaviors, more normal activities, and most of what we see is incremental development, not the great successes. So, I think we need to get away from the over-emphasis on high-tech, high-growth and highly visible successes ... that is really unusual behavior ... we get skewed samples in our research, and we miss the true variation, diversity and heterogeneity in the business landscape – in turn, there is a bias in the models that we develop, and you can't build a science if you only focus on the abnormal behavior ... you can't build a science on forest ecology if you only look at redwoods, that is the last stage in the forest, you have to understand all the other flora involved in creating a forest.

I also think that we focus too much on what I will call "outcome-driven research" based on cross-sectional and static studies. Outcome-driven research is built backwards from the observed outcomes to prior significant events. In this kind of research we have problems, for example, researchers make their selection on the dependent variables, there might be problems in accessing people who experienced the event or relevant records from the past, and it is also difficult for people to recall past events in a detailed manner. On the other hand, evolutionary thinking focuses on processes, and the research is "event-driven" where the explanations are built forward, from observed events to outcomes. The research design in such a study could vary, but should be very dynamic. One good example of such an event-driven study is the PSED project (the Panel Study of Entrepreneurial Dynamics in the US) that Paul Reynolds initiated to study the behavior of nascent entrepreneurs.

In entrepreneurship research we also tend to leave the time and changes rather imprecise and ambiguous ... and we ought to specify the intervals of time during which events occur ... which will influence the frequency of observations needed and the time intervals between them. For example, researchers who rely on archival data often only have data available in one-year chunks, even if we know that events occur more often. We need to specify "pace" – the number of events in a given space of time, and "duration" – the amount of time that elapses for a given event. It is difficult to rely on archival and publicly available data for the study of pace and duration – such data can tell us when an event was completed, but not when people began to work on it – we know the outcome, but not the sequence and pace of events leading up to it. Instead, what we need is fieldwork and real ethnographic studies.

Finally, in entrepreneurship research we need to ask ourselves more often: "What happens next?" Most of our empirical generalization is about the past, not least evolutionary thinking. It is difficult to explain, on the basis of an evolutionary approach, why some companies survive while others do not ... it's not possible to "pick the winners" ... an explanation can only be provided afterwards, as each company has its own specific history and is situated in a specific social context. Many have criticized evolutionary thinking, saying that "evolutionary thinking is backward looking – it only helps us understand what has already happened". My answer to that would be: "When did you collect your data?" and "When did you analyze it?" None of them claim to have written their results before the data were collected. Most research is historically situated although perhaps evolutionary thinking makes it more salient. But we need to build models from our research that help us understand what is likely to happen in the future – our research results are historical artefacts, and until we have tested our models in other periods, we don't know if our results are dependent on unique historical circumstances or not. In this respect I am very confident that the use of simulation and computational modeling can give us the tools we need to test the dynamic implications of our research.

REFERENCES

Entrepreneurship research

Aldrich, H.E., 1992, Methods in Our Madness? Trends in Entrepreneurship Research, in Sexton, D.L. & Kasarda, J.D. (eds.), *The state of the art of entrepreneurship*, Boston: PWS-Kent, 191-213.

Aldrich, H.E., 2000, Learning together: National differences in entrepreneurship research, in Sexton, D.L. & Landström, H. (eds.), *The Blackwell Handbook of Entrepreneurship*, Oxford: Blackwell, 5-25.

Aldrich, H.E., 2001, Who Wants to Be an Evolutionary Theorist?, *Journal of Management Inquiry*, 10, 2, 115-127.

Aldrich, H.E. & Baker, T., 1997, Blinded by the cites? Has there been progress in entrepreneurship research?, in Sexton, D.L. & Smilor, R.W. (eds.), *Entrepreneurship 2000*, Chicago: Uppstart Publishers, 377-400.

Evolutionary perspective

Aldrich, H.E., 1972, Organizational Boundaries and Inter-Organizational Conflicts, *Human Relations*, 24, 4, 279-293.

Aldrich, H.E., 1979, *Organizations and environments*, Englewood Cliffs, NJ: Prentice-Hall.

Aldrich, H.E., 1999, *Organizations evolving*, Thousand Oaks: Sage.

Aldrich, H.E. & Herker, D., 1977, Boundary Spanning roles and Organizational Structure, *Academy of Management Review*, 2, 217-230.

Aldrich, H.E. & Pfeffer, J., 1976, Environments of Organizations, in Inkeles, A. (ed.), *Annual Review of Sociology*, Vol III, Palo Alto: Annual Review Inc, 79-105.

Aldrich, H.E. & Whetten, D., 1981, Organization-sets, Action-sets, and Networks: Making the Most of Simplicity, in Nystrom, P. & Starbuck, W. (eds.), *Handbook of Organizational Design*, New York: Oxford University Press, 385-408.

Boeker, W., 1988, Organizational origins: Entrepreneurial and environmental imprinting at the time of founding, in Carroll, G.R. (ed.), *Ecological models of organization*, Cambridge, MA: Ballinger, 33-51.

Carroll, G., 1983, A stochastic model of organizational mortality: Review and reanalysis, *Social Science Research*, 12, 4, pp 303-329.

Gartner, W.E. & Bird, B.J. & Starr, J.A., 1992, Acting As If: Differentiating Entrepreneurial From Organizational Behavior, *Entrepreneurship Theory and Practice*, Spring, 13-31.

Hannan, M.T., 1986, *Competitive and institutional processes in organizational ecology*, Ithaca, BY: Cornell University.

Hannan, M.T. & Freeman, J.H., 1977, The population ecology of organizations, *American Journal of Sociology*, 82, 929-964.

Hannan, M.T. & Freeman, J.H., 1984, Structural inertia and organizational change, *American Sociological Review*, 49, 149-164.

Hannan, M.T. & Freeman, J.H., 1989, *Organizational ecology*, Cambridge, MA: Harvard University Press.

Murmann, J.P. & Aldrich, H.E. & Levinthal, D. & Winter, S.G., 2003, Evolutionary Thought in Management and Organization Theory at the Beginning of the New Millennium, *Journal of Management Inquiry*, 12, 1, 22-40.

Nelson, R.R. & Winter, S.G., 1982, *An evolutionary theory of economic change*, Cambridge, MA: Harvard University Press.

Romanelli, E., 1989, Organization birth and population variety: A community perspective on origins, in Staw, B.M. & Cummings, L.L. (eds.), *Research in organizational behavior*, 11, 211-246.

Stinchcombe, A., 1965, Social structure and organization, in March, J.G. (ed.), *Handbook of organizations*, Chicago: Rand-McNally, 142-193.

Weick, K.E., 1979, *The social psychology of organizing*, Reading, MA: Addison-Wesley.

Whetten, D. & Aldrich, H.E., 1979, Organization Set Size and Diversity: Links Between People Processing Organizations and Their Environments, *Administration and Society*, 11, 3, 251-282.

Business formation

Aldrich, H.E., 1990, Using an ecological perspective to study organizational founding rates, *Entrepreneurship Theory and Practice*, 14, 3, 7-24.

Aldrich, H. & Auster, E.R., 1986, Even dwarfs started small: Liabilities of age and size and their strategic implications, in Staw, B. & Cummings, L.L. (eds.), *Research in Organizational Behavior*, 8, Greenwich, CT: JAI Press, 165-198.

Aldrich, H.E. & Fiol, C.M., 1994, Fools rush in? The institutional context of industry creation, *Academy of Management Review*, 19, 4, 645-670.

Aldrich, H.E. & Mueller, S., 1981, The Evolution of Organizational Forms: Technology, Coordination, and Control, in Staw, B. & Cummings, L.L. (eds.), *Research in Organizational Behavior*, Vol IV, JAI Press.

Aldrich, H.E. & Wiedenmayer, G., 1993, From traits to rates: An ecological perspective on organizational foundings, in Katz, J.A. & Brockhaus, R.H. (eds.), *Advances in Entrepreneurship, Firm Emergence and Growth*, Volume 1, Greenwich: JAI Press. 145-195.

Ethnicity and entrepreneurship

Aldrich, H. & Cater, J. & Jones, T. & McEvoy, D. & Velleman, P., 1985, Ethnic Residential Concentration and the Protected Market Hypothesis, *Social Forces*, 63, 4, 996-1009.

Aldrich, H.E. & Waldinger, R., 1990, Ethnicity and Entrepreneurship, *Annual Review of Sociology*, 16, 111-135.

Blaschke, J. & Boissevain, J. & Grotenbreg, H. & Joseph, I. & Morokvasic, M. & Ward, R., 1990, European Trends in Ethnic Business, in Waldinger, R. & Aldrich, H. & Ward, R. (eds.), *Ethnic Entrepreneurs*, Newbury Park, CA: Sage.

Light, I., 1972, *Ethnic Enterprise in America*, Berkeley: University of California Press.

Waldinger, R. & Aldrich, H., 1990a, Trends in Ethnic Business in the United States, in Waldinger, R. & Aldrich, H. & Ward, R. (eds.), *Ethnic Entrepreneurs*, Newbury Park, CA: Sage.

Waldinger, R. & Aldrich, H. & Ward, R., 1990b, Opportunities, Group Characteristics and Strategies, in Waldinger, R. & Aldrich, H. & Ward, R. (eds.), *Ethnic Entrepreneurs*, Newbury Park, CA: Sage.

Zimmer, C. & Aldrich, 1987, Resource mobilization through ethnic networks: Kinship and friendship ties of shopkeepers in England, *Sociological Perspective*, 30, 422-455.

Networks

Aldrich, H.E. & Reese, P.R., 1993, Does networking pay off? A panel study of entrepreneurs in the research triangle, *Frontiers of Entrepreneurship Research*, 325-339.

Aldrich, H. & Rosen, B. & Woodward, W., 1987, The impact of social networks on business foundings and profit: A longitudinal study, Frontiers of Entrepreneurship Research, 154-168.

Aldrich, H.E. & Sakano, T., 1998, Unbroken Ties. Comparing Personal Business Networks Cross-Nationally, in Fruin, W.M. (ed.), *Networks, Markets and the Pacific Rim*, New York: Oxford University Press, 32-52.

Aldrich, H. & Zimmer, C., 1986, Entrepreneurship Through Social Networks, in Sexton, D.L. & Smilor, R.W. (eds.), *The Art and Science of Entrepreneurship*, Cambridge, MA: Ballinger, 3-23.

Dubini, P. & Aldrich, H., 1991, Personal and Extended Networks are Central to the Entrepreneurial Process, *Journal of Business Venturing*, 6, 305-313.

Granovetter, M., 1973, The Strength of Weak Ties, *American Journal of Sociology*, 78, 6, 1360-80.

Reese, P.R. & Aldrich, H.E., 1995, Entrepreneurship networks and business performance. A panel study of small and medium-sized firms in the research triangle, in Birley, S. & MacMillan, I.C. (eds.), *International Entrepreneurship*, London: Routledge, 124-144.

Women entrepreneurship

Aldrich, H., 1989, Networking among women entrepreneurs, in Hagan, O. & Rivchun, C. & Sexton, D. (eds.), *Women-owned businesses*, New York: Praeger, 103-132.

Aldrich, H.E. & Elam, A.B. & Reese, P.R., 1997, Strong ties, weak ties, and strangers. Do women owners differ from men in their use of networking to obtain assistance?, in Birley, S. & MacMillan, I.C. (eds.), *Entrepreneurship in global context*, London: Routledge, 1-25.

Aldrich, H. & Reese, P.R. & Dubini, P., 1989, Women on the verge of a breakthrough: networking among entrepreneurs in the United States and Italy, *Entrepreneurship and Regional Development*, 1, 339-356.

Aldrich, H.E. & Sakano, T., 1998, Unbroken Ties. Comparing Personal Business Networks Cross-Nationally, in Fruin, W.M. (ed.), *Networks, Markets and the Pacific Rim*, New York: Oxford University Press, 32-52.

Baker, T. & Aldrich, H.E. & Liou, N., 1997, Invisible entrepreneurs: the neglect of women business owners by mass media and scholarly journals in the USA, *Entrepreneurship and Regional Development*, 9, 221-238.

EPILOGUE

Chapter 13

A RETROSPECTIVE AS A FUTURE OUTLOOK

In the book I have tried to provide a historical-doctrinal review of the development of entrepreneurship and small business research as well as presenting some of the pioneers, who have been influential in the creation and development of the field. I am aware that this review tends to mirror my own subjective view of the development of the field, and the pioneers selected for inclusion in the book are those who have received the FSF-NUTEK International Award for Small Business Research – which may reflect the bias of the scientific committee of the Swedish Foundation for Small Business Research (FSF). However, the first recipients of the FSF-NUTEK International Award are unquestionably pioneers in the field of entrepreneurship and small business research.

One concern that has been raised by many researchers within as well as outside the entrepreneurship and small business field is the problem of defining central concepts in the research, such as "entrepreneur" and "entrepreneurship". Chapter one includes some definitions that have been used in earlier research, which focused on entrepreneurship as a function of the market, the entrepreneur as an individual, and entrepreneurship as a process. My main argument in the chapter was that (i) entrepreneurship is an inherently complicated, vague and changeable phenomenon and (ii) has its roots in many different disciplines, and researchers brought in a range of different definitions of central concepts. Thus, it stands to reason that the definitions of entrepreneurship are ambiguous and changeable and, in common with other more established research fields, we have to learn to live with this lack of clarity – there are "many entrepreneurships" in terms of definitions, but also regarding focus, scope, and paradigms.

In chapter 2 I attempted to describe the roots of entrepreneurship and small business research. This research has a long history, and we can identify the gradual development from being a topic within economic science, to a behavioral science research area, finally becoming a part of management science – thus, entrepreneurship and small business research has its roots in many different disciplines. My main argument in this chapter was that our knowledge of entrepreneurship and small firms seems to develop with certain chronological regularities. Entrepreneurship and small business research thrives and peaks at the end of periods that are characterized by powerful dynamics and developments in society, while it is less conspicuous during periods of rationalization. According to Schön (2001) there is at present a shift toward a new rationalization period, which may indicate that entrepreneurship and small business research will assume a new form with a different research agenda in the future.

Even if entrepreneurship and small firms have for a long time aroused the interest of researchers in different disciplines, it was only during the last decades that the study of entrepreneurship and small business has been conducted in a more systematic manner and that a research field started to emerge. In chapter 3 I described the emergence of entrepreneurship and small business as a field of research (mainly based on a US research context) – from the social turmoil of the 1960s and 1970s toward the scientific maturation of the field during the early 2000s. This development has been characterized by the enormous growth of the research field – largely irrespective of the measurement employed. Chapter 3 showed that:

- The field seems to have been particularly successful in building a strong *social structure*. With an origin in management studies and the business schools in the US, a community of scholars interested in entrepreneurship and small business emerged in the 1970s and 1980s – a community characterized by enthusiasm, individualism and the import of knowledge from many different disciplines. Since these pioneering achievements, the research community in the field has expanded, although to a large extent it has been fragmented and transient. There has also been greater "liberation" from mainstream disciplines, and the researchers have increasingly come to view themselves as entrepreneurship and small business researchers, although at the same time there has been increased segmentation within the field – an "emerging tribes" phase.
- Starting with a couple of pioneering studies within the area that is known today as "small business economics", the *cognitive development* of the field has been characterized by a successive change from a discovery-oriented research approach, i.e. providing descriptions and insights about a previously unfamiliar phenomenon, toward an empirical-oriented research approach, i.e. an increasing number of high quality empirical studies and use of more sophisticated statistical methods. But we have also witnessed an expanding interest in theoretical perspectives that can help us understand entrepreneurship and small business, for example, the evolutionary approach and the resource-based view. At the same

time, US research seems to be achieving convergence in the use of identifiable methodological practices, whereas the level of thematic convergence is still relatively low and unstable (new topics replacing old ones over time).

The main conclusion in this chapter is that, even though the field is still young and eclectic, much has been achieved over the last decades, and we know a great deal more about entrepreneurship and small business than we did twenty or thirty years ago. The field, seen from a US research perspective, has been converging more and more toward a "normal science approach" (Aldrich & Baker, 1997), but at the same time it can be argued that this development counteracts the original openness and interest in experimentation that originally characterized entrepreneurship and small business research. In order to achieve a dynamic research field in the future, entrepreneurship and small business research needs to create a balance between exploration, i.e. the pursuit of new knowledge, and exploitation, i.e. the development of existing knowledge within the field.

As in many social sciences, not least management studies (Engwall, 1995; 1996), entrepreneurship and small business research is dominated by US scholars. However, the growth of interest in the field is an international phenomenon, and we can find an enormous increase in research in Europe as well as in Australia. In chapter 4, I described the development of entrepreneurship and small business research in Australia and various European countries and compared the research in Europe, Australia, and the US. My main conclusion was that even if some similarities are evident, there are great differences in entrepreneurship and small business research between the continents (and between countries) in terms of the contextual conditions for entrepreneurship and small firms as well as differences in research traditions manifested in thematic focus, methodological approaches, and in the incentives for researchers to conduct studies within the field – there is great heterogeneity in entrepreneurship and small business research around the world.

In all emerging fields of research, some individuals appear to have a greater influence than others – researchers who ask the interesting questions, who make new phenomena visible, and who attract other researchers into the emerging field, but also researchers who start to organize colleagues with similar interests, maintain informal contacts with other researchers, train and recruit new doctoral students into the field, etc. – pioneers who create the field. In the late 1970s and during the 1980s many scholars from various disciplines rushed into this promising field, thus the field of entrepreneurship and small business includes quite a few individuals that can be regarded as pioneers. In chapter 5, I present some of these pioneers: pioneers in education, the building of social networks of scholars and in research. As chapter 5 reveals, from the start the field was characterized by heterogeneity –

many different topics and methodological approaches were grouped under the umbrella that we call entrepreneurship and small business research. The chapter concludes with a short presentation of the first recipients of the FSF-NUTEK International Award for Small Business Research – all of whom can be regarded as pioneers of entrepreneurship and small business research – while in chapters 6 to 12 the award winners are presented in more detail.

Pioneers employing macro-level analysis

Chapter 6	David Birch	Award Winner 1996
Chapter 7	David Storey	Award Winner 1998
Chapter 8	Zoltan Acs and	
	David Audretsch	Award Winners 2001
Chapter 9	Giacomo Becattini and	
	Charles Sabel	Award Winners 2002

Pioneers employing micro-level analysis

Chapter 10	Arnold Cooper	Award Winner 1997
Chapter 11	Ian MacMillan	Award Winner 1999
Chapter 12	Howard Aldrich	Award Winner 2000

Why is it that these researchers can be regarded as pioneers within entrepreneurship and small business research? In general, the field does not appear any different from many other emerging research fields – research fields especially in the areas of natural science and medicine are often created as a result of the possibilities brought about by the development of new measuring instruments – which is also true of entrepreneurship and small business research. The late 1970s and early 1980s witnessed a dramatic development in the area of information technology, making it possible to process large amounts of data, which was necessary due to the great number of small businesses. Information databases could now be built on young and small firms, allowing researchers to identify new patterns that were previously impossible to discern. This is similar to Friedel's (2001) reasoning regarding the ways in which serendipitous discovery occurs (pp. 39-40):

– Columbian: serendipity is "when one is looking for one thing, but finds another thing of value, and recognizes that value".
– Archimedeon: serendipity is "finding sought-for results, although by routes not logically deduced but luckily observed".
– Galilean: serendipity involves the use of new instruments or capabilities to generate surprises.

These three approaches are still evident in scientific activities but, without doubt, the use of new data capacity and new data bases (the Galilean approach) has had a strong influence on the development of entrepreneurship and small business as a research field.

Numerous examples of the fact that groundbreaking discoveries are more or less the result of chance can be found in the history of science. However, the pioneers presented in this book are proof that groundbreaking works do not always originate in creative flashes of genius but are the result of being open to ongoing transformations in society as well as "empirical groundwork" – thus they are the results of empirical problem-solving rather than random flashes of genius (Sahlin, 2001). In this connection it is worth noting that several of the pioneers within entrepreneurship and small business research were firmly rooted in an established research field (such as economics, industrial organization, strategic management or organizational behaviour) – they knew the rules of the game and thus challenged conventional knowledge (they had something to "push against"). As in most radical ventures, the pioneers showed a great measure of "courage" in bypassing the rules and knowledge of their research field as well as the necessary motivation to go against the "conventional wisdom" within the field as well as in society at large. The pioneers had also a great ability to communicate their results both to politicians, decision-makers and within science – their works were frequently published and their results presented in renowned journals within their respective research field. Thus, the pioneers within entrepreneurship and small business research presented results that challenged conventional knowledge within the established fields and in society at large – and their findings were interesting.

According to Davis (1971) we tend to think of researchers as great because their theories are true. But this is open to question: a researcher is considered great, not because his/her theories are true but interesting. What makes a theory interesting? In my opinion, interesting theories are those that contradict certain taken-for-granted assumptions and beliefs. For example: What seems to be a disorganized phenomenon is in reality an organized phenomenon. What seems to be a single phenomenon is, in reality, composed of heterogeneous elements. What seems to be a phenomenon that functions ineffectively is, in reality, a phenomenon that functions effectively. What the pioneers of entrepreneurship research have done is to propose interesting theories about the phenomenon known as entrepreneurship and small business – theories that prompt a certain movement in the minds of their audience.

However, interesting theories alone are often not enough – it is also a question of "timing" – society was in turmoil (the industrial landscape was radically transformed, large companies lost their attraction, the importance of new and small firms increased, and new political winds began to blow) – small and young firms were in vogue and there was growing realization of their importance for societal dynamics. Thus the pioneers presented not only interesting theories, but also important ones – their contributions were highly relevant for societal development – theories that had an impact on wealth creation. Thus, what the pioneers did was to focus their efforts on important questions – that had an impact on wealth creation in society – in addition to developing interesting theories about the phenomenon.

The development of the research field during the 1980s and 1990s more or less followed the traditional pattern for the development of new research field development. Many scientific theorists have discussed how new academic fields are created, developed, and sometimes even abandoned. Focussing on the cognitive aspects of this development, Hansson (1993) uses the concepts of "technical" and "theoretical" approaches to knowledge creation. Young fields of research are characterized by a technical approach, the researchers focus their attention on the object of study (as opposed to theories and methodologies), and in their search for "safe" knowledge. The aim of research is primarily to achieve a broad understanding of the study object and to obtain specific outcomes, often in the form of knowledge that can be applied in practical situations. Due to the lack of any conceptual platform, the knowledge is rather fragmented. As a field develops, the research gradually becomes more specialized and clearer definitions are formulated. According to Hansson, mature fields display a strong theoretical approach to knowledge, where immediate applicability is of lesser importance. The research is often speculative, the aim being to move away from simple empirical descriptions and to focus instead on explanations and an understanding of the object of study, in which theories and methodological approaches are central.

According to Hansson's concepts, entrepreneurship and small business research has applied a technical approach to knowledge for many years – with focus on the object of study and the aim of forming a view of the phenomenon of entrepreneurship and small firms. At present, caught between efforts to overcome the drawbacks of newness and the need to achieve maturity, two somewhat contradictory tendencies can be identified in entrepreneurship and small business research. On the one hand, an increased modulation of concepts, but also an increased modulation of our knowledge about entrepreneurship and small business, as well as increased convergence in the use of identifiable methodological approaches – mainly based on a US research tradition. On the other hand, we can find great heterogeneity (and even increased heterogeneity) and dynamics in entrepreneurship and small business research around the world in terms of definitions, thematic focus and methodological approaches.

As I see it, in this situation the efforts to achieve a unified research field are an illusion. During recent years there has been a stronger strive toward achieving coherence in entrepreneurship and small business research. However, there are several arguments against such a development. By definition, entrepreneurship and small business is an inherently complicated and changeable phenomenon, which makes it difficult to find common definitions. The history of the field shows that the research has its roots in many different disciplines, with different theoretical points of departure, levels of analysis and methodological approaches. The review of research in different countries also reveals great differences in terms of contextual preconditions and research traditions. Even if a certain degree of convergence can be identified, not least in the US, the field is extremely heterogeneous, and current efforts toward a more unified science approach tend to counteract the content of entrepreneurship and its different research traditions.

But what are the alternatives? Naturally there are many possibilities but, assuming that entrepreneurship and small business research will follow the evolutionary pattern of many other research fields, there are two possible scenarios:

- The research field is divided in a new way. History shows that the impulse for such a change often emanates from totally different disciplines, which makes one aware that the basic lines of reasoning and theories are the same as those of other disciplines, thus opening up a new way of looking at the phenomenon.
- A splitting up of the subject and increased specialization. Entrepreneurship and small business research is and has long been a heterogeneous research field – many topics and methodological approaches have been accommodated under the heading of "entrepreneurship and small business research" – thus it is possible that we will see a specialization of the subject in the future, not only thematically but perhaps also due to the diverse methodological traditions, which will lead to more autonomous research areas within for example "nascent entrepreneurship", "venture capital", and "firm growth".

In addition, it is not realistic to expect entrepreneurship and small business research to be any different from many other emerging fields in terms of the social structure. Krohn and Küppers (1989) consider research to be a self-organizing system, with the first phase consisting of a "cognitive belief", where the researchers develop basic assumptions about the need for the research, the importance of the study object, and ensuring a certain degree of continuity. In this phase, different research approaches will be developed. The larger the research community, the greater is the divergence of these approaches. Entrepreneurship and small business research has been comparatively successful when it comes to achieve the next phase – "stabilizing the cognitive belief", which implies liberation from main stream disciplines, and the increasing tendency of researchers to regard themselves as belonging to the field. This stabilization of the belief requires ongoing communication by means of conferences, journals and exchange of researchers. This communication within the research community successively leads to a self-image, while increased communication with other research communities results in the development of a mutual image of the other – an "identity" is created, i.e. a body of consistently formulated values and beliefs, by which the research community is guided.

Thus, entrepreneurship and small business research has succeeded in building a social structure, which has resulted in a stabilization of the research; however, the creation of an identity of its own has not yet been accomplished. Of course, this goes hand in hand with the cognitive development of the research field, for example, it is important to develop a "cognitive style" including a professional language and concepts that play a "boundary-establishing" role for the research field. But in order to establish a recognizable identity, it is also essential to develop a "social culture" within the field, which requires a regular and intensive forum for discussions. The informal communication between researchers becomes of paramount importance, and in entrepreneurship and small business research the informal networks are less developed than the formal ones (even if formal networks are often an important prerequisite for the establishment of informal networks). Informal networks are essential for the exchange of "tacit" knowledge – important for the creation of the identity of the field – an argument for the creation of smaller "research circles" in which consensus can be reached regarding the problems of interest, definitions, methodological approaches, etc. Such "research circles" can be achieved through the establishment of research centers, but also through well-developed informal international networks. It is in these "research circles" that a cognitive style can be developed. We have to be aware that many well established disciplines do not offer a picture of unity and coherence but are organized into different research areas, with competing "research circles". (Frank & Landström, 1997)

REFERENCES

Aldrich, H.E. & Baker, T.B., 1997, Blinded by the cites? Has there been progress in entrepreneurship research?, in Sexton, D.L. & Smilor, R.W. (eds.), *Entrepreneurship 2000*, Chicago: Uppstart, 377-400.

Davis, M., 1971, That's Interesting!, *Philosophical Social Science*, 1, 309-344.

Engwall, L., 1995, Management research: A fragmented adhocracy, *Scandinavian Journal of Management*, 11, 3, 225-235.

Engwall, L., 1996, The Vikings versus the World: An examination of nordic business research, *Scandinavian Journal of Management*, 12, 4, 425-436.

Frank, H. & Landström, H., 1997, Entrepreneurship and small business research in Europe – analysis and reflections, in Landström, H. & Frank, H. & Veciana, J.M., (eds.), *Entreprenurship and Small Business Research in Europe*, Aldershot: Avebury.

Friedel, R., 2001, Serendipity is not accident, *The Kenyon Review*, 23, 2, 36-47.

Hansson, B., 1993, *Vetenskapsfilosofi*, Filosofiska institutionen, Lund: Lund University.

Krohn, W. & Küppers, G., 1989, *Die Selbstorganisation der Wissenschaft*, Frankfurt.

Sahlin, N-E., 2001, *Kreativitetens filosofi*, Nora: Nya Doxa.

Schön, L., 2001, Swedish Industrial Growth and Crises in the 20th Century, paper at the workshop Growth, crises and regulation in the European economies, University of Helsinki, 1-4 March 2001.

INDEX